This is a significant evaluative biography of an effective mid-20th century missionary grappling with the changing dynamics of mission in the transition from pioneers to parents to partners in the relations between service agencies and the younger churches. It is a must read for any missionary candidate; any theology student or Christian involved in inter-cultural ministry today; and any informed Christian or supporter of mission seeking to grasp the ways of God in reaching our contemporary world. As the amazing record of the impact of the life of one person totally yielded to God and obedient to his call, it also reflects the missionary spirituality of the time with a particular focus on evaluating Christian leadership issues through the lens of Gil McArthur's life journey.

John Hitchen, Honorary Research Fellow,
Laidlaw Graduate School, Laidlaw College, Auckland

Mission lies at the core of evangelicalism. The call to witness to the Gospel is key to understanding the evangelical community. Figures such as Gilbert McArthur demonstrate this dynamic in their very lives. This book gives us an overdue account of a South Pacific mission visionary. The foundations Gil McArthur laid, now support ministries which are strategic not just for Christian mission, but for the future of the Pacific and its peoples. This is more than a record for those who remember him. It is a narrative of a family's discipleship that all Christians should ponder.

Martin Sutherland, Dean, Australian College of Theology

LIVE IN TENTS — BUILD ONLY ALTARS
GILBERT McARTHUR — HIS STORY

DAVID PRICE

in association with

2019

Published by MST Press (ABN 58 004 265 016)
in association with Pioneers of Australia.
Orders:
MST Press, PO Box 6257, Vermont South VIC 3133 Australia
mstpress@mst.edu.au
Pioneers of Australia, PO Box 200, Blackburn VIC 3130 Australia
info@pioneers.org.au

Copyright © David Price 2019. All rights reserved. Except for brief quotations in critical publications or reviews, no part of this book may be reproduced in any manner without prior written permission from the publisher.

First Published April 2019
Second reprint June 2019

Publication details
Title: Live in Tents - Build Only Altars:
Gilbert McArthur - His Story
ISBN(s): 9780987615480 : Paperback
        98780987640109 : ebook - epub

 A catalogue record for this book is available from the National Library of Australia

Unless otherwise indicated, Scripture quotations are taken from the Holy Bible New International Version of the Bible. Copyright © 1973, 1978, 1984, 2011 by Biblica, Inc. Used by permission of Zondervan. All rights reserved worldwide. www.zondervan.com

Cover and layout by Ivan Smith
Printed by Lightning Source

DEDICATION

To my family –
Margaret, my constant source of love and encouragement,
Our three wonderful children and their spouses,
Andrew & Corrie, Amanda & Julian, Tim & Marisa,
And our grandchildren
Brianna, Chantelle, Finlay,
Jemima, Matilda, Mabel, Elsie,
April, Archer, Cormac,
I love you more than mere words can express.

....

To my Heavenly Father –
There is no one like him,
The Father, Son and Spirit,
Creator, Saviour and Judge,
Infinitely great and good,
Loving beyond our comprehension,
Ever reaching out to a world of lost, rebellious and broken people,
Ever willing to forgive and work his purpose in us,
I urge you to worship him, surrender to him, serve him,
The Way, The Truth and The Life,
And discover more than you could ever hope for.

....

And he [Jesus Christ] died for all,
that those who live should no longer live for themselves
but for him who died for them and was raised again.
(2 Corinthians 5:15)

CONTENTS

Abbreviations	viii
Maps and Diagrams	ix
Foreword	
Tim Meyers – Principal Melbourne School of Theology	x
Foreword	
William Longgar – Principal Christian Leaders' Training College of Papua New Guinea Inc.	xiii
Acknowledgements	xiv
Preface	xvi
Introduction	xix
PART ONE: THE MAN	**1**
Chapter One: The Boy Becomes a Man 1922-1939	3
Chapter Two: The Shaping of the Man 1940-1955	13
Chapter Three: The Qualities of the Man	27
PART TWO: THE MISSION	**35**
Chapter Four: Pioneering Probationer 1955-1956	37
Chapter Five: Maturing Ministry 1957-1963	61
Chapter Six: New Challenge and Vision 1963-1970	87
Chapter Seven: Searching for Land	103
Chapter Eight: Vision to Reality	115
Chapter Nine: Logistics and Consolidation	135
Chapter Ten: Spreading Influence	155
Chapter Eleven: Vision for the Wider Pacific 1 – Developing National Kingdom Leaders	171
Chapter Twelve: Vision for the Wider Pacific 2 – Building Leaders in SSEC and Pacific Evangelical Churches	191
Chapter Thirteen: The New Door and the Final Call 1987-1994	207

PART THREE: THE LEGACY	**219**
Chapter Fourteen: The Legacy of a Leader	221
Chapter Fifteen: Legacy in Church and Community Leaders	233
Chapter Sixteen: Legacy in Infrastructure Builders	249
Chapter Seventeen: Legacy in Theological Educators	259
Chapter Eighteen: Legacy in Missional Business Entrepreneurs	277
Chapter Nineteen: Legacy in the Wider Pacific and Beyond	291
Chapter Twenty: Legacy in Organisations and Ministries	299
Chapter Twenty-one: A Loving Loyal Partner and Family	327
Chapter Twenty-two: A Leader's Character	335
CONCLUSION – TIME FOR MEDITATION?	**349**
APPENDIX ONE Gilbert J McArthur Missionary Diary Extracts, 1-28	353
APPENDIX TWO Pioneers International Core Values	440
APPENDIX THREE Pioneers International Statistics 2017	442
APPENDIX FOUR Gilbert J McArthur – A Biblical Approach to Holistic Community Development	443
APPENDIX FIVE CLTC Mission Statement	444
APPENDIX SIX Graham Salisbury – CLTC Poultry Program	446
BIBLIOGRAPHY	448
INDEX	456

ABBREVIATIONS

AAC	Australian Advisory Council of Christian Leaders' Training College of PNG Inc.
ABFM	Australian Baptist Foreign Mission (later Australian Baptist Missionary Society)
APCM	Asia Pacific Christian Mission
ATA	Alliance Training Association of Papua New Guinea
ATASI	Alliance Training Association of the Solomon Islands
BAM	Business as Mission
BCV	Bible College of Victoria
BCNZ	Bible College of New Zealand
BEM	Borneo Evangelical Mission
CLTC	Christian Leaders' Training College of Papua New Guinea Inc.
CLTCCC	Christian Leaders' Training College Consultative Committee
C&MA	Christian and Missionary Alliance
CMML	Christian Missions in Many Lands
CPBC	Clemton Park Baptist Church
DNG	Dutch New Guinea
EAPNG	Evangelical Alliance of Papua New Guinea Inc
EASPI	Evangelical Alliance of the South Pacific Islands
EWA	East West Airlines Australia Pty Ltd
FSM	Federated States of Micronesia
GiA	Global Interaction, previously ABFM, later Australian Baptist Missionary Society
KJV	King James Version of the Bible
MAF	Missionary Aviation Fellowship, later Mission Aviation Fellowship
MBI	Melbourne Bible Institute, later BCV, now Melbourne School of Theology
MCC	Melanesian Council of Churches
NIV	New International Version of the Bible
NSW	New South Wales - Australia
NZAC	New Zealand Advisory Council of Christian Leaders' Training College of PNG Inc.
NZBTI	New Zealand Bible Training Institute, later BCNZ, now Laidlaw College
NZEDF	New Zealand Educational Development Foundation
PLF	Pacific Leaders' Fellowship
PNG	Papua New Guinea
PoA	Pioneers of Australia
PTI	Pacific Training Institute
RBMU	Regions Beyond Missionary Union
SIL	Summer Institute of Linguistics
SSEC	South Sea Evangelical Church
SSEM	South Sea Evangelical Mission
TEE	Theological Education by Extension
UFM	Unevangelised Fields Mission, later APCM then PoA
WBT	Wycliffe Bible Translators
WCC	World Council of Churches
WEF	World Evangelical Fellowship

MAPS AND DIAGRAMS

The Baliem River Area Dutch New Guinea	44
The Min Area Papua New Guinea	64
Papua New Guinea	88
Pacific Leaders' Fellowship Tours	176
A Christian Leadership Manifesto	188
Dutch New Guinea	360
Holistic Community Development	443

FOREWORD

I cannot recall precisely when it was that I first heard the name Gil McArthur. It's just one of those names that seems to have been woven into the fabric of my own life from my earliest memories, growing up as an 'MAF' kid in Papua New Guinea.

Certainly, he was in our home on many occasions, as indeed were so many of the names that grace the pages of this book; names of men and women whom I now realise, in retrospect, were some of the most remarkable, visionary, strategic and formative leaders in the Australian church and missions history.

Perhaps that's why I found David Price's comprehensive and fascinating account of Gil McArthur's life not only strangely familiar, but so personally moving. For it is, if nothing else, a much-needed commentary on one of the more unique and fascinating seasons in the Australian church, and the mission work that flourished throughout that era. It was a season into which I feel deeply privileged to have been born and raised, and by which I have been inevitably and indelibly shaped. More than that, though, it is an account of the contribution of a quite unique and remarkable man, whose actual role in shaping that 'missional season' will only ever really be fully known in the full light of eternity.

Now, of course, as Executive Principal of both the Melbourne School of Theology (formerly the Melbourne Bible Institute, and Bible College of Victoria), and more recently, Eastern College, Australia (formerly Tabor Victoria), I reflect with even deeper appreciation on just how significant and formative a contribution Gil McArthur made to Christian theological and higher education, leadership development and missional thinking. The legacy of his vision is perhaps no more evident than in the treasured relationship and academic partnership that continues to this day between Christian Leaders' Training College in PNG, and MST. There is absolutely no doubt that I, and many of my own contemporaries in mission, church and theological leadership, have been profoundly impacted by the legacy of his life; his dedication, his uncanny sense of gospel opportunity, his relentless pursuit of new ways of thinking about missional leadership, and his example of a life dedicated to making Christ known.

We owe a debt of gratitude to Dr. David Price for his research into Gil McArthur's life, and his labour of love in recording so carefully a story of great importance to the church, and the work of global mission.

Timothy Meyers
Executive Principal
Melbourne School of Theology,
Eastern College Australia
July 2018

FOREWORD

Gilbert McArthur – His Story is a powerful, heart-warming and deeply inspiring story of a man who calculatingly made a faith decision to make himself available to God as his instrument. Perhaps his major achievement was the Christian Leaders' Training College of Papua New Guinea, Inc.: a collective dream that needed a person with the spiritual stature and calibre, and visionary mind of the Rev Dr Gilbert MacArthur to bring it to fruition. The story is also about the sovereignty of God who directed and superintended the course of history to make the idea become a reality – so that in 1965 the Christian Leaders' Training College of Papua New Guinea Inc. came into being. Envisioning the mission statement of the College, the Rev. Dr. Gilbert McArthur wrote in 1964 the following:

Missionary leaders are faced with the immediate task to ensure the rapid emergence of English educated Christian leaders…
- To provide a well-equipped, spiritually mature, Church leadership for the changing age.
- To ensure the moral and spiritual dynamic of the Christian ethic makes its fullest contribution to the emerging spiritual life.

The Rev Dr David Price, as the author of this detailed and deeply inspiring story, writes as one of the former Principals of the Christian Leaders' Training College of Papua New Guinea, who served this College for sixteen years as a lecturer and later as the Principal, before finally returning home. He is therefore able to re-live the story before us in his own simple and penetrating way. He brings to this story sound scholarship and research, devotion, a deep spirituality, and a simplicity that makes this book must-read mission literature.

It is a book that every person who has had connection with the Christian Leaders' Training College of Papua New Guinea over the years should own.

It should inspire every aspiring young scholar and Christian leader who is visioning a part in God's mission.

William Longgar
National Principal
Christian Leaders' Training College of Papua New Guinea
July 2018

ACKNOWLEDGEMENTS

In May 1967, I was challenged by Gilbert McArthur over a cup of coffee to join the faculty at the Christian Leaders' Training College of Papua New Guinea Inc. (CLTC) in 1968. After many questions, prayers, and very clear confirmations from our Heavenly Father, Margaret and I sensed this was the will of God for us to go.[1] I graduated from the Baptist College in Sydney, concluded pastoral ministry at North Epping Baptist Church, and we were married – all in December of that year! Then the additional transition from Australia to CLTC in Papua New Guinea in February 1968 produced more than two huge sudden transitions in our lives. But that is another story!

My personal links with Gilbert McArthur go back to 1963, when he was appointed the founding Principal of CLTC by the Melbourne Bible Institute (MBI) Council, and I happened to be a first-year student at MBI.

In late 2015, the current CLTC National Principal, Rev Dr William Longgar, asked me to research and write three lectures on Rev Dr Gilbert McArthur, The Man, The Mission and The Legacy, to appropriately inaugurate the Gilbert McArthur Lecture Series at CLTC in April 2017. I am very thankful to William for giving me this opportunity to produce the lectures and this book, although I admit to being a reluctant starter!

To be faithful in any sense to such a task, I felt that I must attempt to walk the story of Gilbert McArthur to understand the life and experiences of this remarkable man and servant of Christ. The resulting fascinating journey of discovery over many months, produced more pages than could fit into the three lectures! Following the delivery of the lectures at CLTC, this book is the result of strong encouragement by numerous people to recount his story in greater detail and represents my best effort to do that.

I am grateful for the help and support of Gil's family in this project (especially daughter Jenny and son Paul). Friends and fellow travellers with CLTC over the past 50 years John Hitchen, Garth Morgan, Will Renshaw and Peter and Margaret Rowse have been a source of immense help and encouragement. John in particular has spent many hours

---

1. Margaret was a student at Sydney Missionary and Bible College and unable to get leave permission for the meeting with Gilbert McArthur.

providing wise counsel, reviewing drafts, answering queries and editing what is an extremely useful index. A large number of Gil's former associates, and others, have researched, read, typed and checked material for accuracy and readability including: Pat Barnden, Gordon Griffiths, John Key, William Longgar, Max Meyers, Berris Clarke, Margaret Rickard, Jayne Wilson and numerous others. Sally Minett's editorial skills have enhanced the flow and readability of the story. Without the help of these wonderful people the task was impossible. I am also thankful for permissions to access the archives of the McArthur family, MBI, CLTC, Pioneers of Australia (PoA), South Sea Evangelical Mission (SSEM), and Global Interaction (GiA – Baptist Mission), among many other sources for information and the photographs included. I am also very grateful for Simon Longden National Director, and PoA for their assistance and encouragement. Ivan Smith with his graphic skills has done excellent work designing the text layout, index, diagrams and cover, and has been ever patient with the multitude of adjustments required. Thank you to all these helpful people.

Margaret, as always, has consistently kept me going when I have wanted to give up living with Gil McArthur in our home every day! I accept final responsibility for what is written, and indeed welcome any corrections or additional insights from readers that will enrich this attempt to tell the Gilbert McArthur story.

Where possible I have tried to allow Gilbert himself to tell his own story, and others who knew and served with him to make their unique contributions. Like all of us, he was not perfect, but his life, like that of the great apostle Paul, calls us to 'follow my example, as I follow the example of Christ'.[2]

David Price
Melbourne
January 2019

---

2. 1 Corinthians 11:1.

PREFACE

'We spend our years as a tale that is told.'[1]

Gil McArthur often drew attention to the phrase in Psalm 90:9b (which only in the King James Version reads) – 'we spend our years as a tale (story) that is told.'[2] Towards the end of his life in 1988 he wrote that this verse:

> ... tells us that we spend our years on this planet 'EARTH' like a 'tale that is told.' This means that each one of us, from birth to the grave, is writing a story-book of life with his or her name written on it. During this short period in time and space we are accountable to Almighty God who has made us in His own image, and endowed us with His own likeness. We are off-spring of Deity with a spiritual capacity for good; and yet entrusted with a free-will that, if not surrendered to the WILL OF GOD, will set in motion a path of disobedience that will take us outside the original plan and purpose that is in the Heart of a Saviour God for each of His children.
>
> It is our Heavenly Father's desire that we should write good and noble chapters in our story-book of life, chapters that will have meaning for both time and eternity.[3]

Unfortunately, apart from his early *Missionary Diary Extracts*,[4] Gilbert McArthur did not write down much of his story-book with pen and paper! He did not think this was a priority. Will Renshaw recalls:

> I clearly remember being with Len [Buck] and Gil whilst we were travelling between meetings when the subject of the writing of

---

1. Psalm 90:9 KJV.
2. In the inclusion of quotations throughout this work, in the interests of readability and those whose first language is not English, the author has updated grammar usage, spelling, and current language trends in gender inclusiveness etc.
3. Gilbert J McArthur, 'A Fellowship of the Committed Ones', 1988, McArthur Family Archives.
4. *The McArthur Diary Extracts* are numbered and dated. They were usually one or two pages, sent out monthly during their time in Dutch New Guinea, and Telefolmin Papua New Guinea 1955-1958, to over 500 recipients. In this book they will be referred to as simply The Diary or Gil's Diary with number and date in the footnotes. See Appendix 1 for the complete original set of The Diary. The originals are held in the McArthur Family Archives by Gil's daughter Jenny Fitzsimmons, Port Macquarie NSW.

memories was raised. Gil's clear response was that he was too busy writing his history by what he was doing than to stop and write it down. Len's silence seemed to imply concurrence with what Gil was saying. Eventually Gil's unexpected onset of dementia, and Len who kept going until cancer resulted in his death, meant that neither had time to write their memoirs.[5]

This book is the story of Gilbert McArthur. He wrote it in action, as one passionately driven by his desire to do the will of God. It is my prayer, and I believe it would be his also, that as you read the chapters of his life, you will be personally challenged and inspired to write your own life story with the one purpose of bringing glory to God.

This book, like the lectures from which they emerged, is in three parts. The first part, *Gilbert McArthur – The Man*, unpacks McArthur's early formative years from his birth on 31 May 1922, through his early life, and the spiritual, vocational, and ministry experiences that shaped him as a man and a follower of Christ, through to his departure for Dutch New Guinea in 1955. Part Two, *Gilbert McArthur – The Mission*, explores his missionary service and leadership from 1955 in Dutch New Guinea (West Irian, Irian Jaya, and now Indonesian Papua), through until his death on 3 February 1994. Part Three, *Gilbert McArthur – The Legacy* traces the impact of his distinctive personality, spirituality and character, his influence on a selection of people, and his legacy in the lasting growth and impact of organisations and ministries he established or shared in.

In *Planting Men in Melanesia*, J Oswald Sanders tells the story of the first decade of CLTC. The opening chapter, entitled *The Shadow of a Man* introduces the sovereign God who is behind every human story including that of Gil McArthur:

> One of the fascinating exercises of the Christian life is to study the interplay of divine providence and human personality. God employs an infinite variety of methods in preparing people He has selected for special assignments. He quietly invades the affairs of men and women and weaves his own perfect plan from the tangled strands of human experience.
>
> God's method in achieving his world purpose has always been through a man or a woman. Not always noble or brilliant, but always a person with capacity for a growing faith.[6]

---

5. Will Renshaw, 'Gil McArthur', Email, 21 December 2015.
6. J. Oswald Sanders, *Planting Men in Melanesia* (Mount Hagen, Papua New Guinea: Christian Leaders' Training College, 1978), 10.

My purpose is not just to tell the story, but also to reflect on how God himself prepared, equipped and worked in and through the life and leadership of Gilbert McArthur for his glory and his world-wide mission to the nations.

David Price
Pioneers of Australia
Melbourne
davidmargprice@gmail.com
January 2019

 # INTRODUCTION

'Live in tents – build only altars'[1]

The LORD had said to Abram,
'Go from your country, your people and your father's household
to the land I will show you.

I will make you into a great nation, and I will bless you;
I will make your name great, and you will be a blessing.

I will bless those who bless you,
and whoever curses you I will curse;
and all peoples on earth will be blessed through you.'

So Abram went, as the LORD had told him; and Lot went with him. Abram was seventy-five years old when he set out from Harran. He took his wife Sarai, his nephew Lot, all the possessions they had accumulated and the people they had acquired in Harran, and they set out for the land of Canaan, and they arrived there.

Abram travelled through the land as far as the site of the great tree of Moreh at Shechem. At that time the Canaanites were in the land. The LORD appeared to Abram and said, 'To your offspring I will give this land.' So he built an altar there to the LORD, who had appeared to him.

From there he went on toward the hills east of Bethel and pitched his tent, with Bethel on the west and Ai on the east.

There he built an altar to the LORD and called on the name of the LORD.[2]

'Story telling is common to all cultures, but the way stories are told and the reasons for telling them, vary considerably between cultures.'[3] The people of Melanesia and the Pacific nations love to tell and listen to stories. They may be about a whole range of topics: gods and spirits; the origins of creation and the first humans; magic and sorcery; ancestors

---

1. Gilbert J McArthur, 'The McArthur Diary Extracts', Number 12, January 1957, 1. McArthur Family Archives.
2. Genesis 12:1-8.
3. Harry Box, *Don't Throw the Book at Them - Communicating the Christian Message to People Who Don't Read* (Pasadena, California: William Carey Library, 2014), 21.

and cultural heroes; tribal myths; famous leaders and warriors etc. The Bible is full of an amazing variety of stories about God and his working in and through people. The unique story of Abraham is one well known story.

God appeared to Abram in the idolatrous city of Ur, calling him with his family to leave Mesopotamia and go to the land he would show them.[4] It was a hard call to leave all that he had known for seventy-five years. But it was a wise and gracious call, given with the threefold promise of the land, a people and the purpose of a loving missionary God to bless all the nations through the descendants of Abram. That is God's specific purpose in calling Abram. Without hesitation or objection Abram went in obedience, and all the Bible story which follows is about how God works out his purpose of blessing the nations through Jesus the Messiah who is born from Abram's people.

God's call on the life of Gilbert McArthur was for the specific purpose of equipping Christian leaders for church, community and nation in Melanesia and the Pacific. He believed this was a critical priority in the young churches of the Pacific. It was a vision and purpose that matured over the years and broadened in scope to reach many of the top leaders of the Pacific nations. Watch for that vision and purpose as you read the story.

When Abram arrived at Shechem, the Lord appeared to him, and confirmed his promise. In response, Abram built an altar to worship and sacrifice. As we follow his story, we find him moving from place to place, pitching his tent and building altars. Tents are light and temporary dwellings – they can be dismantled and easily moved on to another place as needed. They belong to a nomadic lifestyle and speak of Abram's readiness to hold things lightly and move in faith and obedience. Altars, on the other hand are built out of stones, and are rarely moved from one place to another. They speak of a consistent loving heart of worship and sacrificial surrender to the will of God. There is not just one altar in Abram's story, but many along the journey to mark the fresh commitment to worship the Lord and surrender to his will.

At one point in Gil's story, just when he has 'got' the language and is starting to preach the Word of God, he is asked to uproot his family (move his tent), and transfer to another country and a new language. It was a very tough call, but the family moved as the mission leaders directed.

---

4. Acts 7:1-2.

In The Diary to supporters, after conveying the news of their move, Gil closed: *'We must measure our work in the light of eternity. Therefore, learn to live in tents, build only altars'*. These two images of tents and altars pointing to the deeper principles of following Christ in his mission appear consistently in the Gilbert McArthur story. They express two vital foundations that always characterise true servants of Christ. *Live in tents*: be open always to what God's will is, be willing to go where he sends, and hold lightly to transient things. *Build only altars*: the one constant must be our loving worship and praise of the Lord, and our heart surrender as we present ourselves daily as 'living sacrifices'.[5] Altars point to the radical call of Jesus Christ:

> Whoever wants to be my disciple must deny themselves and take up their cross and follow me. For whoever wants to save their life will lose it, but whoever loses their life for me and for the gospel will save it. What good is it for someone to gain the whole world, yet forfeit their soul? Or what can anyone give in exchange for their soul?[6]

During their 48 years of marriage, the family estimates Gil and Pat lived in over 20 different houses in four different countries as they obediently followed the cloud of God's leadership in their lives.[7] They surely did learn to live in tents and build only altars!

Watch for the tents and altars in the story of Gilbert McArthur.

---

5. Romans 12:1-2.
6. Mark 8:34-37.
7. Tamworth NSW, Wentworthville Sydney, Guildford Sydney, Parramatta Sydney, Sentani Dutch New Guinea, Telefolmin Papua New Guinea, East Tamworth NSW, Kingsgrove Sydney, Clemton Park Sydney, Homebush Sydney, Armadale Melbourne Bible Institute Victoria, Banz Christian Leaders' Training College Papua New Guinea, South Carolina Columbia Bible College USA, Epping Sydney, Marsfield Sydney, Lae Papua New Guinea Alliance Training Association x 2 different houses, Beechwood Southern Highlands Province Beechwood Timber Papua New Guinea, Marsfield Sydney, Port Macquarie NSW (Information provided by daughter Jenny and son Paul by email to the author, 27 November 2017).

Gil McArthur – His Story

Part One

The Man

Heredity and early life experience
have an important influence in any life.
In the providence of God, the shaping of a leader
begins before birth.
Jeremiah recognised this sovereign activity of God.

*'Before I formed you in the womb I knew you,
before you were born I set you apart;
I appointed you as a prophet to the nations.'*
(Jeremiah 1:5)

Like Jeremiah, Gilbert McArthur was chosen for leadership,
but soon discovered that his preparation involved
following a long and sometimes difficult path.

1

THE BOY BECOMES A MAN
1922 – 1939

For you created my inmost being;
You knit me together in my mother's womb.
I praise you because I am fearfully and wonderfully made;
Your works are wonderful, I know full well.[1]

Early Years in England

Gilbert James McArthur (Gil as I shall refer to him throughout) was born in a little weatherboard cottage in Randwick, close to the Sydney racecourse on 31 May 1922. He used to say he had 'not stopped running since'. His father was an Englishman and his mother an Australian of Scots parentage. They met in Australia and had a daughter, Joyce, and three years later a son, Gilbert.

Gil's grandfather on his mother's side was James Adams, a well-known Brethren preacher and the founder of the Brethren Assembly at Bondi in Sydney. His parents, Sidney and (Ada) Dorcas McArthur held only a nominal Christian faith. When Gil was around eight years old the family moved to England where Gil's father managed a soap manufacturing business.

Gil's Grandfather J.N. Adams

In his unpublished article, *The Making of a Man*, Gil describes his early childhood:

> Business interests necessitated my father's return to England, and it was there that I spent my childhood. Socially and economically our family would have come within the category of the upper-middle class. I was a student at Waterloo Grammar [in London], a choir boy in the Anglican Church [St Nicholas in Liverpool in

---

1. Psalm 139:13,14.

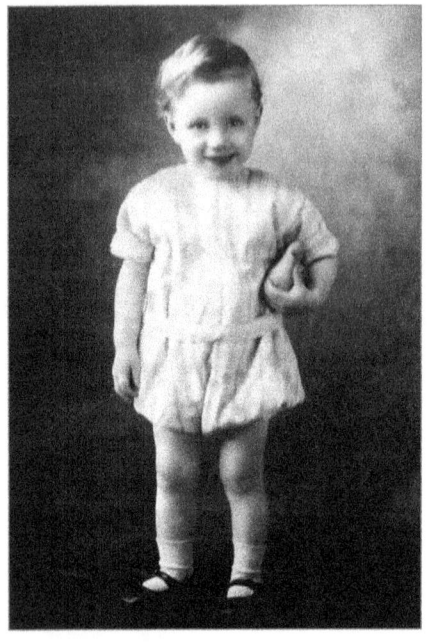

Left: Gil as a young boy and above, as a schoolboy

Lancashire], and lived in a three-storied mansion in a respectable English suburbia.[2]

Gil won a monetary prize at the age of 12 for an essay explaining why he wanted to be a choir boy: 'As a choir boy at St Nicholas' church, my ambition is to be a world-famous singer. I should ask the King and Queen if they would pay for my voice to be trained. Then perhaps I might some-day have the pleasure of singing before them.'[3] This was no doubt a reflection of his strong sense of ambition evident even in his early years.

In May 1936, just before his fourteenth birthday, Gil's life was traumatically turned upside down.

> How suddenly and sometimes how drastically can a person's world change…? Father [Sidney], a strong virile man of forty-two years who boasted of never being ill, had gone to bed with flu; pneumonia developed and within three days he was dead, and with his death the wheels of personal destiny for his fourteen year old son began slowly but inexorably to turn.[4]

---

2. Gilbert J McArthur, 'The Making of a Man', unpublished article, n.d. circa 1968, McArthur Family Archives.
3. Author Unknown, untitled Newspaper clipping, unknown Newspaper, n.d. circa 1934, McArthur Family Archives.
4. McArthur, 'The Making of a Man', 1.

To add to the tragedy, Gil's father's business interests were not very secure, and his partner by 'devious means took all', which reduced the McArthur family to poverty.

Gil's grandfather James, in Sydney, asked the Australian Government to pay part of Gil's fares back to Australia if he paid a share as well. The request was refused. The precarious financial situation brought the destitute family to a tough decision:

> The terms of charity offered by the relatives on my father's side were not acceptable to mother's proud spirit; thus, in a triumvirate of solemn resolve, born of inward hurt and urgent necessity, we met; mother, daughter and son, and there in that dreadful yet glorious moment, we each one committed the other to their own individual resources and the challenge of the unknown. Our covenant of separation was that by all fair means of personal endeavour we would work our way back to the country of our birth, Australia.[5]

His mother and sister secured live-in work to save for their travel to Australia. In May 1936 (just weeks after his father's death) Gil left Waterloo Grammar School where he had been studying Maths, Science, French and the Humanities for three years. His Leaving Certificate awarded in April 1937 indicated that his schooling was cut short by his father's death. Despite this, John Thomas, his headmaster, said in his report, 'I can recommend him as one who will do his best to give satisfaction to his employers.'[6] Gil commenced work at Moore Lane Service Station as an apprentice. He later told the *Argus* news reporter on his arrival in Australia,

> I had a pretty tough time. I was not used to roughing it, but I determined to win through and get back to my mother. I earned 12 shillings a week as an apprentice in the motor trade working from 7.30 in the morning till 9 at night. I tried to save, and all the time I watched the newspapers in case a chance should come of getting passage to Australia.
>
> One day I saw an advertisement asking for men to make up the crew of a trawler, the *St Lolan*, that was to be sent to Australia. I applied to be taken on as a cabin boy.

---

5. McArthur, 'The Making of a Man', 1.
6. J.H. Thomas, 'Leaving Certificate', (Waterloo Grammar School, April 1937), McArthur Family Archives.

Gil on the deck of the St Lolan (inset)

They told me they did not need a cabin boy, and I was too young and inexperienced to be a seaman. But I was lucky and a friend that I met persuaded them to take me on provided I did not want pay – one shilling a month they offered. I was jolly glad to get the chance, and so here I am, going back home at last.[7]

Traumatic Transition

So aged nearly fifteen, Gil signed on as a deck boy on the 150 ton 138 foot long *St Lolan*, which had been purchased to join the fishery fleet owned by Red Funnel Fisheries in Sydney, Australia.

Saying an outwardly brave farewell, I travelled North to the little fishing town of Fleetwood near Blackpool. The wharf was some distance from the railway station and the suitcase containing all my worldly possessions was large and heavy. To make matters worse the handle broke!... I think that first struggle from the train to the ship could be said to epitomise the next chapter of my life: a boy suddenly challenged to become a man![8]

When Gil finally arrived at the wharf, he looked up and down for a tall ship with a gang-way to climb, but nothing like that could be seen. He

---

7. Author Unknown, 'Stranded in England', *Argus Newspaper*, May 1937, McArthur Family Archives.
8. McArthur, 'The Making of a Man', 2.

asked an old sailor if he knew where the *St Lolan* was. He pointed down to a row of fishing trawlers moored together and told Gil: 'clamber down and take the one on the end – that be 'er'. Arriving on deck, Gil asked to be shown to his cabin, but another disappointment was in store as he discovered that his cabin was in fact the officers' mess, and that his share in it was the bunk in the bulkhead behind the sliding doors – a cavity about two feet deep, six feet long and two feet wide with a locker underneath the bench! He was immediately put to work assisting the cook.[9]

Over the next few days, the fourteen-member crew of various nationalities arrived. They sailed from Fleetwood on a voyage of 19,500 kilometres that would take 87 days around the African coast and across the Indian Ocean to Sydney. He had never imagined possible the personal, physical, and moral challenges that journey would bring. The young boy was indeed to become a man!

The first three stormy days of the voyage in the Irish Sea were a nightmare of violent seasickness during which Gil was unable to help himself. He was fed a mixture of bread and condensed milk to overcome the agony of dry-retching, and as they moved into calmer seas he began to find his sea-legs. As he served meals to the officers there were numerous occasions when the lurch of the ship resulted in food being placed anywhere but on the table. He received many 'boots in the backside' until at last he became adept at balancing things under all the changing conditions of wind and sea.[10]

> In many ways I became quite a favourite with the crew; I was generally alert and helpful, and being the 'boy' of the ship, provided an outlet for their butts and jokes. My youthful cheekiness often gave them the opportunity to teach me the necessary lessons of life. One, well remembered, was known as the 'shark bait treatment'. In the glass-like waters of the African coast we often gathered to watch the sharks, as, attracted by the ships offal, they would glide along near the after-quarter. Grabbing me by the legs my crewmates would toss me over the side and dangle me head-first a few inches above the water and the awful denizens of the deep – upon reflection, the crew's laughter, mingled with my screams, would doubtless have kept the hungriest shark at bay![11]

---

9. McArthur, 'The Making of a Man', 2.
10. McArthur, 'The Making of a Man', 3.
11. McArthur, 'The Making of a Man', 3.

While in Dakar on the west coast of Africa, some of the crew decided that young Gil's education should include a visit to a brothel in the red-light area so they could introduce him to the facts of life. After doing the rounds of the town and providing tuition for Gil in the art of beer drinking, they arrived at the brothel. The 'ladies of entertainment' quickly entered crudely into assisting the crew advance 'the boy's essential education'. But when the madam of the house arrived she took pity on his 'youthful bewilderment', bundled him out the back door, and he escaped back to the ship. The episode became a continuing source of mirth for the crew.

Leaving Dakar, they headed for Cape Town. Gil unexpectedly replaced the cook as he had deserted the trawler in Dakar. One morning, as Gil was doing his duty of delivering a 5.00 am cup of coffee to the officer of the watch, he made the mistake of approaching the bridge from the weather side instead of the lee. As he opened the wheel house door a wave hit the ship, and lurching forward Gil tipped a large mug of steaming hot coffee into the lap of the first mate!

> 'You **** idiot,' he screamed as he leaped to his feet in pain, at the same time letting fly with a mighty swipe which lifted me up into the air and sent me sailing off the bridge onto the deck below. Just at that moment the chief engineer appeared. As an Irishman, he was always ready to sponsor any worthy cause, and seeing me groaning on the deck he was well on the way to heading up a minor mutiny when one of the stokers rushed up shouting: 'Fire! Fire in the bunkers!'[12]

Spontaneous combustion had set the bunker coal alight, and for four days and nights they fought the fire and the accompanying smoke and gas. The heat from the fire turned the ship into an oven with steel decks blistering and bulkheads too hot for comfort. The exhausted crew at last brought the still burning ship into Cape Town, where with proper fire-fighting equipment the fire was extinguished. News in the local papers of their hazardous experience made them the centre of attraction, and Gil was befriended by two older ladies who showed him the sights. It was also his first thrilling experience of flying, as he was taken up in a Gypsy Moth for a panoramic flight over the city – a 'harbinger of things to come'.[13]

---

12. McArthur, 'The Making of a Man', 4.
13. McArthur, 'The Making of a Man', 5.

THE BOY BECOMES A MAN

The newspaper clipping of Gil and his Grandfather

Between Cape Town and Durban, Gil celebrated his fifteenth birthday. In Durban, they loaded to the maximum supplies for the long stretch across the Indian Ocean. Two sailors had to be left in Durban due to illness. Two days out of Durban they ran into a 'raging storm', and the heavy ship struggled in the huge seas. The Chief Engineer reported to the Captain that he was having trouble keeping up steam in the boiler, because he believed they had taken on inferior quality coal in Durban. The storm increased in ferocity, and they 'hove to' heading the bow into the wind and sea. But successive heavy waves breaking over the fore peak smashed the hatches, and water began to pour in, so it was all hands to the pumps. Getting heavier, the ship began to bury its bow completely in the oncoming waves, the pumps clogged up and the situation deteriorated to the point where the ship was in danger of sinking. The Captain, deck officers and chief engineer conferred on what to do. There were two choices as the ship dug her nose in deeper every wave: stay hove to and hope they could somehow ride out the storm or try and turn the ship and run for port, a dangerous manoeuvre with insufficient steam up so that the ship could broach (only half turn and so lie side on to wind and sea). The decision was made by the Captain, with 40 years' sea experience, to generate all possible steam, and waiting for the right moment, then to turn the ship. Around they went, keeling over with the starboard gunwale completely underwater. The next wave smacked them hard on the quarter and helped to complete the turn, and riding with the weather they headed back to Durban. On arrival, after some long haggling, the bunkers were refilled with good quality coal, and without further major incident apart from running out of fresh food, they completed the thirty-day trip to Albany Western Australia, and then around the coast to Sydney.[14]

When the *St Lolan* finally arrived in Sydney on 20 July 1937, it was reported in the *Daily Telegraph*, 'Not one of the 14 men on board including the commander (Captain W.A. Boyd) wants to see the ship again… Rats, vermin and shortage of food made us all wish for the sight of Sydney, and a bath'.[15]

The teenage Gil's comment was characteristically much more positive and reflected his love of challenge and adventure. 'It was a wonderful

---

14. McArthur, 'The Making of a Man', 7.
15. Author Unknown, 'Trawler Arrives – Hardships of Voyage', Newspaper Unknown, 21 July 1937, McArthur Family Archives.

trip. I could not have sailed with a better bunch of chaps. Although I was the youngest, no one tried to bully me. They even let me steer the ship. That was great.'[16] He also made a profit out of the trip, because in Cape Town the two women who looked after the 'plucky lad' presented him with a gift of £24!

Thirty years later, however, Gil was able to recall what had become a moment of transition for him in that huge storm out of Durban:

> The pathos of those few awful moments when as but a stripling I stood on the deck of that little fishing trawler as we raced down the crest of a mighty wave into what seemed the very jaws of death, has never left me. In that moment 'a soul was born'; in spirit, the boy became a man, and the man was destined to a life of service for his fellowman, and for his God.[17]

New Beginnings

When Gil arrived in Sydney his grandfather was waiting for him:

> My old scots Grandfather who sailed the 'Cape route' many years before in the sailing ship days was there to meet me. Proudly he witnessed my certificate of discharge and as a true Scotsman offered wise counsel as to how I should invest my 87 days' pay – the fabulous (equivalent) amount of 35 cents: ten cents a month and half month's bonus![18]

His first concern was for his mother and sister still in London. He wanted to get a job with a good wage so that they could join him as soon as possible.[19] But his grandfather had far more than Gil's finances at heart.

> I was soon to discover that this dear man had in fact been the veritable guardian angel of the voyage. Knowing something of the physical and moral hazards of such a journey he had set himself a covenant of prayer: Every day entering the 'quiet place' and there claiming his 'boy' for God – 'The prayer of a righteous man is powerful and effective.' (James 5:16)[20]

---

16. Author Unknown, 'Cabin Boy's Trip to Aid Family', *Daily Telegraph*, 21 July 1937, McArthur Family Archives.
17. McArthur, 'The Making of a Man', 8.
18. McArthur, 'The Making of a Man', 7.
19. Author Unknown, 'Cabin Boy's Trip to Aid Family'.
20. McArthur, 'The Making of a Man', 7.

Gil McArthur:
A 14 year-old cabin boy on the trawler St Lolan

Gil later wrote in his application to the Baptist College of NSW – 'I was led to faith in Christ through the life and witness of a godly grandfather.'[21] He lived in Sydney under the guiding hand of his preacher grandfather, with his mother (who married again) and sister Joyce. He completed his secondary education and became an optical assistant until 22 April 1941, when he enlisted for military service in World War II, putting his birth date back to 21 February 1922 to be accepted into the military forces.[22]

---

21. Gilbert and Pat McArthur, 'Application for Service in New Guinea', July 1951, personal letter cited in Schedule B of his application, Global Interaction Archives.
22. Certificate of the Australian Government Department of Veterans' Affairs. On his transfer to the Navy his birth date was listed correctly on the Navy Certificate of Service.

2
THE SHAPING OF THE MAN
1940 – 1955

*And we know that in all things God works
for the good of those who love him,
who have been called according to his purpose.*[1]

Military Service World War II 1941–1945

When World War II continued to escalate Gil, with his age suitably inflated, enlisted in the Allied Military Forces. In April 1941 he was sent for training to the army base at Tamworth NSW. One Sunday he attended the Brethren Assembly there, and met the Miller family of five daughters – one of whom was a young lady named Pat. Following his training, he was posted to serve in the Middle East with the 5th Field Company of the Royal Australian Engineers 2nd Division.

On the returning voyage to Australia following 18 months' service in the Middle East, he became seriously ill with appendicitis that developed into peritonitis. He was put ashore in India in a small Catholic hospital. His memories of that time were of the nuns faithfully praying at his bedside each time he awoke from his coma. The ship he had been on was later torpedoed and destroyed, with the loss of many lives. God had spared his life twice over.

Because the Navy needed his optical skills, Gil was asked to transfer from the Army to the Navy. From 15 February 1943 until 19 November 1945, he served in an Australian flotilla assigned to the American 7th Fleet under the command of General Douglas McArthur. Following training at the *Cerberus* Naval Base, Gil served on His Majesty's Australian ships, *Kanimbla*, *Doomba* and *Rushcutter*. During these years he contracted rheumatic fever and was warned not to exercise or to be active. His bold response to that instruction was to take up horse riding, boxing and swimming![2]

---

1. Romans 8:28.
2. During his military service Gil qualified for the following campaign awards – 1939-45 Star, Pacific Star, Defence Medal, War Medal, Australian Service Medal, and the Returned from Active Service Badge.

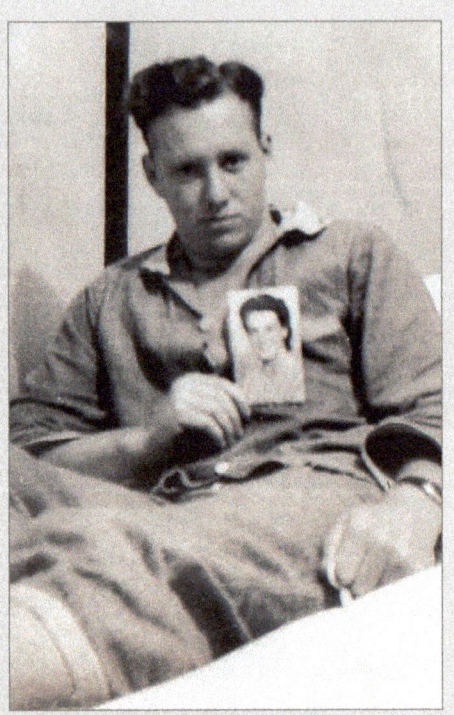

Above:
Gil initially enlisted in the Army for his WWII service

Above right:
Gil in hospital recovering from Peritonitis

Right:
Gil after his Navy transfer

The war years were important in the formation of Gil the man. He faced the tough conditions of war in the Middle East. He was delivered from death by illness, danger and shipwreck, and he was brought into contact with the Pacific Island world for the first time, later a major arena of his ministry. Although converted earlier, the war experiences brought a deeper commitment to Christ as not only Saviour, but Lord. Years later he wrote, 'How glad I am personally that as a young soldier, caught up in the ravages of the Second World War in the Middle East and the Pacific, I was led by the Spirit of God to yield my will to HIS WILL.'[3]

During the War in the Pacific, the Spirit of God placed the peoples of the Pacific on his heart. Thereafter Gil experienced God's protective hand upon his life, keeping him and preparing him for his sovereign purposes in the years ahead.

Marriage, Family and Ministry 1946

Following his discharge from the Navy, Gil again worked as a Dispensing Optician in the Sydney suburb of Bondi. On 15 June 1946, four years after meeting her in Tamworth, Gil married Patricia May Miller at the Jubilee Hall, Tamworth NSW. Pat was a shop assistant at Treloars, one of the large department stores in Tamworth. She was also the right-hand girl for her father Clarry in his transport business, helping to service vehicles and carry out mechanical work. She was very much a hands-on practical person. Pat was to prove to be a tower of strength, and the anchor for the family in their ministry journey together. Gil's son Paul recalls that Pat's family never really forgave Gil for taking Pat away from Tamworth.[4] In 1949 they purchased a home in Tamworth under the War Services Scheme. It was during this time that Gil learned to fly and took out his private pilot's licence.

In the years that followed, Gil and Pat had five children: Robyn Leigh born 2 March 1947 (Eden), Jeanette Patricia born 20 July 1949 (Fitzsimons), Paul Anthony born 19 February 1951, Wendy Elizabeth born 8 June 1955 (Micklessen), and Sandra Joy born 26 July 1958 (died 24 February 2012).[5]

Gil and Pat attended the Baptist Church in Tamworth. The pastor, Victor Barnard, was deeply committed not only to the church, but also

---

3. McArthur, 'The Fellowship of the Committed Ones'.
4. Paul McArthur. 'Gilbert McArthur Memories', Telephone Interview, Queensland, 9 June 2016.
5. Jenny Fitzsimons, 'Birth Dates', Email, 17 May 2016.

The McArthur's wedding day on 15 June 1946

to ministry among the indigenous Australians living in New South Wales. Because Gil had his pilot's licence, and Victor sensed his potential capacity for gospel ministry, Victor often asked Gil to fly him out west for evangelistic outreach to the Aboriginal communities. Under Victor's influence, Gil himself became involved in the preaching, and at times when Victor was unable to go, Gil went on his own. This opportunity was formative in helping Gil understand traditional animistic religion, and how to preach the Bible to the indigenous people.

East West Airlines 1946-1950

Gil moved from optometry, and from 1946 until 1950 worked as the Supply and Commercial Manager with East West Airlines (EWA). This young developing airline was committed to extending air services to outback NSW and connecting the regional cities with Sydney. During Gil's time with EWA, two events in particular indicate his developing leadership qualities.

The first was his involvement in the crash of an EWA aircraft. Gil recorded the sequence of events in his *Early EWA Reminiscences*:

Flight… Took off from the Tamworth showground airfield with passengers bound for Sydney… I was the last one to board and strapped myself into the lift-up hostess seat at the rear of the aircraft. John Rentall was the pilot, and after completing his various flight checks, we commenced our take-off run down the grass airstrip. The lift off and climb procedures were normal, but as we flew down past the cemetery, I recall making a brief reflection of the seeming incongruity of being in an aircraft which by the power of propulsion could 'reach for the sky' while underneath me was the stark evidence of the limited tenure of man's life-span within his experience of time and space.

These personal reveries were suddenly shattered by the discordant noise of the starboard engine as it spluttered and coughed from fuel starvation (which was later determined as being the main fuel line blocked by a hornet's nest!). Within seconds the engine had died and the pilot was involved in a desperate struggle to keep the aircraft flying. It is well known that the single engine performance of the Avro Anson is very marginal and from my own limited knowledge of flying I knew that our attempt to maintain altitude was doomed to failure and that a crash landing was inevitable and, even as I was alerting the passengers to strap-tight and brace themselves, we literally 'fell out of the air'. The port wing and engine took most of the initial crash shock force and after numerous jumps and bumps we came to rest in a water-logged paddock. Calling to the passengers to get out quickly and get far away from the aircraft, I grabbed the fire extinguisher knocked open the rear door and raced towards the pilot.

As I climbed over the starboard wing I noticed the broken fuel lines and smoke and feared that we may be engulfed in flames at any moment. This fear lent wings to my feet and strength to my arms. The pilot was sitting in his seat in open space. The whole front of the aircraft had shattered and collapsed around him. The front instrument panel had smashed into the pilot's face and he was unconscious. I unbuckled his belt and tried to lift him out, but soon discovered that his leg was caught in the rudder pedal and had been partly severed by the metal protrusion.

Left:
Gil learning to fly,
Tamworth

Centre:
A converted Lockheed Hudson bomber at Tamworth 1950

Below:
The East West fleet,
Tamworth 1950

The first was his involvement in the crash of an EWA aircraft. Gil recorded the sequence of events in his *Early EWA Reminiscences*:

> Flight… Took off from the Tamworth showground airfield with passengers bound for Sydney… I was the last one to board and strapped myself into the lift-up hostess seat at the rear of the aircraft. John Rentall was the pilot, and after completing his various flight checks, we commenced our take-off run down the grass airstrip. The lift off and climb procedures were normal, but as we flew down past the cemetery, I recall making a brief reflection of the seeming incongruity of being in an aircraft which by the power of propulsion could 'reach for the sky' while underneath me was the stark evidence of the limited tenure of man's life-span within his experience of time and space.
>
> These personal reveries were suddenly shattered by the discordant noise of the starboard engine as it spluttered and coughed from fuel starvation (which was later determined as being the main fuel line blocked by a hornet's nest!). Within seconds the engine had died and the pilot was involved in a desperate struggle to keep the aircraft flying. It is well known that the single engine performance of the Avro Anson is very marginal and from my own limited knowledge of flying I knew that our attempt to maintain altitude was doomed to failure and that a crash landing was inevitable and, even as I was alerting the passengers to strap-tight and brace themselves, we literally 'fell out of the air'. The port wing and engine took most of the initial crash shock force and after numerous jumps and bumps we came to rest in a water-logged paddock. Calling to the passengers to get out quickly and get far away from the aircraft, I grabbed the fire extinguisher knocked open the rear door and raced towards the pilot.
>
> As I climbed over the starboard wing I noticed the broken fuel lines and smoke and feared that we may be engulfed in flames at any moment. This fear lent wings to my feet and strength to my arms. The pilot was sitting in his seat in open space. The whole front of the aircraft had shattered and collapsed around him. The front instrument panel had smashed into the pilot's face and he was unconscious. I unbuckled his belt and tried to lift him out, but soon discovered that his leg was caught in the rudder pedal and had been partly severed by the metal protrusion.

Left:
Gil learning to fly, Tamworth

Centre:
A converted Lockheed Hudson bomber at Tamworth 1950

Below:
The East West fleet, Tamworth 1950

The fear of fire was heavy upon me as I struggled madly to free him, and in the process probably caused more damage to his foot and leg. His facial injuries were pumping blood onto my suit coat as I prayed for superhuman effort to extricate him from the wreckage. Fortunately help arrived and we were able to lift the battered Johnny Rentell out of the flight deck and laid him on the grass well away from the aircraft. Upon reflection, I believe this was my most traumatic moment, for as we attended to Johnny, so I looked up and saw his wife Peggy racing towards us. She had watched the take-off, witnessed the crash, and run all the way from the airport to reach her husband. Never will I forget the look of sheer agony upon her face as she knelt by her badly injured husband and pleaded for his life. Of such chapters of human pathos were the fledgling days of the young airline as it struggled to fulfil its mandate of linking the country with the capitals.

The sequel to this accident was a somewhat happy one. Johnny Rentell was flown to Sydney by Air-Ambulance where his foot and lower leg were amputated. He was fitted later with an artificial leg and after a lengthy convalescence returned to flying duties with EWA.[6]

The second event took place when EWA wanted to develop their services and move from visual to full instrument flight operations with larger aircraft. The airport at Tamworth in NSW was too short for DC3 aircraft, but they managed to locate six Lockheed Hudson Bomber aircraft at Camden in NSW south of Sydney, which were surplus from the war effort. These aircraft could be modified for civilian passenger use and operate out of Tamworth. They were in stripped-down condition but came with many spares (15 new Pratt and Whitney R1830 engines, many boxes of instruments, engine and airframe spares and many small components.)[7]

In March 1949 the company received news of their successful tender for these aircraft and spares at a very keen price. But the problem was how to get the airframes to Tamworth. One plane was prepared for a ferry flight to Tamworth, and it was Gil's suggestion that he attempt to transport three plane fuselages overland by road to Tamworth, minus

---

6. Archie Smith, *East-West Eagles – The Story of East West Airlines* (Cairns. Australia: Robert Brown and Associates, 1989), 32 ff.
7. Gilbert J McArthur, 'The Lockheed Hudson Saga', unpublished article, circa 1947, 1, 2, McArthur Family Archives.

their wings, on their own wheels. It was a distance of 482 kilometres, a seemingly impossible task. He would also supervise the transport of the wings, and all the other parts and spares. Gil negotiated with the Police and Transport Department for a wide vehicle road permit. But when the aircraft were measured, the authorities responded with a complete negative, which put a cloud over the entire operation. Sometime later, Gil heard that a new Superintendent of Transport had been appointed who was the Honorary Commandant of the Police Boys' Club with which he had previous connections. Not one to give up easily in the face of opposition, Gil placed the East West situation before him. The Superintendent said he would consider the matter subject to three requirements. First, that Gil would make a complete detailed study of the road, paying special attention to the width of bridges over the creeks and rivers, and the sharp bends of the dirt road section to Singleton of 90 kilometres, estimating how many trees would need to be cut down, and where the road would be widened to make room for the towed aircraft to negotiate the corners. Second, that East West would pay for a police motor cycle escort at the front and rear of the convoy to ensure the safety of other traffic. Third, that where it was not possible to negotiate small bridges, the permission of the farmers be sought to cut and repair their fences so they could ford the various rivers and get back on the road. It was obviously a mammoth task!

With these conditions agreed to, Gil and Captain Arch Smith set out on the survey of the road and bridges.

> [It was] a trip which took much longer than we estimated as, in an ex-army jeep, we found ourselves in the dark of night and amidst a raging rainstorm trying to traverse the hills, bends, and fast running creeks of what, in those days, was just a little-used back road. Certainly, the experience of the particular trip did not auger well for the major aircraft towing expedition yet to come![8]

Finally, with all the permissions in place, the aircraft were stripped of their wings, hitched to their Land Rover towing vehicles and towed on their own wheels the 482 kilometres to Tamworth. Gil described this very difficult operation:

> The overall exercise took three arduous days, the highlights of which were overcoming the problem of the numerous wooden bridges that were too small… This required cutting the farmer's

---

8. McArthur, 'The Lockheed Hudson Saga', 1, 2.

barbed-wire fences and winching the aircraft off the road, over the banks, down into the creeks, rolling them on their wheels or floating them across the water, and then winching them up on the other side and on to the road again, after which, of course, the farmer's fences had to be repaired. This difficult exercise had to be repeated many times and the physical demands upon the team were very heavy but, without exception they rose to the challenge of the hour… Special thanks must be given to the members of the police motor cycle escort. These men were worth their weight in gold. They got off their motorcycles and joined the team in every hazardous exercise of the water crossings, and in many instances, their quick action prevented serious danger to the aircraft… It was an exhilarating moment for the transport team when the city of Tamworth at last loomed into view… a large number of the populace came out to welcome the weary cavalcade that had overcome many difficulties in bringing the whole new dimension of arterial services to the country centres.[9]

This amazing achievement speaks volumes about Gil – his vision, ambition, determination, faith to overcome obstacles, and ability to succeed in seemingly impossible tasks. As Kouzes and Posner observe, 'Leaders look for ways to radically alter the status quo, for ways to create something totally new, for revolutionary new processes, for ways to beat the system. Whether leaders are selected for processes or initiate them, they always search for opportunities to do what has never been done.'[10]

These new EWA initiatives brought profound and lasting change in the regional air services in NSW. In the words of Archie Smith, the CEO of EWA, 'These Lockheed aircraft performed a magnificent task for almost a decade without serious mishap during a vital period of the company's development.'[11]

However, one evening travelling home after an EWA Board meeting, Gil asked himself 'how important was it in terms of eternal values if people travelled on an EWA flight?' His pastor, Victor Barnard, had been urging him to consider entering full-time Christian ministry. It was a time of restlessness, as he with Pat reflected on God's purpose for their lives. When Dr J Oswald Sanders delivered a missionary challenge

---

9. McArthur, 'The Lockheed Hudson Saga', 2.
10. James M Kouzes and Barry Z Posner, *The Leadership Challenge*, Second Edition (San Franciso: Jossey-Bass Publishers, 1995), 36.
11. Smith, *East-West Eagles - The Story of East West Airlines*. 36.

at Tamworth Baptist Church in 1950, Gil and Pat talked with him, and the conviction deepened to offer themselves for missionary service. 'Something happened to them in Tamworth that lit a fire in them for mission.'[12]

Baptist (Morling) Theological College of NSW 1951-1954

In 1951, to prepare for what would be a major transition from the commercial aviation industry into mission, Gil and Pat with their two girls Robyn and Jenny, and new son Paul, moved to Sydney from Tamworth to enrol in Theological studies at the Baptist Theological College (now Morling College) where the Principal was Professor George Morling. He later commented, '[Gil] is one of our best men of all time. He has a rich spiritual life, undoubted gifts of administration and outstanding powers of influence. I need not say anything else about this outstanding man.'[13]

In his first probationary year in 1951, Gil was employed on the staff of the Baptist Home Mission Committee under the direction of the Home Mission Superintendent. In July of that year Gil and Pat wrote a joint letter of application to the Australian Baptist Foreign Mission (ABFM) in George Street Sydney. It expressed their deep personal conviction and sense of debt to serve in mission to reach those who had never heard the Gospel:

Dear Brother in Christ;

My wife and I are deeply conscious of our Lord's leading in respect to Him requiring us to devote our lives to the proclamation of His riches, to souls in need where'er those souls may be found.

Being as we are debtors to His Grace, we find ourselves also debtors to the Greeks, and to the Barbarians, to the wise, and to the unwise. To our God then, we have been able to say of a truth; as much as in us is, we are ready to preach the Gospel to those in New Guinea who constantly rise up before us as souls in need.

Having spent nigh on three years in the Islands and being thereby conversant with the Peoples, Life, Climate, etc. I have been able to convey much of same to my wife, so that together we might intelligently count the cost, and then in the light of our debtorship

---

12. McArthur, Paul, 'Gil McArthur Memories'.
13. George Morling, 'Letter to Max Knight from George Morling', n.d., Global Interaction Archives.

to God, count our service not by any means a sacrifice, but a blessed privilege.

In submitting this application, we will deal only with those questions pertinent to the New Guinea field, as having already been examined by the officers of the Union and accepted for service within the Denomination, we therefore look upon this application as the widening only, of our sphere of service.

It is known of course, that my aviation experience would be of some assistance should Aircraft be applied to the Mission work and whilst for myself I sincerely believe that the Lord would have us use Aircraft in His service in New Guinea, in much the way as we use a car in Australia, yet nevertheless this application expresses the desire of my wife and myself to serve our Master in New Guinea where'er and in what'er capacity He would cause the Foreign Mission Committee to use us.

Yours in His Service.

G.J. McArthur & P.M. McArthur[14]

Gil's letter and application papers reveal his visionary interest of pioneering the possible use of aircraft for the Baptist Mission work in New Guinea. He believed this would facilitate the movement of supplies, overcome the heavy time commitment in trekking over mountainous terrain, and with the establishment of airstrips accelerate the evangelisation of the remote tribes. He expressed the conviction in his application that he believed that 'there is a special work for me to do in Telefolmin[15], that not many others are equipped to do.'[16] In addition to Gil, Doug Vaughan, an aircraft engineer was also in College and very interested in being part of the aircraft strategy.

Rev Harry Orr, Secretary of the New Guinea Missionary Committee, spent several hours in conference with Gil discussing all aspects of his aviation vision for PNG. As a result, Gil was asked to research and prepare a full proposal. On 25 May 1951, he presented *The Case for Aviation*

---

14. McArthur, 'Application for Service in New Guinea', Letter to Baptist New Guinea Mission, 17 July 1951. Global Interaction Archives.
15. The earlier spelling (Telefolmin) is followed throughout, but later spelling changed to Telefomin.
16. McArthur, 'Application for Service in New Guinea'. No doubt this was related to his developing vision for the use of aircraft in the missionary strategy and the possibility of his personal involvement in this initiative at Telefolmin.

detailing strategic and financial proposals and a funding strategy for consideration. The Committee saw the aircraft scheme useful for more than the Telefolmin area:

> An important factor in considering this scheme is the development of the Sepik River area. Our ultimate plan is to break into the Roman Catholic strongholds. A suitable vessel would cost upward of £5000. A smaller craft would be needed for lesser waterways. The operation of our own aircraft would be quicker and conserve our missionaries' time, would save the outlay to purchase a suitable craft and would be at least comparable in the cost of maintaining the stations. By that time there should be 4 or 5 stations at least with their own airstrips. The more stations developed the more advantageous the scheme. What we saved in transport would possibly make the opening of other pioneer stations possible… If the Committee approves of this scheme it would seem advisable that it should be set in motion this year…[17]

By 1953 planning had proceeded to the point that a further report indicated that it was proposed to have the aircraft operating in the field by March 1954.[18] In January, Gil was asked to go to New Guinea 'to undertake an exhaustive survey in connection with the projected Aircraft Scheme.'[19] The *Board Decisions* in *Vision* October 1954 reported:

> Readers will have heard of the projected aircraft scheme for our New Guinea field. After a very intensive survey by Mr Gilbert McArthur, the Board has accepted a different scheme for the implementing of this aircraft service. This new scheme will co-operate with the Missionary Aviation Fellowship, and the two Lutheran societies in the area, to bring this much-needed service into operation…[20]

---

17. Harry Orr, 'Aircraft in New Guinea', unpublished report (Granville NSW, 25 May 1951), Global Interaction Archives. Rev Harry Orr was the Secretary of the New Guinea Missionary Committee. Attached to his report were the financial proposal and details prepared by Gil McArthur.
18. Harry Orr and Albert Dube, 'New Guinea Aircraft Scheme', unpublished paper, (Sydney NSW, actual date not specified 1953), Global Interaction Archives.
19. Author Unknown, 'Brief Mention', *Vision Magazine*, March 1954, 10, Global Interaction Archives.
20. Author Unknown, 'Brief Mention', *Vision Magazine*, October 1954, 12, Global Interaction Archives.

But the 'Aircraft Scheme' proposal remained under discussion until January 1958. Missionary Aviation Fellowship (MAF) had been unable to provide the capacity required for the Telefolmin area. Due to the strategic importance of aircraft for the Telefolmin outreach, Gil was still urging that the Baptists start their own program. In a letter from Vic Ambrose MAF PNG Manager to Gil in November 1957, MAF provided assurance that they would adjust their program to give priority to the needs of Telefolmin, but they were interested in the Baptists purchasing an aircraft to lease to MAF to operate for this purpose. In January 1958, the Telefolmin Station Committee agreed (with some reservations) to a trial of the MAF partnership, and the purchase of an aircraft to lease to MAF.[21]

Principal George Morling, Baptist Theological College

During his theological studies Gil was the student pastor at the Wentworthville, Guilford and then Parramatta Baptist Churches. This enabled him to develop his preaching and pastoral skills, which further prepared him for the leadership roles ahead.

Departure for Dutch New Guinea 1955

In November 1955, Gil and Pat sailed for Dutch New Guinea (West Irian, Irian Jaya, now the Indonesian Province of Papua). They were assigned to be part of a joint missions team to trek into the 'Shangri La' of the Baliem Valley to the unreached Dani tribes people, building airstrips, engaging in Bible translation, and training national evangelist/church planters. The call to move their tent to take the Gospel of Christ to those who had never heard found a ready response on the altar of their hearts and compelled them forward. And so begins the next part of the story.

---

21. Vic Ambrose, 'Telefolmin Aircraft Program', Letter, 11 April 1957, Global Interaction Archives.

Gil and Pat's ABFM application photographs

3

THE QUALITIES OF THE MAN

*Therefore, I urge you, brothers and sisters,
in view of God's mercy,
to offer your bodies as living sacrifices,
holy and pleasing to God –
this is your spiritual act of worship.
Do not conform any longer to the pattern of this world,
but be transformed by the renewing of your mind.
Then you will be able to test and approve what God's will is –
his good pleasing and perfect will.*[1]

'Lurking in the murky depths of leadership theory is a question… Are leaders born or made?' The general consensus is that leaders are born *and* made.[2] Born, because there are some features of leadership that emerge in the development of the person in their early life experience. Made, because leadership includes a set of skills that can be learned by training, perception, practice and experience over time. It seems appropriate to pause here in Gil McArthur's story to ask what qualities of Christian leadership have emerged in his first 30 years?

Gil's early life and formative years can hardly be described as ordinary or mundane! In reviewing this formative part of his story we have seen the overruling hand of God's sovereign providence, protection and formation. In these years God allowed Gil a difficult and dangerous pathway and provided for him a wonderful soul mate who was one with him in mind and heart to do God's will. The God who shapes and moulds our lives worked purposefully to equip Gil for leadership, and to prepare his chosen channel to initiate some remarkable ministries that would impact the lives of many and change eternal destinies. As F B Meyer reflects:

---

1. Romans 12:1,2.
2. James Lawrence, *Growing Leaders – Reflections on Leadership, Life and Jesus.* (Abingdon United Kingdom: The Bible Reading Fellowship, 2004), 25.

A providence is shaping our ends; a plan is developing in our lives; a supremely wise and loving Being is making all things work together for good. In the sequel of our life's story we shall see that there was meaning and necessity in all the previous incidents, save those which are the result of our own folly and sin, and that even those have been made to contribute to the final result.[3]

How has God been shaping Gil in these early years? Upon reflection we see him emerging as a man with distinctive values, qualities, experiences and practical skills that equipped him for Christian leadership.

Total Commitment to Christ as Lord

Gil was led to faith as a teenager through the influence of a godly grandfather, and during the painful and stretching experience of war his mature and total surrender to Christ solidified. 'How glad I am personally that as a young soldier, caught up in the ravages of World War II in the Middle East and the Pacific, I was led by the Spirit of God to yield my will to HIS WILL.'[4]

Authentic leadership does not generate from the outside in. It comes from the inside out – from the altar of the heart. For Christian leaders, the foundation of leadership is their personal relationship and walk with the Lord Jesus Christ, and the biblical worldview and values that become the integrating force in their lives. Without strong core beliefs, a leader will be inconsistent, untrustworthy and not willingly followed: in other words, an ineffective leader. A solid base upon which to stand that is clearly communicated to others and matched by their lives provides, under God, the credibility for others to put their trust in those charged with leadership roles.

Gil McArthur's leadership was based on the altar of his surrender to Christ as Lord, and his consistent daily walk in Christ. This total commitment was expressed by both Gil and Pat in their letter to the Baptist Mission: 'this application expresses the desire of my wife and myself to serve our Master in New Guinea where'er and in whate'er capacity He would cause the Foreign Mission Committee to use us.'[5]

Gil understood the warning James Lawrence of Arrow Leadership presents:

---

3. J. Oswald Sanders, *Paul the Leader: A Vision for Christian Leadership Today* (Eastbourne United Kingdom, 1983), 19.
4. McArthur, 'The Fellowship of the Committed Ones'.
5. McArthur, 'Application for Service in New Guinea'.

If we've lost our first love, there is no greater priority than regaining it. Ultimately this is dependent upon God's grace, for it is his gift to us, but our part is to put ourselves in the place where we are open to receiving his grace through believing and acting upon what Jesus said, through exercising spiritual disciplines, through resolving internal issues, and through knowing what we are aiming for.[6]

Discerning Vision and Direction

Leadership by definition involves leading people, so the Christian leader needs to discern God's direction for the future. Walter Wright believes,

> Articulating the vision may be a leader's single most important responsibility. The leader keeps the vision – the mission, the reason the church or organization was formed – before the people, continually asking what we need to do today and tomorrow to live out that vision.[7]

It is important to note that this orientation towards the future may well be more difficult in some cultures, where the emphasis is upon the stories and leaders of the past. Leaders in these cultures will require a greater realignment in thinking to grapple with discerning how God is leading them forward into change. Vision is not just dreaming our own dreams, but actually seeing what **God** is doing, and keeping the main thing the main thing.

From an early age, Gil was a man of vision. He could see the possibilities – whether it was finding his way as a teenager back to Australia by ship to start a new life; or using surplus aircraft from the War effort to convert into passenger aircraft to grow a rural air-service; or moving aircraft overland by road to Tamworth along an impossible road; or using aircraft for more effective mission in the rugged mountainous terrain of PNG.

This capacity to discern God's vision and direction becomes central in Part Two of Gil's story. He could see the opportunities, see a new future, see the difficulties and yet see the Lord as sufficient to overcome them, because he was convinced the plans were not his own but God's.

---

6. Lawrence, *Growing Leaders – Reflections on Leadership, Life and Jesus*, 81.
7. Walter Wright, *Relational Leadership – A Biblical Model for Influence and Service*, Kindle Edition (Carlisle United Kingdom: Paternoster Press, 2009), Kindle Locations 1617-1618.

Wide Breadth of Experience

Gil had an unusual breadth of life and work experience in his formative years. He was a generalist not a specialist as seems often to be the pattern today. Gil was student, mechanic, sailor, optical assistant, soldier, pilot, commercial manager, airline executive, theological student and pastor. 'This kind of diversity manifestly suited a pioneer like Gil. In our day today, with narrow specialisations the norm, we have lost touch with this kind of multi-talented generalist, but DNG and PNG needed exactly this in the 1960s.'[8]

Gil's diversity of life experience equipped him to provide confident leadership in complex organisations and tasks, and a readiness to tackle challenges that he had never faced before – whether it was an 87-day sea voyage as a teenager, enrolling to fight in the war under age, or moving modified Bomber aircraft by road. It seemed nothing was beyond his readiness to 'have a go' in the faith of the pioneer that says 'I can do everything through him who gives me strength.'[9]

Gifted Ability to Communicate and Inspire

Principal George Morling observed that in his time in College Gil had 'outstanding powers of influence'.[10] This was demonstrated in a remarkable gift in oratory, preaching Christian truth, and inspiring and mentoring others to commit themselves to the will of God for their lives.

> Leadership articulates a compelling vision for tomorrow that captures the imagination of the followers and energizes their attitudes and actions in the present. It gives meaning and value to living. Leadership in community focuses the dreams and commitments of the people on a shared vision of the mission that brings them together, and then leadership works with the people to see that that mission is accomplished. Leadership is a relationship of influence that points people to a shared vision that shapes their living today in such a way that the vision is realized.[11]

---

8. John Hitchen, 'Gilbert McArthur Lecture Series for CLTC', Email, 9 September 2016.
9. Philippians 4:13.
10. Morling, 'Letter to Max Knight from George Morling', n.d.
11. Wright, *Relational Leadership - A Biblical Model for Influence and Service*, Kindle Locations 468-472.

One has only to read Gil's sermon notes or listen to his preaching to discover the evidence for this. It is true that often his vocabulary was a challenge for his audience, but his 'influence always came through'.[12] He could paint (or create) word-pictures to provide a sense of the majesty and greatness of his God, and through him the Spirit of God motivated his readers and listeners to think great thoughts about God and his purposes and give themselves in sacrificial service. This also becomes very evident in Part Two of his story.

Resilience

Resilience is defined as the ability to recover from setbacks, adapt well to change, and a toughness to keep going in the face of adversity.

Diane Coutu helpfully suggests that:

> Resilient people possess three characteristics – a staunch acceptance of reality; a deep belief, often buttressed by strongly held values, that life is meaningful; and an uncanny ability to improvise. You can bounce back from hardship with just one or two of these qualities, but you will only be truly resilient with all three.[13]

In addition, from a biblical perspective resilience is not simply generated from personal resources, or from life experiences, but also out of personal knowledge of God and strong relationship with Christ. The great apostle Paul demonstrated remarkable resilience in his life and ministry and eloquently describes it:

> But we have this treasure in jars of clay to show that this all-surpassing power is from God and not from us. We are hard pressed on every side, but not crushed; perplexed, but not in despair; persecuted, but not abandoned; struck down, but not destroyed. We always carry around in our body the death of Jesus, so that the life of Jesus may also be revealed in our body. For we who are alive are always being given over to death for Jesus' sake, so that his life may also be revealed in our mortal body. So then, death is at work in us, but life is at work in you…
>
> Therefore we do not lose heart. Though outwardly we are wasting away, yet inwardly we are being renewed day by day.

---

12. William Longgar, 'Memories of Gilbert McArthur', Telephone Interview, 24 January 2017.
13. Diane Coutu, 'How Resilience Works', *Harvard Business Review*, (May 2002).

> For our light and momentary troubles are achieving for us an eternal glory that far outweighs them all. So we fix our eyes not on what is seen, but on what is unseen, since what is seen is temporary, but what is unseen is eternal.[14]

Gil's early story is marked by the fact that in many ways it was a tough journey – transitioning as a young boy to England; the sudden loss of his father; the betrayal of his father's business partner and total loss of the life his family was accustomed to; the rejection of relatives; leaving school and finding work; saying goodbye to his mother and sister as a teenager; left alone to find his way around the world to Sydney; a long and dangerous 87 day voyage with rough sailors; his unrecorded stressful war experiences in the Middle East and Pacific; near death from appendicitis in a lonely Indian hospital; involvement in an air crash rescue; fulfilling seemingly impossible assignments in his work with EWA; going into College to study, and at the same time serving as a young pastor combining both ministry and study!

Bobby Clinton believes leadership is a 'lifetime of lessons'.[15] These lifetime lessons were difficult and probably sometimes very discouraging days in the first chapter of the Gilbert McArthur story. But in all these experiences, Gil demonstrated resilience, not just to survive, but thrive where others would have given up or become bitter. For Gil, this was a time of anchoring his soul in the hand of God.

It is these emerging leadership qualities of;
- total commitment to Christ as Lord,
- discerning vision and direction,
- wide breadth of experience,
- gifted ability to communicate and inspire, and
- resilience,

among others forged and tested in his early life, that are very evident in Part Two of his story.

At times Gil must have wondered what God was doing as he met challenge after challenge. Maybe you are currently asking that very same question about your own story?

May the Spirit of God speak out of Gil McArthur's early story, rekindle our aspirations, and renew our purpose to trust and thank the sovereign

---

14. 2 Corinthians 4:7-12; 16-18.
15. Bobby Clinton, *The Making of a Leader – Recognising the Lessons and Stages of Leadership Development* (Colorado Springs USA: NavPress, 1988), 40.

THE QUALITIES OF THE MAN

Lord in all that he allows to touch our lives in the lessons of our life and leadership journey, as we surrender to daily live and lead for his glory.

> Leadership for Christians is about God, not about us… We centre our soul in the hand of God – only then are we ready for leadership. Leadership for Christians starts with a vital relationship between the leader and God. Leadership begins by following. This is the essence of biblical servanthood, of servant leadership.[16]

The McArthur family en route to Dutch New Guinea, 1955

---

16. Wright, *Relational Leadership - A Biblical Model for Influence and Service*, Kindle Location 248, 249.

Gil McArthur – His Story

Part Two

The Mission

―⁕―

Like many others before and after,
Gilbert McArthur was in the grip of an insatiable passion for God,
and the ambition expressed by the great apostle Paul:

'He [Christ] is the one we proclaim,
admonishing and teaching everyone with all wisdom,
so that we may present everyone fully mature in Christ.
To this end I strenuously contend
with all the energy Christ so powerfully works in me.
(Colossians 1:28,29)

This ambition for evangelising, making disciples,
equipping leaders and building the Church of Jesus Christ
inspired him to the very end.

Lake Sentani – Hollandia DNG

Dani Warriors – Baliem Valley

4
PIONEERING PROBATIONER
1955-1956

*The exaltation of Jesus Christ to the Father's right hand,
that is, to the position of supreme honour,
provides the strongest of all missionary incentives.*[1]

Transition to Dutch New Guinea

Gil's missionary commitment emerged out of his early spiritual journey under the guidance of a godly grandfather, his personal encounter with the living God through his Word, his diverse vocational and war experiences in the Pacific, the influence of his pastor Victor Barnard, and his growing desire to see Christ known and worshipped by those who had never heard the Gospel. This sense of a personal divine direction into mission became imperative through the ministry of J Oswald Sanders and Principal George Morling. Gil reflected the 'evangelical missionary spirituality' of his time in the sense of strong calling or inner compulsion as a significant part of his missionary motivation.

In April 1958, Gil was asked to write an article from a missionary perspective, attempting to reconcile the Sovereignty of God and the Free Will of Men.[2] This article expressed his understanding of the biblical foundations of his call to mission.

> Having reached this place of inward (not intellectual) reconciliation as to the seeming paradox of the Sovereignty of God and the Free Will of Man, I find no great difficulty in moving beyond the glorious façade of Jehovah God's eternal majesty and power to rest in child-like trust upon the loving heart of a Father, so fully revealed in God the Son and made over to me by God the Holy Spirit.
>
> Let me say now, that it is impossible for one to enter in and oft resort to this place of holy intimacy without being made conscious

---

1. John R. W. Stott, *The Contemporary Christian* (Downers Grove, ILL: Inter Varsity Press, 1992), 366.
2. Gilbert J McArthur, 'The Sovereignty of God and the Free Will of Men', April 1958, McArthur Family Archives.

of the fact that the heart of God longs to make known its 'love call' to the heart of every human, and just as God the Son could not rest upon the Bosom of the Father without coming to reveal the Father's heart, and by the quality of his own life and sacrifice burst asunder every human and Divine barrier that prevented the heart of God reaching the human heart and His life touching ours, so also, are we verily constrained, yea strangely impelled to do likewise – to go and tell, that 'God would have all people to be saved and brought to a knowledge of the truth!' We find that such a 'heart' must be witnessed to, such love must be shared, the story must be told.[3]

This commitment to mission had a clear geographical focus to work among the unreached tribes of Min people around the Telefolmin area in PNG. However, Charles Mellis, an MAF pilot in Wewak, had flown into the Baptist station at Baiyer River, and meeting with the missionaries, urged them to consider taking the Gospel into the interior across the border in what was then Netherlands or DNG. After a survey visit, the ABFM Board[4] agreed to commence work in the North Baliem area. Gil and Pat were asked to join the team pioneering this new work. Unlike PNG, where the government would not give permission to enter a new area until it had been 'pacified', the DNG Governor gave permission for missionaries to enter the interior without government presence.[5]

In February 1955, as final preparation, Gil completed a Wycliffe Bible Translators (WBT) Summer Institute of Linguistics course. The plan was for him to go on ahead to DNG, and Pat and the children to join him soon after. They were assigned to work in a joint missions team to trek into the 'Shangri La' of the Baliem Valley, make contact with unreached Dani tribes people, build airstrips and commence translation work. They would join two other Baptist missionaries, Rev Victor White and

---

3. McArthur, 'The Sovereignty of God...', 1, 2.
4. Australian Baptist Foreign Mission was the original name. As early as 1936 the use of the word 'foreign' had been queried as unhelpful. But it was not until 1959 it was finally agreed that the word must go, and the name was changed to the Australian Baptist Missionary Society (ABMS). Through Gil's time in Sentani and Telefolmin the mission was known as the ABFM. See Eds, Tony Cupit, Ros Gooden and Ken Manley, *From Five Barley Loaves - Australian Baptists in Global Mission 1864-2010* (Preston, Victoria, Australia.: Mosaic Press, 2013), 425.
5. Norm Draper, *Daring to Believe: Personal Accounts of Life Changing Events in Papua New Guinea and Irian Jaya* (Lawson NSW: Mission Publications of Australia, 1990), 201.

Rev Norm Draper who had preceded them.[6] Pat, Robyn, Jenny, Paul and new baby Wendy were to follow soon after.[7] However, their departure was delayed until 22 November 1955, when all the McArthur family finally sailed together on the *MV Sibigo*.

An extract from Gil's Diary three days out provides both some family insights and Gil's mindset:

> We have all settled down well onboard ship; Robyn and Paul have been sharing their meals with the fishes occasionally, but we have no real casualties amongst us, and are really enjoying the hitherto unknown experience of just eating and sleeping with intermittent bursts of reading. Wendy is basking in the sunshine of all the added attention we are now able to give her, and it's going to be hard not to spoil her over these next two weeks. Jenny is obviously going to get the language before any of us, and in her own way will be a real little missionary for whenever we notice her missing she may be found entertaining the Chinese crew, and apparently making herself quite well understood.
>
> It is somewhat hard to realise that we have left our homeland far behind and severed our physical connections with you dear folk with whom we have been so closely united these past years. The parting has not been really hard for us, it has seemed to be but a natural transition into the sphere of service for which we have so long prepared, and in which you are so completely one with us. The sense of our great partnership as together we work out the purposes of God on earth outweighs such things as human separation and distance, and links us all together at the Mercy-Seat in strong eternal ties.[8]

Pitching Tent in Sentani

On their arrival in Sentani, Gil, Pat and the children joined the White and Draper families on 'Missionary Hill' to set up their home. The initial work of establishing the house was already partially done, but it was tough going. Gil described those early weeks in 1955 after their arrival:

---

6. Author Unknown, 'Missionary Movements', *Vision Magazine*, December 1955, 12, Global Interaction Archives.
7. Author Unknown, 'Brief Mention', *Vision Magazine*, February 1955, 12, Global Interaction Archives.
8. McArthur, 'The McArthur Diary Extracts', Number 1, November 1955, 1.

From the day of our arrival here, we have just worked to the limit each day, collapsing into bed at night completely exhausted. The shell of the house was up when we arrived, but the cement floors had to be put in, basic furniture erected (we still haven't got our chairs together), sanitary arrangements effected and water facilities arranged, plus additions to the house, and making same waterproof, etc.

All our goods and chattels were outside in crates, covered with roofing iron. As we wanted something, so we rummaged around, identified the right crate, opened same up, located the article, repacked the crate, covered it up again, and so it went on.

I picked up tinea of the feet whilst up this way during the war years, and although it did not worry me much in Australia, it broke out here again, and during the cementing programme I was foolish enough to work in bare feet for a while. The cement burned into where the tinea had opened up the flesh, and the result was a horrible infection on both feet. Boy! It was just plain agony to have all my weight on those feet whilst I was trowelling out the floors.

When putting in the drainage system the Diary states that I would stand in the blistering sun with the heavy crowbar held in hands that were so sore that every jab at the tough concrete felt like hot

Building house in Hollandia

needles, and I was wondering why I spent five years studying theology and Greek, etc., as a preparation for missionary service.⁹

But this was their 'light affliction for a moment' and remarkably, by the end of December they had moved from temporary quarters to enjoy Christmas and live 'comfortably' in their new home. Gil's Christmas reflection points to the motivation for their coming:

> Tonight, all the folk on Missionary Hill are getting together for a time of fellowship, singing carols etc., and praising God for the gift of His Son. But what about the people way over those great mountains that I can see from here? Locked away in those virtually inaccessible valleys and gorges? They have no Christmas Day, they sing no carol, only the mournful funeral chant comes echoing across the hills. This week in the Baliem Valley seven people died, all over some petty incident. They know of no way of settling their disputes other than by killing. Out of the abyss of their spiritual darkness they unconsciously call us to share with them the true meaning of Christmas – 'God with us'! Oh! Beloved, let us continue to pray, continue to live, in the glory of that great fact – 'God with us!' Firstly, for our own salvation and then with us, that in Christ's stead we may beseech people everywhere to be reconciled to God.¹⁰

An International Partnership

The missionary advance into the Baliem Valley was a partnership of five mission agencies: the Christian and Missionary Alliance (C&MA), the Regions Beyond Missionary Union (RBMU), the Unevangelised Fields Mission (UFM), the MAF and the ABFM.¹¹

The 'vision glorious', perhaps 'unique in the history of the missionary enterprise', was that these five agencies with independent world-wide support, sharing oneness of faith, and no major doctrinal differences, would be entrusted with separate areas of the heavily populated Baliem Valley, and so work together.

There were of course significant difficulties to overcome, including gathering personnel, supplies, finance, and organisational issues. The major problem however was with the Foreign Department of the C&MA Headquarters in New York 'who vetoed the request of their

---

9. Gilbert J McArthur, 'Making a Base', *Vision Magazine*, March 1956, 8, Global Interaction Archives.
10. McArthur, 'The McArthur Diary Extracts', Number 3, December 1955, 1, 2.
11. McArthur, 'The McArthur Diary Extracts', Number 4, February 1956, 1.

field conference that the North Baliem area be conceded to some other evangelical missionary body'.[12] They felt the C&MA had claim to the whole valley, including the North Baliem, yet they did not have the resources to immediately advance into all the Baliem. Gil appealed for prayer that this issue might be resolved quickly. God answered, and by March 1956 a United Evangelical Mission Committee had been formed to co-operate in the mission to the Baliem.[13]

Into the Baliem Valley

An exploratory probe was planned for early April 1956 into the Archbold Lake area, where the UFM was working together with the RBMU. The aim was to cross the Hablifoerie River and trek through to a site four days journey away, where they hoped to construct an airstrip at Bokondini. This would provide opportunity to assess the reaction of the local tribes, and possible further probes in the direction of the North Baliem and Swartz valleys.

Gil was hospitalised with a tropical ulcer for ten days, and then injected himself with penicillin on discharge so he could prepare for the trek. He also completed a course of medical instruction and was certified by the Dutch authorities to perform basic medical treatments, and even minor operations![14]

Further major preparations involved packing gear for aerial supply drops and setting up a radio network. They were able to secure two 56-foot radio masts at no cost to the mission and transported them in one piece five miles from the top of a 2000-foot climb, using a jeep and trailer complete with police motor cycle escort! On 16 April the MAF Piper Pacer aircraft, fitted with a new engine and floats and piloted by Dave Steiger, made the first of twelve flights into Archbold Lake carrying one man and his gear.[15] After a final communion service with families and fellow workers, Gil flew out on 19 April to join the survey team for a two-month separation from the family.[16]

Writing to prayer partners and supporters ten days after Gil's departure, Pat reported the team had experienced a 'lively time' at the

---

12. McArthur, 'The McArthur Diary Extracts', Number 4, February 1956, 1.
13. McArthur, 'The McArthur Diary Extracts'. Number 5, March 1956, 1.
14. McArthur, 'The McArthur Diary Extracts', Number 6, April 1956, 1.
15. In the providence of God, years later David and Janet Steiger were recruited by Gil to come to CLTC to manage the Guest House.
16. McArthur, 'The McArthur Diary Extracts', Number 6, April 1956, 2.

Preparing the floatplane on Lake Sentani

Floatplane landing Lake Archbold

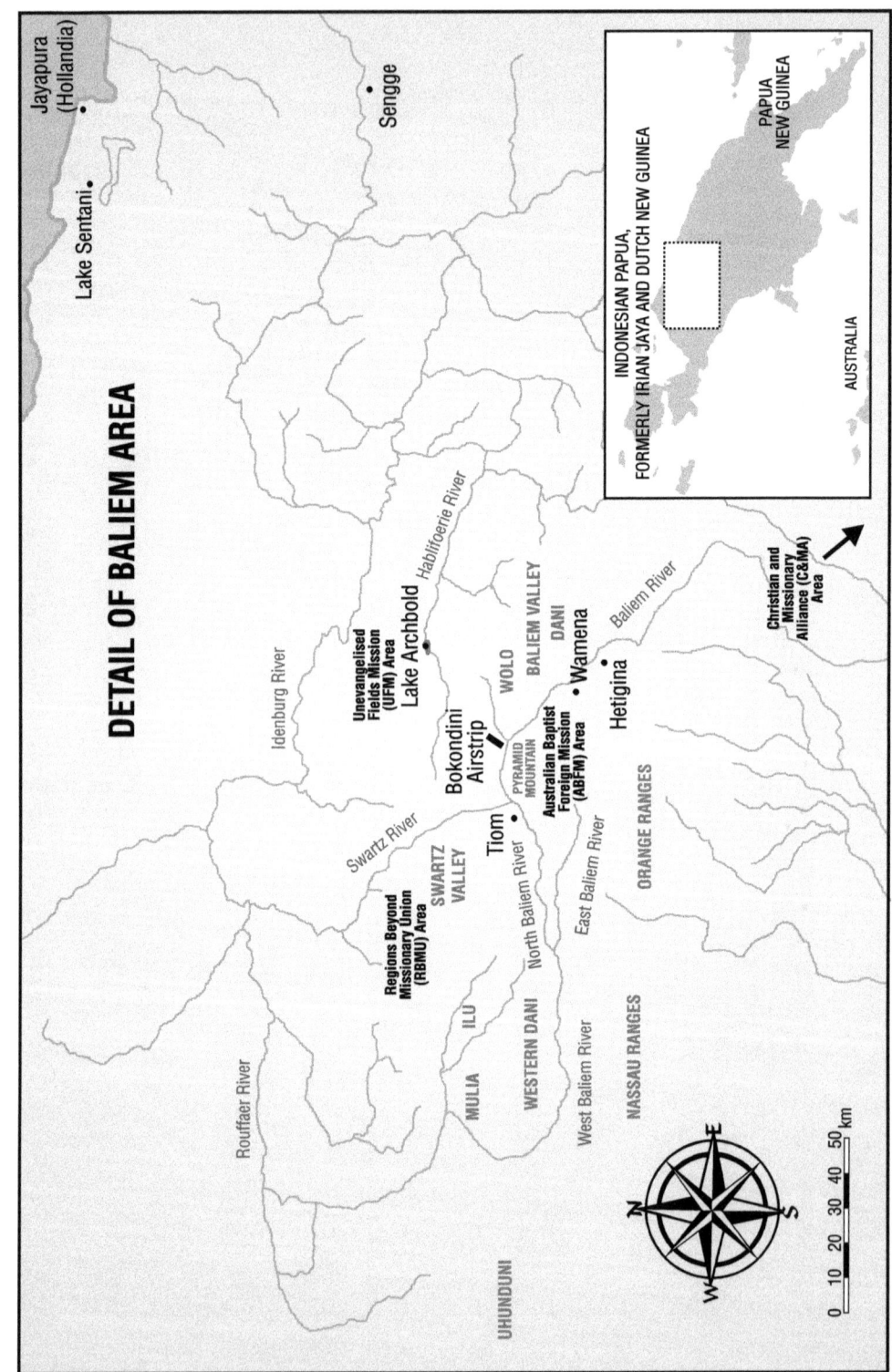

start of the trek in their attempts to cross the powerful Hablifoerie River. Gil's Diary records the extreme challenges and risks in crossing a river which had been in flood for some time, with bridges washed away and no tall timber close enough to bridge the river:

> Garnet, who is a strong swimmer, thought he would try to cross. Boy!! You should have been there – the current caught him and within seconds he was a hundred yards or more down-stream but managed to make his way to the other bank. The next to try was a Christian native boy,[17] but he could not get across the current and managed to scramble out on the same side…
>
> As the water has always been my strong suit, I thought I would have a try because even if I didn't make it I reasoned that I would hit the same bank somewhere down the river and I particularly wanted to test the strength of such a current as it would be valuable experience and help to determine future decisions…
>
> I reasoned that if I could get some place to dive from, that such would give me a good start across the current. So, finding a high bank I threw myself in, hoping that there were no snags.
>
> Boy!! Did I have to swim and when I reached the other bank I found that my new trekking boots had gone… Also, my waterproof watch which I had quite forgotten about, and which had a strong strap, had also been pulled off and was somewhere in the Hablifoerie river.
>
> The recrossing of the river was just as much fun, only this time we had John Betteridge and the native boys to grab us as we got near the bank.
>
> Altogether it was quite an expensive venture but was a valuable experience as now I know just what can and cannot be accomplished in strong river flow crossings. The trekking party would never make it and equipment would be lost.[18]

One can only wonder what Pat and partners back home thought about these risky escapades! But they were the normal pioneer missionary

---

17. We note that terms such as 'native', 'boy', 'master', 'primitive', etc., were not widely regarded as pejorative at the time Gil was writing, and some also reflect popular Tok Pisin words used commonly by English speakers at the time. At later stages of his life, Gil became more sensitive to misunderstandings such terminology can cause.
18. McArthur, 'The McArthur Diary Extracts', Number 7, April 1956, 1.

experience of the time. Being 'obedient to the heavenly vision', they were unstoppable. Their faith and trust were firmly in the Lord who had called them into this situation.

Joining the trekking team was a very significant moment for Gil:

> Last night was a moving experience as the members of the trekking party gathered together for prayer. The setting also added meaning to the moment – that little lake, hidden away up in the mountains, shut off from the rest of the world. The bush timber house set on great foundation poles 8 feet high. Inside on heavy bush chairs which look all askew as they stand on a floor made of strips of bark, are to be seen seven weary men. A closer look made by the light of the tilly lamp reveals that they are all covered from head to toe, and one wonders why, for it is not so very cold. Then is heard the high drone of hundreds of big black mosquitoes and all is understood. A further glance reveals that in every hand is to be seen an open Bible, for these men are servants of the Most-High God, and as such need daily direction from His Word. To the most deafening sound of the tropical rain one after the other of these men rises to pray. In a moment of time, the bounds of time and space are lifted, and heart is joined to heart at the divine meeting place. The content of the prayer is all embracing: confession, personal need, loved ones, mission leaders, other mission groups, prayer partners, and finally a strong confident note is reached as God the Holy Spirit works in the midst and gives to these lonely men the assurance of the faithfulness of God in meeting all the many and varied needs relative to the trek into the unknown. The perils of the river and all that lies ahead, the concern for loved ones left behind are all resolved in the presence of the Lord. Thank God for the place of prayer and daily strength, the 'Open door' has deeper meaning these days.[19]

The next day they tried another river crossing. Gil, Garner and Bert crossed successfully, but the others could not make it. They tried to bridge the gap with trees, but they were swept away. The following day they finally conquered the river using a dinghy on a rope to ferry team members and equipment across.

As they trekked on, they moved through various population groups, and were always met with acceptance by the local people. They reached the Bokondini site on the fourth day, and the MAF aircraft dropped more supplies for airstrip construction. At first sight, after burning the kunai

---

19. McArthur, 'The McArthur Diary Extracts', Number 7, April 1956, 2.

Building the airstrip at Bokondini

The opening of the airstrip at Bokondini

grass, it looked like a long job with thousands of stones, small and large, embedded in the ground. But in answer to prayer, over a thousand local people arrived at the camp. 99% had never seen a white man before, yet all were willing and eager to work for the sum of one cowrie shell per day. After four weeks, an area of 600 by 30 metres was cleared and hardened, and the first successful landings were made. It was planned that UFM would establish a mission station at Bokondini. Early in July, the Baptist group would use this as a base from which to move to Pyramid Mountain in the unreached Northern Baliem Valley. A two-pronged advance was planned, with the Baptist team climbing the range coming in from the north, and a C&MA team moving up river in a flat-bottomed boat to hopefully avoid where local people were constantly engaged in warfare. This would also provide a retreat route if major hostilities were encountered.

Gil was glad to return to the coast and family for a break before the next trek. Although assigned to supply duties on the coast, he was looking forward to finally settling down in the interior, to work on studying the language.[20]

> Learning the language and learning it well is absolutely vital in the course of pioneer church planting… We cannot become 'incarnate' among the people God has called us to love without becoming able to readily communicate with them in their language and in their cultural framework.[21]

Advancing to Pyramid Mountain

On 27 July 1956, Gil and Norman Draper flew from Sentani to Bokondini to join the rest of the Baptist team. After two days assembling their loads for the trek, they left (dog included) in very wet weather. Gil found the climbing very tough and was glad of the carriers who had the heaviest loads.

His Diary describes another very risky and eventful journey – powerfully illustrating the commitment, tenacious faith and toughness of Gil and the others in the team. It is a fine example of a great pioneering missionary journey opening the way for the Gospel to unreached peoples.[22]

---

20. McArthur, 'The McArthur Diary Extracts', Number 8, June 1956, 2.
21. Daniel Sinclair, *A Vision of the Possible – Pioneer Church Planting in Teams* (Waynesboro, GA.: Authentic Media, 2005), 88–89.
22. For this reason, I have only lightly edited the Diary entry on this historic trek, as it reflects so well the way that these pioneers grappled with the many challenges along the way, and the issues involved in first contact with the people.

Monday 30 July. Nightfall of the first day found us moving up the slopes of another mountain and near to a native village. The folk were quite friendly and invited us to stay in one of their huts. We had had enough of the wet by this time, so suppressing any thoughts of pigs, bugs and fleas we crawled into one of the little round houses. The various oddments adorning the walls as revealed in the light of a torch, defy description, but as I endeavoured to clean an area in which to lay my sleeping bag, I had the feeling that on this night, I would be closely associated with the venerable ancestors of the highlanders.

Sleep did not come easily, for reasons best left to your imagination. Also, the men, gathered in one of the adjoining huts, entertained us until 3 a.m. with vigorous, if not musical chants. At last our voices were raised in protest to this prolonged serenade, and to our amazement it ceased immediately. Oh, that we had spoken a few hours earlier! Well, at last the morning dawned, at least finding us dry if not refreshed.

Tuesday 31 July. We pulled on our socks, still wet from the previous day's soaking, ate some boiled rice and tinned fruit, packed our gear, stood for reading and prayer, whilst bewildered highlanders looked on, then off once more to our objective. The natives on these first two days were quite friendly and co-operative, although as we walked down the narrow gorge towards the Baliem River, large numbers of them armed with spears and bows and arrows pressed hard upon the party. For those of us in the rear of the line it was rather eerie to be able both to smell and to hear them whispering together, and then to be startled as they would break into a mighty shout.

By 2 p.m. we had reached a 'No Man's Land' and our local carriers would go no further. So, shouldering the packs ourselves we moved off to the accompaniment of 'Barbi' 'Barbi', which meant that we were going into the territory of the enemy. Below us we could now see the mighty Baliem River, and beyond in the distance, our objective – Pyramid Mountain could be discerned. We walked for about two hours, feeling the silence now as each one was occupied with carrying his load, and perhaps, contemplating what reception would be forthcoming from the next group of people as we came upon them from the country of their enemies.

We had passed through two or three deserted villages and were abreast of another, when we were spotted for the first time by the

Crossing the Baliem River

locals. All these villages are quite strongly fortified by a high wall completely encircling the houses. As the young men saw us, so they immediately rushed for their weapons to the accompaniment of the shrieks of the women and children. However, as we stood and called greetings to them, so they stopped and took stock of us. Finally realising that we were not their traditional enemies but 'white men' they became quite friendly and carried our gear down to the river.

The recent rains had caused the river to rise, and it was running quite swiftly. Whilst considering how we could get across with all our equipment etc., two men appeared on a raft made of three long tree trunks lashed together and propelled by one of the men pushing a long pole into the bed of the river – just like a punt. Rev Norm Draper hopped on and asked them to take him across, but they refused to do so. This stalemate was broken as I, taking hold of the pole, jumped on and commenced to push off. This provided the necessary impetus for one of the chiefs to hop on and take over, which I was quite happy for him to do, as it required skilful and experienced handling to get that thing across the current without capsizing same. Hendrik Noordyke and myself eventually swam the river both ways, just to show them that it could be done without their aid if necessary. However, they were very helpful and numerous trips were made without incident, until at last all our gear was safely across…

Wednesday 1 August. Moving quickly along the river now, our original intention was to contact the C&MA party by radio, thus determining each other's position, and eventually joining forces before converging on Pyramid Mountain, which was known to be a troublesome area. However, we were not able to contact the C&MA party (subsequently we learned that their radio battery had shorted out) and so decided to move towards our objective. As we neared the area large groups of young warriors appeared from all directions, and we had real difficulty in keeping our party with all its equipment from being completely enveloped. Those of us at the rear became hoarse from shouting at them to keep back. On reaching the site we made all sit down so that we could watch them carefully whilst we had another try at making radio contact. We had no sooner turned around than 'lo and behold' the aerial wire had disappeared!

These young warriors were certainly a playful bunch of fellows. Ian Gruber and I went to look for some water, and on returning I had a long stick, pointed like a spear, thrown at me. Fortunately, it ricocheted off the top of my head, a little lower and it might have hurt more than my feelings. Thereafter whenever any of us went to the creek, we would be pelted with sticks and stones by these young bucks hiding in the trees. Then when we erected the tents, long lengths of bamboo were thrown, but no serious damage was done, and we can be thankful that no barbed arrows and proper fighting spears were used. I discovered later that one contributing factor to all this horse-play was, that we white men were considered to be spirits, and they wanted to see if we could really be hurt just like anybody else.

Fortunately, the attention of these young warriors was soon distracted from us by the arrival of the MAF plane which swooped over and drove them all back into the trees. But after our first load of supplies had been dropped and the plane headed back for Bokondini, they soon came out of hiding and crowded around again.

The C&MA party arrived that night and we put them up in our tents around which we had erected an electric fence as a deterrent against night marauders…

Saturday 4 August. Large crowds of natives were around when suddenly a cry went up from one whom later we determined to be the witch doctor. He kept shouting out one word only, which resulted in all the women and children running away and the menfolk separating into two groups, one on either side of the camp.

We were all wondering what would happen next, when into the picture stepped the big chief and beckoned us towards him. As we came near so he motioned us to sit down and the other tribal elders came and did likewise. Fortunately, Mr Myron Bromley, the C&MA linguist, was with us, and though the dialect is somewhat different from that of the other end of the valley where he had been working, he was still able to converse with the chief and interpret the proceedings to us.

It transpired that the elders had ruled that we should stay, but that to do so a ceremony of removing the heat from the ground had to be enacted. We had passed through enemy territory in coming amongst them, and the bad influences of such associations had to be removed if we were to remain. Naturally we had to concede to this request even though we knew not what it might entail. But as it turned out, it was quite a harmless, yet very interesting procedure.

Long lengths of bamboo were placed on the ground, together with pieces of sweet potato. Each one of us in turn was selected to stand alongside one of these lengths of bamboo, whilst a warrior partner was selected to stand opposite and join hands with us. To the accompaniment of much 'mumbo jumbo' on the part of the witch doctor and the chief, the lengths of bamboo were jumped on and crushed. Two separate pieces, representing the alien influences were taken away and dealt with as enemies apparently should be.

All this had the effect of getting the heat out of the ground, and we were then solemnly informed that the ground was now cold, and we could be seated again. But if you had been there sitting out under the blazing sun, you would doubtless have thought otherwise. We now settled down to the serious business of making friends. First there was an exchange of gifts – axes, mirrors, beads, and shells on our part and pigs on theirs. Then came the smoking of the traditional 'pipe of peace' which in this case was a dirty cigarette made of a certain type of leaf. The chief would take one puff and then place it in each of our mouths for us to inhale likewise. The whole thing was really very humorous. I managed to evade this part of the ceremony by telling the chief, in the few Dani words that I knew, that I was only a little fellow of no significance, whilst the fellow next to me was a big chief and better to give him two puffs. Next there followed the 'feast'. The old chief was certainly a persistent fellow and tried to make us consume large quantities of sweet potato, baked banana, sugar cane and a type of spinach which tasted like castor-oil. I was

Above:
Building relationships

Right:
Medical ministry

Below:
Taking the heat out of the ground

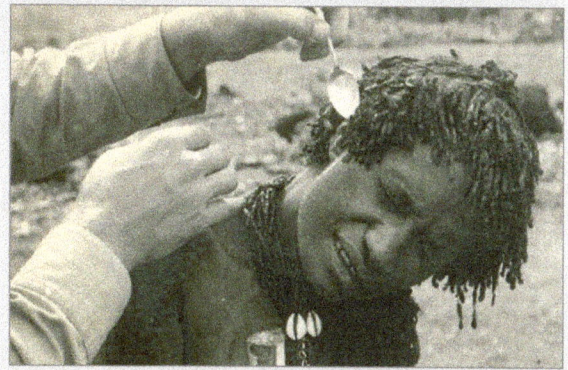

fortunate to have the dog alongside of me, and between the two of us, plus what I managed to give away to the young bucks behind me, I think I acquitted myself rather well and made the old chief proud to have me around.

Sunday 5 August. The feast proceedings continued, but during the course of same Myron Bromley was able to tell them something of the purpose for which we had come and they all quietened down whilst he led in prayer. Also, some of the worst cases of natives suffering from tropical yaws[23] were treated on this occasion. One woman had the whole of her face eaten away, eyes, nose, lips, completely indistinguishable. It will surely be in this field that our best contacts with the people will be maintained during the early days of the work.

We were deeply thankful to our Heavenly Father on this day for the marked change in the attitude of the people. The articles stolen were returned, and the boisterousness of the young men diminished. The evening hours of this day were poignant with meaning. To native eyes watching from the darkness of the trees would be seen gathered under the tent fly and illuminated by two tilly lamps a group of white men sitting down and strangely quiet. One after another would stand, and with eyes closed and face pointed skywards would utter many fervent words. Then one man takes something in his hands – the Bible – and looking at it begins to speak whilst all the rest listen intently. Ah! Little do those dark watchers realise that the coming of this Book marks a new era for them. For the message of this Book is not bound and has penetrated every realm of darkness, coming as it does with power and speaking with its own authority to the souls of men.

It was a very real privilege to be the first to minister the Word of God in this area, and as some words rolled out into the night I could not help but be thrilled and yet strangely awed by the thought of what the content of this Book could, and ultimately would do even for such a heathen community as now surrounded us.[24]

---

23. Yaws is a chronic infection that affects mainly the skin, bone and cartilage, causing disfigurement. The disease occurs mainly in poor communities in warm, humid, tropical areas of Africa, Asia and Latin America. The causative organism is a bacterium called Treponema pertenue, a subspecies of Treponema pallidum that causes venereal syphilis.
24. McArthur, 'The McArthur Diary Extracts', Number 9, August 1956, 1-5.

This latest advance into a new area did not however assuage Gil's burden for others yet unreached, and his vision widened for further advances into the upper North Baliem, another separate and isolated valley system of people not yet contacted.[25]

Leadership Tensions

Norman Draper, the senior missionary and Field Secretary, assigned Gil to be responsible for the supply line from the coast. While someone needed to take this role, it appears that there were emerging tensions between Norman and Gil, as both were eager to be on the pioneering edge of the advance. But because the supply role needed his attention, Gil trekked back to the UFM station at Bokondini. From there he flew by MAF back over their tracks to make another drop of supplies to the team at Pyramid Mountain, where airstrip work was progressing well, and then on to Sentani. On that flight Gil persuaded the pilot to do a little detour to survey other areas, which did not help his relationship with Norman who felt he had no authority to do this.[26] The Baptist team left at Pyramid Mountain consisted of Rev and Mrs Draper, Mr Ian Gruber, Mr H Noordyke, and five Christian national young men they had taken in from the coast.

For Gil, now back on the coast, the spectacular (which he clearly loved) was over for the present, and it was what he described as 'more normal missionary life' – keeping the missionaries inland supplied with everything essential to living. Gil also now had time to work hard on the Indonesian language, and he was encouraged by Pat's mastery of both the grammar and vocabulary.[27]

Given Gil's enthusiasm to be on the cutting edge of mission to the unreached, his new role in Sentani must have been difficult for him to accept. Tensions continued with Norm Draper who was the pioneering leader from the beginning of the Baptist advance into the Baliem. Norm sent a hand-written letter from the Baliem on 11 August 1956 to Albert Dube, Secretary of the ABFM in Sydney, expressing strong concern that in his role on the coast, Gil was stepping across boundaries of Norm's authority as Field Secretary:

> I would like to advise personally that an aerial survey of the complete North Baliem by McArthur, as he was flying to Sentani was done

---

25. McArthur, 'The McArthur Diary Extracts', Number 9, August 1956, 5.
26. Norm Draper, 'Personal Re: Gil McArthur', Letter, 11 August 1956, Global Interaction Archives.
27. McArthur, 'The McArthur Diary Extracts', Number 10, October 1956, 1.

completely without my knowledge. When I heard he had arranged and done it, he commented on cloud formations making the 'detour' necessary. I would appreciate that, if he submits any report on it that it not be considered, as from experience I have found his sweeping generalisations and inexperience very unreliable… I will be writing to him with this mail reminding him again of mission regulations. Not with-standing the above, there are no personal tensions between personalities and as a staff all goes very well.[28]

On 20 August, upon receiving Norm's letter reminding him of 'mission regulations', Gil also wrote to Albert Dube explaining how he felt:

Dear Albert,

From… a letter received yesterday from Norman, it is apparent that he is greatly concerned with the fact that certain mission business is being, or has been, handled by myself.

It may well be that I am deserving of censure in this regard, for it appears, that what Norman has considered to be matters demanding authoritative action alone, I have interpreted as being normal business procedure and actioned accordingly. Some mitigation may also be claimed by virtue of the fact, that due to the present formative nature of our work, and the number of occasions that the Field Secretary has been physically removed from the situation, planning and preparation together with certain adminstrative measures have of necessity, still required attention and action. If my natural enthusiasm for getting the job done has occasioned a breach of probationary etiquette, then I express regret. However, it should be remembered that the situation is not of my making and the constant inference to the effect that I am still a probationary and should remember my place is, I think a little unjust. There has been nothing for me to be a probationary to. The work had to be developed and a system of operation introduced for which there was no precedent, and which called for latent business experience alone.

True it is, to my sorrow, that initially I challenged Norman's competency and right to maintain complete control… But even here it was not a probationary rebelling against a proven and established system of administration, but simply a request to enact certain duties which Mr White had previously indicated that I should take over. Norman, however was not prepared to concede such, and at the time I failed to appreciate such an attitude, for to

---

28. Draper, 'Personal Re: Gil McArthur'.

me, there existed certain anomalous factors due to the inability of one man to effectively handle every aspect of the work. This crisis was resolved in discussion with Mr White, when I undertook to do my utmost to make the existing administrative pattern work until such times as a more democratic procedure be introduced.

In any approach to this problem it should be noted that as a probationary, I have been called upon to fill a position – not asked for nor desired – my contemporaries of which are all field leaders and which by content and location alone tends to represent a challenge to complete control being vested inland.

My God knows that since reconciling myself to the situation in discussion with Mr. White, I have earnestly endeavoured to do all that is required of me and be faithful to recognised leadership. To this I shall continue to adhere, although at times one becomes sick in heart at being involved in such an awkward situation. It is obvious that I represent a mental block to Norman which is not going to be easy to erase. It seems that if I attend to one matter beyond the point of handling stores and posting mail it's interpreted as overstepping my boundaries. It is equally obvious that he has no desire to make use of any previous experience that I may have had in any field, and that his estimate of the position at Base is such that it certainly does not require the services of a Baptist Minister.

Well Albert, I realise that Norman's feelings in this matter are more worthy of consideration than mine, and God knows I need His wisdom and guidance that no untoward attitude of mine shall be allowed to hinder the smooth development of the work. I write now in a purely personal way, requiring no action, only understanding and direction. However, should it be thought necessary, I am quite prepared to raise these issues in the official way. At the moment, I feel however that charge and counter-charge will serve no purpose, and therefore await your advice.

Warmly Yours,

Gil[29]

Albert Dube replied to Gil, trying to settle him down for the moment:

Be assured that the Regional Committee, least of all myself, does not expect you to spend your Missionary days in Sentani

---

29. Gilbert J McArthur, 'Gil McArthur to Albert Dube', Letter, 20 August 1956, Global Interaction Archives.

> looking after Stores, however essential that job may be. However, it is obvious that for the time being someone with ability and intelligence has to do that work to establish the supply line and the system and be available if needed to make contact with the Dutch authorities, and I cannot see anyone else to do the job just now apart from yourself. As the work develops inland so the picture will surely change, and we will be able to recast the Staffing position.
>
> I suggest that for the time being you exercise all the patience you can and work as closely with Norm as possible and refer all matters to him that the Field Secretary should decide and so preserve that essential harmony between the Staff. I'm hoping that it will soon be possible to form a Field Council in DNG and this should help solve the problems. I am not unaware of the difficulties facing you, Gil, nor of your desire to do more direct Missionary work and hope the way will open up for you in the near future. Let us both covenant to pray about the matter and God will surely give grace and guidance.[30]

The final sentence of Gil's Diary Extract 10 in October revealed some suggestion of unrest in the routine work, and the veiled possibility of a coming change – 'Pray with us, that we may be found continuing faithful to the routine tasks at hand, and yet ever sensitive to His voice as new doors of opportunity are opened.'[31]

Transfer to Telefolmin

Two months later in December, as Gil reflected on the amazing achievements of the past year of pioneering work, he reported that he had preached his first message in the Malay language. He also revealed a new door of opportunity the Regional Committee had opened for the McArthur family.

> It is now just twelve months since our pioneering work began in DNG, and after the building of four airstrips and undertaking many treks the great objective of reaching and settling among the people of the North Baliem has been achieved. There are some 30-40,000 people locked away in the rugged mountainous system – pray that God will give us men to match these mountains, and in turn,

---

30. Albert Dube, 'Dube to Gil McArthur – Personal', Letter, 13 September 1956, Global Interaction Archives.
31. McArthur, 'The McArthur Diary Extracts', Number 10, October 1956, 3.

raise up prayer supporters at home to overcome the mountainous problems of supply and support.

Last week I preached my first message in Malay without the aid of an interpreter to a mixed congregation of about sixty. My wife commented that it was the first time she had ever seen me stuck for words!...

It seems to be clearly indicated that it is the will of God for us to leave Sentani and move over to Australian New Guinea, in order to strengthen the work at Telefolmin. Our mission work at Telefolmin has, in the past, been hindered some-what by the unavailability of a suitable linguist to tackle the difficult tonal language. It is the feeling of our Regional Committee that we should be the ones to undertake this work. We surely respect the confidence of our brethren in this and rejoice at such an opportunity for a life of service amongst these people. However, let it be said, that our personal equipment is, at present, not all that it could be in order to break open this difficult language, and we earnestly covet your fellowship in prayer, that the Divine enablement shall be ours.[32]

The Regional Committee's solution to the Draper/McArthur tensions was that the Craig family would be sent across from Telefolmin to exchange with the McArthur family. This would open the door for Gil to pursue his passion for language and frontline pioneering work.[33] At Telefolmin, the McArthurs would join Doug and Rosemary Vaughan (friends from Baptist College days), and Don and Elaine Doull, when the Doulls returned from furlough. A letter from Albert Dube to Gil confirms Gil had communicated that he was 'very happy' about the transfer to Telefolmin.[34] Upon reflection, it was not a transfer without considerable challenge. He was just gaining facility in the language, and now being asked to uproot the family once again and move their 'tent' by faith into a new beginning. Ray Ortlund captures the challenge of faith that is not simply 'creedal faith' but faith in action:

> Personally, when was the last time you made a major decision that was so clearly of God and so clearly not of yourself that your conclusion actually surprised you? Are we shocking anybody by

---

32. McArthur, 'The McArthur Diary Extracts', Number 11, December 1956, 1.
33. Don Doull, 'Re: Dr Gilbert McArthur', Telephone Interview, 29 August 2016.
34. Albert Dube, 'Dube to Gil McArthur – Personal', Letter, 13 December 1956, Global Interaction Archives.

our faith? If God were to show us in one instant the full meaning of living by faith, we might all gasp and say, 'Nobody can live that way, not in this world.' That's why he keeps throwing our lives into upheaval. He wants us to experience what it's like for him to come through when the only thing that will suffice is what is directly and immediately of God. He wants us to be living proof that he is real, as we dare to treat him as the greatest ally in the universe.[35]

Due to the transport arrangements for their goods, it was necessary for Pat and the children to go on ahead of Gil, and they left Sentani mid-January 1957 for Telfolmin, with a great send off from the missionary community. This included father Gil racing the Jeep against the aircraft as it sped down the runway for take-off. Try as he could, Gil could not get the Jeep to leave the ground, as the children laughed at his antics from the plane! Gil later asked Dave Steiger the MAF pilot how the children had coped with their first experience in light aircraft. Dave replied in his usual casual drawl,

> Waal, they did alright I guess, when the kids got all through fighting to look out the window, they just went to sleep… Good thing though they didn't weigh much (the five of them weighed 260 lbs), for when we got to Wewak the Government were flying extra police into Telefolmin to deal with another outbreak of cannibalism in the area, in which thirty odd people were reputedly killed and eaten… But don't get to worrying though, your bunch don't rustle up a good feed between the lot of them![36]

Before leaving DNG, Gil again made a visit inland to where the Baptists had established a station at Tiom in the North Baliem, and then to Bokondini, where he spent a week viewing the progress of the work and was able to spend valuable hours in linguistic revision as he handed over this responsibility to Ian Gruber. Facing the uprooting and transition from Sentani to Telefolmin,

Gil expressed his resilient passion to his supporters:

Keep on keeping on – Ephesians 6 – there's much to do whilst it is day. We must measure our work in the light of eternity, therefore, learn to live in tents, build only altars.[37]

---

35. Raymond Ortlund Jr, *Isaiah: God Saves Sinners* (Wheaton Illnois: Crossway Books, 2005), 211.
36. McArthur, 'The McArthur Diary Extracts', Number 12, January 1957, 1.
37. McArthur, 'The McArthur Diary Extracts', Number 12, January 1957, 2, emphasis added.

5
MATURING MINISTRY
1957-1963

*It is significant that all three of Jesus' temptations had to do
with choosing the will of God over alternate paths.
With the first temptation it was the will of God over
his rights and privileges.
The second dealt with God's will over uncrucified desires, and
the third with God's will over wrong paths to success.
The will of God is ultimately the most important thing in our lives.*[1]

Telefolmin Papua New Guinea 1957-1958

In his final Diary Extract before leaving Sentani in February 1957, Gil recalled:

> Two years ago, whilst attending the School of Linguistics in Melbourne, I received my phonemics examination paper back from the instructor with the following words written on the top – 'Good work Gil, Telefolmin here I come.' He knew my concern for the people of Telefolmin – that they should hear the Gospel in their own mother-tongue and was also aware of the difficulties of such language situation and had promised his aid in the unravelling of some of the technical complexities known to exist. And so, two years from that date, and six years from the time when on returning to my home in Tamworth from a meeting of the Airline Executive and being struck with the amount of time and energy being expended in the business world, I was moved in prayer to promise the Lord that He who is the First shall have the first of my life. Hence College, the ministry of the churches, DNG and now Telefolmin here I come! God grant that the intervening years have wrought something of the character of God into one's life that will be continuously and increasingly revealed in the ministry into which we now humbly and gratefully move.[2]

---

1. Ajith Fernando, *Jesus Driven Ministry* (Leicester England: Inter Varsity Press, 2002), 87.
2. McArthur, 'The McArthur Diary Extracts', Number 13, February 1957, 2.

Gil was finally moving to the place he had earlier sensed was where the Lord wanted him.

Pitching Tent in Telefolmin

Moving across to Telefolmin in the headwaters of the Sepik River in New Guinea, Gil, Pat and the family settled well into a comfortable house that had been built by Don Doull five years earlier. He had first pioneered the Telefolmin station for the Baptist Mission with John Green in 1951.[3] The station comprised two houses, trade store, church, school, sawmill, cargo handler and school dormitories – all built out of bush materials. The sawmill production provided some income, and the timber to construct more permanent station buildings.[4]

The McArthurs joined Doug and Rosemary Vaughan. They had been very busy managing the timber mill, maintaining machinery, running the school program and trade store, plus general station management and the building program. While Gil offered some help in these areas, he spent the major part of his time on language learning so that the people could hear the message of life in their own language. Pidgin English was the only teaching medium, and its usage was limited and provided no bridge to people in the villages. The McArthurs and Vaughans were looking forward to the return from furlough of Don and Elaine Doull and their family to help with the overall program.[5]

Gil, no longer under authoritarian leadership, found a new freedom to engage in his two great loves of pioneering work and Bible translation.

Walking into Danger

The constant tribal wars, animosity to outsiders, and the rugged terrain in the area made it very difficult to bring under government control, and so for five years the mission work at Telefolmin had been restricted to a small radius. But after Doug Vaughan's application 12 months earlier, permits became available (if there were two experienced Europeans in the party) to trek into the Eliptamin and Feramin areas, where two Australian Patrol Officers and five local police had been killed in 1953.[6]

---

3. Don Doull, *One Passion: Church Planting in Papua New Guinea* (Springwood, N.S.W, Springwood Printing Company, 2004), See chapter 6, 'Go West Young Man', 61ff.
4. McArthur, 'The McArthur Diary Extracts', Number 14, March 1957, 1.
5. McArthur, 'The McArthur Diary Extracts', Number 14, March 1957, 2.
6. Author Unknown, 'Pygmy Killers Used Women as Decoys', *Herald Newspaper*, 11 October 1953, 1, McArthur Family Archives.

MATURING MINISTRY

Unloading supplies at Telefolmin

The McArthur home at Telefolmin

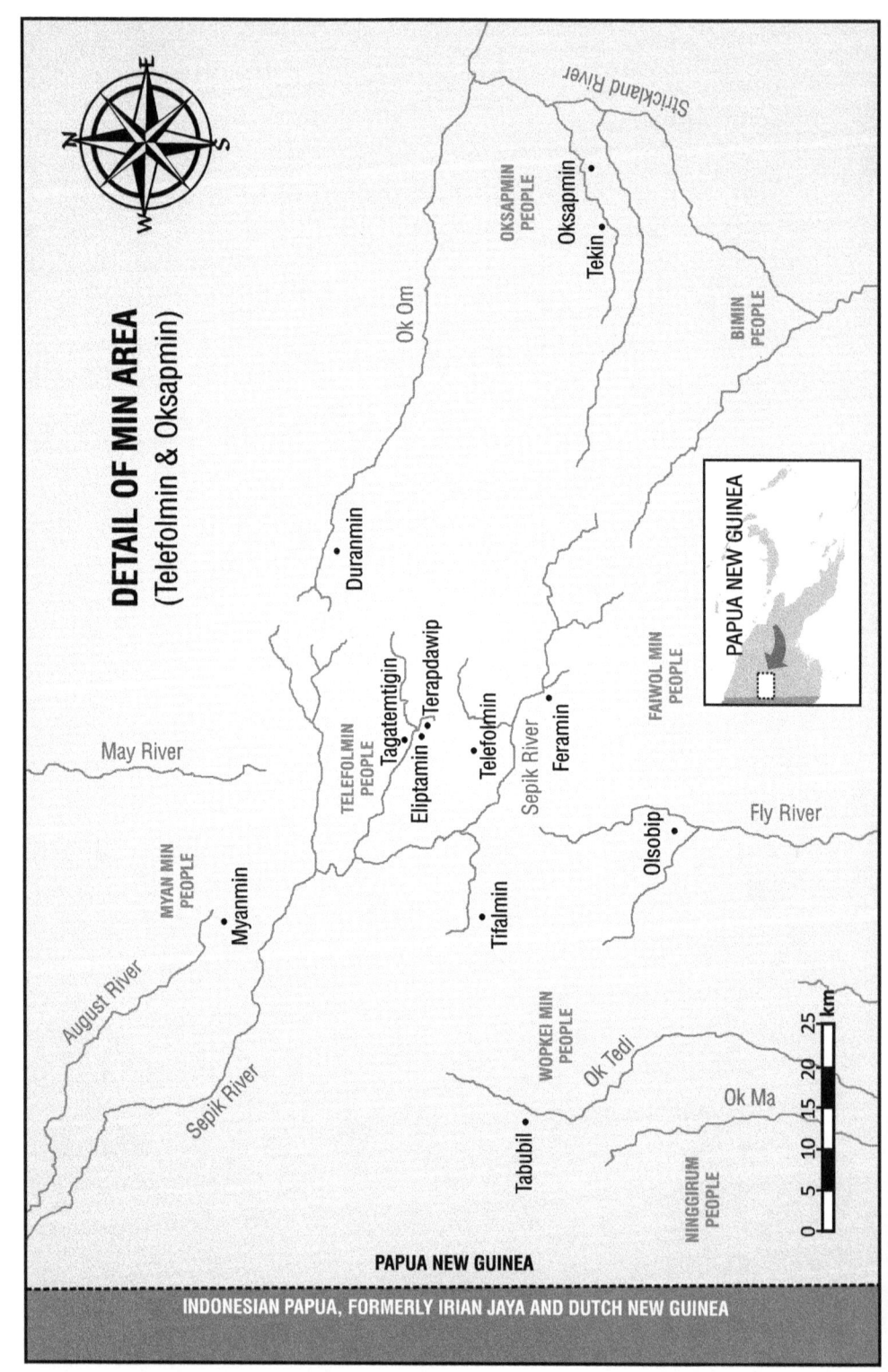

By March 1957, Gil and Doug Vaughan and some of the local school students had been on a trek over the mountains (which was headlined in Australian news as 'Walked into Danger'[7]), holding meetings in the villages, and giving gifts to the headmen to mark their first contact with them. Gil provides insight into what was clearly a step of faith, and considerable risk on the edge of the unknown:

> It was a moving experience to stand on the sites of the previous killings, and to hear from the people themselves the vivid descriptions of what actually took place, and then to have them all sit down and haltingly explain that into this place of violence and death, there had at last come the message of life, love and reconciliation... We do thank you all for your prayer support... and really believe God answered prayer and gave us complete acceptance with the people. Never at any time during the day, or the long night hours as we slept among them, did we have any cause for alarm and we feel there is a rich harvest awaiting us amongst these people.[8]

It seems Gil's eyes were ever on the horizons of the unreached beyond them. In March 1957 he wrote to prayer partners:

> Walking Eastward through the precipitous country for about ten days would bring us to the watershed of the Strickland River System, and amongst the Oksapmin group of people who are reputed to number about 12,000. This is still uncontrolled territory and it will be some time before we are able to work amongst such, but later this year there is a strong Government patrol scheduled to move out into this area, and we hope to be able to join one of our missionaries to the party.[9]

The move to extend out from Telefolmin was a huge challenge for the missionaries involved:

> The missionaries who spread the message in the Upper Sepik had arduous challenges to overcome with hazardous treks to places such as Duranmin, Tifalmin, Mianmin and Eliptamin. All were distant from Telefolmin and the rugged nature of the mountainous terrain made the journeys long and difficult. Beyond these centres lay

---

7. Author Unknown, 'Walked into Danger', *Herald Newspaper*, 3 November 1957, McArthur Family Archives.
8. McArthur, 'The McArthur Diary Extracts', Number 14, March 1957, 2.
9. McArthur, 'The McArthur Diary Extracts', Number 14, March 1957, 1.

another band of villages such as Fiyak, Hotmin, Olsobip, Yapsei and Tumolbil. Until airstrips could be laid in these places, there was no option but to put on the trekking boots and head out.[10]

In Telefolmin there was opportunity for contact with the Government personnel. Gil and Doug took the opportunity to regularly engage in a battle with them on the badminton court, seeking to build trust and open opportunities for witness. 'One dear fellow, who apparently has never been favourably disposed towards missions was invited over, and after having soundly thrashed us in most of the games, went away feeling much happier and decidedly more friendly. You might remember us in our contact with these fellows.'[11]

Vision and Strategy

Gil and Doug both had pilot's licences, and Doug was also a licenced aircraft engineer. Since their time in College, both had been interested in making use of light aircraft in evangelising isolated tribal peoples in areas of large rugged mountainous terrain. After the initial challenge of locating sites and building airstrips, light aircraft could drastically reduce the time in moving from place to place, and facilitate the supplies required to support the evangelisation of the people, the development of the churches and medical and humanitarian services. Don Doull realised:

> Both men [Gil and Doug] could see that the area could be evangelised in a comparatively short period of time if airstrips could be built in the surrounding valleys, where different groups of people lived, and we could visit such areas regularly by plane. In that way we would be able to keep in touch with indigenous pastors and could also take medical missionaries to those isolated areas where they could bring medical help to the people and establish baby health clinics. This was visionary thinking, but Gil in particular, was noted for his gift in that area.[12]

Gil's earlier experience with MAF assisting in opening the Baliem Valley in DNG convinced him that the use of aircraft must be a vital component of their strategy at Telefolmin in PNG. MAF had already begun flying

---

10. Eds, Tony Cupit, Ros Gooden and Ken Manley, *From Five Barley Loaves – Australian Baptists in Global Mission 1864-2010*, 228.
11. McArthur, 'The McArthur Diary Extracts', Number 14, March 1957, 3.
12. Doull, *One Passion: Church Planting in Papua New Guinea*, 111, 112.

in New Guinea in 1951. Other mission agencies chose to use their own aircraft, but after assessment, the ABFM had decided that it would be more economical, safe and efficient to utilise the expanding services of MAF. The use of aircraft became a major platform of the missionary team strategy at Telefolmin. Don Doull recalls:

> Our thinking began to focus on a two-pronged program. First, we must get young men into a Bible School where they could be trained and eventually, by God's grace, become evangelists and pastors in those remote areas. The second aspect of this program was that we must work toward the building of airstrips in the many areas which we only knew about by word of mouth, up until that time.[13]

Gil visited the Baptist station in the Baiyer Valley in April 1957 for Field Council Meetings and two baptismal services. As he watched an old man and his two wives being baptised, he thought deeply about what had brought about the remarkable changes in the lives of the people, and he became convinced of the central emphasis needed in their strategy.

> What mighty weapon had been so effectively wielded, so as to break through the fixed feelings and inhibitions of such a man and his many like-fellows. For on very few mission fields of the world has there been such a marked success with the older generation. The answer, I feel sure, is Educational Evangelism, for whilst there are undoubtedly many contributing factors to be considered, yet central to all, is the emphasis on Adult Education in the local vernacular. This has brought many choice men and women to the stage where they can both read and write in their own language. Then into their hands has come the 'Living Word' – through the eye-gate and penetrating deep into the heart, there producing its own eternal result. The Gospel of Mark is now being translated, each chapter being duplicated and given to the Teacher Boys and other literates to digest and converse upon.[14] And so they do – at work in the gardens, in their home, and around the fires at night. With right wonder and amazement, we 20th Century Westerners may look on and watch this spiritual metamorphosis, as, through the working of the Holy Spirit the 'dynamic' of the Gospel breaks down the

---

13. Doull, *One Passion: Church Planting in Papua New Guinea*, 112.
14. This literal back translation from *Tok Pisin* to English refers to the young men who served as teachers, translators or catechists in the villages after receiving elementary literacy and Bible training in the Bible School.

The McArthur Family Telefolmin

'old' and establishes the 'new', by relating a primitive world to the Saviour God.[15]

Reflecting on their missionary strategy, one is reminded of the encounter of Philip with the Ethiopian Eunuch on the desert road. Philip hears the Ethiopian reading Isaiah 53 and asks the question, 'Do you understand what you are reading?' The response of the Ethiopian is 'How can I unless someone explains it to me?'[16] Bruce Milne, in his commentary on Acts, has a penetrating insight into the significance of this response:

> The verb translated 'explain' (*hodegeo*), is used of guiding people who need to be pointed in the right direction, commonly of leading the blind (Matt. 15:14; Luke 6:39). This little piece of dialogue can be repeated endlessly from every corner of the world in our time. Whether in the context of biblical illiteracy which characterizes much life in the Western world, both outside and inside the church, or among the host of the newly converted or the genuine seekers in the developing world, there is clamant and global need today for

---

15. McArthur, 'The McArthur Diary - Extracts', Number 15, April 1957.
16. See Acts 8:26-40.

'Bible Guides'. Obviously written materials such as this commentary series, radio broadcasts, films, internet connections, and other contemporary media forms all contribute to meeting this need. But there is also, as a primary element, the critical role of the human guide and conversation partner who will 'come alongside' and journey with these new converts or seekers, both young and old, listening to their questions, and sharing the true meaning of God's Word. 'How can I understand unless someone explains it to me?' is a heart cry today, from the neighbourhoods, and the nations, of the world... For some it could be a life-calling; is there any greater?[17]

The strategy of the Baptist missionary team was exactly along the lines of what the Holy Spirit was doing in the ministry of Philip – equipping an army of 'Bible Guides' who could explain the Gospel, and accurately teach the Word of God.

Implementing the Strategy

On his return from Baiyer, Gil was met by Doug with his trekking boots, and they trekked out for another three days among the people of the Eliptamin Valley. They received a warm welcome, due in part, no doubt, to the many who had been treated on their earlier visit for an abundance of ailments and had made full recoveries. Gil and Doug marked out a site for an airstrip, and left the people to work, clearing the area themselves, preparing the site for completion on their next visit.

Back at Telefolmin, Gil took over the school work from Doug, and spent each morning working with the students in Pidgin English. In the afternoons he concentrated a major effort on vernacular language work, although frustrated by the unfortunate loss of his informant. In June Gil sent a Linguistic Edition in his Diary Extract to supporters, which clearly illustrated his concentrated work in researching the language. He had made significant progress with a new informant,[18] Wesani, in analysing basic sounds, constructing a phonetic alphabet that was easy to read, producing a dictionary of 300 words, and drafting a concise Grammar Statement. He also developed twenty questions and answers on the subject 'God the Father'. On Sunday 24 June, he made his first attempt after only five months of language learning, to speak in the vernacular

---

17. Bruce Milne, *Acts: Witnesses to Him to the Ends of the Earth* (Ross-shire, Great Britain, Christian Publications Ltd, 2010), 200-201.
18. McArthur, 'The McArthur Diary Extracts', Number 15, April 1957.

using this material! 'If my speech is understood by the people it will mean a most significant step forward evangelistically. Will you pray for us all on the above date?'[19]

Gil concluded his 'Linguistic Edition' with a quote expressing his reasoned approach to the priority of language and translation work.

> The missionary aims at influencing, not the shallows of a people's life, but the deepest depths – to touch springs of conduct, to reach down to the innermost recesses of their being. There is no path to the heart save through the mother-tongue. The mother-tongue! That in which the mother croons lullabies over the cradle – that in which the infant learns to lisp, that in which he first learns to pray at his mother's knee, that in which he jokes and plays with his fellows, that in which the youth whispers words of love into his sweetheart's ear, that which enters into all the sacred memories of a man's life. The mother-tongue – the music of the heart and home! Men may learn in many languages, but they pray in their own, as they make love [court] in their own. Whenever they wish to express that which is deepest in them they use the speech they drew from their mother's milk. And when the Gospel comes to them in those hallowed tones, it comes with power it can never have in an alien tongue.[20]

In July 1957, Don and Elaine Doull and family returned from furlough. Gil and Doug had been eagerly waiting their return before finally formulating their program for the future as they planned to make the most impact for Christ upon the 'strongholds of Satan':

> Our times of group discussion and prayer were characterised by a real sense of the presence of Christ as the urgency of the need all around us, and the inadequacy of our own efforts, caused us to definitely seek the working of the Holy Spirit in His gracious ministry of illumination, inspiration and guidance. Complete unity in decision and harmony in proportioning for the work was paramount at all times, and it is felt we now stand ready to make positive advances for our God and Saviour amongst these people.[21]

With language progress, the preparation of an orthography, and the first of four Basic Primers done, the team began to plan the building of the

---

19. McArthur, 'The McArthur Diary Extracts', Number 16, June 1957, 3.
20. McArthur, 'The McArthur Diary Extracts', Number 16, June 1957, 2. Citing Edwin Smith, *The Shrine of the Soul*, 1929.
21. McArthur, 'The McArthur Diary Extracts', Number 17, July 1957, 1.

Gil and Wesani translating

Gil and Wesani preaching

Teacher Pastor Training School. Here, selected local people would be trained in language literacy and the Bible stories, so they could share them with those in their villages. By 23 August trainees had reached a standard of literacy in Pidgin and the vernacular where they could secure work with the government for good wages. The missionaries challenged the trainees to commit to continuing in the literacy program (with a small remuneration), which would focus upon Bible teaching and relating the message to the life of the community. To their surprise, only one chose to leave the program:

> You can imagine what a joy it was to us all here on Sunday last to present our 23 Bible School boys, resplendent in royal blue lap laps and white belts, to the local congregation, and inform them that through these boys they would shortly be hearing the Word of Life in their own tongue. We do not expect the battle to be an easy one for Satan will not readily relinquish his seat of authority and demonic control, but we have thrown down the gauntlet before these people, named him and his emissaries for what they are… Be assured then, that our request for prayer is no formal matter, but a plea from the heart to join with us in claiming the outpouring of the Holy Spirit's transforming power upon these people.[22]

Bible School Students

---

22. McArthur, 'The McArthur Diary Extracts', Number 18, August 1957, 2.

Students fly out to preach in villages

The missionaries understood the vital place of prayer in the spiritual battle, both in their regular praying together and in communicating with their partners in prayer. John Piper succinctly expresses the crucial importance of this intercessory prayer; 'Until you know that life is war, you cannot know what prayer is for.'[23]

While teaching the Bible to the men progressed, Pat with the other missionary wives ensured that the women were not neglected. They also received Bible teaching together with practical training in sewing, health and hygiene – 'for unless mothers are reached with the Gospel, then our impact upon the community as a whole is small indeed, being related only to the male population.'[24]

In his language work in October, Gil was excited to identify a suitable word in the vernacular to translate the vital concept of 'propitiation'. In discussion with Wesani his informant, he discovered a word used when an influential man was sick and near death. A pig would be killed, and the blood offered up to the spirit world as an appeasement, in the sense

---

23. John Piper, *Let the Nations Be Glad - The Supremacy of God in Missions* (Leicester England: Inter Varsity Press, 1993), 41ff. See the whole chapter – The Supremacy of Prayer in Missions.
24. McArthur, 'The McArthur Diary Extracts', Number 19, October 1957, 2.

of atoning for the sick man's offence against the spirit world. 'And so, related to Christ, and given deeper meaning, this word "ungkotiwe", to propitiate by sacrifice, will become a gateway to the spiritual enlightenment of these people'.[25] It was in that same month a practical cleansing milestone was achieved and history made with the installation of a bath in the Doull's home. A wet week ensured that all could enjoy it without fear of jeopardising the water supply!

In December 1957, all the Bible School students, now literate in their own language, took the ten biblical stories Gil and Wesani had prepared and went back to their villages in the valleys around Telefolmin to share what they had been taught. The McArthur family took the opportunity to enjoy a holiday at Wewak in the new Baptist Mission Guest House situated just 30 metres from the beach. 'Oh! The beautiful surf, how glorious it is to plunge into the cool waves and be tossed around on the crests, especially for one who spent a good deal of his life-time at Coogee and Bondi.'[26] After this special family time, they faced a tough family goodbye to Robyn and Jenny as they boarded the plane to continue their schooling with Pat's family in Tamworth NSW. They would be reunited when the family planned to go home for furlough at the end of 1958.

Gil felt that this time in Wewak was especially significant, because with Wesani he visited the Telefolmin prisoners who were serving a ten-year sentence for their part in the uprisings and killing of the Patrol Officers and local police in the Eliptamin Valley in November 1953. These men were some of the leaders of the Telefolmin and Eliptamin communities. Gil and Wesani visited them several times, and they listened to the Bible stories and observed how Wesani could read and write. A few expressed the desire to be taught to read the stories in their own language. A Christian lady living in Wewak offered to visit them twice weekly for the next two years, and to keep feeding them biblical material. Gil's hope was that 'under God, it may well be that, in future years, instead of returning to their communities as embittered martyrs, they will come back as messengers of the Gospel'.[27]

Back at Telefolmin, Gil began the year with Don Doull and twelve Bible school students trekking out for a week with the Eliptamin people. They surveyed two airstrip sites and held meetings every day. They were conscious of the Spirit of God moving in the hearts of the people, as they

---

25. McArthur, 'The McArthur Diary Extracts', Number 19, October 1957, 1.
26. McArthur, 'The McArthur Diary Extracts', Number 20, December 1957, 1.
27. McArthur, 'The McArthur Diary Extracts', Number 20, December 1957, 2.

eagerly discussed Bible stories. All the headmen agreed for their people to help in airstrip construction to enable regular visits and Teacher Training stations to be set up. Back at Telefolmin, the missionary team prayerfully progressed the subject of who might be able to go and take up residence among the people and direct the airstrip work. Gil's vision also included keeping the Bible School and Literacy work functioning strongly,

> … so that by the end of the year we may rightly expect to reap a number of boys having both the academic and spiritual qualifications to warrant their being posted as Teacher Boys to the areas of need. We are hoping that we shall be able to send them out equipped with a series of some forty odd printed Bible messages, covering the essential truths of both Old and New Testaments, and giving teaching points to be highlighted in each lesson.[28]

The team devised a plan to keep all aspects of their strategy moving ahead. On Tuesday 18 February, a fully loaded party of carriers, together with Doug Vaughan and Don Doull trekked over the range separating Eliptamin from Telefolmin to live among the people, recruiting and organising local labourers, building a new Teacher Training station for young men, and supervising the airstrip construction. Doug Vaughan would live on-site, but because the government had decreed that two missionaries must always be present, Don and Gil would rotate every two weeks, living with Doug in a 12 by 6 foot log cabin. Each morning Gil and Don would teach their Bible School students, and in the afternoon, assist in the airstrip work. At 12 noon the whistle blew, and everyone downed tools for taro and 'shuteye', and then gathered at 1pm for the daily Church service. Soon it was not the missionary reading the Bible story translation, but now numbers of the young men were standing and preaching the message:

> … the story is being told, clearly and decisively in the language and thought forms of the people, and what is more important perhaps, their own young men – our Bible School boys – are standing forth and fearlessly naming the old evil practices for what they are and telling of the deliverance to be found in Christ the Saviour.[29]

On Sundays, instead of the people coming in, the team went out to

---

28. McArthur, 'The McArthur Diary Extracts', Number 21, January 1958, 2.
29. McArthur, 'The McArthur Diary Extracts', Number 24, April 1958, 2.

the villages – which was no Sunday stroll in the hills! Gil describes the challenge of a visit to Tagatemtigin:

> … leaving the airstrip, we climb down into the gorge, up the other side into the bush. After about half an hour slopping along the muddy track we come to the top of another gorge system. From here we can see the village. All we have to do is to drop down 1000 feet into the river, wander along awhile, and then climb up 1500 feet to the Tagatemtigin village which is way up on the other side of the mountain range... Sitting down under the shade of one of the huts, we gather the folk around and commence to tell them of the Saviour's love. They listen very well…[30]

It was in April that the story of the Crucifixion of Jesus was first translated into the vernacular, and Gil wrote to his prayer partners:

> Do you remember the day when you first realised that there on the Cross of Rejection and Shame, the Lord of Life and Glory died for you – paid the price to set you free from sin and death and hell? All of this coming week will be spent in translating this great fact into the language of the people and making its eternal application in their hearts. Will you join us in prayer? For we are asking that as we come to this point in the teaching syllabus, many of the young men of the Bible School will find it impossible to get past the Cross without a full surrender to its love demand.[31]

By July 1958 the airstrip at Eliptamin was complete, and the first landings successfully made. Doug Vaughan, who had carried the heavy load of airstrip construction, left with Rosemary for a well-earned furlough. Gil and Don now eagerly engaged in starting an adult school and literacy program, with the aim of commencing an itinerant Bible teaching program. This advance would provide the proving ground for the Bible School graduates who would operate in pairs, conducting school in the mornings teaching a printed vernacular Bible School syllabus, doing airstrip maintenance in the afternoons, and involvement in evening and weekend ministries in the villages. The plan also included commencing regular Baby Clinics to break through to the 'Mother's heart', and radically reduce the very high infant mortality rate in the area. The Bible School students also faced very difficult challenges:

---

30. McArthur, 'The McArthur Diary Extracts', Number 24, April 1958, 2.
31. McArthur, 'The McArthur Diary Extracts', Number 24, April 1958, 2.

... those young men of the Bible School are now being subjected to many strains and stresses as the old life makes its claims, and yet is found contrary to the truth they are hearing. But at this point too we have immediate cause for rejoicing. This week out in the Eliptamin, there is being celebrated the most important stage in the initiation of the young men into the rites of manhood. The Government Station lost a number of its men from the permanent cargo line, even though the warning was given that any men leaving would not be re-employed. At the Bible School, this call to tribal manhood was reacted to in different ways. Some openly told their head-men and even their fathers, that they were finished with such practices. Others however, under family pressure, wavered nearly to the point of capitulation. For such as these, prayer was made, and we rejoice to say that to date, not one of our young men has associated himself with these initiation ceremonies, surely another evidence of the enlightenment of the Holy Spirit.[32]

In early July, Pat left for the hospital at Baiyer River for the birth of their fifth child Sandra, who was born on the 26 July. This was a lonely time for Pat, and 'can opening time' for Gil.

Yes! You have guessed rightly – there's a new baby in the McArthur's bamboo mansion viz: Sandra Joy – our little 6lb. 5 oz. daughter. We are most thankful to say, that the complications usually anticipated with an RH-Factor baby did not eventuate, and Pat arrived back in Telefolmin two weeks after Sandra was born. This was much to Paul's and Wendy's delight, and of course Dad was tickled pink, too (the tin opener had become quite blunt). But four girls! Am I going to have trouble in a few years' time! However, Paul and I have agreed to stand together in the uneven contest in future years.[33]

Harvest Time at Telefolmin

'Hallelujah Edition' was the heading of the Diary of August 1958.[34] It began with reference to the wise insight of William Carey. 'It is of significance that every man earnestly engaged in the work sooner or later acquires a personal confidence in the growing triumph of the Kingdom, and in the secret miraculous energy of the Divine Spirit associated with

---

32. McArthur, 'The McArthur Diary Extracts', Number 25, July 1958, 2.
33. McArthur, 'The McArthur Diary Extracts', Number 26, August 1958, 1.
34. Eds, Tony Cupit, Ros Gooden and Ken Manley, *From Five Barley Loaves – Australian Baptists in Global Mission 1864-2010*, 227–229.

West Sepik Baptisms – 3000 in 7 years

Early MAF plane – a vital component in the missionary strategy

his own feeble and seemingly futile endeavours.' Gil continued, 'And what has proved to be true in all places of the earth where Christ is preached, is now being evidenced in this remote valley of Telefolmin. Come and rejoice with us now, as the Diary record leads us into yet another 20th Century Journey into Pentecost'.[35]

Don and Gil had been meeting each morning at 6.30 am to pray specifically for a spiritual awakening among the Bible School students. Those prayers were answered in a remarkable way.

> **Sunday 24, 6.45 am...** A voice at the window, 'Masta Makata, mi laik mekim samfela tok-tok long yu,' (Mister McArthur, I would like to have a word with you). On the way to open the door and let the speaker in, I thought to myself – 'Oh dear! more trouble', for invariably when the Bible School men have come to see us early in the morning, it has meant something amiss during the night. But, 'O ye of little faith', for when I opened the door, there before me were two young men resplendent in their blue lap-laps and white belts, hair washed and combed, and faces aglow with the Joy of the Lord. 'Oh Masta Makata, bel (heart) bilong mifela hapi tumas long Yesus, na mi tufela kam tokim yu.' (Oh! Mister McArthur, two of us men want to speak with you because our hearts are so happy in Jesus). I rejoiced with them briefly and then asked them to sit down in the study whilst I contacted Mr Doull. On Don's arrival, we had prayer with them and questioned them as to their experience. From their joyful answers it was obvious that for some time the Holy Spirit had been dealing with them and facing them up with the challenge of stepping right out for Christ, and there had now come this full surrender to his Lordship, and the desire to let the whole community know where they stood by following their Lord through the waters of baptism... for the Min people to say 'Yes' to the new life in Christ, means saying 'No' to so much of that which hitherto has formed and fashioned their lives. With this in mind we asked the young men viz: Wesani and Yemis, if they would stand up at the Church service, and tell their own people of their great decision. They readily agreed to do so, and we prayed with them asking the Lord to give courage and strength and the right words to say.[36]

It was Don Doull's turn to lead the Church service, and he was preaching the last message in a series on the Crucifixion. After his preaching, and

---

35. McArthur, 'The McArthur Diary Extracts, Number 27, 15-31 August 1958, 1.
36. McArthur, 'The McArthur Diary Extracts', Number 27, August 1958, 1.

then the testimony of Wesani and Yemis, Don felt constrained to issue the challenge of the Crucifixion of Jesus to the 130 people who had now been sitting under consistent Christian teaching for a long time. Don asked them to count the cost, and if they wanted to make a personal response, to come to the School room to meet with Gil and himself that night. Don recorded the wonderful response:

> Nifinin a local headman, who has been a regular attender at church services since we first came to Telefolmin in 1951, came during the afternoon to inquire again what effect a decision for Christ would have on his attitude to the Tambaran. The Tambaran was the centre of their heathen worship and belief. We explained that there could be no compromise.
>
> Now you will understand why we wondered who would meet with us that night. Was the power of evil about to be broken in this valley of darkness? Was the labour and witness of the past years about to yield the first fruits of a great harvest? Could the cross triumph over the seeming impregnable forces of evil which we have witnessed here?
>
> As we moved into the school building, we saw that the front desks were already occupied by five of the Bible School lads waiting quietly in the darkness. Soon we saw groups of people emerging out of the darkness as they came toward the school from their villages. Nifinim, on whose behalf much prayer has been made by friends in Australia, was among the first to arrive. His wife and children, including his son in law, Felepnok, who is himself quite an influential member of the community, came with him.
>
> This in itself was a great victory, but the number was to grow until fifty people were crowded into the school room. Most of the Bible School lads were there, the married ones with their wives, also the parents of some of these young men. We explained further the way of salvation and again pointed out the cost of discipleship. Then calling each person present by name, asked them to answer 'yes' if they were definite in their decision for Christ, and 'no' if they were not yet ready. It was a great thrill to hear fifty Telefolmin people answer 'yes' to the claims of Christ.[37]

Gil believed that the birth of the Church of Jesus Christ among the Min people on Sunday 24 August 1958 was a moment of destiny, the glorious

---

37. Doull, *One Passion: Church Planting in Papua New Guinea*, 118.

fruit of the tireless work of the missionary team and many faithful prayers.

> This was no ordinary appeal (if one may, in this particular case, be permitted to use the term) – it went back to a day in December 1950, when Don Doull together with a party led by Rev A H Orr and Rev Professor Burleigh, had flown across the mountains from Baiyer River and landed in the Telefolmin Valley. The intervening years had been filled with much toil, disappointment, and frustration, even to the complete closing down of the work following the uprising of 1953. But coupled with this was the knowledge that God's Word had been faithfully and consistently proclaimed, and that for the past eighteen months there had been the concentrated village preaching programme, where, through the medium of the Bible School men the message of Redemption had been systematically told forth in the language and thought forms of the people. It was fitting then, that Don should be used of the Holy Spirit to issue this challenge. But knowing all that was involved, Don asked the people to carefully count the cost and then if the answer was a personal one of, 'Christ for me and me for Christ', to come and see us that night and we would meet with them in the school room at the station.[38]

Among the fifty people who responded that evening, there were three village Headmen, and nineteen Bible School men. This was a God-given confirmation of the missionary strategy. It was also clearly divine timing, as it was only that week that Gil and Wesani had completed the final translation of the teaching syllabus.[39] There followed a period of follow-up instruction and answering questions on Sunday afternoons. The numbers soon reached over 100 as more people wanted to become Christians and commit to the radical change of learning to follow Christ.[40]

> Those who have not known the darkness of spirit worship and its fear of evil and malicious spirits with all its taboos and rites and its belief inherited from generations of ancestors, can have no conception of the giant step forward these people took.[41]

---

38. McArthur, 'The McArthur Diary Extracts', Number 27, August 1958, 2.
39. McArthur, 'The McArthur Diary Extracts', Number 27, August 1958, 2.
40. Doull, *One Passion: Church Planting in Papua New Guinea*, 119.
41. Jess Redman, *The Light Shines On* (Melbourne: Australian Baptist Missionary Society, 1982), 154.

As the spiritual movement grew in their area, Gil and Don did not forget the urgent need to press on and reach the surrounding valleys. News of a tribal fight in the uncontrolled Tifalmin valley necessitated a government patrol, and Gil and Don were invited to join them. The ten-hour trek brought them into friendly contact with a large population of completely isolated people. They marked out a site for an airstrip, and left instructions with the local headmen as to what to do in clearing and preparing the main area.

This trek was to prove Gil's last. It had been three years and Gil and Pat were due for furlough. This proved to be a watershed transition under the sovereign purpose of God as he prepared Gil for yet another vital emerging pioneering challenge. It was time to move the tent again. The last Diary from Telefolmin closed with Gil's personal reflection on the impact of the three years since sailing from Sydney:

> We feel that with some real measure of truth we are now able to say – as we have witnessed both the regenerating and moral dynamic of the Spirit of Christ at work in the lives of men – that our hitherto unconscious confidence in self has shifted, and now has for its object the Glorified Christ, ever at work in the world, in the Church and in the believer through the Holy Spirit.[42]

They arrived in Sydney eager to meet up with Robyn, Jenny, family, friends and partners to share their experiences, and tell the story of what the Lord had done.

Pastoral Ministry at Clemton Park Baptist Church 1959 – 1963

In early 1959, Gil and Pat reluctantly concluded that they must resign from the ABFM. The pressing reason was the educational needs of their five children, which could not be adequately met in a return to Telefolmin. The Mission Board meeting on 26 August 1959 recorded the acceptance of their resignation.

> Resolved that the Board record its sense of indebtedness to Mr McArthur for his service in the Netherlands New Guinea and at Telefolmin. Mr McArthur displayed courage and initiative in his share of the pioneering journeys which made possible the opening of our work in the Baliem Valley. At Telefolmin he enthusiastically applied his great ability as a linguist to the problem of reducing the

---

42. McArthur, 'The McArthur Diary Extracts', Number 28, November 1958, 2.

MATURING MINISTRY

Gil and Pat. Gil was called as Clemton Park's first full-time pastor.

The new Clemton Park church.

language to writing. He inspired the development of the work into nearby areas and laid the plan for future evangelism by aircraft.

Mr and Mrs McArthur are assured of the prayers of all members of the Board in their work in the Home Ministry.[43]

On 11 March 1959, Gil was called to be the first full-time pastor of Clemton Park Baptist Church (CPBC), commencing his ministry in August. The CPBC was born on 31 March 1940, when a group of 38 people (28 of whom were local residents) gathered at the Progress Hall. World War II was raging, but despite the difficulties of the times, the Earlwood Church felt there should be a Baptist work in the new district of Clemton Park. Two years after commencement, the church purchased land, and a new church building was opened in October 1942. The church was served by honorary and student pastors over the years, until Gil was appointed the first full time pastor. The CPBC Golden Jubilee Report of 1990 recorded, 'Rev Gilbert McArthur was a man for all seasons; his knowledge of building operations, his pastoral heart and missionary zeal proved invaluable to the new self-governing Church; he was a man sent by God!'[44]

Gil served the church until the end of 1963. He brought with him his vision and passion to reach people with the Good News of Christ, and his broad vocational, pastoral, and mission experience in Dutch New Guinea and Telefolmin. Gil vigorously led the church into a period of strong growth and was significantly involved in the 'hands on' planning and building of the first manse, as well as the new church and education block.

The experience of Gwen Bignold, a long-time member of CPBC, was typical of many in the congregation.

> My personal recollections of Dr McArthur are gleaned through a number of meetings to discuss the youth ministry of the church. He was a gracious godly visionary, with a passion for God and the church, and a deep concern for lost people. He led the church into

---

43. Australian Baptist Foreign Mission, 'Australian Baptist Foreign Mission Board Minutes of Annual Meeting', 26 August 1959, Global Interaction Archives. The focus of the Board's thanks to Gil for his achievements, with the mention of Pat only in the last sentence, is typical of the prevailing culture of the time! See Chapter 21 – 'A Loving Loyal Partner and Family'.
44. Ken Palmer, 'Clemton Park Baptist Church – Golden Jubilee 1940-1990' (Clemton Park, NSW: Clemton Park Baptist Church, 1990), 10.

MATURING MINISTRY

the early years of great growth and impact upon many lives. He laid a theological foundation that enabled the church to grow and impact the then young community at Clemton Park.

We first came in contact with Clemton Park Baptist as we watched the new church being built 'from a distance', at the same time as our new home was being built.

After marriage and a time to settle into the district, we decided that we would visit Clemton Park Baptist Church to see 'what they were like!' Upon entering the new church, we found it to be a very large congregation, with a mixture of young people, young couples, young families, down to the 'more mature' folk and the elderly.

The pastor, Dr. Gilbert McArthur, was a very learned man and very theological in his messages. He always preached from the high pulpit and looked down on the congregation, which was at times rather off-putting. As a young couple in our mid 20's, we found some of his sermons were way above our level of understanding and difficult to follow. However, we soon realised that Gilbert McArthur was a man of God, filled with knowledge, understanding and wisdom from God.[45]

In the purposes of God, Gil's time of leadership at CPBC was short, but it was a period of significant advance. When he arrived, there were 40 members and an aging weatherboard building. In four years the congregation grew to over 400 in attendance, and a new worship centre, education block and manse were built.[46] But it was not to be the long-term ministry call for Gil, as a new challenge to move the McArthur tent yet again was just around the corner.

---

45. Gwen Bignold, 'Memories of Dr Gilbert McArthur', February 2016, 1.
46. Author unknown, 'We Live Our Years as a Tale That Is Told – Notes of Eulogy at the Funeral of Gilbert McArthur', February 1994, 3, McArthur Family Archives.

The Flag of Papua New Guinea

Parliament House in Port Moresby
Photo: www.tokpisin.info

to Banz. They inspected the *Wo* site and found it very wet and unsuitable in many ways. However, they proceeded to mark out placements for the first buildings required. Gil left to try to resolve the lease of the *Wo* land.

The next day Clyde had a visit from Ted Rowse, a Warragul farmer who made a special trip to inspect the *Wo* site and take soil samples back to Melbourne for testing. Returning to Banz on the motor bike, Clyde was unable to avoid a car travelling fast on the wrong side of the road. The bike hit the car and sent Clyde and Ted flying through the air onto the road. Ted was not hurt but Clyde had a bad leg for some weeks. It was a miraculous deliverance from what could have been a very serious accident.[7]

Perseverance and Faith

The second building team member was George Tweedale, a remarkable young man, only 25 years of age when he arrived at Banz in October 1963.[8] His story is important because of the way he first connected with Gil, his divine direction and radical obedience to go to PNG, and the unique part he played in the final 'discovery' of the *Giramben* land on which the College now stands.

George had made his 'bucket list' of things he wanted to do in life and was on a journey of adventure. 'At that time, I thought that if I had all the things I wanted, could do all the things I dreamed of doing, and was able to travel to all the places I wanted to go, then I would have the kind of life that I wanted and would be satisfied.'[9]

In India he met Victor Barnard and his wife, who were independent Baptist missionaries. They invited George to stay with them and began to share the Gospel with him and teach him the Bible. 'Day by day, the Word of God did its work, until at last the truth about Jesus' claim on my life dawned on me.' He had gone to India to study Yoga from the Gurus, but instead was found by Christ and soundly converted! 'I was fully aware that this was an all or nothing commitment.'[10] Victor told George that God had a plan for his life, and in that plan he would find

---

7. Clyde Parkinson, 'Christian Leaders' Training College - October 1962 to October 1964', n.d., 1–4.
8. George Tweedale, *Not Counting the Cost - Missionary Experiences in Papua New Guinea, Ethiopia and Liberia* (Burpengary, Queensland: George Tweedale, 2016), 32.
9. Tweedale, *Not Counting the Cost*, 2, 3.
10. Tweedale, *Not Counting the Cost*, 11.

true meaning and fulfillment.[11] He decided to return to Australia, and on the bus on the way to Delhi asked the Lord what he wanted him to do.

> Straight away, I got the idea that I should go to a Pacific Island and build something beautiful for God. However, it was such a strange idea that I promptly forgot about it until I arrived back from Papua New Guinea about two years later. It was then I realised that I had done what God told me to do on the bus to Delhi.[12]

Before George left India, Victor had given him the address of a Baptist pastor in Sydney urging George to visit him.[13] George wanted to get home to Brisbane, but on arrival in Sydney decided he should give the pastor a call to pass on Victor's greetings. The pastor was Gil McArthur. Gil persuaded George to stay for the weekend. George was surprised to learn that Victor Barnard had been Gil's pastor! Gil told George that after the War he had learned to fly in a Tiger Moth in Tamworth and how Victor had often asked him to fly him outback for Gospel ministry to the Aboriginal people. When Victor could not go himself, he would send Gil on his own, no doubt planting the 'vision seed' in Gil's mind for the possible use of small aircraft in Baptist mission work. He told George how it had been Victor that had urged him to go into the ministry.[14]

On the Sunday evening George shared his testimony at CPBC, and that night Gil told George the story about the new Bible College for PNG, and his call to establish the work.

Later George recalled, 'Gil caught my attention with one of his typical visionary statements: "The CLTC will affect the whole of the Melanesian peoples of the South Pacific!" Then he said, "Will you go there and help build it?".'[15] This was not something George wanted to hear, but he agreed to pray. When he arrived home in Brisbane, he started attending the local Baptist church. The Pastor there was Dick Walker. Dick encouraged George with his own story:

---

11. George's autobiography recounts his conversion and subsequent missionary experiences.
12. Tweedale, *Not Counting the Cost*, 19.
13. Tweedale, *Not Counting the Cost*, 22, 23.
14. McArthur Paul, 'Gil McArthur Memories'. These details about flying and Victor's influence were confirmed by Gil's son Paul.
15. Tweedale, Not Counting the Cost, 24.

> I used to live in a country town about 80 miles north of Brisbane, where I owned a family bakery. The Pastor of the local Baptist church where I worshipped challenged me to go into the ministry. His name was Victor Barnard. It was because of his encouragement, that I sold my bakery business and studied for the ministry![16]

Every time George thought about settling down, Gil's request was 'nagging' at the back of his mind. But a message from Pastor Dick on Luke 9:24, 'Whosoever shall save his life shall lose it, and whosoever shall lose his life for my sake, shall find it' spoke powerfully to George:

> How many Christians fool themselves into believing they are serving God when they choose a path for their life that dodges the sacrifices of the cross by their preference for a path that suits their convenience and comfort zone? I realised that I would not find the life that God had for me if I was going to save my life for my plans and aspirations.[17]

George wrote to Gil and told him he believed that the Lord wanted him to go and help build CLTC. Gil was fascinated to hear that Victor Barnard had also urged Pastor Dick to go into the ministry. What a wonderful example of the providential work and guidance of God in human stories. Who can measure the Kingdom impact of Victor Barnard's mentoring of Gil, Dick, George – and no doubt many others?

George received a prompt reply from Bill Clack, the Secretary of the MBI CLTC Committee:

> We will be glad for your help. There is a man by the name of Clyde Parkinson there already. You should make your way first to Port Moresby. The next day, fly to Lae on the East Coast, and then take a plane into the Highlands. Your destination is a grass airstrip at Banz in the Wahgi Valley. Doug McCraw who is a Missionary Aviation Fellowship pilot and his wife Joyce live in a house near the end of this grass airstrip. Make contact with him.[18]

Pastor Dick was the only one who encouraged George to go, although he was baffled that the letter did not mention any payment for the ticket, support while he was there, or how long George might be needed. George however, was not concerned. This young Christian demonstrated his radical faith and obedience. 'I gave up my carpenter's job, and I took a

---

16. Dick Walker, as cited in Tweedale, *Not Counting the Cost*, 26.
17. Tweedale, *Not Counting the Cost*, 26, 27.
18. Tweedale, *Not Counting the Cost*, 27, 28.

plane for Papua New Guinea two weeks after receiving the letter from MBI. It was four months since I arrived home from India.'[19]

When George arrived, he worked with Clyde on the road into the *Wo* land, and they even began work on a bush house for the building team. But a few days after George arrived, the project came to a 'full stop'. A priest told them that they were working on land that was to become a Roman Catholic Mission compound. Undaunted, Gil headed off to the Roman Catholic Bishop's office in Mount Hagen and arrived just as they were about to have lunch. He introduced himself as Rev McArthur, and the Bishop warmly invited him to join them for lunch, assuming Gil was a priest of his own Church. During lunch, he turned to Gil and said, 'You know we are growing into quite a family!' Gil thought the situation was getting out of hand at this point, so he responded, 'I am sorry, your Grace, but I am not of your faith, I am a Baptist Minister!' The Bishop responded with a hearty laugh at his mistake. Gil then discussed the problem of the *Wo* land with him. He was very gracious, and the team never heard any more about a church being built on that site.[20]

Not wanting Clyde and George to overstay their welcome at the Banz MAF base, Gil found some very basic bush accommodation for them at the Kimel timber saw mill at Bung Village on the side of the mountain overlooking the Wahgi Valley. He set them to work cutting out his house frame at the Kimel saw mill. In the evenings, Clyde helped George understand more of the Bible and what it meant to follow Christ. Time dragged on, and nothing was heard about the land application. It seemed to George that they had been forgotten.[21]

When the Lands Department hearing for the lease of the *Wo* land finally came up in December 1963 in Mount Hagen, a large number turned up who wanted the land for plantation development. They were vehemently opposed to a Christian Bible and Theological College. Len Buck was there, ably presenting the case for the College, stressing the importance of courses which would benefit the community. But the atmosphere of the meeting became very heated, with much arguing, and the members of the Lands Board closed the meeting down. The application was lost. Years later Clyde Parkinson met some retired planters from PNG in Queensland, who asked,

---

19. Tweedale, *Not Counting the Cost*, 28.
20. Parkinson, 'Christian Leaders' Training College – October 1962 to October 1964', 9.
21. Tweedale, *Not Counting the Cost*, 34, 35.

Len Buck inspects the Giramben land in 1964

'Do you remember the big Lands Board meeting held at Mount Hagen?'

'I certainly do', Clyde responded.

'Well,' they said, 'that was the most contentious meeting we ever had!'[22]

The failure of the *Wo* land application was a devastating blow after such a long wait, and the work already begun! Clyde, lonely to see his wife and wanting to help at the Christmas Mount Tamborine Convention went back to Australia. George, a Christian of around six months, was left on his own with $50 in the kitty. His only company were the local people, whose basic medical needs Clyde and George had been attending to with a kit Gil left with them. He learnt much about the Wahgi culture and language. During those weeks alone, George experienced daily pressure from the village single women to seduce him.[23] It was truly a testing time for a young Christian.

Gil returned in February 1964 to look for suitable land up to a hundred miles radius from Banz. He told George that after waiting three years for land, consideration was being given to limit the original plan for CLTC. But Gil and Len Buck had decided 'to hold out in faith, that God would in his time honour the original vision for the College.'

---

22. Parkinson, 'Christian Leaders' Training College – October 1962 to October 1964', 10.
23. George only mentions this particular pressure in the unpublished draft of his autobiography *Not Counting the Cost...* on page 24.

Building the road into Giramben

George shared that same conviction, and so had persevered, living alone on the mountainside. Before Gil left, he arranged for George to go to the Baptist Mission workshop at Baiyer River, to prepare timber so he could usefully make furniture for the College. More equipment had also landed at Banz and George had great difficulty in finding storage for it. The only place was a shed owned by local plantation managers who were very reluctant to help.[24]

God's Remarkable Provision

It was a savage tribal fight over pigs that brought the police and an Australian Kiap (Patrol Officer) to the village where George was staying. While the local police looked for the culprits, George talked with the Kiap over a cup of tea. He knew about the CLTC project and told George about a prize tract of land called *Giramben* that he had just bought from the local people. George became very excited and asked if it might be possible for CLTC to apply for it. The Patrol Officer replied, 'If you get in very quick with your application, I would say a good chance. Very few people know about it yet.'[25] The land was right next to the *Bunum Wo* land that the College had unsuccessfully applied for. George went early

---

24. Tweedale, *Not Counting the Cost*, 49.
25. Tweedale, *Not Counting the Cost*, 61, 62.

the next morning to *Giramben*, and climbed the hill where the local leader, who had been present when the purchase was made, pointed out the boundaries. George felt a strong assurance that this was the right land for CLTC. He quickly advised Gil of his find. Gil soon arrived, and they drove to the land. They sat with *Giramben*'s original owners on the hill for a long time. George remembers,

> Gil explained to me what would be his plan for the College if we got the land. From what he said that day, it was clear that he already knew where most things would go… He was a visionary, a clear and quick-minded strategist… We made our evening meal… Then we had prayer about *Giramben*, praying that the Lord would go before us in the application process. Gil said, 'After breakfast tomorrow morning we will drive down the valley to Minj. I know the Australian Patrol Officer who is in charge there, and he will help us.'
>
> Next morning… we left for Minj. On the way Gil asked me to stop the vehicle at the *Giramben* land. He said, 'Let's go up that hill again.'[26]

But George did not particularly want to walk up through the tall wet grass again, so Gil went alone. In J Oswald Sander's words,

> [Gil's] eyes swept the swampy grasslands where the College now stands, and as he gazed, God spoke the reassuring word to his heart – the same word as he had spoken to Moses: 'Build according to the pattern of the words I gave you on the mountain.' Doubt and discouragement fled, and in faith he claimed the *Giramben* property for the projected College. Never again did his faith waver, nor was it misplaced.[27]

A member of the CPBC congregation recalled Gil's description of his God-given vision on what was later named Vision Hill:

> He shared with [us] how God had spoken to him on top of a mountain in Banz and told him that he had been chosen to build a Bible College in the valley below. We sat amazed and were overawed at Gilbert's description of the vision God had given to him.
>
> Gilbert told us that God stood him on the mountain and showed him a very swampy, muddy valley below. God told him that this valley would become Christian Leaders' Training College. God

---

26. Tweedale, *Not Counting the Cost*, 64.
27. Sanders, *Planting Men in Melanesia*, 38.

showed Gilbert in a vision how he would have to drain the valley, do the plumbing needed, make dams to store some of the water for later use, where to place the buildings, auditorium, lecture rooms and houses for staff and students. God also gave him the vision to develop agriculture, animals, vegetables, fruit, etc., to later feed the College people and how to sell the surplus to gain an income. Many decisions had to be made, but wisdom was given by God to develop this vision of the College in this valley below the mountain.

After Gilbert shared his vision from God with us, he then told us that God had called him to leave Clemton Park Baptist and go to PNG to build and oversee the work and development of the College. Later, Gilbert became Principal of the College and his faith, obedience to God's call, wisdom and hard work became a blessing to many students over many years and continues today. We thank God for knowing this man of God for a short time in our church, but for a much longer time as we followed his work over many years.[28]

After some time on the hilltop Gil returned, and they drove on to Minj. The Patrol Officer gave Gil all the information he needed to lodge an application, and Gil went on the motor bike to see the District Commissioner in Mount Hagen.[29] He told him the story, and how the *Wo* land application which should have been given to CLTC had been poorly handled. He asked if the Commissioner would oppose or stand behind the CLTC application. He replied, 'I am not going to fight you or your God. Go down to Port Moresby.'[30]

When Gil initiated the paper work, he discovered that the Officer was a young man 'whom he had befriended, and to whom he had opened his home in Telefolmin days.'[31] The Officer gave prompt assistance in the survey and documentation, and in a short time the application was sent to Port Moresby. In February 1964 it was reported to the MBI Executive that Gil had lodged another new application for 413 acres of *Giramben* land, and that the hearing would take place on 4 March.[32] The

---

28. Bignold, 'Memories of Dr Gilbert McArthur', 1, 2.
29. Tweedale, *Not Counting the Cost*, 65.
30. Sanders, *Planting Men in Melanesia*, 39.
31. Sanders, *Planting Men in Melanesia*, 39.
32. MBI Executive, 'Minutes of the Executive Meeting of the Melbourne Bible Institute', 25 February 1964.

Administrator's Council confirmed the application on 9 April 1964.[33] 'The transaction could well have taken eighteen months, but it was completed in a quarter of that time.'[34] God had provided a place which proved to be perfectly suitable for the development of CLTC in the years ahead.

George later wrote of his deep disappointment that Gil never spoke to him about the 'vision' he later said he had received that morning. Furthermore, the later account of the story of finding the *Giramben* land omitted to mention George's role in the providential sequence of events that led to the eventual securing of the campus site: the fight over pigs at his bush house that brought the police and Patrol Officer to his village, the cup of tea over which the purchase of the *Giramben* land was discussed which became the basis of his call to Gil, and the final successful application that followed.[35] George's key role and

The building team 1964
Back, L-R: Alan Baker, Peter Ezzy, John Davidson, George Tweedale
Middle: Bob Lockhart, Ken Eden, Rita 'Mum' Eden, Clyde Parkinson, Ian Edridge
Front: Name unknown, Willie Exton, Seloani, Name unknown

---

33. MBI Executive, 'Minutes of the Executive Meeting of the Melbourne Bible Institute', 19 March 1964.
34. Sanders, *Planting Men in Melanesia*, 39.
35. Tweedale, *Not Counting the Cost*, 65.

Vision Hill – Easter Service – 2018

faithful perseverance in the securing of the *Giramben* land for CLTC demonstrates that God can accomplish his purpose through even the youngest Christian committed to him. Vision Hill has continued to be a hallowed place in the life of CLTC.

Years later, George made his first return visit to CLTC in April 2017 to see 50 years of progress in the development of the campus and facilities, share his story with the students, and visit the village and 'bush house' where he formerly lived in 1964. His visit and testimony after so many years had a powerful impact upon staff and students.

George Tweedale returns to CLTC 53 years after the Vision Hill story.
L-R: Jeffrey Wanure, Valeria Elel, Tim Price, George Tweedale, Gordon Tobul, Paul McArthur, Jenny Tobul, Liz McArthur, Garth Morgan, Trevor Pell, Robyn Pell, Simon Elel.

8
VISION TO REALITY

*Leadership is not about wrenching a grudging effort out of
virtual slaves or grandstanding for adoring spectators.
It is about inviting partners to identify with and participate in
bringing about something worth giving your life for.
When people sign up for a vision, everything they have comes with it.
You don't have to wrangle their resources out of them.
Resources follow vision.
You don't have to plead for their loyalty or time.
They are eager to invest. They line up to be involved.*[1]

The People

Well before the term 'mentoring' came into prominence, Gil often spoke of Christian life and ministry as being a 'romance of encounter in life on life' experience. He believed leadership involved investing in the lives of those around him. One of the immediate needs for the commencement of CLTC was suitably mature, gifted, skilled Christians to provide responsible governance, build facilities, develop agricultural projects, draft and teach the training syllabus, administer the organisation, and maintain vehicles, plant and machinery. Clyde Parkinson and George Tweedale were early pioneers in what became a long line of committed people who served to bring the vision of CLTC to maturity. Again and again God answered prayer in providing the right people to meet immediate and diverse needs, and Gil himself had a unique role with most of them in their service at CLTC.

Clyde Parkinson re-joined George in March 1964. Alan Baker from Melbourne and Peter Ezzy from Toowoomba also joined the team and together they cut the road into the property and worked on both the Principal's house and a bush house for the Building Team.

Immediately the issue of the land was settled, Gil was deeply concerned to see the right people in place to construct basic facilities

---

1. Ralph Enlow Jr., *The Leader's Palette: Seven Primary Colours* (Bloomington, Indiana: WestBow Press, a Division of Thomas Nelson, 2013), 73.

and commence classes in 1965 – only a nine-month window of time for preparation! He launched into an extensive program of deputation which began in March 1964 in New Zealand, and included Tasmania, Melbourne, Sydney, Canberra and Queensland in that order, before he planned to depart with his family for PNG in October 1964.[2]

Gil had been active in publicising the commencement of CLTC in Australia, but he also had a growing conviction that he should go to share the challenge in New Zealand. The difficulty was that he was completely unknown there. The initial planning for the meetings disintegrated when the New Zealand businessman who was responsible suffered a family tragedy. It seemed an impossible situation. After prayerful advice from Rev John Searle, Principal of MBI, Gil left for New Zealand. He remembered two Christian friends in Auckland, who provided accommodation and helped him plan an itinerary that proved to have miraculous outcomes in the life direction of numerous people, and the gathering of resources for the work ahead.

> Together, with map in hand, they scanned the Missionary Association Directory, and the Baptist Year Book, to plot an itinerary. After prayer, fifty centres were selected, and fifty letters sent out seeking openings for meetings. As there was no time to await replies, each letter stated the time he would arrive at each place. So that no one should feel pressured, he wrote, 'Don't be embarrassed if you have been unable to arrange a meeting.'
>
> From those fifty hurried letters, more than forty meetings eventuated. 'Looking back on that tour', Dr McArthur recalled, 'I don't think there was one meeting out of which something did not eventually arise for the benefit of the work.' At every meeting, he was conscious of an unusual unction, and a deep sense of God being with him. As he approached each gathering, there was a lively sense of expectancy: 'I wonder who or what God has got for us here?'[3]

It was Easter 1964, and Gil heard that the Ngaruawahia Easter Convention two hours drive south of Auckland, was a strategic place to contact young people with a missionary vision and interest. Although the program was already completed, he managed to secure a three-

---

2. MBI Executive, 'Minutes of the Executive Meeting of the Melbourne Bible Institute', 21 August 1964.
3. Sanders, *Planting Men in Melanesia*, 41–43.

The 1965 building team
L-R: Name unknown, Ian Keals, Bob Watson, John Woodbridge,
Ron Youngman, Seloani

minute slot in the missionary meeting to present the vision and needs of CLTC. His message was simple and powerful:

> I am Gilbert McArthur. I arrived in New Zealand on Wednesday, having come from New Guinea, via Melbourne, where the Melbourne Bible Institute is preparing to undertake the great responsibility of providing this specialised ministry through the establishment of a centralised intermission training college, to be called 'New Guinea Christian Leaders' Training College'. 413 acres of valuable land has now been acquired in the Western Highlands of New Guinea. The establishment of this College is considered to be one of the most strategic missionary thrusts of the 20th Century, and will, through its evangelical emphasis, greatly influence the whole spiritual climate of the young churches in their developing life and witness. It is a venture of faith on the part of the evangelical world of both Australia and New Zealand. You are now invited to share in the inspiration and blessing of this Bible-centred ministry. I have been appointed as first Principal. I am looking for a degreed Bible teacher, a degreed agriculturist, a degreed registrar, builders, farmers and tradesmen.[4]

---

4. Garth and Ruth Morgan, 'Timeline for CLTC for Garth and Ruth Morgan', 3 December 2016, 2.

Gil's passionate plea occupied exactly two minutes and fifty-five seconds. The impact was such, that seven of the young people present subsequently joined the College staff.

Garth Morgan recalls the spiritual power of that brief appeal: 'We went home from that meeting feeling that this was what God wanted us to do with our lives, and five others went home under the same constraint. The others were David and Thea Martin, Thomas Strahan, Ian Keals and Robin Cowie. Not bad recruitment, seven candidates in three minutes!'[5]

> Following the Convention, Garth and Ruth went with Gil to the top of Titirangi in Auckland. They looked over the beautiful harbour on which they had spent many happy hours sailing. Was the cloud about to move for them? They discussed the possibilities of service with CLTC, and where their accounting and administrative skills could best be employed. 'As we talked', Garth recalled, 'I was impressed that here was a man of vision. He seemed to be seeing things a long way off', as indeed he was.[6]

Garth and Ruth's training and experience equipped them in a remarkable way for what became a life-long involvement with CLTC. Following high-school, Garth trained in a Public Accountant's office, attending university part-time. In this period of study and preparation he qualified as a professional accountant, became a member of the Institute of Secretaries and completed cost and management accounting, and a degree in Commerce. Ruth had extensive administrative and accounting machine experience. They had also completed their Bible College training (Garth with a Licentiate in Theology). They applied to join CLTC in April 1964, but 22 months went past before their final acceptance in February 1966, and arrival at CLTC in August.[7]

---

5. Sanders, *Planting Men in Melanesia*, 41, 42.
6. Sanders, *Planting Men in Melanesia*, 42.
7. Morgan, 'Timeline for CLTC for Garth and Ruth Morgan', 1. This timeline also reveals that, at an Easter Camp in 1957, Garth (18) and Ruth (17) clearly sensed God's leading to facilitate a Bible College like the NZ Bible Training Institute in PNG. They went to Bible College as the Lord challenged them through Len Buck's preaching in the Auckland Baptist Tabernacle in August 1961. The delay in the acceptance of their application to CLTC, after Gil's urging them to apply, was that the MBI CLTC Committee in Melbourne were initially not convinced that people with their skill levels were really required, and then a subsequent long delay in their letter of acceptance being received from Melbourne. In the mean time they continued working and following up all Gil's contacts from his visit to New Zealand.

CLTC Campus from Vision Hill 1974

Another New Zealand meeting was attended by Ron and Peg Youngman. Ron had built streets of state houses in the suburbs of Auckland following World War II until 1961 when he 'retired' from commercial building at the age of 40. Peg worked alongside Ron in the office administration. Following his retirement, Ron offered his building experience to Baptist churches in New Zealand. Ron and Peg were powerfully impacted by the vision for CLTC:

> As they listened to Dr McArthur's message, it impressed them in the same way as it had the Morgans. They too felt that God was laying His hand on them for service in Papua New Guinea. In the succeeding years, Ron and Peg gave unstintingly of both service and substance, and many buildings at Lae and at Banz are monuments to their sacrificial labours which, at times, involved considerable periods of separation. The fruit of their work is seen not only in buildings, but in the lives of students and workmen whom they influenced for the Lord.[8]

---

8. Garth Morgan, 'Gilbert McArthur Information', Email, 6 November, 2016. Ron and Peg's response in late 1964 included packing up and crating Ron's joinery factory with all the equipment that he had used to build state houses for 15 years, and gifting it to the College. Garth Morgan physically helped Ron in the packing.

The first meeting in 1964 of the people who had offered their services following Gil's New Zealand visit was held in the Youngman's Auckland home. Later, these meetings became the New Zealand CLTC Advisory Council (NZAC). In 1966 Rev Dr David Stewart became chairman following his commencement as Principal of the New Zealand Bible Training Institute (NZBTI).[9] The NZAC offered strong support for the development of CLTC in the following years.

When Gil went on to the South Island of New Zealand, two other young people, John and Ann Hitchen, experienced the same Spirit-birthed compulsion to embrace the vision for CLTC.[10]

John had served five years with the Youth Department of the YMCA, and following his Bachelor of Arts, entered the NZBTI in 1961, where his call to missionary Bible teaching developed. He completed his Bachelor of Divinity and served as a youth pastor in 1963/64. When Gil visited Wellington, Ann Ross, a nurse who was engaged to John, heard Gil's presentation and felt strongly that CLTC could be the right place for them to serve. When Gil arrived in Christchurch,

> … as in other centres, he enthralled his audiences with a picture of what God could do in Papua New Guinea. John was deeply impressed, and on a memorable Sunday spent two hours with Dr McArthur, asking questions and, incidentally, finding the answers very satisfying. 'Why are you recruiting raw and inexperienced staff and not using experienced missionaries for this task?' he asked.[11] Once again the answer satisfied him. The pioneering nature of CLTC with its novel type of programme needed young people, well qualified, with creative ideas and new approaches. Older missionaries were usually more set in their ideas, and less willing to learn and adapt to new situations.
>
> As the interview continued, John grew more enthusiastic, and apparently there was a reciprocal response in the heart of the Principal-designate. As they were separating, although nothing formal was said, he was suggesting the equipment to bring, and methods of shipment, as though the issue was a foregone

---

9. Garth Morgan, 'A Tribute to Ron and Peg Youngman', 22 February, 2017. New Zealand Bible Training Institute, later became Bible College of New Zealand, and now Laidlaw College.
10. Sanders, *Planting Men in Melanesia*, 41–43.
11. This question was a serious one, asked a number of times by the younger inexperienced missionaries that Gil recruited for his emerging team.

conclusion – as indeed it was. In due course, he and Ann were accepted for service.

The understanding John then had was, that as neither funds nor housing would be available until January 1966, he would not be expected on the field until December 1965. But just as he was about to sit his final B.D. examinations in late 1964, he received a letter from Dr McArthur which ran, 'When you arrive in New Guinea in December'… you will do this and that! Through some failure in communication, he had assumed that he was to commence at the end of 1965, not 1964![12]

When John arrived at CLTC Gil began an intensive mentoring oversight of John's introduction to PNG culture and the vision and ethos of CLTC. John recalls that 'Gil, having first recruited me, then carefully oriented me and developed our mutual working relationship in those first two or three formative years of the teaching programme at Banz.'[13]

J Oswald Sanders provided exactly the right insight on Gil's providential New Zealand visit when he wrote, 'Reviewing that brief and seemingly ill-starred visit, one is left with the unmistakable impression that this was God's time, and Gilbert McArthur was God's man to lay the burden and vision of the Christian Leaders' Training College on the hearts of fellow Christians in New Zealand.'[14] Through that visit the Lord had provided the key people necessary for the initial phase of establishing CLTC: an accountant, office administrator, Bible teacher, agriculturalist, dairy farmer, motor mechanic and very experienced builders and building equipment!

In succeeding years a long line of Australian, New Zealand, and other nationalities, plus a growing core of Papua New Guineans, caught the vision – many through Gil's influence. Following the early pioneers, they developed CLTC to become the leading evangelical Bible and Theological College of the South Pacific, fully accredited by the PNG government as an Institute of Higher Education of PNG, offering courses from Certificate through Diploma, Degree, to Post-Graduate levels.

In recruiting people for CLTC Gil, along with the Australia and New Zealand Advisory Councils, demonstrated discernment in identifying

---

12. Sanders, *Planting Men in Melanesia*, 99, 100.
13. John Hitchen, 'Gil McArthur as Mentor', 22 October, 2016, 1. Further details of John's experience of being mentored by Gil are included in Part Three, 'Gil McArthur – The Legacy'.
14. Sanders, *Planting Men in Melanesia*, 42.

Single student houses

the right people for the right opportunities, and the Holy Spirit exercised a powerful influence in the lives of those who were caught up in the life and work of CLTC. Gil's emphasis was on younger, well qualified people, who may not have had much cross-cultural experience, but who were passionate to serve Christ and totally committed to the vision of CLTC; people he could lead and mould into an effective team to see the vision realised.[15]

Years later John Hitchen in his farewell when Gil left CLTC, spoke of him as a 'moulder of men and women':

> He's had the gift of being able to not only see the potential in another person, but to draw it out of them. It takes a big man to do what Mr McArthur has done. He gathered around him a group of completely inexperienced, mostly young, new missionaries, and yet through them he has developed what is perhaps one of the most strategic works in the whole of the Territory.
>
> In this he has been personally responsible for choosing and selecting almost all the staff at CLTC today. He's moulded us into a team. He has demanded that we become bigger people, that we become bigger in our own thinking, that we become bigger in our skills and knowledge... Mr McArthur has demanded that we become bigger people in our own souls if we want to share with him

---

15. Sanders, *Planting Men in Melanesia*. For a more comprehensive account of the lives of those impacted by Gil in the early days, readers should refer to this book by J Oswald Sanders on the first ten years of CLTC.

in the work of CLTC. He has moulded us to become tools which the Master has been able to use.[16]

The Training Curriculum

Often the term 'training curriculum' brings to mind the cognitive content of training. But that is only one aspect of what must be an integrated holistic program. It can rightly be said that 'the College is the curriculum.' The whole training experience is indeed the curriculum that shapes the learning of the students. This includes the integration of the academic, spiritual and practical aspects of training; the character, integrity and ministry experience of the teaching staff; and the community life of the College itself. In the development of CLTC, this integrated holistic approach has been a primary concern from the very beginning. The MBI CLTC Committee, in guiding the shaping of this new curriculum, had the wealth of MBI's rich biblical training heritage at their disposal to draw upon. In addition, there has been the driving motivation to understand, teach and model what 'Christian Leadership' – leading like Jesus – looks like in the contemporary Melanesian context. J Oswald Sanders notes the primary focus of the mission of CLTC:

> Is it too much to say that the health and prosperity of the Christian Church, and of the newly-born Papua New Guinean nation depend on the calibre of their spiritual leaders? Actuated by this conviction, and in response to the divine injunction to entrust the Word received to 'faithful men who will be able to teach others', the College has formulated courses calculated to provide the best training available for its students. The objective was not merely to draw up a useful and attractive curriculum, but to plan courses that would impart spiritual tone and quality to the students.[17]

The actual foundation stones for the development of the curriculum were clear from the beginning. From 1965, building on the guideline laid down by the MBI CLTC Committee, a pattern of consultation was initiated with evangelical mission leaders in PNG on curriculum development. The key components were established early:

> Biblical and theological study at the centre of the curriculum, as the prime requirement for young evangelical churches growing from the then dominant missions.

---

16. John Hitchen, 'Appreciation of Rev G. J. McArthur', 29 November, 1970, 3, McArthur Family Archives.
17. Sanders, *Planting Men in Melanesia*, 67.

Using English as the language of instruction: both to utilise the one common language uniting students from across the nation, and to equip students with the language and literacy skills to bridge into the wider Christian world. Neo-Melanesian (Tok Pisin), was used for pastoral care amongst students and in College outreach ministries.

Keeping a practical and holistic perspective: equipping leaders both for church and community leadership, but also for agricultural, mechanical, and building ministries – and, in the original plan, even teacher training.

Rooted in Melanesia with a strong self-support commitment: seen at first in developing the money-earning capacity of the property, but increasingly worked out in the curriculum in terms of contextualization – ensuring the teaching is relevant to the cultural settings of Melanesia.[18]

To assist the Principal and ensure that the development of CLTC was connecting with and meeting the training needs of the missions and churches, it was agreed in March 1964 that the MBI Council in consultation with the Principal, would establish a CLTC Consultative Committee in New Guinea (CLTCCC).[19] However, the confirmation of membership and work of the CLTCCC only began in earnest in November 1966, when it met to discuss some urgent questions of the missions and churches.[20] Some were considering setting up their own English programs. Genuine questions were being asked about CLTC training. How would the missions and churches safeguard their particular theological and strategic emphases? What would it cost to send students to CLTC instead of starting their own program? How would students readjust to the village situation after being extracted from their own

---

18. John Hitchen, 'Evangelicals Equipping Melanesian Men and Women: An Interpretation of the Training Ministries of the Christian Leaders' Training College of Papua New Guinea, 1965-2010', in Tim Meadowcroft and Myk Habets (Eds.). *Gospel, Truth & Interpretation: Evangelical Identity in Aotearoa New Zealand* (Auckland, New Zealand: Archer, 2011), 113.
19. MBI Executive, 'Minutes of the Executive Meeting of the Melbourne Bible Institute', 19 March 1964.
20. It continued until 1973 when its functions were absorbed into the PNG based Governing Council.

Faculty Staff team, 1967
L-R: Garth Morgan, Ruth Morgan, Heather Strahan, Pat McArthur,
Gwen Sach, Gil McArthur, Margaret Webber, Ann Hitchen,
Barry McWha and John Hitchen

context for training at CLTC? For what ministry or service was CLTC really preparing students?[21]

Gil discussed with John Hitchen how they might clarify these concerns and ensure open frank discussion at the CLTCCC meeting. John drafted a paper that identified the issues and sought to provide a reasoned way forward for an English training program that would have maximum benefit for all the churches and missions. This was presented and discussed at the November 1966 meeting of the CLTCCC.[22]

It was agreed that inclusion of chosen reading assignments in the students' final year, followed by a 'finishing' year back home would overcome the concern about protecting the particular theological emphases and strategies of the sending missions and churches. To ensure the College's theological position was well understood, students would be required to accept the EA statement of faith. In regard to fees, Papua New Guinea local churches would be asked to supply the monthly allowance, basic kit and travelling expenses. The additional training cost of $150 per year was not regarded as a local church responsibility, or a condition of acceptance. The College would seek to raise these

---

21. CLTC Consultative Committee, 'Minutes of the Christian Leaders' Training College Consultative Committee Meeting', 15 November, 1966, 1.
22. John Hitchen, 'Thinking Aloud - About English Bible School Programmes within the Framework of the Evangelical Alliance', 15 November 1966.

training costs through its fund-raising and income earning programs. This would be far cheaper than churches or missions setting up their own colleges. However, missions and churches were urged to consider partnership in capital expenditure in the establishment phase of CLTC. The CLTC paper, 'The Place of Vacation Ministries – and the Role of the Missionary in such Ministries', sought to ensure that term breaks spent back in their villages were also a vital part of training, so the issues of the integration of students back into village life could be addressed.[23]

The MBI CLTC Committee set broad parameters for the curriculum, and it was under Gil's mentoring that John Hitchen spearheaded the development of the CLTC training programs.[24] As envisaged by the MBI CLTC Committee, and as advised by the Consultative Committee in PNG, the initial program was a four-year Certificate of Church Leadership course, based on a controlled English vocabulary and simple sentence structures. Detailed notes enabled students to gain use of English biblical materials. Up to 25% of the study involved improving their English and general education. There was a strong emphasis on community, and practical ministry assignments that rooted the training in a ministry context.

After ten years, the Certificate course was reduced to three years. Practical internship periods back in their home ministry context were introduced to ensure that the training was focused on practical outcomes, and the development of gifts and skills in ministry. Apart from the first year of teaching, while married student facilities were still being constructed, the students' wives and families accompanied their husbands for a special program designed for student wives, although where education levels were adequate they studied in the English programs. A one-year Certificate of Christian Education course introduced in 1968 offered opportunity for those in different vocations to gain competence in biblical knowledge and basic ministry skills. In these developments, the College was receiving guidance from the Consultative Committee about the training needs of the churches. A higher-level Diploma course was introduced in 1969, and a Single Women's course from 1970.

---

23. CLTC Consultative Committee, 'Minutes of the Christian Leaders' Training College Consultative Committee Meeting', 1966.
24. The curriculum philosophy and development stages of CLTC's theological teaching programme are explained in, John Hitchen, 'Evangelicals Equipping Melanesian Men and Women...', 2011:110-136.

Following further evaluation in 1977, a Bachelor of Theology program was introduced in 1978. Students completing the Diploma at the required level (including six months' practical internship), could then go on to do a fourth and fifth year for the degree. Due to the need for older, mature, experienced pastors to upgrade their biblical knowledge, and reflect on their ministries, a series of six-month Senior Pastors' courses were introduced in 1973. A very significant development has been the introduction of the Master of Theology program in 2008. Overseas Council Australia as a core element of their PASIFIKA Strategy, has provided significant financial contributions for housing and operational expenses for the MTh. CLTC was formally accredited in a process over 2008 to 2010 as an Institute of Higher Education in PNG.[25] As a component of accreditation, CLTC was encouraged to broaden its offerings, and in 2017 introduced a Diploma of Community Development.

Alongside the key residential programs, John Hitchen – influenced by the success of Theological Education by Extension (TEE), in Latin America – produced a staff study paper on how TEE could reach a new group of people across PNG. In 1975, TEE was introduced in pilot courses in Mount Hagen and Port Moresby, and then rapidly developed into a Distance Education Department of CLTC which has touched thousands of students across PNG and beyond in the Solomon Islands and the Pacific. Urban campus programs also developed in Port Moresby and Lae in the early 1980s.[26] The urban programs were a component of the original vision that Len Buck had shared with the MBI Council from the very early days and was later stimulated in 1980 by a visit of Dr Bruce Nicholls of the World Evangelical Theological Commission.[27]

To complete the story of the development of CLTC training, we need to recognise that in addition to the Bible teaching training, there were closely associated vocational programs which were also inherent in the CLTC vision. A Farm Management Course started in 1966 to develop agricultural knowledge and animal husbandry skills to lift the productivity of those in the village communities. The Agricultural program's model farm project and attempts to introduce new projects and technologies had varying success. This program was discontinued after some years but re-emerged in the current Rice Growing and Community Development programs. Mechanical, technical and building training

---

25. Hitchen, 'Evangelicals Equipping Melanesian Men and Women...' 114–18.
26. Hitchen, 'Evangelicals Equipping Melanesian Men and Women...' 118–19.
27. Renshaw, 'Gilbert McArthur Lecture – The Mission', 4.

was present from the beginning, and students equipped with these skills have provided much needed help at this level in their own communities. Later these developed into apprenticeship training schemes.[28]

Over the years, Gil and his teaching team were proactive in responding to a number of issues.[29] First, the potential problems of an 'extraction' model of theological education were recognised from the beginning.[30] However, in a clan-based society, learning can be more effectively achieved in a social process. The campus-based College provided a community of learners, both students and faculty, which stimulated learning and provided opportunity for faculty to invest time with students. In a country like PNG, the geographic isolation of communities and churches, plus the difficulties of transport, mean campus training does offer access to limited resources not available in isolation. At the same time an awareness of the need for flexible delivery required to train different kinds of Christian leaders has been important in planning programs for different leadership needs. It is also recognised that the highest academic level is not the only strategic requirement and both formal and informal programs have been used over the years. Gil pioneered this diversity in his leadership development work with the Defence and Police Forces.[31]

Second, Gil's leadership team emphasised the importance of Melanesian integrity and the contextualization of CLTC's programs. 'Contextualization means relating the never-changing truths of Scripture to ever-changing human contexts so that those truths are clear and compelling. It is the process of engaging culture in all its varied dimensions with biblical truth.'[32] Was the CLTC learning process

---

28. Hitchen, 'Evangelicals Equipping Melanesian Men and Women...' 120–121.
29. For a more complete discussion of these issues please refer to Hitchen, 'Evangelicals Equipping Melanesian Men and Women...', 121-128.
30. The 'Extraction Model' requires that students leave their normal living and work situation to receive their training in a college. The Banz campus training at CLTC involves extraction from their home and church communities, whereas students in the urban centres are not extracted from their normal living situation – especially those who are part-time.
31. For example, CLTC has also used and adapted Development Associates International leadership materials for informal leadership seminars and conducted Graduates' Refresher Courses and other events to encourage renewal and lifelong learning.
32. Craig Ott and Strauss, Stephen J, *Encountering Theology of Mission – Biblical Foundations, Historical Developments, and Contemporary Issues* (Grand Rapids Michigan: Baker Academic, 2010), 266.

First CLTC Graduates 1968
Back, L-R: Tuata Iosep, Mandalaga Giawasi, Isaac Burai, Naba Bore
Middle: Samson Mahien, Kongoe Sipwanje, Kawaki Kamaya, Kyapo Roepe,
Pyau Grepure. Front: Neksep Fapkilok, Levi Wadah, Jezreel Filoa,
Traimya Kambipi, Silas Blaisip

designed with deliberate reference to Melanesian culture, and the context of ministry in which graduates serve? Due to the recruitment of some faculty who had no previous experience in PNG, Gil knew that this sensitivity and understanding needed to be intentionally developed. Faculty were mentored in their developing understanding of Melanesian culture, and very early were made aware that curricula could not simply be imported from abroad, or even just handed down unchanged from the past. The abstract approach to biblical concepts evolved into a strong focus on the narrative story of God's revelation of himself and his mission in Scripture, which rooted theology in the historical events and experiences of God's people. Faculty also pursued post graduate work in different aspects of grappling with this issue, which provided deeper insights for curriculum development and class-room teaching.

Third, Gil understood the importance of continuing interaction with the missions and churches and the need to adjust training processes in the light of this dialogue:

> The curriculum should be designed to meet the present needs of the community, not some idealistic situation which is still far distant. In effect, this means that courses need to be geared to cycles of training which will progress as the general levels of education,

literacy, technological experience and skill are lifted. This will probably also mean that institutions will need to run two or even three levels of training during these years of transition.[33]

This interaction to identify 'present needs' first took place through Gil's individual contacts, and then through the CLTCCC. This formal level of dialogue developed further through the EA annual conferences held on the campus, and the input of national Council members following the incorporation of CLTC in PNG in 1973. Vacation ministries and the movement of faculty around among the churches also ensured that faculty were personally involved in this process.

Fourth, from the early days Gil was committed to the localisation of the College governance, faculty and staff. His approach to Joshua Daimoi while still a student at the Baptist College in Sydney led to Joshua's appointment in 1968 as the first national faculty member. Numerous other tertiary sponsorships of national people and appointments to faculty followed. Gil's last report to the CLTC Council appended his 'Localisation Plan', which served to stimulate even further the professional enrichment and localisation of faculty and staff, as subsequent principals followed his lead.

Finally, Gil's personal spiritual passion and devotion to Christ meant that he was not interested in merely an academic process but equipping that placed personal spiritual formation and Bible at the very heart of the curriculum.

> Processes and structures for discipling, regularity of quality spiritual input, communal attention to failures and to forgiveness and restoration, concern to sustain the College's prayer life, evident sorrow and heart searching when discipline or dismissal were necessary are all found regularly in the official documents.[34]

In each of these issues it is profoundly significant to reflect on the way Gil's leadership and influence has flowed through into the rich heritage that CLTC has brought to PNG and the Pacific. The unity of vision shared first by Gil and Leonard (Principal and Chair of the MBI CLTC Committee) was fully endorsed by the faculty team at the College and implemented accountably under the guidance of the MBI CLTC Committee through the annual College Council meetings. It was enriched by the practical

---

33. Gilbert J McArthur and John Hitchen, 'Leadership in Rural Communities in Melanesia', March 1967, 4, CLTC Archives.
34. Hitchen, 'Evangelicals Equipping Melanesian Men and Women...', 127.

Faculty 1971
Back, L-R: Ivan Shepherd, Garth Morgan, Adrian Rickard,
David Price, Barry McWha, John Hitchen, Isaac Burai
Front: Jill Gordon, Keith Liddle, Kay Liddle (Acting Principal),
Ernie Brainwood and Dorothy Tweddell

wisdom of the Consultative Committee, providing an effective process through which Gil's leadership established the necessary integrated curriculum. 'The central Bible teaching ministries of the College have thus developed to embrace many levels, to serve people at every stage of involvement in Christian service, and to do so through various modes of delivery in several locations across the nation.'[35]

The Students

In early discussions with the MBI Council on identifying intakes of suitable students for CLTC, Gil drew attention to a key systemic issue in the thinking of mission and church leaders that would need to be overcome to see the right students enrol, and the best outcomes for the churches.

> One matter… which gives cause for concern, is the evidence that the major emphasis in the educational training programme of most missions is aimed in the direction of producing suitable candidates for teacher-training, and the resultant benefits of a government subsidy. There is an evident dearth of any well-planned teaching, spiritual encouragement or challenge, being presented to the young churches in regard to the need for setting aside the very best

---

35. Hitchen, 'Evangelicals Equipping Melanesian Men and Women..', 119–20.

material for the work of the ministry. Quite unconsciously, there seems to be the acceptance of the fact that all academic ability should be channelled into remunerative positions, whilst literacy in the vernacular or trade language is sufficient for positions of church leadership. Such a trend, if continued, will produce adverse repercussions in each church and community life, and one of the immediate ministries of the College should be to provide the forum for top level discussions and prayer on the subject of mission strategy as it relates to the establishment of balanced leadership-training programmes.[36]

Through the CLTCCC and the emergence of the EASPI annual conferences at CLTC, the above difficulties were largely overcome, especially as the flow of graduates into the churches proved the value of CLTC training.[37]

Kay Liddle, veteran Brethren missionary, provides an independent and objective assessment:

A training institution's value can be fairly evaluated by the quality and effectiveness of its graduates. The College has produced hundreds of graduates, both men and women, who have made and are making their mark on Papua New Guinea and other nations of the South Pacific. I have personally met many of them on the job and been most impressed by their spiritual maturity, faith, diligence, generosity and humility. Many have returned to their home areas to serve God and their grass root churches and communities faithfully and well as pastors, evangelists, agriculturalists, community workers, teachers and health workers.

---

36. MBI Council, 'Minutes of Council Meeting of the Melbourne Bible Institute', 19 November 1963.
37. The core founding churches (and the missions from which they grew), included: Baptist Union of PNG (Australian Baptist Missionary Society); Evangelical Church of Papua New Guinea (Unevangelized Fields Mission/Asia Pacific Christian Mission/Pioneers); South Sea Evangelical Church(SSEM); Christian Brethren Churches (Christian Missions in Many Lands); Churches of Christ PNG (Australian Churches of Christ); Assemblies of God; Apostolic Christian Churches (Apostolic Christian Mission); and Evangelical Church of Manus (Manus Evangelical Mission). Students were drawn from these and a wide circle of other churches including the Church of the Nazarene; Wesleyan Church; various Synods of the United Church, and a number of independent churches and mission groups. Growing numbers of students from other mainline churches in PNG have enrolled as students in more recent years.

Joyce Walker teaching student wives

Some have become principals and lecturers in vernacular and Tok Pisin or English language regional Bible schools. Some work as Bible translators. Some are filling national leadership roles in their respective denominations. One such was, at the time of his death, President of a denomination of 400,000 adherents and 1,600 local churches. Others have served as political representatives of the people at Local, Provincial or National levels. Others have functioned as God's salt and light in the arenas of education, health, business and commerce.

A significant number are engaged in missionary service overseas, being supported by their home communities. The *Deep Sea Canoe* which first brought the Good News of Jesus Christ to Papuan shores from the Cook Islands, Samoa and Tonga has been re-launched and Melanesian missionaries from PNG now serve in Indonesia, India, Africa, the Middle East and even in Australia and New Zealand.

Yes, to God be the glory, great things he is doing, using CLTC as part of his plan![38]

---

38. Kay Liddle, *Into the Heart of Papua New Guinea: A Pioneering Mission Adventure, Book One* (Auckland New Zealand: Kay Liddle Trust, 2012), 348–49.

9
LOGISTICS AND CONSOLIDATION

Leadership breaks the mission up into human-sized assignments and seeks to influence followers to accept responsibility for one piece of the mission. This delegation allows followers to take ownership for the mission and measure the accomplishment of their work.[1]

Right from the first stage of developing the campus site and facilities, the MBI Council, then Gil and his small team were faced with what J Oswald Sanders later called 'three pioneering problems':

> How do you get supplies and building materials the 300 miles (480 kms) from the coast to the College site in the mountain enclosed Wahgi Valley?
>
> How do you get sufficient timber to build the rapidly growing College?
>
> How do you maintain vital vehicles, machinery and equipment to enable the needed development to go ahead?[2]

In addition, we should add:

> How do you raise the financial support necessary for the capital and continuing operational expenses of a College in the highlands of PNG?
>
> How do you develop the vital partnership of praying and giving people to ensure that all the above is provided through our dependence upon God, that his Word is clearly taught, students' lives are transformed, their ministry impacts the church and nation, and the work is 'all of God, and not of us'?

All these challenges were very clear to the MBI CLTC Committee, and at the forefront of Gil's mind and that of his emerging team. Under the

---

1. Wright, *Relational Leadership – A Biblical Model for Influence and Service*, Kindle 2093–95.
2. Sanders, *Planting Men in Melanesia*, 160. Will Renshaw (MBI Treasurer and Council member at the time) comments that the questions asked by J O Sanders had been asked and faced by the MBI Council, right from the acceptance of the challenge to establish the College.

oversight of the MBI Council and Gil's leadership, these challenges were met through dependence upon God, obedient steps of faith and sacrifice by many people.³ One by one these impossibilities were overcome. In each instance it is salutary to observe how the Lord used Gil's interaction with people to call out those equipped to address these challenges.

Transport

> How do you get supplies and building materials the 300 miles
> (480 kms) from the coast to the College site in the mountain
> enclosed Wahgi Valley?

The cost of flying timber and building materials in from Madang by air was exorbitant.⁴ Even commercial trucking from Lae was very expensive. The ultimate answer was for CLTC to establish its own transport operations.

Bill Clack MBI Men's Superintendent and Secretary of the MBI CLTC Committee, and Peter Rowse leaving MBI to drive the 'original' tractor and trailer to the wharf for shipment to PNG.

---

3. MBI and CLTC Councils, Gil, staff, students, short term volunteers, prayer and financial supporters etc.
4. Sanders, *Planting Men in Melanesia*, 161.

*MBI CLTC Committee on Vision Hill
L-R: Gil McArthur, Bill Clack, John Fawckner, Jack Garrett,
Alfred Coombe with Ron Youngman*

In 1963 Gil visited a young Gippsland farmer and his wife, Peter and Margaret Rowse. Peter was involved in a very successful flower growing, horticultural and family dairy business. (Peter's father Ted had made an earlier visit to PNG, when the search for the land was on). Gil saw in Peter a highly creative, capable, multi-skilled, energetic and hardworking young man. He believed Peter could make a vital contribution in the agricultural and business development of the College.

Peter, through his many farm contacts in 1963/64, assisted Gil and the MBI CLTC Committee in bringing together a new David Brown tractor and trailer that was filled with agricultural implements to gravel the roads and start cultivation for agricultural projects. This, together with a brand-new Holden EH Station Wagon donated by General Motors, was to be shipped to Lae, and then driven up the primitive and dangerous highlands highway to the College at Banz. Peter's cousin Ian Rowse (a missionary with UFM at Tani in the Southern Highlands), met Peter in Lae to drive the two vehicles to the College. The story of that epic and dangerous journey could fill another book!

Gil wanted to source timber from Mount Hagen, and asked Peter to do a weekly trip with the tractor and trailer. Peter refused, as the road was very dangerous and it was a long 65 kilometre journey each

*Tractor bogged!
Peter Rowse and Ian Edridge to the rescue*

way on the tractor. Peter told Gil 'you need a truck!' Trucks were in great demand, but Peter found an old Thames Trader in Mount Hagen. It needed work, and only had brakes on one front wheel! The price was £900. When Peter told Gil, he immediately asked, 'Where do you think you are going to get that from?'

Peter replied, 'How much did you want to pay?'

Gil shot back '£250!'

They bought the truck. Peter and Margaret personally paid the £900 out of their own funds. Later, the money was reimbursed by Peter's sending church.[5] Towards the end of 1964 the Thames made weekly timber runs to Mount Hagen. Peter and Brian Eden then pioneered a trip to Lae. This was the start of regularly carting supplies in from Lae. Sometimes the round trip of 1,000 kilometres could take up to three weeks, depending on the road conditions! It was after the initial trip that an exhausted Peter returned home to his family.

In 1964, Gil visited Syndal Baptist Church in Melbourne to share the vision of a central Bible College in PNG. His visit sparked a response from Graham and Joyce Walker. Graham had been in the landscaping, excavation, and trucking business for many years.

---

5. The Ellingbank Methodist Church near Warragul.

As we prayed about it we felt personally challenged, as there appear to be so many things which occupied the time of staff workers, and to some degree burdened progress in their particular work… My wife and I wish to apply for service so that we might assist and in some way fill the gaps in the work… Over the last twelve months we have felt a challenge and desire to be more involved in the Lord's work. At CLTC, there are many things to do similar to those in which we have gained experience, and we earnestly believe God is calling us to do them.[6]

Early in 1965 they paid a visit to the College, and realised something of the challenge and magnitude of the task that was being faced… The seal of God was on this move, and a month later Graham was able to write, 'We are now endeavouring to wind up our affairs as quickly as possible, and the Lord is taking a hand in a wonderful way. So far, we have sold our caravan, small boat, refrigerator, TV, washing machine and the house without one advertisement… before we put it on the market'.[7]

Possessions sold, they arrived at CLTC in October 1965 with their children, Liz, John, Carolyn, and Rick (Narelle was born later in PNG). The arrival of the Walker family brought great relief for Gil. The gift of a brand new International Acco truck enhanced the transport capacity, and the loan of a front-end loader for excavation work greatly assisted the property development. Garth Morgan recalls that Graham was so convinced of the need to bring supplies up from the coast by road that he challenged the MBI based CLTC Committee to 'match' the Walker gift of a brand new International Acco (single, dual wheel rear axle drive) truck by purchasing a second one. They agreed as the two trucks could work better than one, travelling in convoy for safety and assisting each other in the rough road conditions.[8] The Walker family came in a voluntary capacity for an initial period of two years. But it proved to be God's call for the rest of their working lives!

With the addition of two new trucks it was now possible to transport supplies for other missions and business groups looking for safe, reliable, economical transport. Under Graham's competent management (and no doubt with Gil's zeal and encouragement),

---

6. Sanders, *Planting Men in Melanesia*, 162.
7. Sanders, *Planting Men in Melanesia*, 161–63.
8. Morgan, 'Gilbert McArthur Information'.

> ... the services division of the College showed unexpectedly rapid expansion and development. The fleet of trucks increased, and drivers were recruited from the South. The maintenance of the trucks, together with the agricultural and other vehicles used in the work of the College gave birth to another training programme in which trainees were initiated into the skills of mechanical engineering... The 23 Lae trips, which carried 136 tons of supplies into the Highlands in 1965/66 year, increased to 70 trips moving 480 tons in 1966/67, and continued to soar in 1968 to 241 trips and 1,923 tons and in 1969 to 340 trips moving 2,733 tons of cargo... All this was achieved at an economic figure 50% below that of any other highland based enterprise.[9]

The success of the transport operations provided funds to grow the business and undergird the development and operations of the CLTC student program. However:

> The very success of the enterprise made increasing demands on the Principal, the Executive and the finance and accounting staff, as well as the transport workers. Almost inevitably tensions developed, and slowly the impression grew that there was a real danger of the Services Department overshadowing or even diverting the College from its primary objective of Bible training for Church leadership. Would it not be in the best interests of the College if the Services Division were physically separated from it?[10]

Following careful and prayerful consideration, and the urging of Gil and Len Buck who could see new possibilities, the CLTC Council agreed that 'the highest interests of the College would be best served by a complete separation of the Services Division from the College campus.'[11]

The result was the birth of the Alliance Training Association (ATA), a new organisation with a freight terminal to be based in Lae. Graham Walker was appointed General Manager, and later Gil himself became Executive Director when he concluded his role as Principal of CLTC in 1970. The continuing links of ATA and CLTC were clear in the three basic aims of ATA:

> To provide efficient road freight and other services to CLTC and other missions and churches.

---

9. Sanders, *Planting Men in Melanesia*, 163, 164.
10. Sanders, *Planting Men in Melanesia*, 164.
11. Sanders, *Planting Men in Melanesia*, 165.

LOGISTICS AND CONSOLIDATION

Student Saturday duties – Draining the swamp

Pioneering road transport

> To provide in-service technical trade training, to send Christian businessmen out into the business world of the young nation, and to localise ATA's own staff.
>
> Through its efficient operation to earn substantial profits from which contributions can be made to underwrite Christian training in Melanesia – particularly CLTC.[12]

Garth Morgan's research indicates the very significant contribution of the transport operations to the early development of CLTC.

> The arrival of the two international trucks in 1966, plus the additional six trucks that progressively were added to the fleet, using depreciation provision funding, earned net profits, totalling $87,178 during the four financial years ending June 1970. That amount funded more than the total training costs since 1965 and represented 26% of the total funds that the College had available from all sources for its operations and ongoing development.[13]

The ATA quickly became a thriving business and training ministry which had a spreading influence and lasting personal impact on the lives of many nationals and expatriates, as well as on the developing economy of PNG: a remarkable solution to the CLTC transport predicament.

ATA trucks and drivers 1969
L-R: Keith Chambers, Graham Ross, Noel Griffin, Keith Hitchen, Graham Walker, Arthur Stacey, Norm Bartlett, Warren Richardson

---

12. Sanders, *Planting Men in Melanesia*, 167.
13. Morgan, 'Gilbert McArthur Information'.

Geoff Webber and National workers – Sawmill

Timber

How do you get sufficient timber to build the rapidly growing College?

Initially, the only way for CLTC to get timber was to buy trees from the local people, cut them down, and have them processed at the sawmill at Kimel. The first building erected was a sapling pole and pitpit (split bamboo) walled building, that one early resident called 'Rats' Castle'. The second building was the Principal's house, with office space underneath. The flooring had to be trucked in from Goroka.

A cheaper and more cost-effective way was vital to provide the timber needed for the proposed campus buildings. But God was already going before in providing for this vital need. In 1964, Geoff Webber, a student at MBI in his last year of studies, heard about the need for a saw-miller to set up a mill at CLTC. Gil was then living on the MBI campus, engaged in deputation and preparation for departure to CLTC when the Principal's house was ready. Geoff recalls:

> I first met Gil in mid-1964, when I was directed by Uncle Bill Clack to the house a couple of 'doors' down Munro Street from MBI. I had been convinced from Isaiah 41:15 that God was directing me to offer for service at CLTC as a saw-miller.[14] Gil kindly listened

---

14. *'See, I will make you into a threshing sledge, new and sharp, with many teeth. You will thresh the mountains and crush them, and reduce the hill to chaff.'* Isaiah 41:15.

to my story and encouraged me to continue to pray about the possibility.

Eventually… I arrived at the Banz airstrip to be greeted by Gil, and at CLTC I soon became part of the family in Rats' Castle, sharing a room with Peter Ezzy. Over the course of the next few months, Gil accompanied me often together with Thomas Strahan on sorties into the hills on the north side of the Wahgi Valley in search of trees suitable for milling. I always admired his willingness to trek around the bush and appreciated his encouragement and company.

I also appreciated the fact that when I eventually was given the go ahead to construct a sawmill, Gil left me to 'my own devices' in going about that project, and always respected my plans and ideas, supporting me with any special needs for equipment that I needed purchasing from 'down south', or manufacturing in our workshop.

I confess to not being the easiest person to get along with and had to apologise to Gil on more than one occasion for intemperate outbursts. These he bore with great grace, which made me feel all the more guilty! And he too was not above apologising on occasion.[15]

The Thames Trader truck purchased by Peter Rowse was also used in the early days to pick up logs from Kimel, Sigri and Kudjip. But the longer-term solution to the timber supply for development was found in the establishment in early 1965 of the saw-mill on campus by Geoff Webber (with help from Hap Skinner and Graham Walker),[16] and the approval to purchase a timber lease at Nondugl, 40 kilometres further down the valley from the College. Brian McPherson and Keith Chambers, graduates of Tahlee Bible College, arrived in December 1966 to build a log chute and loading bay, and start felling timber. A small house was built, and Bill (MBI graduate) and Helen Miles lived 'rough' in the wet Nondugl bush. When the lease was no longer economical, it closed in late 1968, but not before it had provided 598,000 log super feet for the College buildings.[17]

---

15. Geoff Webber, 'Some Hazy and Some Vivid Recollections of Rev Gil McArthur', Email, 20 January 2016. While at CLTC, Geoff married Margaret whom he had first met in Melbourne. Margaret followed him to CLTC using her nursing skills to provide much needed medical care to staff, students and the local people.
16. John Hitchen, 'Early Timber Sources', Email, 15 August 2016.
17. Sanders, *Planting Men in Melanesia*, 163.

Equipment and Technology

How do you maintain vital vehicles, machinery and equipment to enable the needed development to go ahead?

The challenge of the technical infrastructure requirements of a growing College campus in the remote Wahgi Valley has always been a present reality for CLTC, and still is! Gil knew the importance of this aspect of growing the College, and the result has been a continuing process of technical and infrastructure advance through the years. But this was not without significant moments of crisis, whether it was shortage of skilled tradesmen, or breakdowns of generators, water pumps, vehicles, agricultural or communications equipment etc.

Again, in ways that can only be described as miraculous, the Lord has moved his people and a variety of funding groups to donate many of the vehicles and technical equipment required – tractors, agricultural implements, trucks, buses, bikes, pumps, generators, computers, telephone equipment and the list could go on – often at great sacrifice to the donors.

But in addition to the flow of donations, there has been the flow of skilled people, both long-term staff and short-term working groups, called by the Lord to serve in the maintenance and technical side of the program. Due to the remoteness of the campus, there has often been evidence of creative genius in producing the required results. Sam Lamont was the first of a long line of motor mechanics and engineers that came to CLTC over the years, without whom the primary objective of equipping leaders would never have been achieved. Even today as I write, Karl Venz, a skilled mechanic with previous experience at CLTC/ATA/Beechwood, is travelling to CLTC for repairs to the main generator.[18] The flow of short-term teams continues.

As in the provision of other needs, under Gil's leadership the maintenance side of the work gave birth to a Technical Training program that equipped national young people with these skills. Consequently, these graduates provided their urgently needed skills to the church and communities across PNG, as well as serving as national engineering staff members of CLTC.

---

18. Karl and his family earlier served with the CLTC family in ATA and then Beechwood in the 1970s.

Finance

How do you seek to raise the financial support necessary for the capital and continuing operational expenses of a College in the highlands of PNG?

The MBI Executive in 1961 had noted that the reason for the application for such a large parcel of land for CLTC was so that 'this acreage could in time make the Bible Institute self-supporting in food.'[19] The lease document for the land specified that 300 of the 413 acres should be set aside for agricultural development.

Brian Brandon and agricultural students – vegetable production

In the constitution, under which CLTC was incorporated in 1973 in PNG (when MBI handed over governance of the College to a CLTC PNG based Council), one of the mission objectives of the College reads:

To provide for the financial support of the College through business programs which positively contribute to the physical and economic wellbeing of the people of Papua New Guinea. Such programs will

---

19. MBI Executive, 'Minutes of the Executive Meeting of the Melbourne Bible Institute', 27 June 1961.

Council and College Executive 1979
Back, L-R: Graham Walker, Will Renshaw, Neville Andersen, Ted Fletcher (visitor), Napelye Kuri, Rob Thompson, Don Moseley, Adrian Rickard, Garth Morgan
Centre: Suren Martin, Gil McArthur, Sione Kami, Oswald Sanders, Len Buck, Bill Clack, Joshua Daimoi, Stan Utting
Front: Mapusiya Kolo, Charles Horne, Bafi Womaneso, Kevin Kasimbua, Judah Akesim, Ossie Fountain, Kasawa Kikia and David Price

provide in-service training for employees and aim to compliment the financial partnership with the churches we serve.[20]

John Hitchen explains:

> The original vision saw three sources of income as necessary for the College's financial viability. The students, together with their sending churches, should accept a proportion of the training costs. Student fees, student travel costs to and from the College and personal living allowances were seen as the student and local church responsibility. Partnerships with Christian friends and churches overseas – mainly Australia and New Zealand – would be potential sources of College administered student scholarships, and donations for capital development or special projects. But the major operational, education and staffing costs were to be funded by commercial support programmes utilising the agricultural potential of the Banz property. While overseas donations were crucial in the early days, the College has very largely achieved the expectation that as overseas donations decreased, the income from within PNG,

---

20. Rule 2(iii) of the CLTC Constitution – 2008 update. CLTC is legally incorporated under the PNG Associations Ordinance of 1966.

particularly from the College's support programmes, would increase to meet the operational costs.[21]

Gil was never one whose vision was curtailed by the question of financial provision. He had such confidence in God providing for the work that he stepped out in pioneering faith on countless occasions just as had characterised his work in DNG and Telefolmin in earlier days. This bold faith initiative sometimes left others wondering about his sense of responsibility or maybe even his sanity! Sometimes to Council members it may have appeared that his philosophy was 'it is easier to ask for forgiveness later, than for permission first!' Looking back over 50 years, one can see the outcome of his pioneering faith in the lasting legacy of CLTC and numerous other ministries.

Garth and Ruth Morgan, who arrived in August 1966, came as a direct result of Gil's presentation at the 1964 Ngaruawahia Easter Convention in New Zealand. Their education and experience uniquely prepared them for the oversight of the financial affairs of CLTC. It lifted to another level in 1987 when Garth was appointed Council Treasurer taking over from Will Renshaw. He continued until he declined nomination in 2016 so that a PNG member could take over this responsibility.[22]

For over 50 years since those three momentous convention minutes Garth and Ruth have provided key leadership and accounting management in the development and oversight of the financial and support projects of CLTC, both in times of great testing and great blessings. When he concluded as Treasurer, Garth had been present either as a staff member or council member at all 51 Council meetings (except for five) – a remarkable commitment.[23]

For the 50th Anniversary celebrations of CLTC in 2015, Garth wrote a summary 'History of CLTC's Funding Over 50 Years', which tells in a nutshell the remarkable story of divine leading and provision, pioneering faith, human creativity and obedience.[24]

---

21. John Hitchen, 'The Christian Leaders' Training College of Papua New Guinea – A Case Study of a Christian Contribution to Economic Development and to Theological Change at World View and Social Imaginary Levels for Sustainable Development in Melanesia – A Paper Presented at the "Woven Together" Conference on Christianity and Development in the Pacific, Victoria University Welllington, New Zealand, 9-10 June 2016', 6 September 2016, 2.
22. Morgan, 'Timeline for CLTC for Garth and Ruth Morgan', 18.
23. Morgan, 'Timeline for CLTC for Garth and Ruth Morgan', 20.
24. Garth Morgan, 'CLTC Financial History 1965-2014', 25 February 2015, CLTC Archives.

Initially, the Council of MBI publicised the CLTC story, and in faith trusted the Lord for the funds needed for the establishment phase of CLTC. When Treasurer John Fawckner reported at the MBI Annual Meeting in 1965 that 'Never before in our history, has a year ended with both the General and Building Funds showing such a substantial credit balance' the entire congregation stood to their feet and enthusiastically sang the doxology. He reported this evidence of God's faithfulness was in addition to £38,000 already received for the establishment of CLTC and revealed that a further £28,000 would be required for CLTC in the next 12 months if the development were to continue as planned. He said, 'We believe that with the prayers and support of the Lord's people, and the promises of God, there will be sufficient to meet that large need.'[25] The establishment of the New Zealand Advisory Council also saw increasing funds and volunteers flowing from New Zealand. It is remarkable that eight years later in 1973, when with great thanksgiving to God, the Council of MBI handed over the newly constituted Christian Leaders' Training College of PNG Inc. to a PNG based CLTC Council as a fully operational College, it was completely clear of any debt.

CLTC Entrance

---

25. Gilbert J McArthur, 'New Guinea Christian Leaders Training College', *New Life*, 9 February 1965, 1, Melbourne School of Theology Archives.

Student fees (a nominal amount), fares and monthly student allowances came from the PNG churches, but covered little more than residential accommodation. Partial support for the training costs of the students were generated through student support sponsors in Australia and New Zealand. Volunteers from both countries also contributed very large amounts of funding by being self-supporting as they served at CLTC.

Gil was proactive right from the start of the College to explore and develop ways in which the CLTC property could produce not only food for staff and students, but also agribusiness profits to contribute towards the training costs. Since 1965 the College has initiated the following funding activities: sowing peanut crops to help prepare the soil for pasture and gardens; producing and selling 20,000 tea seedlings for one cent each to plantations; selling garden vegetable produce on back loading by air to Madang stores and surplus kaukau (sweet potato) production to local plantations; developing the transport operations carting fuel for Shell and British Petroleum from the coast at Lae to Mount Hagen in the Western Highlands for 2/6 a gallon, as well as fish, rice and other trade store goods; producing bridge planks and other timber for sale ex the CLTC saw mill; selling produce from the Model Farm in the Agricultural training program; dairy farming providing fresh pasteurised and flavoured milk to Hagen & Banz, and weaned calves for MAF transport to remote mission and church cattle projects; developing poultry production to provide table eggs to highlands stores and mission groups, and later meat birds and a hatchery development producing day-old meat chickens for urban stores and rural projects; developing a piggery for selling to the highlands sing-sing and bride price markets; upon closure of the dairy program moving to beef cattle with abattoir facilities for the sale of dressed beef and chickens; rabbit production for meat sales; development of rice farming alongside a Rice Training Program for rice sales and to facilitate rice growing in rural communities. Fortunately, not all these programs have operated simultaneously! Different projects were initiated according to the changing market opportunities over the years. But this summary is a remarkable record of over 50 years of creative response to business opportunities, diligent planning, careful management, hard work, sacrifice and faith.[26]

---

26. Garth Morgan, 'Christian Leaders Training College of Papua New Guinea Inc. 50th Jubilee Celebrations 2015 - A History of CLTC's Funding Over 50 Years' (Auckland New Zealand, 25 February 2015), 1, 2.

Garth's research reveals that over 300 Australians and New Zealanders have poured a part of their lives into CLTC and ATA, training and mentoring PNG staff, and developing business opportunities, 'which have provided (in the first 35 years), 56% of the total funding available to the College, with fees providing 8%, PNG donations 6%, and overseas donations 30%. The costs of training have used 53% of this funding, and 47% has been invested in the development of the College facilities at Banz, Lae and Port Moresby.'[27]

> The next 15 years [from 2000] saw very significant increases in the cost of training at higher academic levels, with increased PNG faculty, a decrease in residential expatriate participation and an increasing commercial competition for our agricultural products. These changes have impacted the total funding available to the College, with the College's business earnings dropping to 44%, fees increasing to 24%, PNG donations reducing to 4%, and overseas donations remaining reasonably constant at 28%. The more significant change is that 99.5% of the past 15 years funding was used in funding training operations, leaving 0.5% for any development, despite the annual funding in 2015 being 238% more than it was in 2000.[28]

In the light of these trends, Garth in his role as Council Treasurer sought new ways (humanly speaking) to 'future fund' the College. In 2011 negotiations took place with Exon Mobil to fund an expansion of the hatchery. But Exon Mobil did not proceed, so NZ$660,000 was raised in loans to build an additional 650 square metres to the hatchery. These loans were repaid by the end of 2015. During 2014, negotiations took place with Mainland Holdings, a major PNG poultry producer, encouraging them to work with CLTC, rather than be a competitor in the Highlands egg and day-old chicken markets. Those negotiations were formalised in a decade-long Poultry Management Contract commencing early in 2016, which brought greater stability for the College in sustaining the income from its agricultural resources.[29]

Behind the scenes of this financial journey, the College has walked a path through times of abundance and plenty and on other occasions times of great financial testing for varying reasons. The fact that CLTC continues today is testimony to God's great faithfulness, the

---

27. Morgan, 'Gilbert McArthur Information', 2. Update provided by Garth Morgan to his original report in 2015.
28. Morgan, 'Gilbert McArthur Information', 2.
29. Morgan, 'Gilbert McArthur Information', 2.

vision, creativity and plain hard work of the MBI CLTC Committee, the Advisory Councils, Gil and his team, and the sacrificial giving and service of many faithful obedient servants of Christ.

Partnership and Prayer

How do you develop the vital partnership of praying and giving people to ensure that all the above is provided, and that God's Word is clearly taught, students' lives are transformed, their ministry impacts the church and nation, and the work is 'all of God and not of us?'

Alongside the responsibility of practical thinking, planning, management and hard work was the engagement with the spiritual dynamic of the Kingdom of God. Gil was a man of prayer – as indeed were those who first conceived of the College, and those who shouldered the load of the establishment and rapid growth of CLTC. Gil knew from practical experience the vital place of prayer in the spiritual battle. So right from the birth of CLTC prayer, especially intercession, was front and centre of the spiritual strategy.

In collaboration with Bill Clack and the MBI CLTC Committee, Gil launched *College News*, a simple, regular news-sheet about CLTC happenings and items for prayer. Subsequently, through Gil's deputation and that of Bill Clack, and later many others both in Australia and New Zealand, there arose an army of prayer and financial partners who prayed regularly for CLTC – and still do to this day using the *Monthly Prayer Notes*.

In the regular life of the College Gil also introduced a Monthly Day of Prayer, when all work and study ceased and the whole community gave themselves to offer praise and thanks to the Lord, and to pray specifically and intentionally about every aspect and need of College life. Nothing was too small to pray about: 'in everything by prayer and supplication with thanksgiving'.[30] Not only did this see the Lord answer, but provided a great practical teaching model, when students saw prayer in action and central to the life of the CLTC community. Classes would always begin and end with prayer, in recognition that CLTC was not simply a secular educational institution, but also an arena of the spiritual conflict of the ages, in which it was recognised that only the power of the Spirit of God through the Word of God could open and transform the minds and lives of the students and equip them for ministry.

---

30. Philippians 4:6-7.

CLTC Administration Building

Glory to God – A Remarkable Achievement!

What was achieved by the efforts and commitment of the early builders and staff in the development of the campus under Gil's leadership was extraordinary. Bill Clack visited CLTC for meetings with Gil in July 1965. He reported to the MBI CLTC Committee his concern that 'the Rev McArthur had lost weight and showed evidence of the strain of the immense task he had accomplished. The Committee consequently sought to modify the time table for the future development of the College.'[31]

However, there appears to be little evidence that the development process slowed down, as Gil pressed on with his team to bring the vision for the campus and facilities to reality.[32] The initial consolidation of the

---

31. MBI CLTC Committee, 'Minutes of the New Guinea Christian Leaders' Training College Committee of MBI', 24 August 1965.
32. Right from the start of campus development and construction there has been a long line of carpenters, builders and other trades people coming and going from overseas over the years including Clyde Parkinson, George Tweedale, Alan Baker, Peter Ezzy, Brian Eden, Ken and Mum Eden, Ian Eldridge, Bob Hargreaves, Thomas Strahan, Robin Cowie, John Davidson, Bob Lockhart, Willie Exton, Erec Rosser, Sam Lamont, Ron Youngman, John Woodbridge, Graham Walker, Ron Finger, David Brunton, Brian Perry, Ray Eland, Howard Martin, Lindsay Olding, Geoff Given, Ian Keals, Bob Watson, Seloani, Peter Rowse, Bob Elphick, Geoff Webber, Bill Miles, Malcolm Hotchkin, Malcolm Wrigley, Brian Brandon, Alex Conlin, Bruce Wilton – and others too numerous to mention! It is also important to recognise the tremendous contribution of the national carpenters and builders over the years who carried the main workload.

minimum necessary facilities was complete in 1967, with the dedication of the new Administration building, which included a Recording Studio and flat to accommodate Director Geoff Baskett, and the growing ministry of Kristen Redio.[33] Gil's Annual Report to the MBI Council for 1967 revealed there were 44 students enrolled in the Certificate of Church Leadership Course, 14 in the Farm Management Course with 10 wives and 18 student children on campus. Twelve different mission agencies had sent students.[34]

The dedication of the Administration Block to the glory of God who had given the vision and provided so abundantly, served as a public occasion for the College to be formally recognised by the District Commissioner Tom Ellis, who stood in for Sir Paul Hasluck, the Australian Minister for External Territories. This was just prior to Gil leaving for a period of study leave at Columbia Bible College in the USA. The administration building had been completed from start to finish in just 12 weeks – a remarkable team effort![35]

District Commissioner Tom Ellis addressing the opening of the Administration Building July 1967

---

33. Gil believed the growing ministry of Kristen Redio provided a great opportunity for the CLTC students to assist in preparing programs in English and vernacular languages for broadcast across the nation.
34. Gilbert J McArthur, 'Christian Leaders' Training College Annual Report for the Year Ended 30 June 1967.' (Melbourne, 25 July 1967), 2, MBI Archives.
35. Sanders, *Planting Men in Melanesia*, 56.

10
SPREADING INFLUENCE

> *But thanks be to God,*
> *who always leads us as captives in Christ's triumphal procession*
> *and uses us to spread the aroma of the knowledge of him everywhere.*[1]

The spreading influence of Gil and the ministry of CLTC continued to steadily grow and gain the acceptance and confidence of the evangelical churches. The July 1966 MBI Annual General Council Meeting noted:

> The entire Council stands awed and solemnized by the rapid growth in stature of CLTC; by the Lord's provision of workers, material resources and money; by the evident maturing of the national student body; and by the wide influence the College is already exerting through its Principal, the Rev GJ McArthur, on the Christian vision and strategy for Papua New Guinea, and indeed the whole of Melanesia.[2]

Gil's wide and influential connections across PNG and beyond in 'selling' the vision of CLTC and the critical strategy of developing leaders is illustrated by the fact that on Sunday 13 July 1969 the Governor General of Australia, Sir Paul and Lady Hasluck, together with the Administrator of the Territory of PNG, Mr David Hay, visited CLTC during Sir Paul's four-day tour of PNG.[3]

At the CLTC farewell to Gil and Pat in November 1970, John Hitchen reminded the CLTC community that Gil's ministry involved a wider national impact across PNG:

> Perhaps not even many of the staff understand what Mr McArthur has been doing on the various trips away from the College, and it might be helpful to list some of the other aspects of God's work in the Territory that Mr McArthur has been responsible for establishing and building up in the last six years.[4]

---

1. 2 Corinthians 2:14.
2. MBI Council, 'Minutes of Council Meeting of the Melbourne Bible Institute', 26 July 1966.
3. Morgan, 'Timeline for CLTC for Garth and Ruth Morgan', 6.
4. Hitchen, 'Appreciation of Rev G. J. McArthur', 1.

Gil's CLTC involvement brought him in touch with a series of PNG-wide holistic needs and opportunities which this chapter outlines. These can be seen in a number of specific areas: his involvement with the development of the Evangelical Alliance; his chaplaincy and leadership training with the Police and Defence forces; his time out for study and reflection in the USA; his leadership with Len Buck, Graham Walker and Bill Conley in the growth of ATA; and his encouragement of Christian Education in Schools and Kristen Redio programs. These areas of influence and involvement paved the way for his later post-CLTC ministries.

The Evangelical Alliance of Papua New Guinea

As Principal of CLTC, Gil was acutely aware of the growing evangelical community and the vital need to equip national leaders for the emerging churches. The Evangelical Alliance of the South Pacific Islands (EASPI) was born just as Gil was beginning to establish CLTC. He had experienced the impact of the Evangelical Alliance in Australia and knew that the role of the EASPI was vital in CLTC's relationship with the churches. He became actively supportive of the EASPI from the time he arrived to live in PNG in late 1964.

Don Doull, with whom Gil had served at Telefolmin in his Baptist Mission days, describes the first of two concerns that led to the formation of the EASPI:

> It was during the early to mid-sixties that I became increasingly aware of the fact that the Christians in Telefolmin, isolated as they were from Christians in other parts of the developing nation of Papua New Guinea, would soon have to take their place among other believers coming from a variety of churches, many of whom were evangelical in doctrine and practice, as we were within the Baptist Churches. Arising from that awareness I saw the need to bring about some sort of loose organisation which would help Christians like the Telefolmin believers to know that they were one with other believers, even although they worked within another organised church and carried another name.
>
> My initial thought was that there should be a 'Union of Evangelical Churches' within PNG, which could be the voice of evangelical churches across the nation, and so give some structure to our oneness. I knew that many other missionaries shared my concern and so wrote to the ABMS in Australia and raised my concern.

Evangelical Alliance Conference at CLTC 1983

Their reply was that the initiative for such a move should come from the field, and so the Telefolmin Field Council authorised me to make an initial approach to some of the missionary societies with whom we felt a real oneness, and suggest a meeting to test the waters.

I subsequently wrote to representatives of the Unevangelised Fields Mission, the South Sea Evangelical Mission, Christian Mission in Many Lands, and Churches of Christ Mission, suggesting a meeting. We eventually met in Wewak on 25-26 October 1963. The outcome of that meeting was a decision to establish an Evangelical Alliance in PNG, and I agreed to draw up a suggested constitution based on information available from other EAs… We met again in March 1964, when the suggested constitution was discussed and finalised. The above-mentioned missionary societies were all acting, as we were, on behalf of the churches which were coming into being in their respective areas of activity. The initial group were soon joined by other groups, and the idea was soon a reality, joining together a host of likeminded groups of believers. This structure represented a whole host of churches and gave a framework within which we were able to take our place and function as a group of like-minded churches who could work together and represent our position within the emerging nation.[5]

---

5. Doull, *One Passion: Church Planting in Papua New Guinea*, 153, 154.

Apart from this danger of isolation from one another, Kay Liddle (also involved in the formation of the EASPI right from the start), points to the second concern that stimulated evangelicals to express their corporate unity:

> In the early 1960s, we were hearing some disturbing reports of the activities of the World Council of Churches in some third world countries. Educated church leaders were being offered scholarships to attend theological seminaries recognised for their liberal theology. Sending a delegate to an ecumenical conference was regarded as reaching self-determination in the religious arena, similar to sending a representative to the United Nations in the political sphere. It conferred recognition and status. The Pacific Council of Churches with links to the World Council was already functioning in the South Pacific. Concern was being expressed by the leaders of the South Sea Evangelical churches in the Solomon Islands and their SSEM missionaries over a forthcoming visit of WCC representatives allegedly to link all national churches to the World Council. These concerns were shared with evangelical mission leaders in New Guinea.[6]

The actual formal inauguration of the EASPI took place in Wewak on 14 November 1964. Mr Norman Deck, a former missionary in the Solomon Islands, and Director of SSEM based in Sydney, represented the SSEC churches of the Solomon Islands. The EASPI later officially registered under the PNG Associations Incorporation Ordinance in 1966.[7] Dudley Deasey (UFM) was elected Chairman, and Kay Liddle (CMML) was appointed Secretary. In that same year EASPI applied for membership with the World Evangelical Fellowship (WEF).[8]

Kay Liddle recorded in his diary at the time:

> The main purpose of EA is to promote greater cooperation and fellowship among like-minded evangelical missions and churches. It is clearly understood that the Alliance does not aim at church

---

6. Liddle, *Into the Heart of Papua New Guinea: A Pioneering Mission Adventure*, Book One, 366.
7. The name Evangelical Alliance of the South Pacific Islands (EASPI) was re-incorporated in May 1974 and it remained until it was changed and incorporated on 14 February 2005 as the Evangelical Alliance of Papua New Guinea Inc (EAPNG). Between 1990 and 1993 with a temporary relocation of the office from CLTC Banz campus to Port Moresby there was also an attempt to change the name to National Council of Evangelical Churches, but that was not successful.
8. Liddle. *Into the Heart of Papua New Guinea*, 366.

union, nor would it interfere with the beliefs and practices of any segment of the Church to which its members respectively belong. It does aim at promoting fellowship and maintaining evangelical witness to Scriptural truth. It will also provide opportunity for cooperation in such fields as literature and radio witness. It did much more than that.

He estimated that, 'by 1966 the EA represented approximately 400 European missionaries, a constituency of over 100,000 in New Guinea, and 285 local churches in the Solomon Islands.'[9]

Although most missions and churches established their own vernacular and trade language Bible schools for the training of pastors, CLTC became the recognised EASPI College for training to advanced levels. It also became the natural meeting place for EASPI conferences for many years.

While the EASPI was not Gil's brain child, from the time he arrived in PNG he understood the crucial contribution it brought to the unity and vitality of the evangelical churches. He shared in the EASPI leadership on the Executive as Vice-President from 1965-67, and as President in 1968. He was involved in almost every part of its ministry, including the establishment of the EASPI Regional Committees in Port Moresby and Lae. It was largely Gil's vision which brought into being the Evangelical Alliance Special English Course at Lapolama, to train men in English to prepare them for their studies at CLTC.[10]

Gil's passion for growing emerging leaders through a mentoring relationship alongside the missionaries is reflected in the EASPI Annual General Meeting minute of 1966:

> *Participation of nationals at the Alliance meetings:* It was felt that there was a great advantage in having a reasonably large group of nationals participating, as the best method of teaching them is to have them alongside us... McArthur moved: 'That at the next meeting of the Alliance all member missions and churches endeavour to bring at least one national representative.'[11]

Following Gil's departure from PNG, by the mid-1990s the influence of the EASPI in keeping the evangelical churches together seriously declined. In 2005 Kay Liddle one of the original founders of the EASPI

---

9. Liddle. *Into the Heart of Papua New Guinea*, 366.
10. Hitchen, 'Appreciation of Rev G. J. McArthur', 1, 2.
11. Yandit, '"Ownership" and Support of Theological Educational Institutions in Papua New Guinea...', 54.

was invited to speak at a 'Leadership Summit' in Port Moresby on the 'Birth and Influence of the Evangelical Alliance'. In concluding his paper, he asked some tough questions and offered some thoughtful reflections on the way forward:

> What is the state of EAPNG [formerly EASPI] today? Do you still have such respect for one another? Do you still strengthen and encourage each other? Or, have you lost the vision? Have you drifted from the moorings? Is the evangelical voice still being heard by those in authority? What impact are you having on the nation? If you are not happy with your answers to those questions, what are you going to do about it? I am not here to tell you what to do. I am not suggesting you should do the same things that were done in the past. They are recounted to inspire you as examples of what God has already done through the cooperative effort of his people in this land. Today is a new day. You face new challenges. I am asking you to consider this question: 'How does God want us to respond to the opportunities that face us today?' It has been suggested to me that we missionaries may have over emphasised the business agenda at EAPNG meetings and that national church leaders had more than enough problems in leading their own churches, without adding those of the EAPNG to their agendas. Perhaps we should have left you with a different model and focused more on spiritual growth and the mentoring and developing of leadership. That is a thought worth considering in the context of this conference, and as you look to where you should place some of your emphasis in the future.[12]

While in recent years the EAPNG has lost focus on the role of bringing the churches together for teaching, mutual encouragement and action in addressing national issues, there are currently serious attempts to re-energise the movement and recover a national voice and influence.

Chaplaincy and Leadership Development in The Defence and Police Forces

Gil's army experience and passion for leadership development at the national level led to his involvement in both the Army and Police Chaplaincy and leadership training.

He served as the Senior Chaplain of the United Churches of the Papua New Guinea Command and as such was responsible for developing the work of chaplaincy in both the Pacific Islands Regiment and the Papua

---

12. Liddle, Kay. *Into the Heart of Papua New Guinea,* Kindle Locations 5124-5134.

New Guinea Volunteer Rifles. He was also on the committee which introduced the first University Chaplaincy in the new University of PNG in Port Moresby.

Furthermore, Gil was the Honorary Secretary of the Police Chaplaincy Board from its inception and gave guidance to the establishment of a chaplaincy program within the Police Force. It is not generally known that the Police Commander of PNG asked Gil to draft a new format for recruiting and training expatriates for the Police Force of Papua New Guinea. Gil then ensured his suggestions were implemented by negotiations with the Administrator and the Police Commissioner.[13]

At the request of Police and Defence Force leaders, Gil developed and initiated Leadership and Character Guidance Courses for the Police Force, the Army and other members of the Administration. In this role he had a formative influence on national leaders along with others involved in facilitating these training events.[14]

Brigadier John Hunter, Army Commander of the Papua New Guinea Command, commended Gil's contribution to chaplaincy in the armed forces and encouraged his study leave in the USA as important for his work with the Army:

> The Reverend Gil McArthur is also Senior Chaplain (United Churches) in my Headquarters. In this capacity he is a source of great strength and I value his counsel, and he has proved his worth in organizing the chaplaincy work in Army units of Papua & New Guinea. He has also assisted the training team in their task.
>
> Our current task is to examine every facet of the problem of… providing an optimum stability, reliability and motivation of a truly national Army for this country, an Army that is truly a servant of the government and the people. There is a need for a deep and complete understanding of the Pacific Islander, but we have need of more detailed research and analysis of the Melanesian culture assumptions, inhibitions and resultant sociological motivations.
>
> The area of investigation and research to be undertaken by Mr McArthur in his overseas study programme is closely aligned with the general sociological, ethical and character guidance requirements in the Papua & New Guinea Command. I will be looking to Senior Chaplain McArthur to provide the subject

---

13. Hitchen, 'Appreciation of Rev G. J. McArthur', 1, 2.
14. Hitchen, 'Appreciation of Rev G. J. McArthur', 2.

material to support the training programme in the fields of moral and ethical concepts, basic to the building of a national Army, founded upon the principles of personal discipline, integrity, justice and good will.[15]

Gil also played a large part in the development of the Christian Education in Schools Curriculum, which was used in Administration Schools throughout the Territory. He also encouraged the whole work of the Christian Broadcasting Service by providing facilities in the CLTC Administration building for Kristen Redio, and personally helping Manager Geoff Basket and others working on Christian programs for broadcasting.

Gil's commitment to developing leaders marked by integrity in the central structures of society came into greater prominence in his thinking and ministry focus following his time at CLTC. His conviction was that the well-being of societal health was directly connected not only to the quality of leaders in the Christian communities, but to the character and integrity of leaders at every level of national life.

Time Out for Study and Reflection

In the initial years of the establishment of CLTC, Gil developed a growing desire for time out for study and reflection, particularly focused on interpreting Biblical Ethics for Melanesian churches. This research would not only directly enrich the CLTC curriculum but also feed into his leadership in the EASPI, and his leadership formation work with the Army and Police.[16]

While it was not easy for the new College to be left without the visionary oversight and energetic leadership Gil provided, the MBI Council agreed:

> that the Rev R V Merritt [then current MBI Vice Principal] be seconded to CLTC, to relieve the Rev G J McArthur for six to nine months from August 1967, whilst Mr McArthur is in America for further study. Resolved that Mr Merritt be made available for this task.[17]

Moving tent once again, Gil enrolled in the Bachelor of Biblical Education and Master of Arts programs at the Columbia Bible College (now Columbia

---

15. Brigadier Ian Hunter, 'Commendation of Rev G. D. McArthur', Letter, 30 January 1967, McArthur Family Archives.
16. Hunter, 'Commendation of Rev G. D. McArthur'.
17. MBI Council, 'Minutes of Council Meeting of the Melbourne Bible Institute', 25 October 1966.

Auditorium funded by 1969 Columbia Bible College students

International University) in South Carolina. He was in many ways unique among the students, and from his strong faith and vast experience, had a profound impact upon many in the College community. He lived in the College President's house for some of that time, and Pat was able to join him. In 1968, the Columbia students chose CLTC for their missionary project, and raised US$10,000 which paid for the construction of the Auditorium on the Banz campus.

Gil grappled with the issues of Biblical Ethics in Melanesia and wrote his MA thesis on *Applied Christian Ethics for Melanesian Churches*. He declared his intentions in the introduction:

The thesis will cover three main areas.

The **first** will provide a general outline of the historical situation which has determined the birth and growth of the young churches up to the present.

The **second** will set forth the biblical imperatives, define the areas of tension arising from the encounter with certain facets of Melanesian culture; then, in a series of constructive syntheses suggest the basic content of teaching necessary to meet the need.

The **third** will aim at presenting a general philosophy of how to best define the problem, measure its moral and spiritual significance, and effectively apply the ethic to the crucial areas. Since most of the missionaries know the customs of their particular tribe, no detailed

> attention will be given to citing examples of various customs other than where it is necessary to make a specific point, or, where it is of an unusual character.
>
> However, it is also recognised that many will not have had an opportunity of adding the tool of anthropology to their missionary equipment, and that this lack is perhaps a prime cause of the inability to define and remedy the tension areas within the young church. The suggested philosophy of application will therefore lay down certain anthropological guide-lines which may prove helpful in fulfilling the missionary task.
>
> The biblical and spiritual conclusions will, it is hoped, engender an increased sensitivity to the fact that it is the Lord who is building his Church; that its form and function is finally the responsibility of the Holy Spirit working through the local believers, and not that of the missionary or his particular Home-Board.[18]

In his thesis Gil outlines the basic biblical imperative of a relationship with God, and then discusses four key biblical ethical imperatives: the sanctity of life, the family, sex and marriage, possessions and speech. Each is discussed in the framework of the Biblical view, the Melanesian view, and a proposed constructive synthesis. His work concludes with a proposed *Philosophy of Application*.

> Allowing for a proper identification with the mores of another culture having been made, consideration must now be given to what is involved in properly applying the ethical demands of the Word to the life of the young church. The popular view of 'situational ethics', which allows for the situation itself to determine the degree of ethic, is fraught with danger and must be rejected. The Christian's answer to the ethical concept of cultural relativism is to state categorically his belief that there is a body of biblical principles which are super-culturally valid and binding upon all people of all cultures. The application of the Christian ethic to any given culture will therefore evidence the following:
>
> 1. The large body of beliefs and practices which are out of moral harmony with biblical truth must be declared as belonging to the kingdom of Satan and put away (Romans 6:16-18; 2 Corinthians 5:17).

---

18. Gilbert J McArthur, 'Applied Christian Ethics For Melanesian Churches', (Columbia Bible College M.A. Thesis, 1968), McArthur Family Archives. Emphasis and paragraphs added for easier reading.

2. The residue of custom, which though culturally repellent to the missionary is nonetheless ethically neutral in respect to biblical imperatives, should be left alone. There must be confidence in the inherent dynamic of the Word to produce any necessary change from within the culture itself. It should not be imposed from without.[19]

The opportunity for study and reflection in the USA enabled Gil to mature his thinking in the areas of Bible, culture and ethics for a new level of influence in his teaching ministry. At the request of many missionaries, the thesis was published by Stanmore Missionary Press. It also provided Gil with the opportunity to develop international relationships in his participation in the Presidential Prayer Breakfasts in Washington.

Alliance Training Association

With the rapid growth of the transport operations of CLTC, the MBI CLTC Committee agreed that this department should be separated from the College structure and campus. ATA was incorporated as a separate charitable Christian business and training organisation and became another dimension of the spreading influence of Gil's vision for leadership development.

In 1970 CLTC gifted ATA all eight trucks, together with a $20 deposit to open a bank account. ATA then borrowed $10,000 from the bank to finance their ongoing operations and development.[20] Len Buck, who had been Chairman of the CLTC MBI Committee from the beginning, was also a driving force in this development and appointed Chairman of the new Board of ATA.

The birth of ATA was the opportunity for Len Buck (Chairman), Gil (Executive Director), Graham Walker (General Manager), and Bill Conley (Finance Manager) to pursue their entrepreneurial vision for the diversification of ATA into subsidiary companies, specialising in related commercial opportunities. They were a team with a proven record of leadership together, and saw the opportunity for ATA not only to grow as a business in serving other agencies, but with a clear vision for the

---

19. McArthur, 'Applied Christian Ethics for Melanesian Churches', 64.
20. Alliance Training Association, 'Minutes of the Annual Members Meeting', 26 October 1971. The Directors of ATA appointed at this meeting were – Len Buck (Chair), Bill Clack, Will Renshaw, Jack Garrett, Charles Sandland, Peter Rowse, Gil McArthur (Secretary), Traimya Kambipi, Glaimi Warena, Ron Youngman, M. Blinman, Donoma Azila, the Principal and Registrar of CLTC.

Beechwood Timber

formation of Christian leaders for the business and professional world of the developing nation.[21] At Gil's final CLTC Graduation in 1970, John Hitchen spoke of ATA as 'Dr McArthur's new love' – to establish it as an organisation that will be able to underwrite the continuing work of training Christian workers in the Territory.[22]

ATA relocated its operational base and head office from the CLTC Banz campus to Lae, occupying the two houses and the duplex that Ron Youngman had previously built for CLTC on Bowerbird Road, providing five families with a home, a transit flat for the drivers, and an office. A warehouse was rented for the truck depot until Ron Youngman later supervised the building of a large complex at Omili to accommodate the depot, workshops, larger offices and living quarters.

ATA negotiated the purchase of the timber yard in Mount Hagen, belonging to Highlands Timber and Hardware, and used that as an ATA highlands depot, while continuing to sell timber provided by the

---

21. Later in 1973, when MBI handed over the CLTC property and all its assets to a new PNG Board of CLTC incorporated in PNG, Len Buck was unanimously appointed the Chairman of the new PNG CLTC Council, indicating the desire to retain his strong leadership as CLTC continued to grow. At that meeting Gil moved a motion of thanks for the leadership that Len Buck had given to CLTC right from its conception and birth. There is no doubt that Gil and Len Buck had a special friendship and relationship in their heart commitment to the work of CLTC and ATA.
22. Graduation Commissioning Service, Sunday 29 November 1970.

sawmill. When Gil, Graham and Bill became aware that the sawmill was coming to the end of its lease, they began negotiations to purchase the existing, but not yet operating timber lease owned by Beechwood Limited at Kauapena in the Southern Highlands. Nearby for sale was Dillingham's road construction campsite, with workshops and five modular-built houses for staff accommodation, which ATA purchased for AUD$25,000. Following approval of the ATA board, the Beechwood lease and sawmilling plant was purchased for AUD$70,000, birthing an ATA subsidiary, Beechwood Limited, together with the mammoth task of assembling all the machinery and developing the timber lease operations.

With the future supply of timber renewed, ATA established Timberline Limited, providing kiln dried and all grades of timber, building hardware, furniture making, residential and commercial construction (including the Kagamuga airport passenger building which was demolished for replacement in 2015), while training apprentices in all those areas, under Werner Mienel's leadership.

The expanding ATA highway transport department was incorporated as Transwest Limited to develop and encourage the concept of owner drivers, assisting some villages to purchase the truck driven by one of their own ATA trained young men.

The birth of Highway Motors Ltd naturally followed, providing all the services to keep highway trucks operating – truck servicing, auto electrical services, spare parts, new truck and vehicle agencies – culminating in Highway Motors securing the Kenworth truck agency for PNG.

In this rapidly spreading organisational influence, ATA continued to fund CLTC. Between 1971 and 1979 ATA contributed the equivalent of $135,000 in donations to supplement the $139,000 CLTC earned from its agricultural support programs, together providing 42% of the total training costs of CLTC's biblical training programs.[23]

The influence of ATA was not only seen in the commercial activities, but also in the fact that the workforce had increased from 30 in 1970 to 250 in 1979, 90% of whom were national employees.[24]

---

23. Garth Morgan, 'Re: ATA 1970-1979 - McArthur', 20 September 2017, 1.
    I am grateful to Garth Morgan for providing the details of the growth and spreading influence of ATA in this section.
24. Alliance Training Association, 'ATA Minutes of the Ninth Annual Meeting of Directors', 27 March 1979. The Staff Handbook and History were approved at this meeting.

Time to Move Tent Again

Once the vision of CLTC was initially established and making solid progress, Gil began to look to other emerging challenges. He concluded as Principal of CLTC at the end of 1970. His final report to the Council again clearly expressed his passion for the priority of developing national leaders, particularly within CLTC itself. 'Appended to his report was a *Localisation Plan* for all the key faculty and staff positions in the College, to be achieved within 15 years.'[25] This catalyst served to stimulate intentional plans for in-service training, study leave provisions, and support for achieving higher qualifications and experience for national staff in virtually every area of College ministry.

When Gil resigned, he was appointed by the MBI Council to the position of Australian Representative of CLTC for two years. He was also appointed a CLTC Council member, and the Executive Director of ATA. He continued to make a key contribution as a CLTC Council member and Executive Director of ATA, among other activities, until his final illness.

In his role as a member of the CLTC Council he demonstrated a passion to ensure CLTC remained true to the original vision. In the 1982 Council meeting, when the training programs were under review, Gil moved a resolution that expressed his conviction of the unique influence of the College in the history of the nation of PNG, and the story of God's global mission. In part, it read:

> In considering the College curriculum, we should not forget what Almighty God has already done through CLTC. We should remember the way He has done it, and the kind of people He has used in doing it. We should not make any big changes quickly, unless there is the very clear sign of His Spirit guiding and directing us. The testimony of mission history in the South Pacific should be recorded. We are those who have been privileged to live within the historic era of missionary outreach…
>
> It should be noted that the mighty missionary exploits of evangelism, church planting and discipleship were born of a 'method of missions' that would, for the most part be unacceptable to the modern methods of cross cultural identification and

---

25. Hitchen, 'Chapter Five: Evangelicals Equipping Melanesian Men and Women: An Interpretation of the Training Ministries of the Christian Leaders Training College of Papua New Guinea, 1965-2010', 126.

contextualisation, missiology, etc. What is it then, that was so signally honoured of God in planting the church in the South Pacific?

The clear answer from history is that these were men and women of 'the Book'. For example, the South Sea Evangelical Mission in the Solomon Islands conducted its literacy and Bible training program in the so-called archaic language of the Authorised (KJV) version of the Bible – a cardinal sin in the thinking of many modern missiologists. And they even established separate Christian villages to ensure vitality of life and faith, free from the soul-destroying disease of religious syncretism. But let the record speak… for they are surely one of the most vital, witnessing churches of the Pacific.

To avoid a student study-intake which is more of the head than of the heart, the testimony of the past is that there is no substitute for the engrafted Word… the major emphasis must always be line upon line, truth upon truth, thereby providing that gathering momentum of truth by which the living Word may come with its own power, speak with its own authority, and produce its own eternal result in the human spirit (Hebrews 4:12-13).

The fundamental responsibility… is to ensure that every student graduates as one who has been 'enlightened, who has tasted the heavenly gift, who has shared in the Holy Spirit, who has tasted the goodness of the Word of God and awakened to the powers of the coming age' (Hebrews 6:1-5). By this means alone will the doctrine of God and His Christ become determinative upon life and practice, faith and witness.[26]

Gil and Pat moved their 'tent' back to Sydney, where Ron Youngman built a home in Marsfield for them. In the years following he returned to Papua New Guinea/Solomon Islands and other Pacific nations many times for meetings, and several extended stays in Lae and Mt Hagen to help establish or support commercial projects under ATA, and in his later roles as Executive Director of SSEM, and Pacific Director for World Vision.

These broadening areas of involvement in establishing evangelical cooperation between churches, grappling with the moral and spiritual needs of Armed services and Police personnel and equipping local

---

26. Will Renshaw, 'Rev Dr Gilbert McArthur', Melbourne Notes and Comments, Issue No. 7, 20 June 1994.

Christians for business and economic development across the life of Melanesian society, were each significant in themselves. But they were also indicative of Gil's developing vision which, from this point, would take the same concerns to yet wider spheres of influence.

Graham Walker and Gil looking across to the Beechwood Sawmill at Kaupena

National workers at the Beechwood Sawmill

Gil and Len Buck encourage progress on Beechwood bush road construction

ATA Workshop Lae – preparing a new Kenworth for the road

11

A VISION FOR THE WIDER PACIFIC 1:
Developing National Kingdom Leaders

1971 – 1987

> *He was a man of vision.*
> *Throughout his life he seemed to see what the crowd did not see, and*
> *to see wider and fuller than many of his own day.*
> *He was a man of far horizons.*[1]

Gil's growing international leadership involvement is indicated by his active participation on the boards of CLTC, ATA PNG, ATASI, Gospel Recordings, MAF, Kristen Kaset, Kristen Redio, SSEM, and his work with the SSEC churches in PNG and the Solomon Islands. He regularly attended the Presidential Prayer Breakfasts in Washington, taking national Pacific leaders with him. He was also a Chaplain Major in the Australia/PNG Defence force until independence in 1975 and continued conducting leadership seminars for them. A number of these responsibilities continued alongside his developing Pacific role with World Vision.

World Vision South Pacific

Arising out of his war experiences, mission in DNG and PNG, and the development of CLTC, the Spirit of God stirred in Gil a broader vision for developing leaders across the Pacific with a holistic kingdom mindset. It was the time when many Pacific nations were moving towards independence, and leadership development was critical.[2] Gil was concerned that communities and nations develop physically, culturally,

---

1. Lettie Cowman, *Charles E. Cowman: Missionary Warrior* (Los Angeles, California: The Oriental Missionary Society, 1928), 259. The author believes that this description of Charles Cowman also seems a very appropriate one for Gilbert McArthur.
2. Independence dates - Fiji 1970, PNG 1975, Solomon Islands 1978, Vanuatu 1980 etc.

economically, politically and spiritually, and enter independence with biblical Kingdom values at the heart of their life and governance. His conviction and passion aligned with that of World Vision, who sought his advice on how to proceed with holistic community development projects in the region. In this period Gil developed a biblical framework for holistic community development, 'I am my brother's keeper – The Covenant Community'. His foundations were the transcendent realities of: the Fatherhood of God, evangelism and spiritual nurture, social justice, the brotherhood of man, and 'the worth of the individual in the sense of being and the joy of doing'.[3] Gil's presentation concludes:

> World Vision Community Developments projects provide for a number of integrated ministries geared to the needs of the whole person in terms of their spiritual, physical, mental, social, cultural and economic needs.
>
> These various streams of ministry sensitively applied in concert impact the community life over a period of time. The result is an enrichment of life that is mysteriously greater than just the sum of the individual parts.
>
> This may be called the 'Divine Mystique': that God given 'Extra Dimension' which happens when we all work together for the common good.[4]

In 1973, Gil was appointed the first Field Director for the World Vision South Pacific Office based in Sydney. He travelled extensively through the region, advising churches and communities, and initiating many World Vision development programs aimed at enhancing community economic self-reliance and self-determination. In his travels, he met many South Pacific leaders, and a new vision for the enhancement of Pacific political leaders emerged – the Pacific Leaders' Fellowship (PLF). Fundamental to this vision for the PLF was Gil's conviction that,

> If we are to impact the nations for good, then we must begin at the Leadership level – for it is a fact of history that the hungry and suffering masses of the world are the direct result of 'man's inhumanity to man' through the abuse of Leadership Power. It is

---

3. See the Appendix 4 for the complete diagram of his biblical approach to Holistic Community Development.
4. Gilbert J. McArthur, 'Holistic Community Development', n.d. McArthur Family Archives.

imperative that a way be found to restore the image of God in man through the Servant Leadership of the Man – Christ Jesus.[5]

Rev John Key, who was to become Gil's Associate Director recalls:

> Gil recognised that many of the national leaders now called to high office were either committed Christians or had been educated in Christian or mission schools and colleges. Many of these men he knew personally, some he had taught or mentored, all he prayed for. He believed they would derive great strength through relating to one another as brothers in Christ and supported through an unofficial network (Pacific Leaders' Fellowship) where they could meet for occasional informal, intimate gatherings, including study and discussion of biblical leadership and sharing of specific issues they faced in guiding their nations.[6]

John had previously been in PNG in the Anglican ministry, and Secretary of the Melanesian Council of Churches (MCC). He first met Gil in 1969 in the early days of CLTC. He returned to church ministry in the UK, but in 1981 was surprised to receive the invitation from Gil to join him as Associate Director. He arrived in Sydney in January 1982, and by July of that year Gil had persuaded World Vision to give John his job as Field Director, so Gil could focus full-time on the establishment of the PLF.

Pacific Leaders' Fellowship

In implementing his vision for the PLF, Gil found his model in an unexpected place: Washington DC. Every year in February, political, business and community leaders from around the USA and the world gathered for the National Prayer Breakfast, hosted by the President. Surrounding this event was a network of informal breakfasts and other groups coordinated by a team of evangelical leaders known unofficially as 'The Fellowship'. Gil had attended these Presidential Prayer Breakfasts for several years and had developed a very close friendship with Doug Coe who was responsible for issuing invitations to leaders from the South Pacific. Gil believed there was a powerful dynamic at work in these gatherings that could be adapted to the needs and opportunities in the Pacific. For several years he managed to secure for himself, and

---

5. Author Unknown, 'Double Honour for Baptist Minister', Publication unknown, 1986, McArthur Family Archives.
6. John Key, 'Dr Gilbert McArthur – Some Recollections by John Key', February 2016, 1.

various Pacific leaders invitations to the National Prayer Breakfast in Washington.

> One year Gil brought eight Papua New Guineans – one of which was the Chief of Police in the capital, Port Moresby. Another year, several Christian leaders from Asia Pacific Christian Mission came and others from the South Sea Evangelical Church. Sir Peter Kenilorea, the Prime Minister of the Solomon Islands, was invited one year.[7]

John Key recalls the amazing privilege of these opportunities. 'One year I had the task (quite formidable), of hosting King Taufa'ahau Tupou IV of Tonga at the Breakfast and a special dinner in his honour. I found him good company, a committed Christian and a scholar of British colonial history.'[8]

As he began to implement his PLF strategy, Gil's first major challenge was to identify the key leaders and persuade them of the value and importance of meeting together. Gil had partially achieved this through his visits across the Pacific in his role with World Vision, and by inviting key leaders to the Washington Prayer Breakfasts where friendships could form with other Pacific and international leaders. In 1980, to make connections, build relationships with national island leaders and confirm their commitment to the PLF, Gil with funding support from World Vision chartered an aircraft for a Pacific Tour. Ed Lumsdaine who had been an MAF pilot in PNG for many years was then flying with Norfolk Airlines. Gil approached Norfolk Air to charter a Beechcraft Super King Air (which was turbine powered and had pressurised air conditioning) for the tour. Gil told management they would get the job if Ed Lumsdaine could be the pilot because Ed had often flown Gil around PNG with MAF. For Ed it was a once in a lifetime chance for such an experience – 'there was a lot of salt water out there and you can see a long way at 30,000 feet!' Departing Brisbane on 16th April, they flew to Port Vila (Vanuatu), to Suva (Fiji), to Tonga, to Niue (over the date line), to Pago Pago and Apia (Samoa), to Funafuti (Tuvalu), to Tarawa (Kiribati) (over the date line and equator), to Honiara (Solomon Islands), to Lae (PNG), to Mt Hagen, to Port Moresby, returning to Brisbane 26th April. The tour involved a total of 34 hours flying time

---

7. John Fletcher, 'Gil McArthur - as Told by Peggy Fletcher to Carin LeRoy', 27 April 2018, 1.
8. Key, 'Dr Gilbert McArthur - Some Recollections by John Key', 1, 2.

over 10 days (see map next page).⁹ One of the of the team members was Maika Bovoro, a Fijian who was then General Secretary of the Bible Society of the South Pacific, based in Fiji. It seems that Doug Coe and his wife from the USA, and Sir Peter Kenilorea were also involved. The names of other team members are not known. John Key recalls that Gil often referred to the value and impact of this first tour.¹⁰

Gil's second PLF development challenge was to gather a small team willing to travel for PLF meetings and securing access to aircraft at reasonable rates. Gil decided to call Max Meyers. Max had first met Gil as a school boy passionate to become a pilot. But Max's pastor, Alan Tinsley, thought Max should enter the ministry. Alan knew Gil understood both vocations, and put Max in contact with Gil, who urged Max to continue to follow his 'God-given' passion to fly. That led Max into a journey in the Royal Australian Air Force, and then into mission aviation with MAF. They had contact over the years, but when Gil was thinking about the PLF in 1979, Max was then CEO of MAF Australia. With typical bold confidence, Gil called Max and said, 'I am coming down to Melbourne to see you. I have something to tell you that will change the rest of your life!' That caught Max's attention. But despite his best efforts to get Gil to talk over the phone and save the airfares, Gil insisted he had to see him personally. When Gil reached Melbourne, Max asked, 'So what do you have to tell me that is about to change my life?'

Gil replied, 'My research shows that in the Pacific Islands, almost every head of state and cabinet member in the emerging nations has received their education in Christian Schools or Colleges.'

'Fascinating,' Max responded, 'But why is that going to change my life?'

'Because,' replied Gil with characteristic bluntness, 'you are going to come with me to visit them!'

He then shared his vision for visiting Pacific leaders with a small team to encourage them in the challenges they faced, and to focus their attention on Kingdom values and Jesus' model of servant leadership in the context of prayer and fellowship. But he needed help. Would Max join the team and would MAF consider providing a suitable aircraft

---

9. Gordon Griffiths, 'More on Gil McArthur', 19 September 2016, 1. This email contained Eddie Lumsdaine's personal report of this first Pacific Tour.
10. John Key, 'Re: Gil McArthur Question', Email, 3 September 2018, 1.

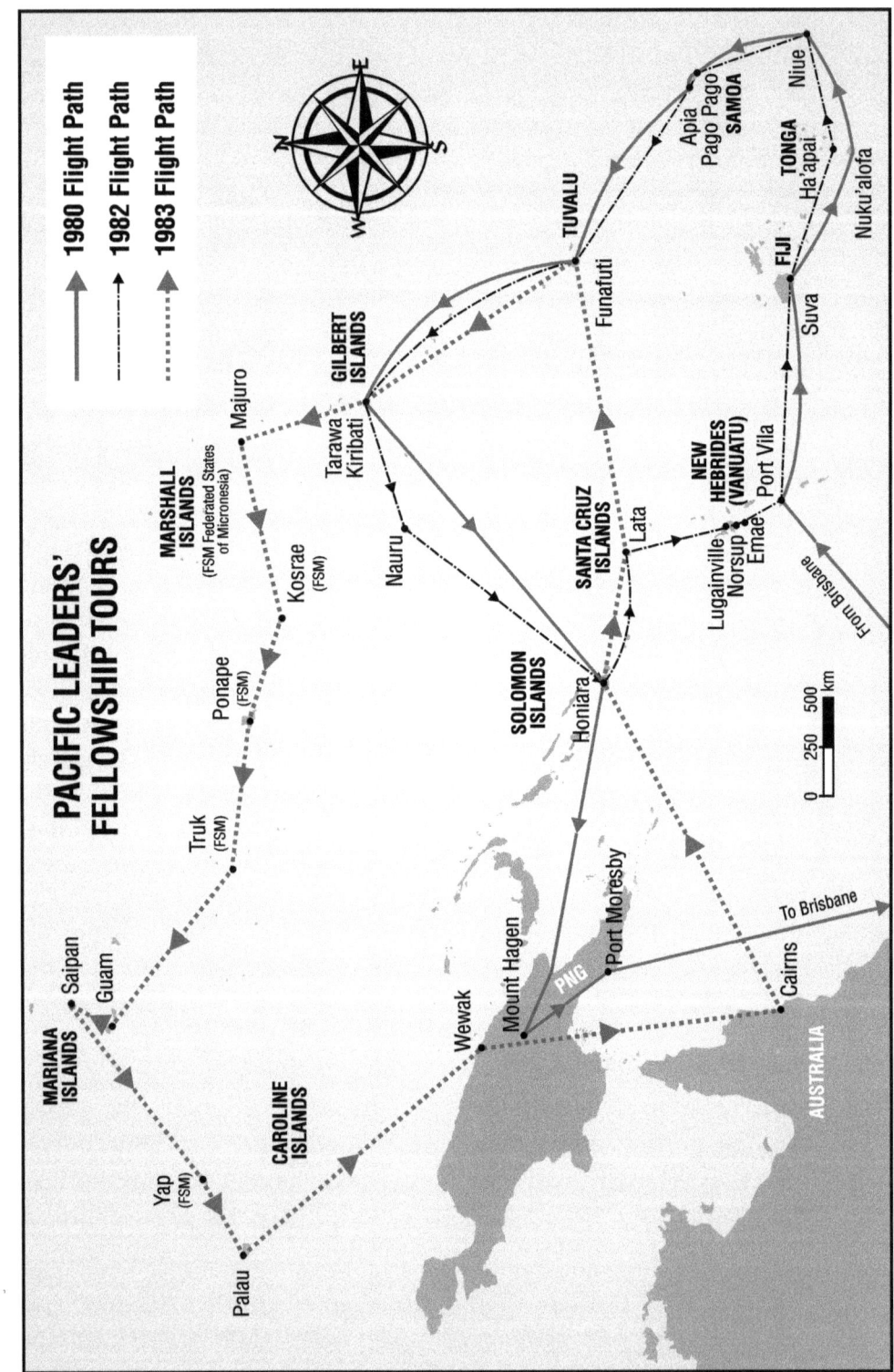

when needed?[11] With the encouragement of the MAF Board, Max became a core member of the PLF team, and MAF agreed to make an aircraft available, even though it was not their core business. Bruce Redpath, a leading Australian businessman, was a board member of both World Vision and MAF at the time and was able to 'oil the wheels' of the PLF proposal. Bruce was also a team member in some of the PLF team visits.[12]

Gil's third challenge was funding for the considerable expenses involved. John Key remembers that it was, 'with typical prophetic persistence that Gil persuaded World Vision Australia to catch the vision and to fund the work of the PLF for a five-year period, as a strategic contribution to the development of the island nations then emerging.'[13]

> Gil aimed to identify key leaders and potential emerging leaders in all the island nations of the South Pacific, build a network of relationships, and so invite them to participate in the PLF. He began with leaders he already knew, and they became an unofficial executive. This group took the lead in arranging events and approaching their peers: a wise and effective strategy.
>
> The undoubted and anointed leader was Sir Peter Kenilorea, several times Prime Minister of the Solomon Islands, an outstanding statesman and excellent communicator. Others included Father Walter Lini, Prime Minister of Vanuatu, Prince Fatafehi Tu'ipelehaki, Prime Minister of Tonga, Ratu Sir Kamisese Mara, Prime Minister of Fiji, and Sir Mari Kapi, Deputy Chief Justice (later Chief Justice) of Papua New Guinea. For me it was a huge blessing and a great joy to sit down with men like these for times of study, sharing and prayer! Almost always everyone was ready and willing to learn, to grow, to be vulnerable and to care for each other.
>
> Over the five years 1982 to 1987 Gil organised (with logistical support from our World Vision South Pacific Office) a series of retreats and meetings in amazing venues across the Pacific, hosted by the leader of that nation. The first was held in Port Vila (Vanuatu) in 1982, with the Prime Minister, Walter Lini, and the

---

11. The details of Gil's contact with Max were provided in a personal discussion with the author and Max Meyers in early 2017.
12. Much of the detailed information for this paragraph was provided in a phone conversation with Max Meyers in Melbourne on 9 June 2017.
13. Key, 'Dr Gilbert McArthur - Some Recollections by John Key', 1.

MAF 402 aircraft – Gil, Sir Peter Kenilorea and MAF pilot Tony Holloway

Gil with Malekula Island church leader

President, George Sokomanu, as hosts. I cannot remember the dates of the other meetings, but the venues included the Coral Coast (Fiji), Nuku'alofa (Tonga), Port Moresby (Papua New Guinea), Honiara (Solomon Islands), Honolulu (Hawaii), Pohnpei (Federated States of Micronesia), Upolu (Samoa) and Gilbulla (NSW, Australia)...[14]

It is worth noting that in every venue, Gil took care to connect with local church leaders, such as Rev Dr Joshua Daimoi in PNG, Dr Sione Havea in Tonga and Rev Maika Bovoro in Fiji, in order to involve them where appropriate, and to build fruitful relationships with their national leaders.[15]

In preparation for the summits and retreats in specific locations, Gil (with the help of Max Meyers) sourced aircraft for the Pacific tours of a ministry team. Their purpose was to meet leaders in their own situations, preparing the way for the leadership gatherings and introducing the ministry of the PLF to island leaders in the threefold 'call to prayer, call to fellowship, and call to servant leadership'.[16]

The second PLF tour through the South Pacific on 6-24 May 1982 was in a Cessna 402 MAF aircraft from PNG. The MAF pilot was Tony Holloway, and the team comprised Sir Peter Kenilorea as leader, Gil McArthur and Max Meyers. The flight path indicates the extensiveness of this second tour to develop the PLF. Starting in Honiara (Solomon Islands), they flew to Lugainville the capital of Vanuatu via Santa Cruz, Norsup on Malekula Island, Emae in Vanuatu (passing the Ambrin and Epi islands), to Vila in Vanuatu, Suva in Fiji, Tonga, the Ha'apai island group in Tonga (which had been severely impacted by cyclone Isaac), Niue (a self-governing independent island still officially under New Zealand's care), Pago Pago in American Samoa, Apia in Western Samoa, Funafuti in Tuvalu, and Tarawa in Kiribati (both formerly the Gilbert

---

14. Micronesia in July 1983, Western Samoa October 1983, Hawaii March 1984, Philippines June? 1984, Port Moresby August 1987, other event dates for Coral Coast Fiji, Nuku'alofa Tonga and Pohnpei FSM are not known – but probably in the latter part of the 1982 to 1987 period.
15. Key, 'Dr Gilbert McArthur - Some Recollections by John Key', 2. I am grateful to John Key for providing much of the information on Gil's formation of the PLF. Sadly World Vision advised that they held nothing in their archives of Gil or his work with them, which I find both disappointing and astonishing.
16. Max Meyers, 'South Pacific Leaders Tour Report' (Box Hill Melbourne: Missionary Aviation Fellowship, May 1982), 3.

and Ellis Islands), and Nauru, before finally returning to Honiara in the Solomon Islands (See Map). The impact of the tour is evident in the report which names 139 'key people' that attended meetings, apart from many other useful contacts.[17]

In each place meetings were held with key government, community and church leaders. Max Meyers' account of their meeting in Vila with President George Sokomanu provides an example of these remarkable encounters, and the purpose of the PLF:

> I wonder how many countries would have a President who would readily invite visitors to sit down and discuss immediately the spiritual welfare of his nation and the place that it was taking in national and international development? It was a great privilege to sit in his sitting room and discuss the things of God…
>
> The objectives of this dinner gathering were, to discuss the role of Christian leadership in the South Pacific… to encourage leaders to go on with Christ… to encourage them in their personal relationship together in a recognition that God has called them to their task…
>
> We had an excellent meal with a marvellous 'inch thick' steak… but much more marvellous was the fellowship in Christ. Whilst Peter, Gil and myself spoke to them, there was a very wonderful attitude of acceptance and fellowship. The main objective in this meeting was to gather support for a 'Summit of Pacific Leadership' to be held in Suva in October. Peter Kenilorea, as Chairman of the South Pacific Leaders Fellowship, was invited on this trip to make these contacts to encourage and support other Christian leaders in the region, and to hear their suggestions and input.
>
> Gil McArthur, who really, behind the scenes, is the encourager in most of this activity, and Peter Kenilorea and I, were delighted with their response as, almost to a man, this group of leaders in this remarkable new nation were totally supportive and pledged themselves to pray and commit themselves to the concept of peer group fellowship in political leadership in the South Pacific.[18]

On 3-7 November 1982, leaders from fifteen Pacific Oceania nations gathered together at Hideaway Island Resort in Port Vila for the first

---

17. Max Meyers, 'South Pacific Leaders Trip Report'.
18. Meyers, 'South Pacific Leaders Trip Report', 7.

A VISION FOR THE WIDER PACIFIC 1

Sir Peter Kenilorea and Gil discussing plans en route to Vanuatu

Gil – time for a sleep!

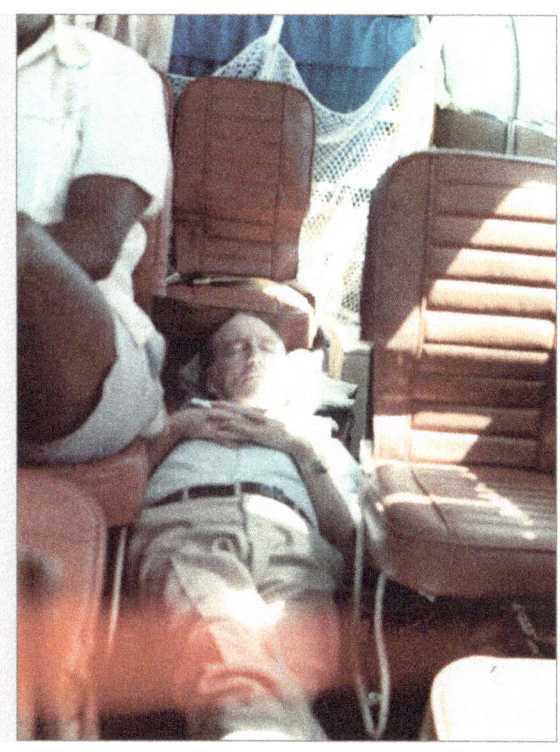

Summit Meeting of the PLF. The theme was 'In God alone we stand, without him we can do nothing'. It involved a call to prayer, a call to fellowship and a call to servant leadership. The Government of Vanuatu had agreed to be the host country at the request of Sir Peter Kenilorea the Chairman of the Coordinating Committee.

> Gathering from the different nations, leaders met together in a most informal, relaxed 'hats off'… even 'shoes off' atmosphere at Hideaway Island… There were Heads of State, Prime Ministers, Presidents and Deputy Presidents and Deputy Prime Ministers, Ministers of State and leaders of both the Judiciary and United Nations Delegations. Predominantly these were Pacific Islanders. There was also a member of the Australian House of Representatives and a four-man team of coordinators under the capable and dedicated leadership of Dr Gilbert McArthur…
>
> Servant-Leadership, epitomised by the life and style of Jesus, was one of the main thrusts of the study material. One cannot possibly measure the historical significance of the political and national leaders of the Pacific relating their own leadership responsibilities and styles to that of the Christ of Galilee…[19]

In Vanuatu the PLF team agreed on the concept of further regionalised meetings with a broader spectrum of leadership including church, business and government.

On 22-24 April 1983 Gil coordinated a PNG South Pacific Leaders' Fellowship Retreat at the Kokoda Trail Motel outside Port Moresby. Over 60 leaders from PNG, the Solomon Islands and Australia attended. Sir Peter Kenilorea presided over the program, which included group studies and plenary sessions covering the Priority of Relationships, the Value and Dignity of Man, and Servant Leadership. Generous time was provided for fellowship and prayer, so that the leaders could get to know each other.[20] Sir Michael Somare, Prime Minister of PNG, was the Fellowship Dinner Speaker. In his address he expressed his interest in the aims of the PLF and affirmed the value of bringing leaders together. After outlining the positive influence of Christianity in the story of the nation, he warned against an 'idealistic Christianity' in which people

---

19. Gilbert J McArthur, 'South Pacific Leaders' Fellowship: The Fruit of Mission in the South Pacific', *Not in Vain*, April 1983, 1, 2.
20. South Pacific Leaders' Fellowship, 'South Pacific Leaders Fellowship – Daily Program', 22 April 1983, McArthur Family Archives.

A VISION FOR THE WIDER PACIFIC 1

*Gil with Fiji Governor-General Ratu Sir George Cakobau,
Micah Bovoro and Sir Peter Kenilorea*

*Max Meyers, Gil, Sir Peter Kenilorea and
Prime Minister of Fiji Ratu Sir Kamasese Mara*

Sir Peter Kenilorea and His Majesty King Taufa' Ahau Tupou IV of Tonga

Gil, Sir Peter Kenilorea, The Hon Robert Rex, Premier of Niue Island, Max Meyers and Fiji Government Secretary Terry Chapman

do not give practical expression to what they profess to believe. He concluded with a strong challenge for self-examination and a call to action:

> I think that you, the Christian leaders, should examine your own conduct and actions. Are your beliefs practical? Are you achieving anything or are you just adding more words to the never-ending round of arguments about where we should be heading? As a leader, you should be able to mobilise people. You should be able to get things done. Are you? Are you applying these Christian ideals which so many espouse but so few put into practice? I believe members of a group like this must face up to these questions. They must test themselves against the real world – the daily grind of Business and Government. You must apply Christian principles not just preach them![21]

A third PLF Pacific Tour visited Micronesia 13-26 July 1983, in a Turbo Commander 690B aircraft owned by Stan Lindgren of Cairns, North Queensland. Stan, a highly qualified airline captain, a Christian and a member of the Gideons, flew the aircraft.[22] The other members of that team were Sir Peter Kenilorea, Chairman of the PLF and leader of the Opposition in the Solomon Islands; Laupepa Malietoa, a member of the Parliament of Western Samoa; Bernard Narakobi, former Judge of the Supreme Court of PNG; Bruce Redpath, Chairman of Mayne Nickless Ltd; Max Meyers, General Director of MAF Australia; and Gil, the PLF Coordinator. The list of participants provides a window into Gil's broad Pacific networks. This visit aimed to draw the South and North Pacific together. The tour departed Cairns and then to Honiara (Solomon Islands), Santa Cruz Islands, Funafuti Tuvalu and Tarawa Kiribati, Majuro in the Marshall Islands (Federated States of Micronesia FSM), Kosrae, FSM, Ponape FSM, Truk FSM, Guam, Saipan in the Mariana Islands, Yap FSM, Palau in the Caroline Islands, Wewak PNG and return to Cairns (See Map).[23] The team received a warm welcome at every stop.

---

21. Michael Somare, 'Speech by the Prime Minister, Mr Michael Somare, at the South Pacific Leaders Fellowship Dinner', 22 April 1983, 3, 4, McArthur Family Archives.
22. The team completed well over 20,000 kms of trans-oceanic flying without even the slightest unserviceability of the aircraft, sickness of any of the party or any other major problem.
23. Max Meyers, 'South Pacific Leaders Fellowship Micronesian Tour Report', (Box Hill, Melbourne: Missionary Aviation Fellowship), July 1983.

Max Meyers' Report listed 103 names of key political, business and church leaders who gathered with the team apart from many others they met on their journey.

> [At Kosrae] we met the Lieutenant Governor and his Ministers. A most encouraging discussion with them. They had not known what to expect but were very warmly approving of our submission to them. We each had the opportunity to speak. Church and State are very close in Kosrae. All leaders to whom we spoke are also involved as leaders in the local Church. It was extremely gratifying to hear the Lieutenant Governor make the statement… 'seeing your level of commitment and perceiving how much it has meant for you to come so far, this visit you are making will perhaps turn out to be the most honourable visit that Kosrae State has ever had'.[24]

In March 1984, Gil was invited to nominate a leading South Pacific figure to speak at the Governor's Prayer Breakfast in Honolulu. The result was an invitation to Peter Kenilorea first Prime Minister of the Solomon Islands and President of the PLF. Gil took the initiative to organise a mini conference of the PLF during the weekend. Representatives came from the island nations like PNG, New Caledonia, Vanuatu, Solomon Islands, Tonga and Fiji. A small number of Australians and Americans were also present. There were two thousand people at the Governor's Prayer Breakfast. Sir Marcus Loane Archbishop of Sydney was one of the PLF speakers and in his report reflected on his impressions.

> Sir Peter Kenilorea gave a splendid address on the basic need for a strong and definite Christian commitment. In the various sessions of the PLF Dr McArthur unfolded plans for 1984 and invited frank and open discussion. This led to a fascinating contribution from the Island Leaders, each of whom spoke from his own particular standpoint, but with an obvious desire for the support and goodwill of others…
>
> I was deeply impressed by the remarkably rapid way in which a warm understanding relationship was established between all who were at the Conference, and by the overflowing generosity of Christian people in Honolulu.[25]

---

24. Meyers, 'South Pacific Leaders' Micronesian Tour Report', 7, Will Renshaw Personal Archives.
25. Marcus Loane, 'Pacific Islands Leadership', *Not in Vain*, May 1984, 4.

It was probably around June 1984 that the Supreme Court Judge of the Philippines Mr Justice Teehankee invited Sir Peter Kenilorea to lead a Fellowship Retreat among the Judiciary and many other Filipino leaders.[26] The theme of the conference was 'Looking at the Needs of Asia-Pacific through the Eyes of Christ'. John Key recalls,

> Gil led a small group of island leaders, headed by Sir Peter Kenilorea, to Manila (Philippines), to connect with national leaders there, communicating the Kingdom message. I remember attending a wonderful dinner event, at which Sir Peter gave his personal testimony as a national leader and as a Christian. Gil's efforts to persuade President Marcos to attend were, for once, not successful! But I sat next to a Filipino who was much impacted and who later rose to high office in the Philippines.[27]

In August 1987, 35 PNG leaders attended a second PNG Leadership Retreat also held at the Kokoda Trail Motel. The theme was 'Leadership Integrity'. Gil coordinated the retreat, and the Bible studies were led by the former Anglican Primate of Australia and Archbishop of Sydney, Sir Marcus Loane. The Chairman of the PNG Leaders' Fellowship, Chief Justice Sir Buri Kidu welcomed those present, and a challenging keynote address was given by Deputy Chief Justice Mari Kapi on 'Foundations for Nation Building'.

> Mr Kapi said that many saw the need for development of natural resources, for more overseas aid, and for good management skills, and the like. Others saw the need for a proper moral foundation, honesty, and respect for the law. Even more important was the need for Christian leaders to concentrate on the view that, whilst the nation could have all those things, unless there was a personal relationship with the Lord Jesus Christ, and individuals became new creatures in Him, they could not become instruments for the Holy Spirit to use. True integrity in leadership would not be effected until a person gave his life to Christ.[28]

Arising from these PLF Encounters, Gil and Bruce Ogden drafted a Leadership Code. Leaders were asked to covenant and pray together

---

26. This event was reported in the August 1984 edition of the SSEM *Not in Vain* magazine, but the exact date not given.
27. Key, 'Dr Gilbert McArthur - Some Recollections by John Key', 2.
28. Will Renshaw, 'PNG Leadership Retreat', *New Life*, 24 September 1987, Vol 50, No 17, 1, Will Renshaw Personal Archives.

that such a code would, under God, result in a new 'Leadership Mode', for the glory of God and the blessing of their nations.[29]

> **A CHRISTIAN LEADERSHIP MANIFESTO**
> *Integrity from the 'Royal Law'*
>
> | | |
> |---:|:---|
> | GOVERNMENT | Established by Righteousness |
> | POLITICS | Controlled by Principle |
> | POWER | Transformed by Love |
> | JUDGEMENT | Determined by Truth |
> | JUSTICE | Tempered by Mercy |
> | KNOWLEDGE | Balanced by Character |
> | EDUCATION | Enlightened by Faith |
> | WISDOM | Endowed by Grace |
> | WEALTH | Gained by Work |
> | BUSINESS | Governed by Ethic |
> | PLEASURE | Safeguarded by Conscience |
> | SCIENCE | Ennobled by Humility |
> | RELIGION | Expressed by Compassion |
> | WORSHIP | Enriched by Sacrifice |
>
> *This is the outworking of the 'Royal Law'*
> *James 2:8; Matthew 22:37*

The Decline of the Pacific Leaders' Fellowship

Gil moved from the World Vision International office across to World Vision Australia on a consultancy basis for his last couple of years, while keeping the PLF group moving through their strategic gatherings. John Key worked closely with Gil on PLF matters from 1982 until John was moved to Bangladesh in 1987. Gil retired from his consulting role with World Vision in 1988 moving into 'partial retirement' in Lake Cathie NSW, with a new vision and strategy emerging from his PLF experiences to further equip Pacific leaders.[30]

---

29. PNG Leaders' Fellowship, 'Leadership News', *PNG Leaders' Fellowship Newsletter*, September 1987, 3, McArthur Family Archives.
30. South Sea Evangelical Mission, 'South Sea Evangelical Mission Director's Meeting Minutes', 24 July, 1987, Melbourne School of Theology Archives.

In July 1991 Wal Denton, one of Gil's friends, wrote to Gil following his visit to the Solomon Islands, lamenting the decline of the influence of the PLF and proposing how it might continue. As Sir Peter Kenilorea was leaving politics to take up a position in Forum Fisheries, he would have time to devote to the revival of the PLF relationships. Such was Wal's conviction about the value of the PLF, that he expressed his readiness to work together with Sir Peter.[31]

However, this plan did not gain any traction. John Tanner recalls that it was the Australian Prime Minister Bob Hawke who helped demolish the PLF by refusing to allow it to continue to convene directly after the South Pacific Forum political meetings. This meant travel costs formerly funded by World Vision could not be covered by the South Pacific Forum, and so funding for meetings for the PLF became an obstacle to its continuity.[32]

It appears that despite the enthusiasm of some, Gil's declining health and Bob Hawke's opposition led to the eventual demise of the PLF. It had served its purpose, brought to birth by God through Gil and his colleagues for the enhancement of the leaders of the newly independent South Pacific nations.

Missionary Aviation Fellowship
Wings of the South Pacific Leaders' Fellowship

---

31. Wal Denton, 'South Pacific Leaders Fellowship', Letter, 18 July 1991, McArthur Family Archives.
32. John Tanner, 'Re: Dr Gilbert McArthur', Telephone Interview, January 17, 2017.

Joshua Daimoi addresses SSEC Leadership Conference 2011

Leaders in discussion groups (women leaders met separately)

SSEC March of Witness in Honiara 2011

12

A VISION FOR THE WIDER PACIFIC 2:
Building Leaders in SSEC and Pacific Evangelical Churches

> *Leadership development **never** happens accidentally.*
> *It only happens when some leader has a white-hot vision for it,*
> *when his or her pulse rate doubles at the very thought*
> *of pumping into the organisational system*
> *a steady stream of competent leaders.*[1]

From the beginning CLTC provided training for key emerging leaders from the South Sea Evangelical Church (SSEC), both in PNG and the Solomon Islands. Gil's early contact with the SSEM and the SSEC convinced him that there was a level of maturity and spirituality in the Solomon Island Churches that was needed in other churches in PNG and the Pacific. Right from the start he was keen to see Solomon Islanders coming to CLTC for further training as they lived alongside students from other churches. He wanted SSEC Solomon Island leaders involved in providing leadership to the SSEC churches in the Sepik area of PNG. In the December 1972 edition of *Not in Vain* he observed:

> In the Solomon Islands, the new wine of the Spirit has been flowing in life-giving power and blessing to the young churches, and through them to the heathen villages. The 'signs following' have had all the marks of a true Pentecostal effusion, but there has also been the inevitable spiritual trauma, resulting from the devil's counterfeits.
>
> The national church in New Guinea has much more recently been brought to birth from the raw material of primitive animism. Pioneer missionaries have august experience of being co-workers

---

1. Bill Hybels, *Courageous Leadership* (Grand Rapids Michigan: Zondervan, 2002), 122, 123.

with the Holy Spirit, as the New Wine of Truth has liberated so many from their long dark night of bondage.[2]

In August 1970 there was a mighty outpouring of the Holy Spirit upon the SSEC churches in the Solomon Islands following the ministry of Muri Thompson, a Maori evangelist from New Zealand. The SSEC students who came across from the Solomon Islands after this time had an even greater impact on the spiritual vitality of the CLTC community, and on the PNG churches visited by Senior SSEC pastors and SSEC CLTC graduates.[3] Revival movements broke out among the churches of the Baptist Union of PNG, Evangelical Church of PNG, Christian Brethren, United Church and other smaller groups. Both 'the blessings and curses of revival' were in evidence in these movements, which highlighted the need for competent leaders to bring sound biblical teaching to guide and mature these movements of the Holy Spirit.

South Sea Evangelical Mission – A New Style of Leadership

In March 1971, soon after his return to Australia from CLTC, Gil was appointed a Director on the Board of SSEM to help initiate a different style of leadership following the earlier and ongoing revivals that the SSEC had experienced. Ken Griffiths had been the Executive Director since 1943. He resigned as Chairman of SSEM in June 1970 but continued to attend to executive affairs until a replacement CEO was identified. In January 1972 Gil requested release from his role as Australian CLTC Representative, to accept the invitation of the SSEM Board to take up the position of Chief Executive Director.[4] The minute of his appointment noted, 'Dr McArthur has had ministry on both fields, in the Solomon Islands and New Guinea, so he is quite well known by most of our missionaries and many national Christian leaders. His appointment as Executive Director is warmly welcomed by the mission staff.'[5]

Before Gil took up his Executive Director role he visited the Sepik field to familiarise himself with the ministry of SSEM and attend a

---

2. Gilbert J McArthur, 'New Wineskins for New Wine', *Not in Vain*, December 1972, 4.
3. For an excellent history of these revival movements, see, Alison Griffiths, *Fire in the Islands: The Acts of the Holy Spirit in the Solomons* (Wheaton, ILL: Harold Shaw Publishers, 1977). Gil became involved with SSEM when these revival movements were taking place - see especially chapters 19-24.
4. MBI Executive, 'Minutes of the Executive Meeting of the Melbourne Bible Institute', 25 January 1972.
5. John Wiggins, 'Section One: Gilbert J McArthur', 25 January 2017, 1.

missionary conference at Brugam in August 1971.[6] He strongly believed that 'the mission must see its vital role as "facilitator" and rise to new levels of involvement'.[7]

Gordon Griffiths, the SSEM Training Director and Board member in 1991 (son of long-serving missionary and SSEM Chairman, Ken), recalls:

> As Gil took up his new role as head of a mission he had the feeling the relevance of missions was increasingly being challenged. He also felt that a duplication of effort by missions was resulting in a heavy expenditure of Christian resources which disturbed many and resulted in a decreasing support for missions. He believed that there were many other areas of genuine concern that confronted and even confounded those charged with the responsibility of decision-making in the overall work of mission. He wanted to honestly determine the priorities of SSEM, and then ensure that all resources were directed to those essential tasks.[8]

Strategic Planning for Mission and Church

In March 1972 Gil wrote extensively in the SSEM *Not in Vain* about the strategies he believed the Evil One might use to destroy both the charter and conduct of Christian missions such as SSEM. This formative message revealed Gil's vision and thinking about his strategy for the future, and the type of leadership he hoped to bring to SSEM.

Gil believed that the devil worked by two strategies. The first through false gods,[9] because humanity has forfeited its spiritual birthright and embraced the 'strong delusion' that pervades a fallen world:

> The mind boggles, the heart is moved and tears spring to the eyes as one faces the awful fact that the greater part of the world's 3.72 billion people do, at this very moment, 'believe a lie'. The god concepts of the third world (the rising nations of Africa, Asia and South America) hold the masses in bondage to deities who, whilst requiring to be propitiated by the blood sacrifices, can at the same

---

6. Gordon Griffiths, 'Information and Observations about Gil McArthur', Email, 25 January 2016. Gordon is responsible for the archives of the SSEC, and provided very helpful details related to Gil's ministry with SSEM/SSEC.
7. Gilbert J McArthur, 'SSEM Centenary - 100 Years, 1882 - 1982', *Not in Vain*, August 1982, 3, SSEM Archives.
8. Gordon Griffiths, 'More on Gil McArthur', Email, 21 August 2016.
9. Romans 1:22-25.

time be manipulated by man. There is no understanding of a Moral Being who is Creator, Judge, and (via the Cross) a Holy Saviour.[10]

Gil believed the devil's second strategy was the infiltration of the Western 'mother' churches by 'traitors within': the curse of passivity and apathy. Great numbers profess with their lips but fail to live out their commitment. They need conversion bringing a compelling sense of mission. 'Woe is me if I preach not the gospel' or be 'doubly damned'.[11]

Gil spoke of applying a strategy of 'Greater Power'. Yet at the same time he confessed his own preoccupation with strategy and the temptation to place too much confidence in technique and methodology. Prayerful reflection led him back to the centrality of Christ and the Gospel,

> All our thinking, planning, praying, and actioning, if it is to
> have eternal meaning, must be Christocentric. It would be both
> fitting and salutary therefore to replace strategy and strategic with
> CHRISTOPHY and CHRISTOPHIC, and to reserve their usage
> solely for significant mission enterprise both at home and abroad.[12]

By a 'Christophy', or a Christ-centred mission strategy, Gil believed that fragmentation and duplication in missionary effort that wasted resources must be rejected. Responsible leaders need to engage in a fearless and honest assessment of the Christ-centred priorities of mission, and all resources used for the agreed essential tasks. This involved what he called Truth in Action.[13] Gil argued that:

> Apostolic succession is only valid in the sense of the truth as it is
> in Jesus being shared and passed on to another life. The apostles'
> doctrine is a teaching of the 'truth once for all declared' and with
> it comes both the charisma and the dynamic of the Holy Spirit.
> Therefore, a CHRISTOPHY OF MISSION must be centred in the
> biblical principle of truth in action, namely, the making of disciples
> who in turn will make disciples, who will make disciples, who will
> make disciples, who will make…[14]

Gil proposed *'training in the faith'* was the starting point in this law of spiritual multiplication. The apostles' doctrine, the recorded revelation

---

10. Gilbert J McArthur, 'Mission: Stratagem and Strategy', *Not in Vain*, March 1972, 2, SSEM Archives.
11. Hebrews 10:28-31.
12. McArthur, 'Mission: Stratagem and Strategy', 3.
13. 2 Timothy 2:2.
14. McArthur, 'Mission: Stratagem and Strategy', 3.

of God's redemptive acts in Jesus Christ, involves the disciple in a 'discipline of learning', which builds maturity in Christ. Without this discipline of learning, the result is an immaturity susceptible to the devil's strategies. But a 'spiritual competence' in being able to teach others involves conviction about the historic basis of faith, and a personal surrender to Christ that inspires a commitment to obedience to Christ in life and mission.

Gil was convinced that the application of these principles in a Christ-centred teaching program with the young churches had to focus on the development of a national leadership:

> The three 'self-principles' propounded by Roland Allen have long been accepted as fundamental… However, it has not been found easy to apply the principles… For example, the principle of self-government… is not achieved simply by passing a resolution on the mission books, or by forming a church constitution and appointing a church council with the authority to govern its own affairs. The mantle of responsibility, without the confidence and general well-being that comes only by acquired skills, can prove more of a curse than a blessing. It is dangerous to personality and character when **office and function** cannot be backed up by **knowledge and ability**. Relating this to the subject of indigenous church leadership certain vital factors emerge:
>
> 1. Self-government is meaningless without the spiritual competence that comes only through deeper insight into truth.
>
> 2. The availability of the Word of God in the lingua franca and a reading facility for a significant proportion of the church constituency is essential for any real degree of self-determination in the realm of church life and order.
>
> 3. A continuous stream of spiritual leadership must be recruited, trained, and channelled into the life of the church at all levels.[15]

In the light of these three vital factors, Gil called for prayerful discussion and planning between mission directors, missionaries and national church leaders to agree on priorities and methodologies for the following:

1. The recognised central objective of 'a biblically taught, spiritually mature church'.

---

15. McArthur, 'Mission: Stratagem and Strategy', 4.

2. Formulating and implementing a five (or ten) year program of action involving all mission and church resources.
3. The placement of missionaries and national leaders on the basis of their individual gifts and abilities, including a drastic review of the policy of placing workers only where mission facilities are located.
4. Establishing all the internal training facilities required for a continuous systematic in-depth teaching program for the life and order of the village churches, including the recruitment of staff needed.
5. Fully utilising external training institutions for more advanced teaching in Bible, Theology and Christian Education.
6. The establishment of a post-graduate course of cultural and contemporary meaning for selected church leaders who would major in: A Biblical Ecclesiology for Young Churches; An Interpretation of Biblical Ethics for Young Churches; The Charisma and Communication of the Gospel; Prophecy – the Judgment, Hope and Destiny of the Nations; Administration and Finance; Leadership and Man-Management.
7. The establishment of a scholarship fund to underwrite these Christ-centred training programs.[16]

In concluding his missiological framework, Gil expressed the challenge for his readers:

> … we reaffirm that the human catastrophe resulting from the devil's stratagems can only be met and overcome by a programme of mission that is of Christophic proportion. May the Lord God Almighty challenge us and the Spirit of Christ empower us so to plan and direct our strategies of mission that they may indeed be clothed with such spiritual content as to have meaning for both time and eternity.[17]

Flowing from this vision of mission, and the coming of independence to Pacific nations, Gil worked to help develop the indigenous leaders of the SSEC and move the churches towards greater autonomy. He established a Leadership Training Fund to resource this need, and there was a strong response from SSEM supporters. He also advocated for the potential return of MAF planes to the Solomon Islands. Unfortunately, this vision

---
16. McArthur, 'Mission: Stratagem and Strategy', 4.
17. McArthur, 'Mission: Stratagem and Strategy', 4.

did not materialise. The amphibious plane purchased by MAF for this purpose crashed when landing on the Sepik River with the wheels down, and so was no longer available. Despite concerted efforts to progress the MAF application, there were also regulatory difficulties for MAF operations in the Solomon Islands. Undaunted, Gil also had a vision for a 'South Pacific Boat Ministry' which he hoped would demonstrate the viability of a boat ministry over the whole of the Pacific. Although this proposed program did not come to fruition, perhaps it sowed the seeds for the 'Deep Sea Canoe' mission movement that was initiated by Pacific Islanders in the late 1980s.[18]

At the Annual Field Conference at Brugam in the Sepik District in August 1972, Gil chaired a meeting at which important steps were taken towards the autonomy of the Sepik SSEC churches. He presented a Constitution and Church structure with a National Council and four District Associations. It was adopted after discussion, and the 110 village congregations adopted the name of SSEC (PNG) establishing fraternal links with the SSEC (Solomon Islands).[19] Plans were made to launch new church planting initiatives in the palm oil plantations in Cape Hoskins, New Britain. CLTC graduates were then among the significant leaders appointed for the Church and Bible School.[20] While CLTC training was providing for the younger generation, Gil was also concerned to see older senior national leaders – 'the proven men of faith' – given the opportunities of specialised training. He proposed that each year for the next five years a selected number of these leaders participate in carefully prepared leadership seminars at CLTC and other courses in Australia. 'The deeper insights provided by these training courses will equip the senior Pastors to give a true biblical direction for the young church during the difficult and turbulent days of early independence.'[21]

In 1975 Gil reported in *Not in Vain*:

> During the last three years, I have made a number of visits to the SSEM work in the Sepik District of Papua New Guinea. Resulting from these visits, prayerful in-depth studies have taken place on the part of the missionaries and national church leaders to determine

---

18. Gordon Griffiths, 'Update on the SSEM Part of the Story', Email, 24 January 2017, 3.
19. It was both national and expatriate missionaries from the SSEC Solomon Islands who planted the SSEC in PNG.
20. Gilbert J McArthur, 'New Guinea Churches - An Historic Moment', *Not in Vain*, December 1972, 2, 3, SSEM Archives.
21. McArthur, 'New Wineskins for New Wine', 3–6.

an overall indigenous church strategy that will provide for real spiritual growth and evangelistic outreach.

The first things that had to be done were to develop the Church Constitution, set up District Associations, determine the place and function of the pastoral ministry, define a culturally relevant structure for the church, and agree upon a meaningful role for its leadership cadre. We are thankful to the Lord for His gracious leading in all these things, now bringing us to the point where the identity and function of the national church has been clearly established.

Parallel with this, a great deal of prayerful assessment has been necessary with a view to determining the place and function of the SSEM as a continuing mission identity in the Sepik. In September 1974, at the General Conference of the SSEC in Brugam, and at subsequent meetings of the Church Council, it was clearly and positively enunciated by the young church that the mission and its missionaries are needed for a long time to come. A basis of separate identity and responsibility, together with a definite framework of 'partnership in the work of the Gospel' was established.

Arising from the above, the SSEM has been invited by the SSEC to assume immediate development of, and operational responsibility for, the following programme of *Sepik Advance*.[22]

The report specified the areas where the mission would take this 'operational responsibility'. This included outreach to various unreached peoples of the Sepik, medical, women's work, child welfare, village pastor training, Bible training programs, literacy work, a special education program for young people to take them to Form IV level, and agricultural training. It was indicated that the SSEM Field Headquarters and Home Base, would 'undergird and coordinate' these programs.[23] Considering the broad nature of these assigned 'mission' functions, questions might be raised about the responsibility of the SSEC churches themselves, and how the partnership relationship actually worked out in practice in these areas of ministry. It is difficult to answer those questions without access to historical data from the actual situation in the Sepik. But Gil initiated

---

22. Gilbert J McArthur, 'Sepik Advance', *Not in Vain*, March 1975, 9, 10, SSEM Archives.
23. McArthur, 'Sepik Advance', 10.

his vision for expanding the ministry of SSEC into other areas of PNG. The same edition of *Not in Vain* that contained the *Sepik Advance* details, also reported:

> Dr and Mrs McArthur have established an SSEM Regional Office in Lae. Dr McArthur will be helping the Sepik field in the development of the programme as outlined in this issue and will also spend considerable time this year in the Solomon Islands. It is hoped, that, at a later date he will be able to present a programme of Solomon Island Advance.[24]

But a *Solomon Island Advance Report* as such never appeared. The situation in the SSEC in the Solomon Islands was quite different to that in the Sepik. Their church was more mature, their structure had been in place since 1964, and the leadership of the church was in the capable hands of gifted national leaders. Indeed, it is clear that there were some rising tensions between the expatriate missionaries, the SSEM, and some national church leaders. It appears that Gil's influence in the Solomon Island SSEC was in moderating church/mission leadership tensions, encouraging and developing the national leaders, and opening opportunities for sharing their spiritual vitality with other churches across the Pacific.

Alliance Training Association of the Solomon Islands

In 1976 Gil was also responsible for establishing the Alliance Training Association of the Solomon Islands, a business company with similar objectives to ATA in PNG that was born out of Gil's time at CLTC.[25] The aims of ATASI were to free the SSEC from the need to be involved in commercial activities, provide training for Islanders in business and financial enterprises, and help fund the ministries of SSEC. In the following years, the relationship between ATASI and the SSEC did not remain as strong as Gil had hoped, and later became more and more challenging. This may have been due in part to the fact that a person who was an 'outsider' to SSEC was brought in to develop ATASI and did not fully understand the importance of the relationship with the SSEC. While ATASI did provide ministry funding to the SSEC, the tensions increased to the point where, following the visit of the SSEM Chairman to the Solomon Islands in 1985, he expressed the view that the SSEC should 'leave ATASI to go its own way'.[26] Similar relational tensions also gradually

---

24. McArthur, 'Sepik Advance', 9.
25. Gil was also still very much involved in ATA PNG as the Executive Director.

developed between ATA and CLTC in PNG, following the move of ATA off the CLTC campus to operate as an independent company.

Vision for a Pacific Training Institute

In Gil's complex involvements during this period, we have noted that he resigned as Executive Director of SSEM in March 1976 but remained a director until he retired from the SSEM Board in 1982. He continued his involvement with the Pacific Leaders' Fellowship and in 1986 the SSEM appointed him as Special Ministries Director, and unanimously approved his emerging vision to establish the SSEM Headquarters and a Pacific Leaders' Training Institute (PTI) at Laurieton, near where he was now living. This new vision developed out of Gil's experience with Pacific leaders, and his passion to continue to equip them for the challenges they faced. In addition, the decline of the PLF due to funding issues for travel, and Gil's resignation from World Vision in 1988, were also catalysts for this new project. He hoped his PTI plan would enable him to continue involvement in training Pacific island leaders, as well as developing strong, independent, self-reliant, self-determining and self-propagating island churches.[27]

In November 1986, Aubrey Coster, a Christian landowner at Laurieton NSW and a friend of Gil's, believed he was directed to offer some of his best land to the Lord. As a result of his contact with Gil, and Gil's new vision to provide advanced training for Christian leaders from across the whole Pacific world, he 'donated a beautiful 140-acre site to the SSEM on which it is proposed to establish a Leadership Training Centre and Mission Headquarters… Just half an hour's drive from Port Macquarie on the western side of North Brother Mountain, the location was ideal for the planned facilities.'[28] It was only after a long period of uncertainty, heart searching and prayer that the SSEM Directors had agreed to the move to Laurieton in 1986.[29]

---

26. South Sea Evangelical Mission, 'South Sea Evangelical Mission Management Committee Meeting Minutes', 27 September 1985, Melbourne School of Theology Archives.
27. South Sea Evangelical Mission, 'South Sea Evangelical Mission Management Committee Meeting Minutes', 27 September 1985.
28. South Sea Evangelical Mission, 'Only the Best for God', *Not in Vain*, November 1986, 2, SSEM Archives.
29. South Sea Evangelical Mission, 'South Sea Evangelical Mission Director's Meeting Minutes', 15 July 1986, Melbourne School of Theology Archives. The proposal indicated that the development of the site at a cost of $170,000, would result in a saleable asset of $3.25 million.

The Executive Secretary of SSEM, Ross Carlyon, wrote in his reasoned recommendation of the PTI proposal to SSEM supporters, 'Ideally, such training should take place as close as possible to the trainee's home. However, there will be the need for a number of SSEC leaders to come overseas to find the level and type of training required.'[30]

In the SSEM *Not in Vain* in May 1987, Gil answered the question 'Why a PTI in Australia?'

The aims of this Institute will be:

1. To bring together men and women, in positions of responsibility and influence from the nations of the Pacific Basin, for a semester programme of leadership and administration education, in the context of an integrated experience of prayer, Christian spirituality, and Holistic community development.

2. To conduct occasional seminars, retreats, and workshops of shorter duration around specific themes relevant to contemporary life and service.

3. To provide a centre of Christian renewal where individual persons may come for periods of varying duration for personal reflection, study and prayer in a setting of global ministry.

Continue to pray with us for God's blessing on this mighty venture.[31]

Gil's retirement from consulting work with World Vision in 1988 meant he could live in his Lake Cathie home and give himself to PTI programs for Pacific leaders, together with co-ordination of the PLF.[32] The official opening of the facilities of the PTI took place on 25 September 1988. By this time, through the sacrificial giving and hard work of many supporters of SSEM, staff houses, a meeting room and accommodation for leaders had been completed. Visitors from many places within Australia joined with Pacific Island representatives among whom were Sir Peter Kenilorea, the Deputy Prime Minister of the Solomon Islands, Rev Maika Bovoro, a Fijian Church leader who was on the staff of the Bimbadeen College, and Pastor Ossie Cruse, representing Aboriginal

---

30. Ross Carlyon, 'Evangelism and Church Building', *Not in Vain*, November 1986, 2, 3, SSEM Archives.
31. Gilbert J McArthur, 'Why a P.T.I. in Australia?', *Not in Vain*, May 1987, SSEM Archives.
32. South Sea Evangelical Mission, 'South Sea Evangelical Mission Director's Meeting Minutes', 24 July 1987.

Christians. The official opening was followed by the first leadership course.³³

There were, however, those who did not fully agree with 'Gil's new brain child', as Ray Laird later described it.³⁴ They expressed their concerns about the lack of consultation on the project, the foreignness of the site from the Pacific context, the distance from an Australian international airport, the cost of travel into Australia for the young churches, the need for suitable teaching staff who could establish and teach the curriculum, the overall cost of training in Australia and whether such training should use the best of Pacific national leaders as the key facilitators. Other agencies in the Pacific, such as Development Associates International, CLTC and some denominations were developing similar programs for more advanced leadership training that were more directly contextualised in the Pacific.

Will Renshaw recalls that when Gil took him to the top of the hill overlooking Laurieton and outlined his plans, he asked Gil, 'Aren't you reversing the principle of training people in their own culture as was done at CLTC?' Will says: 'I can't recall his answer, but I knew he was fixed on the vision he had, probably because of the way the land had been provided.'³⁵ Gil's PTI vision does seem to reflect a change in his earlier strong view that leadership development ought to take place in the participants' traditional cultural context.³⁶

John Tanner, Chairman of the SSEM Board, sensed that the establishment of the PTI was 'a bit patronising' in that the underlying message to the Pacific leaders seemed to be 'if you want excellence in leadership training, then you need to come here to Australia.'³⁷ In the period that followed, it did not attract strong support from the Pacific churches and leaders.

It seems that one of Gil's weaknesses was the way he moved from one role to the next, without trying to continue within a ministry he had established if that involved working alongside or under someone he had once led or mentored. This pattern worked well for him until he became

---

33. Pacific Training Institute, 'The Official Opening', *Pacific Training Institute Newsletter*, Volume 1, No 5, n.d, 1. Will Renshaw Personal Archives.
34. Ray Laird, 'An Era of Change', *Not in Vain*, December 1990, SSEM Archives. Referred to in an email from Gordon Griffiths.
35. Will Renshaw, 'The Mission – Last Section', Email, 20 October 2017, 1, 2.
36. Renshaw, 'The Mission – Last Section', 2.
37. Tanner, 'Re Dr Gilbert McArthur'.

older. In the early years after leaving CLTC he did have regular influence as a Council member, but he did not really stay closely engaged with the growing child he had left behind. Was he, in fact, creating a new ministry for his own needs instead of facing the need to transition to a new pattern of relationship with the agencies already involved? Did he feel that he could only work in situations where he was the chief organiser? A leader needs to learn to continue working with those he has thrust into leadership trusting them to take his 'brain children' to new levels. John Hitchen believes it is the difference between a Paul and Barnabas leadership style… 'and maybe why in Acts 2 and Joel it says "young men will see visions, but the old men are to dream dreams".[38] Dreams need others to implement them. Visions can be implemented only if you have the energy at full strength.'[39] It seemed to some of Gil's contemporaries that the PTI concept was out of touch with the dynamics of mission at the time.

Despite all of this Gil held tenaciously to his vision for the PTI. In 1989, at a gathering on the PTI campus at Laurieton, following the Federal Parliamentary Christian Prayer Breakfast in Canberra and a Leadership Seminar at Laurieton, Gil asked:

> The question now is, where do we go from here? The overall picture is, that in the fellowship of kindred spirits we have been led to embrace the wider world of Christian encounter. The flow on from Canberra and the Pacific Training Institute will have its issue by the development of 'Leaders Retreats'. This will provide the opportunity for members of the Parliamentary Christian Fellowship to reach out across the Pacific and fellowship with their political peers. These Fellowship Forums will also provide for a mix of significant voices that, be they white, black or brindle, they will be brothers and sisters together in Christ and who by the indwelling of the Holy Spirit, have discovered the wonder, the glory of a cross-fertilisation of life and purpose for the work of the Kingdom… May I then suggest to you that 'the Lord enabling us' we will covenant to meet together annually on this campus of the Pacific Training Institute, with the view to strengthening our fellowship links with our Pacific Island brethren, and also our Canberra Parliamentary

---

38. Joel 2:28, Acts 2:17,18.
39. John Hitchen, 'Part Two: The Mission', Email, 4 October 2017, 3. In this email John raises the question about a possible weakness in Gil's leadership in his later years. His comments, with which I agree form the basis of these paragraphs.

> Fellowship Groups… and we may therefore dare to believe that these encounters of life touching life, and heart responding to heart, will continue to enrich our respective ministries within the wider fellowship of South East Asia and the Pacific Islands.[40]

Due to his declining health Gil retired from his position as SSEM Special Ministries Director in 1988. The SSEM Board and Chairman Ray Laird faced a very difficult situation when due to his deteriorating health, Gil was unable to continue to lead the PTI:

> The Mission had taken the step to set up the PTI in Laurieton. With the site and the buildings in place and all ready to roll, and with no Gil to give the lead to the development of his project, my reaction was, who could do this? Frankly, I could not identify anyone in SSEM as suitable for it. I was exceptionally busy at the time, still Principal of Tahlee Bible College, finishing my MA with Newcastle University, and moving to become the Principal of the Bible College of South Australia in Adelaide in the following year or so. The only person I thought might handle the task was John Tanner: I think he was Principal of Onepus [SSEC Bible College on Malaita, Solomon Islands] at the time… In the event the Mission decided to go ahead with a make-shift appointment – no condemnation of the person who was appointed. Very few people could do what Gil had in mind, and our network had failed to bring up any other choice.[41]

Despite the serious attempts to carry on the vision of the PTI, without a suitable inspired leader and support from the Pacific churches, the SSEM decided that the PTI could not continue. John Tanner, who followed Ray as Chairman of SSEM had 'the terrible task of persuading the mission to sell Laurieton'.[42] It was subsequently purchased by New Tribes Mission for a Head Office and Training Base.

Was this the end of the remarkable SSEM story? It began in 1882, when a young girl named Florence Young was burdened for the Pacific Island cane workers on her brother's cane plantation in Queensland and dreamt of the day a mission movement would spread across the Pacific Islands. In 1904 she arrived in the Solomon Islands to begin the work.[43] Now, in the 1980s the SSEM Directors were recognising that

---

40. Gilbert J McArthur, 'Address to the Gathered Community at the Pacific Training Institute at Laurieton', September 1989, McArthur Family Archives.
41. Ray Laird, 'Gil McArthur', 13 January 2017, 2.
42. Tanner, 'Re: Dr Gilbert McArthur'.
43. Pioneers of Australia, 'Our Story', Brochure, n.d., 7, 8.

with the establishment of the SSEC in the Solomon Islands and PNG, SSEM missionary numbers and funds were depleting. Chairman Ray Laird observed in 1990,

> The churches have come of age and are quite capable of managing their own affairs. Then, too, these churches have tasted revival. Therefore growth has accelerated. Problems peculiar to revivals have reared their heads and cast church leaders on the Lord in a way nothing else could do. This means they have outstripped strategies for growth and moved into advanced phases of development before normally expected. Under these circumstances a decline in missionary numbers and missionary control had become a necessity. The Board has steadfastly pursued a philosophy of mission which would not hinder the development of the leadership of the churches. We did not rush to supply personnel at the merest suggestion of the churches. We asked them to pray and think long and hard before acceding to their requests.[44]

The question for the SSEM Board now was 'where to send new cross-cultural workers?' The mission changed its name to South Pacific Partners and the directors explored potential new opportunities in New Caledonia, French Polynesia, Philippines, Vanuatu, India and Nauru. But nothing seemed to clearly come into focus.[45] But in 1997 a new and wide door opened in the sovereign purposes of God in the merger of South Pacific Partners (SSEM) and APCM with a young emerging mission in the USA. This gave birth to a new international mission thrust to reach unreached peoples around the world. This new advance began not with a single woman, but with a husband, wife and four children totally committed to the vision God placed on their hearts, and *very* significantly, their contact with Gil McArthur. But this leads into a new chapter in the story.

---

44. Laird, 'An Era of Transition', 1.
45. South Sea Evangelical Mission, 'SSEM Annual Conference Minutes', 1984, Melbourne School of Theology Archives.

LIVE IN TENTS — BUILD ONLY ALTARS

PACIFIC TRAINING INSTITUTE

KEEPING YOU UP-TO-DATE WITH OUR ACTIVITIES... PLANS... PEOPLE AND PROGRESS

A MINISTRY OF THE SOUTH SEA EVANGELICAL MISSION

VOL. 1. No. 5

THE OFFICIAL OPENING

With only weeks to go, the Pacific Training Institute is coming close to completion ready for the official opening on Saturday, 24th and Sunday, 25th of September.

This weekend will mark the beginning of a new chapter in the history of the work of SSEM, and will bring together many of you who have shared this vision with us, having prayerfully and practically given us your support, for which we are most thankful.

Visitors from many places within Australia are expected to join with visitors from Pacific Island countries. Church leaders from the Solomon Islands and Papua New Guinea will be attending the official opening and they will be the very first to participate in the initial course of the P.T.I. immediately following the opening.

The two days set aside for the opening will be a time of praise and thanksgiving to our God as we acknowledge His goodness in the provision of these lovely facilities which will be used for the building up and encouragement of our Pacific Island brothers and sisters. It will also be a time when the purposes of the Pacific Training Institute's program can be outlined more fully.

It will be a privilege to have Sir Peter Kenilorea, the Deputy Prime Minister of the Solomon Islands; Maika Bovoro, Fijian Church leader and currently on the staff of Bimbadeen College; and Ossie Cruse, representing Aboriginal Christians, as special guests taking part in the Commissioning Service on the Sunday afternoon.

We eagerly look forward to sharing this time of celebration with you and anticipate that the opening of these facilities will be a time of fellowship and great encouragement in the Lord's work.

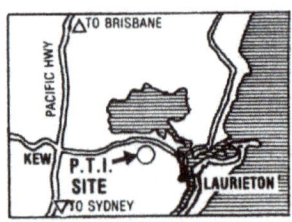

With the initial leadership course immediately following the official opening it has been imperative that the dormitory accommodation be completed in good time. A volunteer worker has been constructing the cupboards and desks for each of the bedrooms while the other rooms within the building have been moving towards completion too.

During August it is planned that another team from Mobile Mission Maintenance will come to help with the work. Progress on the administration/classroom building is temporarily at a standstill until the arrival of this team.

The third week of July saw the Bitupave trucks eventually able to tar seal the roads and parking bays on the property. The ever present rain had caused several delays to this work and also meant that prepatory work was damaged to some extent which needed repairing before sealing. However the roads now are well protected from any future rain damage.

The sewerage works are now all but complete, for which we are extremely grateful to council. The pumping station, the final piece of work has been built and is just waiting on the electrical system to be fitted.

Continue to pray with us for the granting of our request to reduce the speed limit along Kew Road, something we, along with many other members of the local community, believe is necessary in the interests of public safety.

13

THE NEW DOOR AND THE FINAL CALL
1987 – 1994

*I have fought the good fight,
I have finished the race,
I have kept the faith.
Now there is in store for me the crown of righteousness,
which the Lord the righteous Judge, will award me on that day –
and not only to me, but also to all who have longed for his appearing.*[1]

It has been said that 'there is no best leadership style… but different styles of leadership that are called for in different situations, at different stages in an organisation's life, or even different periods of a leader's life.'[2] In the later years of his vision for the PTI, perhaps Gil could not see how a passion for growing leaders for the Pacific churches and mobilising them into mission could take a different path to the one he was proposing. Despite Gil's failing health and the lack of a suitable person to progress the work of the PTI, the sovereign Lord was already at work opening a new door for an even wider influence than Gil could have imagined.

The New Door

In December 1952 American Evangelist Billy Graham visited the US Forces fighting in the Korean War. It was an eleven-day visit, but there was only one meeting when he addressed the Marines fighting on the front lines. Billy later reflected on the events of that cold Korean morning:

> I will never forget that first meeting at the front. Many of these men had been on patrol duty the night before… many had travelled

---
1. 2 Timothy 4:7,8.
2. Wesley Granberg-Michaelson, *Leadership From Inside Out - Spirituality and Organizational Change* (New York: The Crossroad Publishing Company, 2004), 11.

on foot from their trenches and bunkers to attend the service…
Everyone had his rifle and was in full fighting gear. They were
extremely responsive and interested in the message. Not once did
I use any humour or any emotional stories. There was no need.
These men were ready for the Word of God.

When I gave the invitation, more than one-third of the men stood
to their feet in front of their buddies to accept Jesus Christ as
Saviour. Many were weeping unashamedly, men who had faced
death just hours before; big strong, tough Marines, weeping
because of their sins and need of a Saviour.

Never in my ministry have I preached with more liberty or power.
The Spirit of God seemed to fall on that meeting.[3]

One 21 year old Marine was gripped by Billy's Gospel message. Following a bloody-battle two weeks earlier, he had been struggling with the question, 'I am licensed to kill, but am I ready to die?' He later told of the significance of that meeting:

With burning intensity, [Billy's] eyes searched the crowd as he asked
if we were ready to meet God. He seemed to be looking at and
talking directly to me. Up to this point in my life, I had considered
myself a Christian. Growing up, I attended Baptist, Methodist,
Presbyterian, and Episcopal churches, prayed whenever I needed
to, and lived a good life. None of that seemed to matter now.
I knew I was not ready to meet my Creator. I was lost and in need
of salvation, and none of my good works could earn it for me.[4]

The young marine stood in response to Billy's challenge and surrendered his life to Christ. His name was Ted Fletcher. Discipled through the Navigators program Ted began to understand that God had given him a new mission in life – he was now licensed to serve the living God. Following the war cease-fire, Ted returned home to Pittsburgh, Pennsylvania and studied business administration. In 1956 he married Peggy Close. Ted became a successful area sales representative with Mobil Oil, and in 1963 was employed by the prestigious Dow Jones

---

3. Billy Graham quoted by Ted Fletcher (*When God Comes Calling – A Journey of Faith*, 10, 11) from *I Saw Your Sons at War: The Korean Diary of Billy Graham*, Billy Graham Evangelistic Association, 1953, no page number.
4. Fletcher, *When God Comes Calling*, 8, 9.

Ted and Peggy Fletcher with J Oswald Sanders at CLTC 1979

and Company who owned *The Wall Street Journal*. Ted was appointed a District Manager and later National Sales Manager.[5]

Since the mid-1950s, Ted and Peggy felt a strong call to missionary work among unreached tribal peoples. But their applications and enquiries had met dead ends and discouragement: you are too old, three years seminary is required, you have too many children, just stay at home in your good job, pray and send others. It seemed the door was closed – perhaps locked! But in Revelation 3 the risen Christ says to the Church at Philadelphia, 'These are the words of him who is holy and true, who holds the key of David. What he opens no one can shut, and what he shuts no one can open.' This is possibly the basis for the popular saying among some Christians 'When God closes a door he always opens a window.' To this some add, 'but you need to stop looking at the closed door and look around to find the open window, or a new door.[6]

While based in Detroit Michigan in 1968, Ted and Peggy attended a Basic Youth Conflict Seminar. Ted overheard two staff discussing

---

5. Fletcher, *When God Comes Calling*, 10, 11, 26-31.
6. Woodrow Kroll, 'When God Closes a Door He Always Opens a Window', n.d., https://www.christianquotes.info/images/woodrow-kroll-quote-closing-a-door/#axzz56HgD4Q90.

who might host their Australian speaker, and enthusiastically offered accommodation.[7] The speaker was Gil McArthur. Peggy recalls:

> After hosting him in our home, we became interested in Gil's work and ministry. Ted had a special burden for tribal people and was also interested in supporting national leaders in ministry. Soon Gil and Ted became good friends… As Gil came for visits to the US, we became a contact of hospitality for him. He stayed with us many times over these early years… He became a mentor to Ted in many ways, and Gil also recognized a special gifting in Ted and the ability to move through different circles than even Gil. On his visits with us Ted tried to connect Gil with people who might be interested in funding his ministry vision at CLTC.[8]

Ted describes Gil's influence as they struggled to find a door to become involved in cross cultural ministry to unreached peoples. Ted had wondered 'Could someone who was rejected by several mission boards start his own?'[9] He recalls:

> God often sends influential people across our paths at pivotal cross-roads in our lives… Dr Gilbert McArthur was another. Gil was Executive Director of the South Sea Evangelical Mission in Australia and a brilliant visionary. When he visited our home in 1968, he told us about the Christian Leaders' Training College in the highlands of Papua New Guinea – 400 acres of almost uninhabitable swampland that he and others transformed into the premier training facility of the South Pacific. Gil was CLTC's first Principal and was instrumental in raising funds to keep it going. He wouldn't say it about himself, of course, but he was like a David Livingstone of the South Pacific – a pioneer who blazed paths that others followed. Peggy and I decided to sponsor a student to attend the Christian Leaders' Training College, a young man named Silas Erikali.
>
> Gil encouraged me to refuse to let go of my dream to become a missionary myself. He was a lone and welcome voice in the midst of many who were urging me to forget my dream and instead stick to making money to fund missions. The Lord knew Gil was the right one to break through to me as he confronted me with one of

---

7. Fletcher, John, 'Gil McArthur - as Told by Peggy Fletcher to Carin LeRoy', 1.
8. Fletcher, John, 'Gil McArthur - as Told by Peggy Fletcher to Carin LeRoy', 1, 2.
9. Fletcher, *When God Comes Calling*, 49.

Ted Fletcher with CLTC Leaders 1979
L-R: J Oswald Sanders, Gil, Len Buck, Ted Fletcher and David Price

his favourite Scriptures: 'We spend our years as a tale that is told' (Psalm 90:9 KJV).

'Ted, how are you writing the story of your life?' Gil asked me. 'What is the next chapter that God might have for you?'

His question startled me, and in the weeks that followed, God wouldn't let me forget it. One May morning in 1968, I was alone in our Detroit, Michigan, living room reading my Bible, and when I came to Psalm 2:8, I stopped: 'Ask of me, and I will make the nations your inheritance, the ends of the earth your possession.'

The words had such a terrific authority that I knew God was speaking directly to me. I wrote in my Bible next to verse 8, 'God's promise to me'. The words of course, were originally a promise to the Messianic King, Jesus, that the domain of His kingdom would someday extend around the world and include all the nations (or literally the 'peoples') of the earth. The missionary task – sharing the Gospel and making disciples – was how God the Father would give the nations to his Son.

I also took this verse as a promise to me, and I knew that through it God had come calling in my life. He was giving me a promise and asking me to trust only Him, because humanly speaking there was no mechanism for its fulfilment.

Yet nothing happened…[10]

---

10. Fletcher, *When God Comes Calling*, 43, 44.

It was to be a period of waiting and 'wilderness wanderings' for the next eight years. Gil's regular visits to the Presidential Prayer Breakfasts in Washington, together with other Australian mission leaders Len Buck, Bill Clack and Will Renshaw, brought continuing encouragement to Ted. He was responsible for the national sales of the prestigious *Wall Street Journal*, but the question he pondered night and day was, 'What difference does it make how many people read the *Wall Street Journal* as far as eternity is concerned?' Ted knew that he had to step out of his comfort zone. In December 1973, he resigned his position, and together with Peggy began the journey of faith which gave birth to a new mission agency, The World Evangelical Outreach, which later changed its name to Pioneers, 'to reflect the desire not to follow worn paths, but to blaze new ones.'[11]

Through Gil, the vision and passion of the 'missionary God' touched and challenged Ted and Peggy Fletcher at this vital point in their lives. God is still writing the amazing story that flowed from their availability to him as over the years Pioneers has rapidly grown to become one of the largest interdenominational mission agencies in the world (more of this story later). Ted, like Gil, was a man of vision and faith. Following Ted's sudden death in 2003, Peggy wrote:

> Three decades ago, when Ted and I answered God's call, we did so without the training, degrees, and experience that one would normally expect of someone who would start a new mission agency. We ventured down this path by faith, just two ordinary people with no idea where God would take us and no master plan to guide us. We clung solely to God's promises and did not doubt that He would bless our humble efforts to be faithful. Today, I marvel at all the Lord has done, shaping the original vision, increasing the numbers of workers, and expanding the work in ways we never dreamed possible. Winston Churchill once said: 'To each there comes in his or her lifetime a special moment when they are tapped on the shoulder and offered the opportunity to do a very special thing, unique to them and fitted to their talent given by the Lord, and the strength to do it. What a tragedy if that moment finds them unprepared or unqualified for that which could have been their finest hour.'[12]

---

11. Fletcher, *When God Comes Calling*, 77.
12. Fletcher, *When God Comes Calling*, 147.

Gil was not to know that, in the sovereign working of God, his mentoring of Ted and Peggy would open the new door for the day in 1997 when Pioneers USA would merge with South Pacific Partners (SSEM) and the Asia Pacific Christian Mission (formerly UFM Australia), creating an international agency (Pioneers International) which would send people to the ends of the earth in gospel ministry to unreached peoples. Gil's hopes and dreams for further leadership training were thereby redirected into even more fruitful pathways for declaring the glory of God to the nations.

The Final Call – 3 February 1994

Gil's son Paul recalls that in his final years Gil regretted that he had not been able to find the time to write the story of his life and experiences. He had been too busy living it.[13]

His last public preaching engagement was at the Clemton Park Baptist Church 50th Reunion which he attended with Pat in May 1990. It became obvious to close family that he was having trouble in certain situations being able to get his thoughts together, especially public speaking, praying and reading. At first Gil thought it was a side effect of the Glaucoma treatment he was undertaking, but after assessment in July 1992 it was confirmed that he had Alzheimer's disease. After this his health seriously declined. For a man who was such a deep thinker and powerful communicator, alive with energy, it is difficult to imagine how hard this must have been for him, his family and friends. He personally expressed that he felt useless and of no value. Ray Laird describes the deep anguish many felt about Gil's decline:

> It was a sad day when I discovered that Gil was a very sick man...
> I became aware of how critical his ailment was in the late 1980s.
> It was at an SSEM Board Meeting, when discussing various items on the agenda. I had noticed that, most unlike Gil, he had hardly said a word all night. Then suddenly, out of the blue he burst into a rambling speech, totally irrelevant to the item on hand, about some incident some thirty years before. That, I thought, is the end of Gil, this servant of God with a brilliant mind. He had gone. I went home and I wept. I still do at the memory of it. The treasure of Melanesia, the dear man who had given his life to those people, had developed some form of Alzheimer's. That great psyche had become silent,

---

13. McArthur, Paul, 'Gil McArthur Memories'.

Gil and Pat in later days

no more on this earth to share his plans for the next advance of the work of the Mission.[14]

Pat was his loving and faithful carer during his illness right until the end, with family as involved as they could be, providing relief for Pat, and valuing time with Gil. Paul remembers it was like all the 'heap of ambition and ego', the driving energy that was behind his life and work, was now gone. What was left was just the 'real Gil'. Paul, along with Robyn, Jenny and Wendy spent time with their Dad in conversation, playing the guitar, going for walks, and reading the Psalms to calm him and instil hope when he became agitated.[15]

The family were all together for Christmas, 1993. Soon after, Gil contracted pneumonia, and at the end of January was moved into a Salvation Army High Care facility. He was only there for nine days. It was on Pat's birthday, February 3, that Gil finished the final chapter in his earthly story. At 4.23pm Gil moved his tent one last time, into

---

14. Laird, 'Gil McArthur', 2.
15. McArthur, Paul. 'Gil McArthur Memories'.

the presence of the Lord he loved, served and proclaimed so well. His daughter Jenny said, 'God in amazing ways cared for Gil and prepared the way for him to go from us. As in life, God's plan and direction were worked out in Gil's death'.[16] Finally leaving his 'earthly tent' he received the promise of an eternal dwelling in heaven.

> *For we know that if the earthly tent we live in is destroyed, we have a building from God, an eternal house in heaven, not built by human hands. Meanwhile we groan, longing to be clothed instead with our heavenly dwelling, because when we are clothed, we will not be found naked. For while we are in this tent, we groan and are burdened, because we do not wish to be unclothed but to be clothed instead with our heavenly dwelling, so that what is mortal may be swallowed up by life. Now the one who has fashioned us for this very purpose is God, who has given us the Spirit as a deposit, guaranteeing what is to come.*[17]

Member of the Order of Australia 1986

---

16. Jenny Fitzsimons, 'Re: Gilbert McArthur's Last Days'. Information for the above paragraphs was provided by Telephone Interview with Gil's daughter Jenny.
17. 2 Corinthians 5:1-5.

Recognition

Gil's influential life and unique ministry was widely recognised in the Christian and broader community across the Pacific.

In 1971, in recognition of his pioneering work in the establishment of CLTC, Gil was awarded an LLD Doctor of Laws by Wheaton College USA.

In June 1986, he was made a Member of the Order of Australia (AM) by the Australian Government 'for service to the community, particularly in Papua New Guinea and the Pacific Islands'.[18]

In October 1986, Gil was presented with a Community Service Award by the Mayor of the Municipality of Hastings NSW where he lived, 'in recognition of a lifetime dedicated to holistic community development and leadership advancement in the Australia-Pacific region'.[19]

In the Queen's PNG Honours List of January 1987, he was awarded the Order of the British Empire (General Division) 'for community service and emergency relief work by the Government of Papua New Guinea'.[20]

The McArthur Family Archives contain many letters of congratulations for these awards from prominent Christian and Community leaders from around the world – powerful evidence that his influence was international in his impact upon so many.

On 3 February 1994, as he finally crossed from time into eternity, Gil received the most significant affirmation of all from the Lord Jesus Christ he so faithfully and passionately served. 'Well done, good and faithful servant.'

What Chapter are you Writing in your Story Book of Life?

One of the few things Gil did write in his later years was a one-page testimony, *A Fellowship of the Committed Ones*, which provides an eloquent conclusion to his 'twilight chapters', and his continuing passion to serve in mission with Pat alongside him to the very end:

---

18. See the Australian Roll of Honour Database.
19. This was the Municipal Council in which Gil lived at Lake Cathie, NSW. Australia – today known as Port MacQuarie-Hastings Municipal Council.
20. Authors Unknown, Various Articles, n.d. circa –1986, 1987, McArthur Family Archives. Information for this paragraph was sourced from various articles in the McArthur Family Archives which did not provide details of the publication or dates.

THE NEW DOOR AND THE FINAL CALL

> My story-book of life became rich and wonderful, as by the Grace of God, I began to write chapters of theology, anthropology and linguistics – all of which equipped me, together with my missionary colleagues, to open up the hinterland of Dutch New Guinea and bring the message of the transforming Power of the Resurrected Christ to thousands of unreached cannibalistic tribes-people, who at that time, had never seen a white man.
>
> How happy I am that those missionary chapters are written down in my personal story-book of life, and thereby written down in Heaven.
>
> In June 1988, my wife and I will celebrate 42 years of married life. We have been blessed with five children and fourteen grand-children, and are now writing the 'twilight chapters' of our story-book of life – and all these rich chapters of life and meaning are ours forever, why? Because in our early days we discovered the Fatherhood of God, the Lordship of Christ, the indwelling of the Holy Spirit, and the life enriching fellowship of our brothers and sisters in the Fellowship of Mission.
>
> The above testimony of the past requires for my wife Pat and I to affirm our availability to SSEM/SSEC for the development of the strategic ministries of mission that we believe the Lord will raise up through the medium of the Pacific Training Institute at Laurieton. We dare to believe that the Lord will provide young, well qualified persons to lead the Mission and National Churches into the next century. However, while we wait for these 'chosen ones' to emerge, we oldies would, as the Lord enables, declare our commitment to stand in the gap wherever necessary.[22]

Gil did not believe in 'retirement'. His God-given vision and burden to grow and equip leaders never lost its motivating fire as a critical strategy in the mission of God to the nations.

The personal question for you, the reader, to prayerfully ponder is – what chapter are you writing today with God in the story-book of your life? Is the Lord calling you to step out in faith, take new steps of obedience, and write a new chapter for the blessing of others and the glory of God?

---

21. McArthur, 'The Fellowship of the Committed Ones'. The last lines indicate Gil's life remained on the altar of complete surrender and commitment to the will of God – whatever it takes!

Gil McArthur – His Story

Part Three

The Legacy

Kingdom servant leaders are much more interested
in the growth and fulfilment of others than their own.

*'For what is our hope, our joy, or the crown
in which we will glory in the presence of our Lord Jesus
when he comes?
Is it not you?
Indeed, you are our glory and joy.'
(1 Thessalonians 2:19,20)*

Gil's life and leadership opened new territory
and charted new pathways in grappling with the bigger issues
around mission in his day.
In so doing his legacy remains in the lives and ministries
of those he touched and influenced.

14
THE LEGACY OF A LEADER

*Therefore, everyone who hears these words of mine
and puts them into practice
is like a wise man who built his house on the rock.
The rain came down, the streams rose, and the winds blew
and beat against that house,
yet it did not fall, because it had foundations on the rock.*[1]

At the end of his great Sermon on the Mount, the Lord Jesus Christ contrasts building on rock or building on sand. Build we must – our characters, ministries, destiny and legacy. Gil McArthur left a legacy built upon the rock of Christ, his Word, his call and his life of obedience in mission empowered by the Holy Spirit. That legacy has a diverse and continuing impact today.

A leader's legacy is established by leaving something behind of enduring influence on people, organisations, or ministries. A legacy may be material or immaterial, positive or negative. This discussion will focus on the positive aspects of Gil's legacy. Like the rest of us, he was not without weaknesses and failure, but our purpose is to give thanks for the impact of his life for the Kingdom of God.

What do we mean by 'legacy'?

The very nature of leadership means that every responsible leader is driven by a desire to lead towards something better, leaving a legacy of influence for good. Essentially then, legacy for our purpose is about influence, enabling people to become all that God intends them to be and making a difference for the advance of the Kingdom purposes

---

1. Matthew 7:24, 25.

of God. It is not about the fame or fortune of the leader. In fact, in opening a discussion about legacy it is vital to note at this point that 'in leadership and in life nothing that we accomplish is singular. *No one ever got anything extraordinary done alone. A leader's legacy is the legacy of many*'.[2] Gil's life touched many who together with him saw God do something extraordinary.

It is helpful to differentiate at least three aspects of a leader's legacy:[3]

First, the leader's distinctive personality, spirituality, and character. It has been said that 'the life you lead is the legacy you leave'. Life expresses itself from the inside out: it starts with our worldview, values, allegiance and spiritual heartbeat.[4]

Second, the lasting influence on others. When discussing Gil's legacy with his son Paul, his response as quick as a flash was, 'Hands down, people are his legacy'.[5] There is no doubt that Gil's legacy lives on in the lives of those who were impacted (often quite radically) by God's Kingdom purposes through him.

Third, the lasting impact made in the birth and/or growth of the organisations and ministries in which the leader has been involved.

This threefold framework is helpful in reflecting on the legacy of Gil McArthur.

The Legacy of the Leader's Distinctive Spirituality and Character

It can be said that 'we are all children of our times'. Gil's conversion to Christ, his missionary preparation and his subsequent ministry took place in the decades from 1940 through to the late 1980s.

Part One of this book, 'Gil – the Man', highlights influences that were formative in his development as a person, his distinctive personality and growing faith and commitment to Christ. Those earlier observations flow through into this discussion about his legacy.

Part Two, 'Gil – the Mission' traces his ministry/missionary journey from departure for Dutch New Guinea in 1955 until his death in early 1994. In his missionary work Gil was impacted by and emulated the 'evangelical missionary spirituality' of his day. What does this mean?

---

2. James M. Kouzes and Barry Z. Posner, *A Leader's Legacy* (San Franciso: Jossey-Bass Publishers, 2006), 11. Emphasis added.
3. Although in reality, they are deeply interwoven.
4. James M. Kouzes and Barry Z. Posner, 'We lead from the inside out', *The Journal of Values Based Leadership*, 1, Winter/Spring (2008), Article 5.
5. McArthur, Paul, 'Re: Details about Gil McArthur', 16 October 2016.

A Google search on 'definition of spirituality' will result in over ten thousand hits! Some background perspectives are important in understanding the legacy of Gil's distinctive evangelical spirituality.

> Spirituality is not a word which would have been found on the lips of evangelicals until recently… Many would even question whether evangelicals have much to offer by way of spirituality. Evangelicalism appears to be such an activist faith that the essential characteristics of spirituality can too easily appear to be squeezed out. From a distance, it can look as if evangelical spirituality consists solely of the 'quiet time', a daily devotional time of Bible reading and prayer, before the Christian rushes out to get on with life. But there is much more to it than that, as, to take but one item, the concern for holiness, which has been such a major preoccupation of evangelicals down the centuries suggests.

> What is spirituality?… Spirituality has to do with the inner life, the vision of God, encountering God in mystery and devotion, mystical theology, contemplative prayer and loving knowledge. It is designed to bring the head and the heart together, to encourage a spiritual journey and to lead to spiritual formation.[6]

John Stott believes the two great distinguishing marks of evangelicals are that they are 'Bible people and Gospel people'.[7] Robert Johnston says, 'Evangelicals are people who are convinced that the gospel is to be experienced personally, defined biblically, and communicated passionately.'[8]

Derek Tidball, in concluding his book *Who are the Evangelicals?* outlines six key themes that are expressed in evangelical spiritual life and experience:

Grace – the word that captures the heart of evangelical spirituality, and which points to God's amazing love to underserving sinners in making salvation freely possible through the death of Christ on the cross.

---

6. Derek J. Tidball, *Who Are the Evangelicals? Tracing the Roots of Today's Movements* (London: Marshall Pickering, 1994), 196.
7. Tidball, *Who Are the Evangelicals?*, citing John Stott, 12, in *What is an Evangelical?* (London: Church Pastoral Aid Society, 1977).
8. Tidball, *Who Are the Evangelicals?*, citing Robert Johnson, 13, in 'American Evangelicalism: An Extended Family' in *The Variety of American Evangelicalism*, Eds Donald Dayton and Robert Johnson (Knoxville: University of Tennessee Press, 1991), 261.

Assurance – the confidence (not arrogance) based on God's grace (not human good works), that God accepts those who repent and believe in Christ as Saviour and Lord, and grants forgiveness of sins, and the gift of the Holy Spirit.

Holiness – the dying to self, and rising to live a new life in Christ, that is expressed in the experience of obedience to please and glorify God in all of life.

Bible – the inspired authoritative channel through which God continues to speak to people today, and how they listen to him and encounter him: the source of truth, nourishment, protection, direction, correction and life change.

Prayer – the vital connection of the Bible and Prayer expressed in personal and corporate prayers of adoration, confession, intercession, contemplation and supplication.

Obedience – the understanding that spirituality is about doing as well as being, expressed personally and in the body of Christ in holy living, evangelism and mission at home and overseas.[9]

Gil's 'evangelical spirituality' was certainly characterised by these six, but he would want a greater emphasis on mission:

Mission – the commitment to world mission because it is central to our understanding of God, the whole Bible, the Church, human history, and the ultimate future destiny of humanity. Believers, with the whole Church of Jesus Christ are called to participate in the mission of God, who is calling out a people for himself from among the nations of the world. The Gospel is God's good news for the whole world, and by his grace believers are sent to obey Christ's commission, to proclaim it by word and works to all peoples, and to make disciples of every nation. Christian mission is both a natural result of, and inherent in, authentic evangelical spirituality.

Historian David Bebbington helpfully identifies four primary characteristics of evangelicalism:

Conversionism: the belief that lives need to be transformed through a 'born-again' experience and a life-long process of transformation in following Jesus,

Activism: the expression and demonstration of the gospel in missionary and social reform ministries,

---

9. Tidball, *Who Are the Evangelicals?*, 197–205.

Biblicism: a high regard for, and obedience to the Bible as the ultimate authority,

Crucicentrism: a stress on the sacrifice of Jesus Christ on the cross making possible the redemption of humanity.

These distinctives and theological convictions define us – not political, social or cultural trends.[10]

All these insights combine to provide helpful background in understanding the evangelical heartbeat and context which shaped Gil's spirituality. It was an important aspect of the legacy he passed on to others. He was converted through the influence of his grandfather, a leader in the strong conservative Bible-based Brethren movement in Sydney, receiving much of his early biblical grounding in the Brethren movement. Later he was impacted by the ministry of J Oswald Sanders, the General Director of the Overseas Missionary Fellowship, and a leading evangelical missionary statesman of his day. It was through Sanders' ministry that Gil discerned God's call to missionary service. The Principal of the Baptist College in Sydney (now Morling College), where Gil trained for ministry was George Morling, another evangelical theologian and teacher who had a profound influence on Gil in his formative College days. Morling was:

> … possessed by a continuing aspiration for immediacy in his experience of God. He thirsted for holiness of life, made available by the work of Christ and applied by the Holy Spirit. It was this that drove him to a study of mystical theology and caused him sometimes to be styled a mystic… Many were attracted to him because they sensed spiritual reality in him and desired to share his secret.
>
> He was an excellent teacher, because he was able to communicate the excitement he felt for what he was teaching. He informed, but more than that, he inspired. He was convinced that theology had to be lived, not merely thought, that doctrine meant little unless it was experienced… He wrote in his Diary, 'there must be a very strong stand taken for doctrinal-experimental truth. I believe that God is calling me to this distinctive work both in College and church'. His particular theological emphases were the Holy Spirit, and the soul's union with Christ. These were the staple of his wider

---

10. National Association of Evangelicals, 'What Is an Evangelical?', 30 November 2016, http://nae.net/what-is-an-evangelical/.

public ministry. His ability as an inspirational Bible teacher was widely recognised. On numerous occasions he was a featured speaker at Keswick-type conventions… Though he stressed God's transcendence, he set over against it his conviction that God is to be seen as immanent, not only in Christ and in creation, but also in the church and the Christian. He was concerned that believers should know God in Christ indwelling them by his Spirit.[11]

Those who knew Gil well would testify that the passions and convictions of George Morling became very evident in Gil's life and ministry, and they became a legacy passed on to others in his sphere of influence over the years.

The Legacy of the Leader's Influence Upon Others

The Bible has many examples of the influence of leaders and the mentoring of younger leaders. Gil often spoke of the impact of 'life upon life'. One only has to think of Moses and Joshua, Elijah and Elisha, David and Jonathan, Jesus and the twelve and also the inner circle of Peter, James and John, or Barnabas and Paul, or Paul and Timothy, to mention only a few.

J Oswald Sanders, in his classic *Spiritual Leadership*, notes the legacy Paul imparted to the younger Timothy:

> Travelling with Paul would bring Timothy into contact with men of all kinds, men of stature, whose personalities and achievements would kindle in him a wholesome ambition. From his tutor, he learned how to meet triumphantly the crises which seemed routine in Paul's life and ministry. He was accorded the privilege of sharing the preaching. He was entrusted with establishing the group of Christians at Thessalonica and confirming them in the faith. Nor did he fail to justify this expression of confidence. Paul's exacting standards, high expectations and heavy demands served to bring out the best in Timothy and probably saved him from mediocrity.[12]

The survey of the ministry of Gil McArthur has shown clear evidence of his strong commitment to the development, growth and maturing of those he led. Before considering specific examples, we should highlight one all-embracing outstanding impact of Gil's life upon others. When

---

11. E. Ron Rogers, 'Morling, George Henry (1891-1974)', *Australian Dictionary of Evangelical Biography* (Evangelical History Association of Australia, 2004).
12. Sanders, *Spiritual Leadership*, 139.

asked the question *'Reflecting back, what do you think was the major impact of Gil's life upon you?'* there was normally one resounding response; *'It was Gil's vision and faith, and his capacity to inspire others to embrace the vision and strive for its fulfilment.'*[13]

The Legacy of Vision and Faith

Joshua Daimoi, the first Melanesian Principal of CLTC says:

> I believed and continue to believe that Dr McArthur was God's hand-picked man to establish the CLTC of Papua New Guinea and the South Pacific. Dr McArthur was a firm and clear-sighted visionary, full of faith and love to see Papua New Guinea become a God loving nation.[14]

Garth and Ruth Morgan (New Zealand) were impacted by Gil's vision in 1964:

> Gil had an amazing capacity to impact people with a vision. Gil's turn to speak came after seven other missionaries, all of whom were passionate about seeking something from over 1,600 convention attendees on Easter Sunday afternoon in 1964 at Ngaruawahia, NZ. In just three brief minutes, he shared the vision of the College, and seven of his future staff responded to his invitation.

> Gil so impacted us with his vision for the College and its development during the five years that we worked with him, that 50 years later, I still find myself reminding the present College Council members of the detailed 'plan' of the campus layout, that God gave Gil, as he stood on Vision Hill early in 1964![15]

Kay Liddle, New Zealand veteran Brethren missionary with CMML, who worked in association with Gil in PNG affirms: 'Gil McArthur was a man fully committed to God, with a big vision and a strong work ethic which drove him and others around him.'[16]

Don Doull who served with Gil at Telefolmin and knew him in his Baptist College days in 1952, says, 'I believe Gil had a vision to stir the Australian churches and the churches of the Pacific to be aware of the

---

13. This conclusion is based on the response to this question which was in a questionnaire to a number of Gil's friends, family and fellow workers.
14. Joshua Daimoi, 'Recollections of Dr McArthur', 5 April 2017, 2.
15. Morgan, 'Gilbert McArthur Information', 3.
16. Kay Liddle, 'Gil McArthur References in Kay Liddle's Books', Email, 27 August 2016.

Great Commission.'[17] In *One Passion: Church Planting in Papua New Guinea*, Don describes the visionary thinking Gil (with Doug Vaughan) brought to developing their team strategy at Telefolmin:

> Both men [Gil and Doug], could see that the area could be evangelised in a comparatively short period of time if airstrips could be built in the surrounding valleys, where different groups of people lived, and we could visit such areas regularly by plane. In that way we would be able to keep in touch with indigenous pastors and could also take medical missionaries to those isolated areas where they could bring medical help to the people and establish baby health clinics. This was visionary thinking, but Gil in particular was noted for his gift in that area.[18]

Peter Salisbury, who served with Gil for over ten years in his later period with SSEM recalls, 'Gil was a tremendous visionary, and always had far reaching ideas and plans.'[19]

Ray Laird, Board Chairman of SSEM agrees:

> Gil was a great Visionary. He was always looking to the future, thinking of what was required for the development of the indigenous churches of PNG in the Sepik and Rabaul, and the SSEC of the Solomon Islands. Although he was dedicated to the Melanesian world, he also looked beyond to the nations of the Pacific Ocean to provide some encouragement to them in an ever-changing world.[20]

When Paul appeared before King Agrippa, he recalled his moment of destiny on the Damascus road, and the Lord's commission, 'I am sending you to the Gentiles'. This was an astounding about-face for a passionate Pharisee. Paul then affirmed, 'so then King Agrippa, I was not disobedient to the vision from heaven'. The vision to reach the Gentiles for the glory of God was the compelling driver in Paul's missionary obedience.[21]

Whatever else vision means, it has to do with what we can 'see'. It is more than just physical vision. It is seeing what others do not yet see. The Old Testament story of Elisha and his young servant illustrates this well. His young servant could only see the armies of the Arameans, but

---

17. Don Doull, 'Re: Gil McArthur', Letter, 29 January 2016, 3.
18. Doull, *One Passion: Church Planting in Papua New Guine*a, 111, 112.
19. Peter Salisbury, 'Gil McArthur', Email, 27 October 2016.
20. Laird, 'Gil McArthur', 1.
21. See Acts 25:23-26:32 for the full account of Paul's encounter with King Agrippa.

THE LEGACY OF A LEADER

Elisha boldly affirms 'Those who are with us are more than those that are with them'! Elisha could 'see' more than his servant could! Then he prayed, 'O Lord, open his eyes that he may see.' And the Lord opened the servant's eyes, and he looked, and 'saw' the hills full of horses and chariots of fire all around Elisha![22]

Read the story of any significant Christian ministry, and you will trace the origin back to people who had a God-given vision. Ex-wartime pilots saw remote areas of PNG opened to the Gospel through the use of small aircraft in MAF. Missionary leaders saw the need for growing national Christian leaders, and a partnership of missions and churches together providing the kind of excellence in leadership development through CLTC that they could not achieve on their own. Or take the Dow Jones USA executive in a pin stripe suit, gripped by a passion for mission to the unreached peoples of the world, who establishes Pioneers – a new and dynamic mission agency to the unreached.

Vision is not about maintenance in ministry, it is the inspiration of moving towards a future that is different from the present. It involves:

A clear understanding of the present, otherwise the vision is not linked to reality but is in fantasy land.

Sensitivity to the guidance and direction of the Holy Spirit in discerning the vision and pathway to its implementation.

Understanding both the modern, post-modern, and cross-cultural contexts, and how those cultural systems work through the dynamics of change.

The ability to develop the skills and gifts of a team, building a united confidence in the leader's role to birth the vision with the team, identifying and affirming the undergirding values.

Strong faith in the guiding and protecting presence of the living Lord.

The freedom to fail with dignity, in the context of taking risks in faith and moving ahead.

All of these characteristics at varying levels were evident in Gil's vision and faith. He was inspired by a 'God honouring, kingdom advancing, heart thumping vision',[23] *focused on the development and equipping of*

---

22. See 2 Kings 6:8-23.
23. Hybels, *Courageous Leadership*, 31.

East West Airlines advertisement, Gordon's Air Guide, *July 1953.*

leaders for the advancement of the Kingdom of God. It took on a specific focus in the different contexts of his ministry.

In his early business life with East West Airlines, Gil led and inspired others to accomplish a seemingly impossible task.[24] In his passion to see the Gospel reach the people of the Baliem Valley in DNG he pioneered with others into the unknown, facing dangerous challenges and hardships. Once the people were contacted he worked on translation so they could have the Bible in their own tongue, and evangelists and Bible teachers were equipped to be deployed among the people as airstrips were established. His transfer to Telefolmin saw a similar strategy born in his partnership with Don Doull and Doug Vaughan. Later his call to Clemton Park Baptist Church was not just to maintain the status quo, but to advance the leadership and witness of the church through a period of rapid growth, missionary involvement, and the development of new facilities.

His appointment as the founding Principal of CLTC in PNG saw the maturing of the strategy he had followed in his years in the Baliem

---

24. See chapter two for the details.

and Telefolmin pioneering work, where the development of national evangelists and pastors was one of the three critical planks in the strategy platform. But in responding to the vision of CLTC, he was seeing the pinnacle of a bigger picture: pastoral leadership health impacts church health and church health impacts community and, indeed, national health. He was convinced that this strategy was both biblically true and theologically valid, a critical strategy which he followed in the establishing of CLTC, and which drove him forward in the years of serving with World Vision and SSEM, and his work with Pacific national leaders in the PLF.

Gil once expressed the profound breadth of his vision in this way:

One of the most vital resources of any nation is its leaders. The social fabric of any society is a reflection of its moral and spiritual values. The political, economic and spiritual life of a nation revolves around the behaviour and actions of the leaders at every level of society (elected as well as the non-elected).[25]

But Gil was not only possessed by what he fervently believed was this God-given vision, he was also an example of pursuing its fulfilment in faith, total commitment, discipline and plain hard work. This commitment had an impact upon Gil's relationships and the demands he made on his team. Garth Morgan quotes a well-known saying among those who served under Gil's leadership:

'Where there is Gil, there is always a way'. If there was a challenge or a difficulty, we learned as his 'lieutenants', that you never give up until you have pursued every possible avenue or person who may have some information or contact which may lead to some solution. And when you receive a negative response, do not be turned aside from your vision or goal.[26]

Gil's passionate pursuit of vision, and just getting on with it, meant that on at least one occasion in his relationships with his governing Council he decided to explain later, rather than ask permission first! Garth recalls a situation in 1968 when:

Gil arrived back at College at the end of May 1968 [following his study leave in the USA], having obtained permission on the way

---

25. While this quotation from Gil is used in an old PowerPoint on the CLTC story, I have been unable to source the original context in which it was made, emphasis added.
26. Morgan, 'Gilbert McArthur Information', 3.

from the Melbourne-based College Council to build the much-needed College guest house. Gil called a special College Executive meeting, as he was accustomed to do, and tabled the basic plans of the approved guest house complex.

Gil announced, 'The Melbourne men will be here at College for the Annual Council meetings at the end of July'. Then the directions: 'Graham, you will have to remove the top of the hill next to the flats and get the logs and mill the timber for the project. Ron, all the foundations must be completed, and the wall framing needs to be up with the roof trusses in place, before these men arrive here in eight weeks, so they cannot change what we are going to build. Here is the approved plan. But we are going to double everything. Two guest flats not one. Eight guest rooms not four. And we are doubling the size of the dining/lounge area!'

When the men arrived from Melbourne, the roof was in place! And we, the members of the College Executive never saw Gil for the first morning of the Council meetings, due to him being fully occupied explaining why and how the guest house had doubled in size![27] Those who have enjoyed the hospitality of that facility, will appreciate the foresight that Gil exercised on that occasion, and what it may have been like to seek forgiveness afterwards, rather than permission first![28]

It is important to understand that this incident should not be seen as evidence of a breakdown of trust or respect between Gil and the Melbourne CLTC Committee. It was never that. Gil always held the men of the MBI leadership group in the highest esteem, and greatly valued their godly wisdom and input into his life and leadership. Rather, the Guest House story is evidence of the way, when Gil mulled over an issue, he sometimes came to a fresh conviction about what was needed, or how something should be done. In these situations, he feared the opinions of no one in pursuing his sense of what the Lord wanted him to do. If that meant having to defend his actions at a later date, he was more than willing to do so, forcefully, humbly, but unapologetically. It was that unusual mix which made Gil the leader he was.

---

27. Gil carefully guarded his right as Principal to be the one and only conduit between the College and the MBI Committee. Other senior staff would not have dreamed of communicating directly with the Melbourne MBI Committee.
28. Morgan, 'Gilbert McArthur Information', 3.

15
LEGACY IN CHURCH AND COMMUNITY LEADERS

Pastoral health affects church health;
church health affects societal health.
This statement can be upheld as biblically true and theologically valid.
Can it also be strategically critical for global ministry today?[1]

It was both his faith-filled vision and practical, unswerving total commitment to its fulfilment that defined Gil's life in every phase of his ministry. It became a multi-dimensional legacy that impacted all those around him. It is impossible to touch on the lives of all those Gil influenced, so it will be necessary to confine this review to some examples. These examples vary in length and depth due to the information available to the writer. The purpose is not simply to tell individual stories, but to appreciate Gil and his leadership style in greater depth. As the members of the staff team during Gil's leadership were mainly expatriates, this is reflected in the people whose stories are recorded below. The following categories provide understanding of the breadth of his leadership influence:

Church and community leaders in PNG,

Church and community leaders in the Solomon Islands,

Infrastructure builders,

Theological educators,

Business entrepreneurs and financial managers,

Mission leaders in the wider Pacific Region and beyond,

Pioneering missionary leaders to reach the Unreached,

National leaders in the wider Pacific and beyond.

First, we consider examples of church and community leaders in Papua New Guinea.

---

1. Ramesh Richard, 'Training of Pastors', *Lausanne Global Analysis*, September 2015, 1.

Wesani Iwoksim

Baptist Church Telefolmin, House of Assembly of Papua New Guinea

Wesani Iwoksim and family

In the early pioneering days in Dutch New Guinea and Telefolmin, the major thrust of Gil's strategy was the development of national evangelists and leaders who could carry the main responsibility of evangelising and making disciples. In an address to the students of Columbia Bible College in 1974, Gil spoke of his investment into the life of Wesani Iwoksim in Telefolmin, who was one of the first to respond to the Gospel and the challenge of leadership in the emerging church:

> I remember working with my informant Wesani and coming to John chapter ten. We spoke about the Lord Jesus Christ as the Shepherd, and he loved that analogy, that truth. And then I went on to share with him that Jesus Christ was not only the Shepherd, but that he knew his sheep by name, and would call them out and each one was known in heaven, and that the Lord Jesus Christ, the great majestic Creator of the universe whom he had come to know... That the Lord of the universe should deign to know this unknown tribesman of the hinterland of New Guinea and know him by name. And I saw Wesani nourish his own soul with this truth. Constantly he would be talking about it and sharing it with others – this great discovery that Wesani was known in heaven, that he was named within the counsels of the Godhead, and that he was a subject of the divine conversation. And as he began to think about it his theological understanding began to grow. He realised that if this was so, then the one true God of heaven is not remote, that he cannot love from a distance, he has to draw near, to find a way to reach the object loved, that such is the motivating power of his own nature that he cannot just love by an edict from glory, but he must come down into our world, and enter into a flesh and blood experience, and become part of our history and enter into our experience that he might touch life as we have to live it at every point.[2]

Wesani was one of the first to respond to the Gospel and became one of the key leaders in the young church in the Telefolmin Valley. He also had a deep commitment to the work. After Gil left, Wesani partnered with Don Doull in the contacting of new tribal groups who were still unreached. Don records the first contact with the Faiwolmin people who lived on the other side of the Victor Emmanuel mountain range which had always been a great barrier between the Min people to the south and the Min people to the north. The southern side of this range was a precipitous limestone escarpment, which stretched for many kilometres both east and west. For years it was regarded as impossible to cross.

> Wesani and I set out with a number of Bible School men to cross over that range… Some of our escorts knew the way across and were able to guide us in a two-day walk over this limestone range, where great sinkholes made the going dangerous all the way across the top of the range… Having negotiated the descent, it took only an hour or so to reach the villages where many of the Faiwolmin people lived. I spent some days making contact with the people… Wesani and I left the villages before dawn, walking as quickly as our legs would carry us. We climbed the limestone escarpment, crossed the top of the mountain range and down the other side, then walked on into the night hours, finally reaching Telefolmin in the one day. It took about 15 hours of walking altogether; the toughest day's walk I ever did![3]

In 1964, when Don was on furlough, Wesani visited Australian Baptist Churches for three months to share the story of what God was doing among his people. Wesani was present at Don's ordination in the Sydney Town Hall in September 1964.[4]

After CLTC commenced, Wesani was sent there for advanced training. Gil was the Principal, and the enrolment of Wesani as the first pastor from the Telefolmin area to attend CLTC must have been a great encouragement to Gil, as the one who had been part of his conversion at the beginning of the harvest time at Telefolmin.[5]

Wesani had such standing as a community leader that later in the preparations for independence in PNG he was elected as a member of the House of Assembly.

---

2. Gilbert J McArthur, *The Dynamic of the Word of God in Action*, Audio CD (Student Chapel Address at Columbia Bible College South Carolina, 1976), McArthur Family Archives.
3. Doull, *One Passion: Church Planting in Papua New Guinea*, 137, 138.
4. Doull, *One Passion: Church Planting in Papua New Guinea*, 151.
5. Doull, *One Passion: Church Planting in Papua New Guinea*, 153.

Traimya Kambipi

Baptist Church Lumusa, PNG House of Assembly then Member of PNG Parliament

Traimya Kambipi

Traimya with his family

Another of the very early graduates of CLTC was Traimya Kambipi. He was nominated to the PNG House of Assembly in the first election in 1964. He did not win that election but had a deep sense of God's call upon his life to represent his people. He came under Gil's influence when he applied to CLTC in 1965 and was accepted in the first group of students. He had completed three and a half years of the Certificate in Church Leadership Course, when he was released for the next election:

> I stood again in the next election (1968). A lot of unbelievers and some of my fellow-Christians were against me, but I left my burden with the Lord. I trusted Him that He would work out his plan for my life. I am sure he has given me this work, for it is His will for me to do the work of a Member of the House of Assembly for His glory.[6]

Traimya was elected in the *Baiyer/Kompian* open seat and became an influential leader in the House. He was particularly outspoken about what he felt was the early push for independence. He boldly said that the visit of Gough Whitlam, the Prime Minister of Australia was only 'to stir up trouble!' He supported a Highlands 'go slow on political independence' group.[7]

---

6. Sanders, *Spiritual Leadership*, 153, 154.
7. Woolford, Don, *Papua New Guinea: Initiation and Independence* (University of Queensland Press, 1976), Chapter 7.

Judah Akesim

South Sea Evangelical Church of Papua New Guinea, Member and Minister in the National PNG Parliament

Judah Akesim

Judah Akesim was a pastor in the South Sea Evangelical Church from the village of Musendai in the Sepik Province. He applied for entry to CLTC and arrived at the College in January 1969 to commence his studies. However, shortly after his arrival, Gil received news from his sending church that Judah had been accused of involvement in an inappropriate relationship in the past, which the church regarded as a serious impediment to any continuing pastoral leadership.

Gil agonised over the situation. Judah had come so far with his family at great expense. When Judah was approached by Gil and another faculty member, he was humble, quick to confess his failure, and prepared to return home and submit to the direction of the church leaders. Gil spent some time with Judah encouraging him from the Bible that 'failure was not final', and that the College would accept him to return for his studies when the church agreed. Judah and his wife and family returned home. Subsequently, they were approved by the church to return a year later, and on completion of the Certificate of Church Leadership in 1972, he returned home to pastoral ministry. Gil later had significant contact with Judah when Gil was the Executive Director of SSEM.

Judah became widely respected as a leader in his community, and in 1997 nominated for the *Ambunti/Dreikikir* open seat in the PNG national parliament. He was elected and appointed Health Minister for a period. He held office in the Parliament until the 2007 election.

Due to Gil's influence at a crucial time in his life, Judah demonstrated in his faith and perseverance that, like Peter in his denial of Jesus, indeed 'failure is not final'.[8]

---

8. David Price, 'Judah Akesim – Personal recall of the author', David was personally involved with Gil in this situation with Judah.

Sir Mari Kapi

Deputy then Chief Justice of Papua New Guinea, United Church, Pacific Leaders' Fellowship

Sir Mari Kapi

Sir Mari Kapi (GCL KCMG CBE), was born at Keapara village, in the Rigo District, Central Province of PNG. He was entirely educated in Papua New Guinea, graduating from the University of Papua New Guinea in 1972. He was employed as a lawyer with the Office of the Public Solicitor, and on 1 January 1978 at the age of 29, became the first Papua New Guinean national to be appointed a justice of the Supreme and National Courts of Papua New Guinea. He was appointed Deputy Chief Justice in 1982, and served as the fourth Chief Justice of the Supreme Court of Papua New Guinea from 16 August 2003 until his retirement in 2008 due to his deteriorating health.[9]

During his university days, Sir Mari was deeply involved in the founding and leadership of the Tertiary Students' Christian Fellowship and the ministry of the Everyman's Centre in Port Moresby. Sir Mari met Gil and Len Buck on their regular visits, when they often preached at the Centre. The three became firm friends, sharing the same passion and vision to see the development of leaders of good character and integrity in the servant leadership of the nation. Len Buck had a vision to start the work of Prison Fellowship in PNG, and Sir Mari was appointed the founding Chairman of Prison Fellowship PNG, and member of the Board of Prison Fellowship International. He received the President´s award for Ministry Statesmanship, recognizing his impact and influence in advancing the cause of doing justice with mercy.

It was Gil's vision and passion for building Kingdom leaders around the Pacific that lit the flame in Sir Mari. He led a prayer group of leaders every Wednesday from 6 to 7 am, and was involved in the PNG Leaders' Fellowship, organising regular seminars and special events for PNG leaders. At the PNG Leadership Retreat in 1987 he gave the keynote address and challenged the leaders present:

---

9. 'Chief Justice Sir Mari Kapi', *Wikipedia*, accessed 6 June 2017, https://en.wikipedia.org/wiki/Mari_Kapi.

It is clear that God intends that all nations prosper, but there is a condition that leaders and people must live righteous lives before Him. All the problems that we face in all areas of development in any country can be dealt with under the guidelines given by the Scriptures. We can trace a moral root cause in the problems that face us in our nations. Think of all the problems caused by greed. When we understand the mind of God in everything we do, this will have a profound effect on the actions we take in our responsibilities.

What steps do we need to take to make this a reality in the life of our nation?

Two important questions need to be asked: What is the role of the leaders in establishing a spiritual foundation for development? What is the role of the people?

In response to the first, it is clear that the leadership must do two things. First, they must apply the spiritual values in their own lives. Second, upon this basis, they must encourage the people to do the same.[10]

Sir Mari also travelled with Gil's team in some of the Pacific Island circuit visits to encourage Pacific leaders in their commitment to Kingdom values and servant leadership.

Second, we consider examples of church and community leaders in the Solomon Islands.

Unity Unasi (Blakey)

South Sea Evangelical Church, Afio Girls' Bible Institute, Girls' Brigade

Gil had the insight and discernment to see others' potential to develop and grow in ministry. Unity is one such example of this. Gil opened a door for Unity Unasi that led to a remarkable ministry. John Wiggins, a former SSEM missionary told her

Unity Unasi Blakey

---

10. PNG Leaders' Fellowship, 'Leadership News', *PNG Leaders' Fellowship Newsletter*, 2.

story at the Thanksgiving Service for her life in Canberra in 1988.

In 1966 Unity had determined to commit her whole life to Jesus Christ, and began training at Afio Girls' Bible Institute, (Maramasike Island, Malaita Province, Solomon Islands) – then run by Joan Gruber of SSEM. After graduation, at the end of her two-year course, Unity served at Araki and Gwaidinale Bible Schools on Malaita Island.

Dr Gil McArthur, Principal of CLTC in New Guinea, visited the Solomons, met Unity, and was so impressed with her Christian character, that he offered her the opportunity of further training in New Guinea. At first, her people felt it was too dangerous for a woman to go to a foreign environment, but they finally agreed. So Unity, after a lot of discussion, was sent and became the first Solomon Island woman student to train at CLTC. After graduating at CLTC at the end of 1972, Unity gladly used her gifts and abilities at Afio Bible Institute, serving this time as fellow-staff member with Joan Gruber.

Unity was not afraid to accept new challenges, and not unwilling to answer God's call to take up new responsibilities. She became the first Solomon Island Principal of Afio Girls' Bible Institute. Her steady growth in maturity was evident in the way she handled this new and demanding role.

Janet Kent, Girls' Brigade Officer in the Solomon Islands needed a Solomon Island co-worker and Unity took up this work in 1976. She lived in Girls Brigade Headquarters, in Honiara. Her small home was always neat and tidy. There were flowers in the front and the vegetable garden down the back, and always plenty of chatter and laughter.

Our primary school age children, with Lady the dog, loved to visit Unity, cooking kaibia puddings, telling stories, and playing games. She was a great friend to all who came and was very generous to all.

During the period up to 1980, she established Girls Brigade in Western Solomons, PNG and other Pacific countries. She also visited New Zealand and Australia. She had the ability to touch people's lives with her love, joy and sparkle. She never felt threatened, inferior, or intimidated. She had a quiet authority, and an appreciation of all things good. People would talk long after about some aspect of her visit. 'She did something for me. I'm not quite sure what it was, but it was good.'

She served on the staff of Goldie College, run by the United Church of PNG and the Solomon Islands. There she showed a clear testimony of honesty, fearless integrity, and a loving way of witnessing for her Lord that attracted many people to put their faith and trust in Him.

At about this time she met Ian. It is said that when Ian asked her family for permission to marry Unity, they decided to set a test for him. 'If you can sail this small dug-out canoe without falling out, then you are fit to marry a salt-water girl'. Ian was an accomplished bush walker and canoeist, so had no trouble passing the test.

After their marriage, Ian and Unity began an involvement with Scripture Union in the Solomons. In February 1983, Nathan was born; then in August 1985 Micah was born. In 1986 the family moved to Australia. They had a great test of faith in December when Joel was born. He was not expected to live, and Unity became seriously ill. In all of this her faith was an encouragement to Ian and others.

We shared a meal in their home earlier this year. Unity shared with us: 'I was washing up, Ian was away at study, and the children were around me. I thought, "How are we going to cope? We have so many needs—a home, finance, study, transport, education, and what about the future?" I became very discouraged. The Lord spoke to me at the sink; "Come, spend time with Me, leave the dishes." I went to my Bible and it opened at Proverbs 3:6 "In all your ways acknowledge him and he shall direct your paths." As I read and prayed, the Lord assured me again that He was still in control, as He had proved in many crises in my life. I went back to my dishes with joy and anticipation and confidence in my heart. He would deal with the problems.'[11]

Following the relentless advance of a genetic degenerative disease, Unity died on Sunday 25 September 1988. The challenge of her life lives on, a legacy made possible (from a human perspective) through Gil's discernment and encouragement. Gil knew the vital importance of developing women in leadership as well as men.

---

11. John Wiggins, 'Tribute to Uniity Unasi (Blakey) at the Thanksgiving Service for Her Life', *Not in Vain*, 1988, 10.

Jezreel Filoa

South Sea Evangelical Church, Christian Leaders' Training College Papua New Guinea

*Jezreel and Bethemek Filoa
L-R: Aburi, Taeasi, Nellie (in arms) and Anilafa 1968*

The story of Jezreel Filoa in his published obituary was titled, *The Loss of a True Leader – The humble saltwater boy extended the work of his parents by being a pioneer missionary*.[12] Jezreel was born on the small island of Ngongosila east of Malaita, in the Solomon Islands in 1933. Through the Christian heritage which came from his parents Joash and Crystal Filoa, he came to know the Lord at a very young age. The story was told that if local heathen kids wanted to share their material goods with him they had to come to church. Jezreel understood right from that time that active Christian witness began when a person committed to following Jesus Christ.[13]

In 1939, he was with his parents (SSEC missionaries) establishing Christian villages on the island of Makira.[14] These teaching missions had a deep impact on him. After the war, he was a student at Su'u Secondary School. In 1947 he became a member of the crew of the mission ship *Evangel*, before becoming a cook at the SSEM headquarters at *One Pusu*. It was there he met Bethemek who had been at the Girls' Training School at Afio. They were married in 1955,[15] and served as missionaries on East Malaita alongside his parents. After they had been married two weeks, Jezreel told Beth he believed that the Lord was calling them to go to New Guinea as missionaries. They prayed, and the door opened for them to go to One Pusu Bible College to prepare.[16]

---

12. Fangalasuu Kaoni Siche, 'Obituary – Jezreel Filoa – The Loss of a True Leader', Unnamed Newspaper, October 1995, SSEM Archives.
13. Siche, 'Obituary – Jezreel Filoa'.
14. In the early history of the SSEC, those who responded to the Gospel and became Christians were forced out of the pagan villages and formed their own Christian settlements far away from the animistic environments. See Alison Griffiths *Fire in the Islands*, 23.
15. Jezreel and Beth had seven children over the years, one of whom was born, died and buried at CLTC.
16. Griffiths, *Fire in the Islands*, 155.

In 1949, following an initial survey, SSEM sent Ken Finger in to open their second mission field in the Sepik District on the north coast of New Guinea. The early missionaries were Europeans who had been working in the Solomon Islands. No Solomon Islander had been asked to go as a missionary to PNG, but Jezreel and Beth, supported by their own people and backed by SSEM, went to the Sepik in New Guinea in 1959. They were the first Solomon Islanders to be sent overseas. Between 1959 and 1964 Jezreel and Beth served alongside the missionaries in the Sepik. Then he was given four years' leave of absence, and (with Gil's encouragement) was accepted into the first intake of students at CLTC. He was appointed Senior Student, and graduated in 1968.[17] During his time at CLTC, he and another student Glaimi Warena, were invited by the MBI CLTC Committee to visit Australia to share the story and their experiences of CLTC. It was a mind-blowing adventure for them to see western culture for the first time, and they received a very warm welcome from many churches. Jezreel reflected on what the missionaries had left behind:

> I have learnt a great lesson, when I was down South. My first night in Melbourne I was amazed to see many coloured lights in the streets and in the tall buildings. It looked very pretty. Also, I saw many good homes, many modern things which make the life down South so easy and comfortable.
>
> When I saw these things, my thoughts went back to the missionaries in New Guinea and in the Solomon Islands. A question came into my mind: 'Why is this, that the missionaries left their beautiful country, and went to live in the jungle of New Guinea, and in the Solomons, among the primitive people?'
>
> As I thought of this question, the answer came to me in the verse in Romans 5:5 Paul says, 'Because God's love has been poured into their hearts, through the Holy Spirit which has been given to them.' Also, Philippians 2, verses 3-4, were real concerning them: 'Do nothing from selfishness or conceit, but in humility count others better than yourself. Let each of you look not only to his interest but also to the interest of others.'
>
> Dear friends, let us learn this great lesson from our missionaries. If God calls us to serve Him in any part of our country, here in New Guinea, or in the Solomons, let us obey Him. If we have the

---

17. Jezreel Filoa, 'Islanders Called to New Guinea', *Not in Vain*, June 1970, 6, Rickard Family Archive.

love of God in our hearts, let us show it by responding to God's call. Christ shows how much He loved God by response to God's call. He came on earth to die on the cross for our sins. Our missionaries show their love for God by response to God's call; they left their beautiful country and their modern way of life and living, and came to dwell among the primitive people of Papua, New Guinea, and in the Solomons.

Let us thank God for those missionaries who have sacrificially offered their lives to live in our uncivilised country to save men and women from going to hell, by preaching the Gospel.

'Let this mind of Christ be in us.' Philippians 2:5[18]

Gil had observed Jezreel's leadership potential, and following his graduation invited him to become the CLTC Student Supervisor. Gil was excited to have such a mature student from the SSEC in the College community.[19] Jezreel's time at CLTC developed his leadership skills and teaching gifts. The family returned briefly to ministry in the Sepik, before returning to the Solomon Islands in 1973. In the following years, Jezreel

SSEC CLTC Graduates Reunion November 2011 in Honiara

---

18. Jezreel Filoa, 'Visit to Australia', *Not in Vain*, September 1968, 10.
19. Griffiths, *Fire in the Islands*, 155.

was the representative of the SSEC churches on the CLTC Council and had a continuing influence into the life and development of the College.

In 1974, he was appointed SSEC General Superintendent, the most senior leadership position in the SSEC. He served five terms in this capacity until 1987, making him the longest serving head of the SSEC church. Because of a restructuring of the SSEC leadership in 1987, he did not seek re-appointment. From 1987 to the end of 1994, he was the Assistant Pastor at the large SSEC Central Church in Honiara. During these years he served under three younger pastors who had also graduated from CLTC – Roy Funu, Festus Suruma and Eric Takila. His involvement in the church only lessened when his health began to fade towards the end of 1994. On 3 October 1995, after celebrating the birthday of one of his grandsons, he prayed with all his children, telling them he was leaving. He then died peacefully and entered the presence of the Lord Jesus whom he loved and served.[20]

Sir Peter Kenilorea

South Sea Evangelical Church,
Member of Parliament,
Pacific Leaders' Fellowship

Sir Peter Kenilorea

Peter Kenilorea was a remarkable leader for the Solomon Islands in his time and enjoyed a unique association with Gil. Sir Peter was born in Takataka village on Malaita. He trained as a teacher for the SSEC in New Zealand. Later he was a co-founder of the Solomon Islands Christian Association. While he was a school teacher, he began to develop political interests and became president of the Civil Servants' Association, an organization that provided the basis for the Solomon Islands United Party he later helped to found.

After nominating but failing to gain a seat in the 1970 and 1973 elections, he was elected unopposed in 1974/1975 when he won the *East 'Are'are* seat, which he held until his resignation from Parliament in 1991.[21]

---

20. Siche, 'Obituary - Jezreel Filoa'.
21. Clive Moore, 'Pacific Islands Autobiography: Personal History and Diplomacy in the Solomon Islands', *Journal of Historical Biography* 10 (2011), 7.

In 1976, Peter Kenilorea became the second chief minister of the Solomon Islands, and the first Prime Minister at independence on 7 July 1978. Kenilorea was Prime Minister until August 1980, returning again from October 1984 until he resigned in December 1986 after he lost the confidence of his cabinet due to his handling of French relief funds. He continued as deputy Prime Minister from 1987 to 1989, and also served as Foreign Minister for seven years of this period [1988-1989, and from 1990-1993].

In 1991, he resigned from Parliament to take up a three-year appointment as director of the South Pacific Forum Fisheries Agency, a regional diplomatic position based in Honiara. He then took a year off before becoming Ombudsman for five years from 1996, and was intimately involved in negotiating the peace process during the political crisis years, 1998 to 2003. He became speaker of the National Parliament in 2000 and served two terms until September 2010.[22]

Clive Moore, who edited Sir Peter's autobiography, points to his powerful influence on the nation:

> Sir Peter is the great survivor of Solomon Islands politics and the nation's elder statesman. He is an old-school national leader who survived only on his salary, rare in modern Solomon Islands politics. He guided the birth of the nation, but says that he was an unwilling politician and entered politics out of a sense of duty as a member of the new educated elite. Since he resigned from Parliament in 1991 he has held a string of influential positions and has been constant in holding the nation to the letter of the National Constitution. With the help of the Public Solicitor's office, he has mounted many important private court cases against the government when it has abused its authority under the Constitution.[23]

In his Editor's Preface, Moore writes specifically about Sir Peter's Christian commitment:

> Sir Peter is a committed Christian and has always involved God in his decision-making at a personal and professional level. He is a member of the South Sea Evangelical Church, a post 1964 iteration

---

22. Moore, 'Pacific Islands Autobiography', 8.
23. Moore, 'Pacific Islands Autobiography', 9, 10.

of a Mission by the same name founded in 1907, based on an earlier Mission begun in Queensland, Australia in the 1880s. The SSEC is non-denominational and based on fundamental biblical beliefs. Sir Peter is a lay preacher and staunch member of his church. When he handed over the first draft of the manuscript, I asked him if he had used references. 'Yes,' he said, with a twinkle in his eyes, 'all from the Bible'. While this is not quite true, scriptural references certainly make up a large number of his footnotes and indicate his strong Christian beliefs.

This is the autobiography of a passionate and committed Christian and will also serve as a benchmark study of Christianity in the Pacific.[24]

In the context of his strong Christian commitment and passion for integrity in leadership Gil had a close association with Sir Peter in the ministry of the PLF. They had a deep relationship and influence upon each other which began through contact at the USA President's Prayer Breakfast.[25] Doug Coe, whom President George Bush referred to as 'his unofficial ambassador to the world', was the USA coordinator who arranged invitations for key leaders from the South Pacific to attend the Prayer Breakfast. Gil met Sir Peter at one of these gatherings, and they became firm friends with a mutual burden to see Pacific Leaders brought together for fellowship, discussion and prayer about Christ-centred servant leadership.[26] Sir Peter and Gil drove the vision of connecting Pacific leaders for Christian fellowship from Gil's position in World Vision as the Consultant and Pacific Co-ordinator for the Leadership Enhancement Ministries of the PLF. Sir Peter travelled on each of the PLF trips, and was a very effective leader in building relationships, taking leadership in their gatherings, and providing a strong credibility base to the ministry. The influence of these gatherings bore fruit in a continuing legacy in the lives of the leaders who attended. Max Meyers (then MAF CEO), another key member of the travelling team, comments on the impact of their visit to Fiji in a meeting they had

---

24. Peter Kenilorea, *Tell It as It Is: Autobiography of Rt. Hon. Sir Peter Kenilorea, KBE, PC Solomon Islands First Prime Minister*, Edited by Clive Moore (Taipei, Taiwan: Centre for Asia-Pacific Area Studies, 2008), xxx, xxxi.
25. Will Renshaw, 'Chief Justice Mari Kapi and his relationship with Gil McArthur', Personal Interview, 10 October 2017.
26. Will Renshaw, 'Re: Gil McArthur and Sir Peter Kenilorea', Email, 27 December 2016.

with the Governor General Ratu Sir George Cakobau:[27]

> An old man, the Governor General is extremely friendly and openly acknowledges a faith in God and a need for effective leadership in the South Pacific to be committed to one another in Christian principles… He… listened very attentively to what Peter Kenilorea was saying and agreed very warmly and encouraged Peter to continue his efforts to exert a strong Christian ministry in the South Pacific. It was a privilege to be asked to pray before we left. I guess I never thought that I would have the opportunity of commending a Governor General to Christ and have him thank me most warmly for doing so.[28]

In the last months of Sir Peter's life, William Longgar, current Principal of CLTC, was able to visit and pray with him. William had met Sir Peter at one of the early PLF gatherings that Gil had arranged in Port Moresby, and William had been impacted by Sir Peter's clear challenge and call for integrity in leadership. During his visit Sir Peter told William about the deep friendship he had enjoyed with Gil, and how Gil's personal friendship and work in the PLF had left a legacy in his own political life and service.

---

27. George Cakobau's great ancestor was the strong leader opposing the Gospel and giving the first missionaries to Fiji a very hard time until he was converted to Christ in 1854. It was hearing the story of Seru Epenisa Cakobau's conversion read in Sunday School that stirred James Chalmers to make his teenage commitment to mission in the Pacific.
28. Meyers, 'South Pacific Leaders Trip Report', 10.

16

LEGACY IN INFRASTRUCTURE BUILDERS

Buildings and facilities are God-given necessary resources, and those who establish them vital partners in teaching the Word of God, and training people for ministry and mission.[1]

Gil's vision for leadership development in the Pacific required huge resources to enable the programs to function effectively. Many who caught the vision through Gil became personally involved in establishing the required infrastructure, often at great personal sacrifice. This is clearly apparent in his pioneering mission involvement in DNG and Telefolmin in PNG, in his ministries at CPBC, in the birth and establishment of CLTC, and in his later ministries with ATA, SSEM, World Vision, the PLF and the PTI. Here we reference a few outstanding examples.

George Tweedale

Christian Leaders' Training College Papua New Guinea, Sudan Interior Mission Ethiopia

George Tweedale

We have already recounted the story of George Tweedale's remarkable conversion through the witness of Australian missionary Victor Barnard, while on his journey seeking spiritual truth and fulfilment in India. George later reflected:

> At the start of my travels, I did not realize that I was looking for the truth about life, and I would never have guessed that only Christ could fill the emptiness in my soul. However, God knew the real stirrings of my

---

1. David Price, December 2017.

soul, that deep down I had a desire to find the truth and to do what was right. He knew that I would respond positively to the gospel after I had come to the end of my list and found that the things I was trying to fill my life with would never be enough. As many others have found, I found that our souls are restless until they find their rest and peace with the God of the Bible.

Instead of being unfulfilled, I became complete in Christ who had a plan for my life. Best of all, I gained assurance of sins forgiven and a heavenly destiny. As I neared the end of my list, I began to see the meaninglessness of my youthful desires. This led me to ask, 'Then what is real life meant to be?'[2]

Leaving India, during a 'reluctant' weekend with Gil at Clemton Park Baptist Church in Sydney on his way home, George was challenged with the vision for CLTC. He agreed to pray about helping in the initial building of the College – and we know the story which followed his prayer and surrender to God's will.[3] It is amazing how God can turn the direction of our lives around: a word of Scripture, meeting with a stranger, a cup of coffee, an unavoidable question, the urging of a Christian we greatly respect; all under the gentle guidance of his Spirit.

In his faithful and persistent service, while living on his own in a Wahgi village, George was in the right place at the right time to hear about the availability of the Giramben land and conclude the long frustrating search for a site to establish CLTC. Then with Clyde Parkinson, and other CLTC 'pioneers' who joined the team, George worked in very difficult conditions providing the first level of infrastructure required in the establishment of CLTC. This included the initial road making, and building the Principal's house, the building team's house and the first student house. After 18 months George returned home to prepare to enter the MBI in 1965, and later served as a missionary in Ethiopia. He demonstrated personal vision and faith in his unique contribution to the infrastructure required to bring CLTC to reality.

---

2. Tweedale, *Not Counting the Cost*, 12.
3. Tweedale, *Not Counting the Cost*, 24. See Chapter Seven for details.

Peter and Margaret Rowse

Christian Leaders' Training College Papua New Guinea, CLTC Australian Advisory Council

*Peter and Margaret Rowse 2017
L-R: Sue, Andy and Paul*

In 1963, Peter and Margaret Rowse, another couple profoundly influenced by Gil's faith and vision were particularly interested in Gil's plan to see the 413 acres of ground being used productively to support the leadership training ministries of the College, and at the same time provide agricultural training that would produce leaders who could enhance the development of their own communities.

Following the hazardous journey to deliver the shipment of tractor, car and agricultural machinery to the College site in 1964, Peter stayed on for a period gravelling the access road and ploughing ground to plant crops to provide food for the students and staff. Peter found Gil's pressure to see results somewhat unreasonable at times. When Gil arrived on campus in 1964 and inspected what had been done, he said to Peter,

'There's a few hours on this thing [tractor], but I don't see much land ploughed up!'

Peter replied, 'That's because I have been flat out carting timber for your house, and gravel for the road!'[4]

Gil had high expectations not only of himself, but of his team. Most were able to measure up. But sometimes Gil could not appreciate that everyone did not have the same capacity that he did! One who worked closely with him believed, 'Gil was a general, not a sergeant, and thus having anointed someone whom he thought adequate to the task, he expected them to forge on without adequate personal supervision. Perhaps I am wrong'…[5]

Peter's commitment to the vision and establishment of CLTC continued. He returned again for a few months in 1965 to help in the

---

4. Rowse, 'Peter Rowse re Gilbert McArthur'.
5. Gordon Griffiths, 'Ray Laird's Response to the SSEM Part of Gil's Story', Email, 28 January 2017, 1.

agricultural development, and was told by Gil the night he arrived, 'Your task, is to split timber posts and do as much fencing as you can.'[6] Peter returned again in 1967, bringing a second brand-new David Brown tractor donated by the Rowse farm. In 1968 Bill Clack told Peter that he was again needed urgently at the College, and they would like him to arrive by the next Monday! When Peter told Margaret, her response was, 'Over my dead body!' She believed that it would not be fair on the family for him to be away yet again. Peter prayed and asked the Lord for a clear sign by providing for the whole family to go. The very next morning he received a bonus from the farm. This unmistakeable provision covered all their fares, so he returned with Margaret and the three children in 1968. At the graduation weekend before they were to return to Australia, Gil asked if they would come back again, this time to live in Lae and manage the College Lae Base, as the transport support program was rapidly developing. Margaret responded saying that they were not sure they could do this, as Peter's father needed him on the farm. Gil wisely suggested they go home, pray about it, and talk to his father. He could see that Peter's mature faith, strong work ethic, business experience, relational skills, and a no nonsense 'we can do it' approach were exactly what was needed. At first Peter's father was totally opposed to him leaving the farm for another extended period. But after a struggle in prayer, he agreed to release Peter and the family to go to Lae where they served a further three and a half years.

Gil's vision and faith totally changed the life direction of Peter and Margaret Rowse. The family finally returned to their Warragul Victoria farm in 1972, after managing the CLTC Lae transport department transition to the head office of ATA in Lae. But such was Peter and Margaret's commitment to CLTC, that Peter served on the CLTC Council and Board of Directors of ATA and Beechwood for some years. He has continued to spend periods at CLTC, assisting in the mechanical, electrical and water infrastructure needs, the agricultural program and mentoring the national staff. He has earned the nickname of 'Mr Hurry Up' around the campus, and workers have been known to take a detour past his office for fear of being given yet one more job to do! Since 1964 Peter has always been a resource for locating equipment and is still sourcing spare parts from Australia for the College. He is passing on the vision, now encouraging younger people to go and mentor the PNG

---

6. Rowse, 'Peter Rowse re Gilbert McArthur'.

engineering College staff. Over the years, 15 items of farm equipment (including two tractors), donated by the Rowse family to CLTC amount to an original cost of A$54,500.[7] Peter continues as a member of the CLTC Australian Advisory Council, of which he was a foundation member. In July 2017, he was awarded the Order of Australia Medal for his Christian service in PNG, and agricultural leadership in Australia.

Ron and Peg Youngman
Christian Leaders' Training College of PNG, Alliance Training Association

Ron & Peg Youngman

Gil met Ron and Peg Youngman on his first whirlwind visit to New Zealand in March 1964.[8] In November 1961, following retirement from commercial building, Ron and Peg set up Roskill Christian Trust, gifting the Trust their two factories in Carr Road Mt. Roskill. Ron had built one for pre-cutting and to make all the window joinery, kitchen and bathroom fittings and doors for his building business, and the other for commercial lease. Ron then offered his building experience to the Baptist Churches of New Zealand to help them with expanding existing or erecting new church buildings.

When Ron and Peg met Gil they were impressed with his vision and were challenged to offer their experience and equipment to the development of the College campus in PNG.[9]

Later in 1964 Ron drove Robin Cowie, Thomas Strahan, and Garth Morgan around the Waikato, dismantling and collecting milking machine equipment from the old sheds of farmers who had upgraded to the new technology of herringbone milking sheds. Claude Evans at Alfa Laval in Hamilton rebuilt a 4-bale walk-through milking plant

---

7. Garth Morgan, 'Re: Peter Rowse', Email, 16 January 2017.
8. Gil spoke at over 40 meetings around New Zealand.
9. I am indebted to Garth and Ruth Morgan for researching and writing 'A Tribute to Ron and Peg Youngman', (22 February 2017) for most of the material in this section.

from the array of parts that were deposited on the floor in front of him! The completed milking unit, together with most of the building and joinery equipment from Ron's factory, was crated and shipped arriving at CLTC in May 1966.[10] Much of Ron's equipment is still being used today, over 50 years later! That gift was of enormous value because it has facilitated the construction of every building, and every piece of joinery and furniture including tables, chairs and beds since 1966.

Ron and John Woodbridge arrived at CLTC in April 1965. Ron first built three 58-foot-long trusses for the sawmill roof, and similar trusses for the original lecture room block. Then he went to Lae with mechanic Sam Lamont.[11] They spent a month in Lae rebuilding an old 'Blitz' army truck from World War II, fitting it with a tip tray, then driving it up the Highlands Highway to the College where it was used for carting gravel and delivering supplies to the campus building sites. Ron built the foundations for two more student houses, and for the expatriate single women's house. He became seriously ill with dysentery and was hospitalised in Goroka for two weeks. In September he returned to New Zealand but was back at CLTC with Peg in May 1966 for Ron and the team to erect the frame for six two bedroomed flats to house the rapidly growing staff numbers. This was followed by a poultry house, two more student houses, and a new lecture room before leaving for New Zealand in November to join Peg who had gone ahead of him.[12]

While in New Zealand, before his next visit to CLTC in 1967, Ron, now in his mid 40s, took himself to welding school so that he could design and construct trusses by bending and welding steel pipe and rods. They became known as *Youngman Trusses* to span large open floor

---

10. The shipment included Ron's timber thicknesser; a 25 KVA generator given by Reckitt & Coleman, NZ, Garth Morgan's former employer; and a chest freezer especially built to operate on 5 hours of power per day, in Thames, NZ, by a Mr Gane Griffen, who met Gil in his April 1964 visit.
11. Sam met Gil McArthur in 1964 at Opotiki in NZ and he was now the CLTC mechanic.
12. Morgan, 'A Tribute to Ron and Peg Youngman', 2, 3. The July 1967 CLTC Field Conference reports record that in the 12 months to 30 June 1967, 12,500sq ft (125 squares) of buildings were erected, costing $23,200. That was a 30% increase in buildings erected from the previous year. The expatriate building hours in the 1967 year totalled 45 months, with Ron contributing 10% of that time (4.5mths). The 1967 expatriate building hours were 20% less than in 1966, yet 30% more building was accomplished. The reason given for this significant improvement, was the efficiencies created by the wood-working machinery donated by Ron.

areas.[13] Commencing in May 1968, Ron was involved in constructing the guest house with its two, two-bedroomed, self-contained flats, eight 2 or 3-bed guest rooms, men's and women's bathrooms, kitchen, dining and lounge areas and its underground concrete rain water tank of around 50,000 litres capacity.

Meanwhile Gil, with his entrepreneurial mindset, had successfully encouraged about nine people who were interested in the College to apply for nine residential blocks of land (sections in NZ terms) in the Bowerbird Road area of Lae early in 1967. During Ron's 1968, 1969 and 1970 visits, six three-bedroomed houses were pre-cut at the College, trucked down the Highlands Highway and erected in Lae on six of those properties. Four properties were sold on the open market for about $8,000 each. The profit from those sales funded the two houses and three remaining vacant blocks CLTC kept. On these, for $15,000, Ron built a two-level four flat duplex with a vacant block on either side, which later became the CLTC Lae Centre. Besides building, Ron and Peg (who accompanied Ron in 1970) were the College's Lae representatives during their 1969 and 1970 visits, prior to Peter and Margaret Rowse arriving in Lae to release Ron to concentrate on building.

In 1971/72 Ron headed up ATA's building team to construct the ATA Omili Lae freight terminal, workshop facilities for servicing the highway trucks and accommodation for PNG staff.[14] Garth Morgan observes:

> It is a testimony to Ron's skill as a builder, that he designed, cut the steel pipes for the trusses, welded everything together and drilled the holes for the bolts that would hold the trusses in place one with the other for the two-level Omili L-shaped freight depot, on the grassed land adjacent to the CLTC duplex in Bowerbird Road, without any shelter from the sun, heat and humidity. The completed trusses were transported to the building site, craned into position and bolted together, without any adjustments having to be made, in less than four hours. Ron's design ensured there were no supporting

---

13. Ron used the 'Youngman trusses' in building the Hazel Nate Community Centre 1967, the main auditorium in 1969, the first library building in 1970, the present library in 1981, and the Alliance Training Association freight depot and workshop buildings in Lae during 1971-1973.
14. Alliance Training Association, 'Minutes of ATA Directors' Meeting', 17-19 August 1972, held in Lae. This ATA terminal, Omili, Lae, including plant and equipment, had all been constructed for $48,047, an average cost of $3.19 for 15,050 sq. ft. of building, some of it double storied.

posts in the middle of the L-shaped floor, to make it as easy as possible for the highway trucks to move throughout the complex.[15]

During 1972/73, Ron supervised the building of the Mount Hagen Christian Bookshop, on behalf of ATA who, by then, were operating the ATA Timberline Ltd yard in Mt. Hagen.

In 1981 Ron and Peg returned to CLTC (lived with the Morgans) and supervised the building of the present Leonard Buck library. Their son, Keith, designed and drew the detailed plans, maximising the flexible use of the floor space for shelving, tables and desks.

The Yougmans at the opening of The Leonard Buck Library 1981

Ron was called Home on 23 August 2011, two months before his 90th birthday. However, his contribution to CLTC had not finished. Early in 2016, the trustees of the Roskill Christian Trust agreed to distribute all the capital of the Trust to the Christian organisations that Ron and Peg had been supporting in New Zealand. Due to the New Zealand tax laws at the time, the 1961 Trust Deed did not allow the funds to go to overseas organisations. Ron had overcome that problem in 1964 and during the following decade by giving CLTC of himself and Peg. But CLTC had a New Zealand need. Two PNG CLTC faculty families enrolled at Otago University for three years of Doctoral studies in June 2015. Peg was

---

15. Morgan, 'A Tribute to Ron and Peg Youngman'. 1, 2.

able with her daughter Christine and Garth Morgan (three trustees), to encourage the Trust's Chairperson to give the last NZD$45,000 of the Trust's capital to help fund three years of Doctoral biblical studies for the two families. Upon graduation they will return to CLTC and teach bachelor and masters level PNG students in the campus and library facilities to which Ron and Peg contributed so much from 1964 to 1981.[16]

Gil's influence on Ron and Peg Youngman resulted in a complete change of direction and an enormous contribution made to the infrastructure of CLTC and ATA, without which neither ministry could have functioned effectively. Later we will speak of the years following Ron's return to New Zealand, when there emerged another legacy from his association with Gil: a legacy that those close to him believe is even more significant than the infrastructure he provided for CLTC and ATA in PNG.

Aubrey Coster
Pacific Training Institute

Aubrey Coster

Gil's later vision for a training institute for Pacific leaders in Australia required the provision of suitable facilities. In November 1986, he approached Aubrey Coster and shared his vision for training Pacific leaders. He encouraged Aubrey to consider donating 140 acres of his land at Laurieton NSW, for the establishment of new SSEM headquarters, and a training centre where leaders from across the Pacific and within Australia could be further equipped for their leadership roles. Aubrey was inspired by Gil's vision, and open to hear the Lord's will for him to make such a valuable gift. He agreed to make his land available.[17]

The PTI was established on this land and opened in 1988. Unfortunately, as we have read, due to Gil's declining health the ministry of the PTI was not able to continue. Instead, the campus was sold to the New Tribes Mission and today training missionaries to work amongst unreached people groups continues in the beautiful Laurieton setting.

---

16. Morgan, 'A Tribute to Ron and Peg Youngman', 3.
17. Gordon Griffiths, 'Ray Laird's Response to the SSEM Part of Gil's Story', 1, 2.

The stories in this chapter provide examples of people whose hearts were open to the Lord, with gifts, skills or resources that made possible the development of a diversity of ministries and organisations. In each case Gil was the one the Spirit of the Lord used to awaken and move people into his Kingdom work. Their legacies endure and provide the significant facilities by which leaders are equipped for ministry in PNG and across the Pacific.

Students and staff lifting the frame of the Library into place

The completed Leonard Buck Library with Vision Hill behind

17

LEGACY IN THEOLOGICAL EDUCATORS

How may we quicken the pace of pastoral training,
(a challenge to formal pastoral training models)
while increasing the quality everywhere
(a challenge to ad-hoc, non-formal pastoral training initiatives)?
May I suggest that collaborative and multiplicative pastoral training
of large numbers of pastors
can effectively address the opportunities and dangers in four realities:
More evangelists required to reach the large numbers
of unreached peoples,
Biblically mature pastors able to disciple those responding to the Gospel,
Gifted leaders and teachers to preserve the fruit of church planting
in expounding God's Word,
Multiplying mature biblically based Christian pastors
and leaders who can equip others.[1]

Gil's legacy in developing leaders lies not only in his equipping national students for various ministries and vocations in PNG, but also in his faculty and support team who were prepared for later leadership in theological education and Christian leadership training programs in PNG, New Zealand and Australia.

John and Ann Hitchen

Christian Leaders' Training College Papua New Guinea, Bible College of New Zealand /Laidlaw College, CLTC New Zealand Advisory Council

We have already heard of Gil's meeting John and Ann Hitchen during his whirlwind 1964 visit to New Zealand, and their call to CLTC. That

---

1. Raymesh, 'Training of Pastors', 2, 3. I have slightly adjusted the wording in this quote to reflect in a succinct way the content of the author's challenge – essentially advocating that leadership development is a critical strategy in God's mission today.

one encounter with Gil bore a long-lasting legacy for CLTC, PNG churches and later in New Zealand.

While John had some good ministry experience and sound academic and spiritual preparation for the CLTC assignment, he had never set foot in PNG! When he arrived, Gil took him through a careful orientation process to induct him into PNG culture, the needs of the churches, and the ethos and vision of CLTC. John describes this process in some detail, providing a great example of Gil's purposeful development of his key staff members:

John & Ann Hitchen with daughter Cate

> From my earliest days at CLTC from 5 January 1965, Gil sent me out with his wife, Pat, on her kaukau (sweet potato) and vegetable buying rounds in the landrover through the surrounding villages. This did much more than motivate me to study Mihalic's Grammar and Dictionary of Neo Melanesian, or Tok Pisin. I saw first-hand the village life, the bartering process, the mutual diplomacy skills of PNGns and whiteskins in creative tension, the interplay between older women and the younger men in the buying and selling processes and learned about living conditions in the valley.
>
> Gil set me to analysing the use of controlled English in the Bible in Basic English which we used initially as our classroom text, blending with the insights from Dennet's Word List for developing our controlled English Bible and Theology lecture notes. I had completed at NZBTI a course on 'Missionary Methods and Practice' taught by Rob Kirkby, recently returned from service in Vanuatu. Now, at Gil's suggestion, I extended my familiarity with Eugene Nida's *Customs, Culture and Christianity* from the NZBTI course, to grapple with the communication principles of Nida's *Message and Mission* and *Religion Across Cultures*. We also gleaned what we could from the new studies on 'English as a Second Language' under the constraints of living in pre-internet days in the PNG highlands.

Gil and I developed a working relationship in which we would discuss, usually briefly, the need to clarify an issue, or our approach to things like lecture patterns, the content and order of courses, the College contribution to a seminar, input for an upcoming conference, or reports and recommendations for the Melbourne Committee of CLTC. I would then draft up those initial comments into a proposal or paper or teaching materials, then Gil would read, comment, re-orient or endorse the draft, for further development to produce the finished product. If I had an idea or suggestion, I soon learned it was best to prepare a brief outline of contributing factors, suggest alternative ways we might handle the problem, and then give it to Gil to think over. He would usually decide his preferred way to address the issue, re-arrange the factors to consider, and add other comments supporting his preference. Then he would present his recommendations to our College leadership team. As a group, we would agree to the inspiring way Gil had presented the issue, and I would be tasked to prepare the necessary paper, report or materials for wider presentation or implementation. In this way, I gained a wealth of insight from Gil, and he internalised, embraced and promoted as his own the approaches we had agreed on. I came to enjoy seeing ideas suggested to Gil work through the alembic of his mind and come out with his mature flourish and his distinctive texture to influence key people on a much wider front than I could have imagined at the beginning.

Gil arranged orientation to Melanesian culture for me beyond the College, especially through the vacation ministries of our early students. In our first teaching year, 1965, during one break between terms, Gil led our first 'Commando Team' of students accompanied by me, to the Baptist Mission area of Baiyer River. Meeting experienced missionaries like Ken Osborne and Rob Thompson; seeing our students from that area preaching and teaching in their vernacular language; visiting Kwinkia, Kumbwareta, and Lumusa village churches; and spending five days on 'retreat' in a bush camp with 50 first generation Christians, now the experienced pastors of the nascent Baptist Church, was a huge experience and learning curve for me. Gil's Dutch New Guinea and Telefolmin experience were evident as he was back in a grass-roots teaching setting, and I 'caught' more fundamental insights from my mentor. For the second 'Commando Mission' at the end of the school year, Gil sent me with the team to the Western Province, where, again, seeing in situ the UFM stalwarts, Dudley Deasey, Alwyn Neuendorf, Brian Tucker and the younger ones like Bruce and Kathy Shields, at Balimo, Awaba, Pangoa (Lake Murray) and Rumginae was an invaluable opportunity to observe, discuss and absorb a wealth of cross-cultural mission wisdom. Again, seeing the students speaking Gogodala, Zimakane and their other dialects, and moving freely between them in different locations, and then talking over how they were translating into those various dialects the English concepts we had discussed in the College classroom, was shaping my understanding daily. Not to mention living on sak-sak (sago); travelling in dug-out canoes; and being stranded for an extra week at Rumginae and thereby missing my wife's birthday and our first wedding anniversary in PNG. The raw, naïve, youngster who had landed in PNG twelve months before had been through a richly formative first year – all under Gil's overseeing eye.

The second and third years went further. Not only another student team ministry to the Christian Brethren work in the West Sepik region, but, with the Evangelical Alliance budding and blossoming with regular Executive and Annual meetings at CLTC, Gil was involving me with wider networks of mission leaders, including Charles Horne and Bill Merriweather (of UFM), Kay Liddle and Colin Cliffe whom I already knew quite well (of CMML), Don Doull and Keith Bricknell (ABMS), John Pearce and Dieter Volz (SSEM), Norman Dietsch (Manus Evangelical Mission), Erwin Yungen (Swiss Evangelical Brotherhood Mission), Wallace White and Bruce Blowers (Church of the Nazarene), and many more of that early generation of post-World War II evangelical mission leaders. Gil was at the same time pushing me to prepare papers and resource material for the concerns their young churches were facing – on the place of anthropology and cultural study in Christian service; on the challenge of legalism as new converts carried over old, fearful attitudes to dominant spirit powers and ancestors into their new encounter with Christ; on the place of inter-connected levels of Bible teaching for the churches of Melanesia; on the role of vacation ministries in CLTC's training; why English as the medium of instruction; how cross-cultural communication works; and, at the heart of it all, what is Christian leadership in rural PNG? My focus was on serving the churches and missionary teams through these papers. Gil knew that, probably just as significantly, I was having to grow in my understanding to be equipped for long-term ministry through CLTC. He challenged me to broaden my thinking and grow into the opportunities he was creating by his own leadership, net-working and broader vision for the Evangelical Alliance and cooperation between the missions and churches in PNG.

Increasingly, Gil trusted me with more of the curriculum development, and thinking through the practical issues we faced as the College developed and he pursued aspects of his wider vision. But he never let me forget who was in charge, and he always expected full commitment, commensurate with his own single-minded dedication. I could go on almost indefinitely, but I trust my point is clear. John Hitchen's contribution at CLTC was the fruit of Gil McArthur's choice, mentoring and trust, and an expression of Gil's appreciation of his own role and its dependence on a group of lieutenants under him to achieve what he envisioned.[2]

John was appointed Principal of CLTC when J Oswald Sanders retired at the end of 1974. Across the years he has provided vital leadership under Gil's early orientation and mentoring: in the development of courses and syllabi, writing and presenting conference papers, facilitating great learning and growing experiences for students, and building a competent expatriate and growing national faculty team over the past 50 plus years, which he continues today. John's legacy is evident in the strong biblical focus, spiritual emphasis, cultural relevance and academic excellence of CLTC programs today.

From 1979 to 1984, the Hitchen family went to Aberdeen for John to engage in PhD studies. On completion of his research and writing on James Chalmers, one of the early pioneer London Missionary Society missionaries to Rarotonga and New Guinea, John and the family returned to New Zealand.

Unable to go back to CLTC full-time due to health issues, John served with Rutland Street Chapel before appointment to BCNZ (now Laidlaw College) as Dean of the Christchurch branch in 1987. He served as National Principal from 1990 to 1998, and since then has provided strong leadership in the post-graduate programs at Laidlaw. However, with God's enabling John has also been able to continue to teach and consult with CLTC right up until today. He is a Life Member of the Council, and a member of the Academic Advisory Board, advising and

---

2. Hitchen, 'Gil McArthur as Mentor', 1–3.

developing the introduction of the CLTC postgraduate programs. In this process John has taught courses, advised on maintaining excellence in academic processes, and supervised CLTC postgraduate students in their research and writing at both Masters and Doctoral levels – thus contributing significantly to the legacy of a qualified faculty team to continue the vision of CLTC.

Joshua and Mone Daimoi
Christian Leaders' Training College Papua New Guinea, Bible Society Papua New Guinea, Tokarara Christian Fellowship, Evangelical Alliance of PNG, Melanesian Council of Churches, Leadership Link, Boroko Baptist Church

Joshua and Mone Daimoi

Right from the birth of CLTC, Gil's eye was on the horizon of his vision that saw CLTC under the leadership of competent and qualified Melanesians and Pacific Islanders. In 1962, Gil first met Joshua in their home at Lakemba in Sydney. Joshua was a student at the Baptist Theological College of NSW. He was from Irian Jaya (now Indonesian Papua) and had gone to Port Moresby in PNG to train as a medical doctor. In Port Moresby he experienced the reality of faith in Christ and became involved in the Boroko Baptist Church.

Sensing a call to ministry (even hearing a voice that asked, 'What about the others?'), Joshua was offered the opportunity to study at the NSW Baptist Theological College (now Morling College). During that time, Gil shared with him the vision for CLTC, and the involvement of Melanesian/Pacific people. Due to the Indonesian takeover of Joshua's country, and the oppression of traditional leaders, it was not safe for Joshua to return home, so he was drawn in the direction of PNG and CLTC.

In 1967, while waiting for a visa to enter PNG, Joshua received a letter from CLTC that read, 'If Joshua believes God has called him to CLTC he should come immediately.'[3] He arrived mid-1968 – the first

---

3. Daimoi, 'Recollections of Dr McArthur'.

Melanesian on faculty. 'Joshua's affinity for the cultural background and awareness of the challenges involved in applying biblical insights relevantly within Melanesian societies made a deep impact on students' lives. His commitment to serious biblical study and sound teaching of the scriptures pioneered a pathway many graduates have followed since.'[4]

Joshua met Mone, a High School student from the Baiyer River Baptist Church. After appropriate cultural negotiations were completed, they were married after Mone had completed a year of study at CLTC. The CLTC faculty assumed the cultural obligation of Joshua's tribe in assisting provision for the bride price. In 1971, he received a letter from the Boroko Baptist Church, inviting them down to Port Moresby to start a new outreach ministry program at Tokarara. Joshua went with some trepidation to see Gil, as the week before he had written a letter thanking him for bringing him to CLTC, helping him readjust to his own culture. Gil agreed he should go, although at the time it was a considerable loss for CLTC. But on reflection, Joshua sees Gil's decision as very strategic:

> Eternity alone knows the real significance of the decision I made, and Gil's part in approving it, for Mone and me to come down to Port Moresby in June 1971.
>
> The importance of the decision made unfolded as follows. After being in Port Moresby for three years serving at Tokarara, we received word from CLTC Banz requesting us to return to the College. At the same time, Bev Burke who was in charge of the Bible Society, asked me to become the Executive Secretary of the Bible Society of Papua New Guinea. After consulting Mone, we agreed to take on the Bible Society's offer.
>
> This opened the door for me to visit all the big churches in PNG, sharing with the heads of the churches on the importance of God's Word for our people. It enabled me to get to know all the heads of the churches in PNG. In this way God prepared me for the responsibility I was to take up at CLTC in the years ahead. For one thing, the heads of the churches would know who I was, so they would not be afraid to send their students to be trained at CLTC.[5]

At the end of 1983, after being sponsored by CLTC to complete his ThM at Fuller Seminary School of World Mission, Joshua became the first

---
4. John Hitchen, 'Joshua Daimoi - Comments from John Hitchen', 4 September 2017.
5. Daimoi, 'Recollections of Dr McArthur'.

Melanesian Principal of CLTC.[6] He later completed his PhD through the University of Sydney and continued to serve CLTC through to his retirement. In his later years he was appointed the Director of Leadership Link which was based in the CLTC Port Moresby campus. Today he still holds the title Principal Emeritus of CLTC in appreciation for his long service to the College. Joshua's personal relationships with a wide range of church leaders, and his continuing service to national church and political leaders in his Bible Society, CLTC, urban pastorates, and Leadership Link specifically serving national leaders in Port Moresby, reflect how deeply he had imbibed Gil McArthur's vision that leadership development is a critical strategy in God's mission today.

In 2015, Joshua was honoured by the PNG Government. He was made an Officer of the Order of the Logohu OL (an award for distinguished service to PNG) for his contribution to theological education and the Baptist Church. He was presented with the award by the Govenor-General at Government House in March.

Rev Dr Joshua Daimoi at the award ceremony with the Governor-General.

In expressing his personal tribute to Gil, Joshua says, 'I am very grateful to God that Dr McArthur's vision to train Papua New Guineans and Pacific Islanders as students, teachers and leaders has become a reality. For Mone and me, CLTC will always remain our home and our training ground.'[7]

David and Margaret Price

Christian Leaders' Training College of Papua New Guinea, Bible College of Victoria, Pioneers of Australia

A cup of coffee with Gil McArthur in May 1967 dramatically changed life direction for David and Margaret. David came to faith in Christ as a

---

6. Joshua followed David Price who was appointed Principal when John Hitchen left for his study leave in 1979. David was asked to join the faculty of the Bible College of Victoria and commenced in 1984.
7. Daimoi, 'Recollections of Dr McArthur'.

13-year-old and this commitment matured during Billy Graham's 1959 Crusade. He graduated in Commerce and began work as an Accountant planning to join the family business. Margaret can never remember a time she did not love the Lord Jesus. She completed secondary teacher training and taught at St Marys and Condell Park in the western suburbs of Sydney.

David & Margaret Price

After only working for a few months David became increasingly restless under the conviction that following accountancy and the family business was not God's plan for him. After some struggle about direction David resigned and became a student at the Melbourne Bible Institute in 1963/64. This time proved a rich preparation for service in studying God's Word and developing both new friendships, gifts and skills in ministry. It was also the time when a connection was made with CLTC. MBI was in the process of appointing Gil Principal of CLTC. The McArthur family lived on the MBI campus, while Gil raced around on deputation until they departed for PNG late 1964. The MBI students heard about the vision, prayed for the needs and raised the funds for the first single student house. Bill Clack, for some unknown reason, asked David to go with Peter Rowse as they drove the Principal's new car and new tractor and trailer filled with implements down to the wharf for shipment to PNG. David had no idea he would later serve at CLTC.

Following MBI David was led to the NSW Baptist Theological College (now Morling College) from 1965-1967 to complete his BD and prepare for pastoral ministry. It was there he met Joshua Daimoi who was one of the Senior Students. David became the Youth Pastor at West Ryde Baptist Church, and then Pastor of the North Epping Baptist Church 1966-1967. In February 1966 Margaret's parents moved from the Church Missionary Society Conference Centre at Katoomba to become the cooks at the Baptist College. Margaret was teaching Maths/Science at Condell Park High School, and David met her over the kitchen servery! They were engaged in December 1966, expecting the Lord was leading them next into pastoral ministry. Margaret finished her teaching bond and became a student at Sydney Missionary and Bible College in 1967.

It was in May 1967 that David received the invitation to coffee from Gil McArthur who was passing through Sydney at the time. Margaret was unable to get permission to leave College during the week, so David went on his own. Gil spoke persuasively about the critical strategy in world mission of training and developing leaders, showed the pictures, and shared the vision of CLTC. He explained that they needed another Bible teacher to start in 1968. 'Would you, David, pray about coming to join the faculty of CLTC?'

It was remarkable that Margaret, as a nine-year-old, had experienced a definite 'call' to be a missionary in PNG. She told everyone that she would become a doctor and marry a pilot who could fly her around PNG to care for the people! David, however, like John Hitchen and others, had serious questions about why Gil wanted young inexperienced people, rather than those who had proven missionary and Bible teaching experience in the PNG cultural context. Like Moses he felt totally inadequate, and that Gil and the MBI Committee should find somebody else.[8] However, prayer together brought the conviction that the Lord was saying that this was simply a matter of obedience. If he was opening this door, then the response should be to obey – not to decide whether they were competent or not. For 'the one who calls is faithful, and he will do it'.[9]

With this solid assurance, David and Margaret finished their biblical studies. David graduated, concluded pastoral ministry, was ordained, and they were married 9 December 1967. After their honeymoon, they went to Melbourne to farewell David's family, returned to Sydney, packed up, and arrived at CLTC in early February 1968 – only seven weeks married, and somewhat stressed after the turbulent weeks preceding their departure, including a fire on the Sydney wharf which reduced more than half their personal effects to ashes! Gil was away on his study leave in the USA, and Roy Merritt was Acting Principal (He was the Vice Principal at MBI when David was a student). Because their house was yet to be built, David and Margaret initially lived with Roy and Dora Merritt in Gil's house.

John Hitchen quickly took the initiative, beginning the process of mentoring them into the culture and their new ministry roles at CLTC (as Gil had with him). After ten challenging but exhilarating years at

---

8. Exodus 4:13.
9. I Thessalonians 5:24.

CLTC, during which their three children were born, David was granted study leave to enrol at Fuller Seminary School of World Mission. He had been in contact with Alan Tippett and commenced core courses seeking help in better understanding Gospel/Cultural issues that seemed vital in the emerging church life in PNG.

While at Fuller in Pasadena, David and Margaret were put in contact with Ted and Peggy Fletcher and their family who lived nearby in Arcadia.[10] As we have seen, Gil first met Ted and Peggy in 1968 when they were struggling with the 'sense of call' to start a new mission agency. He had strongly encouraged them to step out, follow the vision, and write a new chapter in their story book of life. Although the Fletcher family children were older, the two families became firm friends. Ted and David enjoyed many hours of discussion on mission, and Ted was hungry for news of the unreached tribes in PNG. David and Margaret returned to CLTC in July 1979, and when John and Ann Hitchen departed for his PhD studies in Aberdeen in August, David was appointed CLTC Principal. Ted and Peggy started their new mission agency, and they came for a personal visit to CLTC and the Pacific in August 1979. This was followed by later sending their first short term missionaries out to PNG, including Ted's own children – Ginny, John, Arlene and Carol. John returned as a long-term missionary to PNG, as did a number of other short-term visitors.

When David was appointed Principal of CLTC, he sensed it was to be for a short season to mentor his lifelong friend Joshua Daimoi to be appointed as the first National Principal. Joshua was appointed in 1983, and David and Margaret responded to the invitation to teach missiology on the faculty of the Bible College of Victoria. Again, they found themselves in the roles of training and mentoring Christian leaders – the passion that God had implanted in their hearts through Gil. After eight years David was appointed Principal of BCV in 1990, a position he held until January 2005.

Over the years, Ted Fletcher had often said to David and Margaret 'when are you going to join Pioneers?' It finally came to fruition in July 2005, when David and Margaret accepted an invitation from Australian Director Tim Meyers to join Pioneers of Australia. Sadly, it was after

---

10. This contact was organised through Bill Clack, Len Buck and Gil. Gil had met Ted earlier, and his friendship with Ted continued in visits to the President's Prayer Breakfast in Washington where Ted also met Len Buck, Bill Clack and Will Renshaw. They urged Ted to make contact with David and Margaret.

Ted's death in 2003. David and Margaret served in the Member Care/Development team and were also involved in the InTent International leadership development program for key Pioneers leaders from around the world. After some nine years, Margaret needed more time to care for her mother, but at the time of writing David continues as a part-time volunteer. Again, their role in Pioneers has been the outworking of Gil's challenge – the critical strategy of developing mature and effective servant leaders for the mission of God to the nations of the world.

Bruce and Retta Renich

South Sea Evangelical Mission and South Sea Evangelical Church Papua New Guinea, Christian Leaders' Training College Papua New Guinea

Bruce & Retta Renich

'It only takes a spark to get a fire going' – so goes the line of the song. Gil McArthur was the instrument for the spark of the Spirit in the lives of Bruce and Retta Renich in moving them out of the USA into cross cultural ministry in PNG.

Retta is the daughter of Egerton and Betty Long. Egerton's parents were missionaries to the indigenous people in the work of the Aborigines Inland Mission (now Australian Indigenous Ministries). In preparing for Christian ministry, Egerton left Australia to study at the Moody Bible Institute in Chicago. There he met Betty Hankins who became his lifelong partner in 1942. Together they served in ministry in Australia and the USA for the whole of their 72 years of marriage. Daughter Retta followed the example of her father and moved to the USA to become a student at the Moody Bible Institute. There she met Bruce Renich. They married in 1968 after finishing Bible College. Bruce went on to do his undergraduate studies at Trinity University.

Retta's father became a good friend of Gil. In 1970, when Wheaton College awarded Gil an honorary Doctor of Laws for his work in establishing the ministry of CLTC, Retta's father called Retta and Bruce to ask if they would look after Gil on his visit to Wheaton to receive his award. Gil stayed with Bruce and Retta and shared with them the story and pictures of the development and work of CLTC.

Gil's visit and vision for the ministry of CLTC aroused in Bruce and Retta a keen interest in CLTC. Could they be involved, was there a place for them? They already knew God wanted them as missionaries, but where? In 1971 they wrote and asked Kay Liddle (the Acting Principal) if there was an opportunity for them at CLTC? The reply came that CLTC did not have a need for them at this particular time. Some months later, when Bruce had completed his studies, he was settling into his teaching position and they were starting to put down roots where they were. But they still sensed a call to mission and felt that instead of just waiting for something to open up for them they should take the initiative. They were in process of discussions with The Evangelical Alliance Mission when one night their phone rang at 2 am. It was Retta's excited father calling to say that Gil had called him to ask what they were doing. Gil asked Egerton to call Bruce and Retta and tell them SSEM wanted them right away to work in Youth ministry with the SSEC in the Sepik Province of PNG. How soon could they come? Sensing that this was God's intervention, things moved fast. They do not recall filling out application papers before leaving the USA for Australia, but they may have done so in Sydney. It seemed that Gil's endorsement was enough.

Retta's father was the pastor of Hornsby Baptist Church in Sydney and Gil preached there at the commissioning and farewell service for Bruce and Retta in early 1973. His powerful message unsettled many as Gil spoke of the isolation, desolation and privation that this young missionary couple would face in the remote location of their assignment in PNG. Gil met Bruce and Retta in March 1973 when they arrived in Wewak and flew out with them to Yagrumbok airstrip and mission station. He encouraged them to get involved with the Trade Store, so they could learn Pidgin and PNG culture. Retta recalls this was a tough period for her in what was a 'man's world', but the experience they gained at village level was excellent preparation for teaching and relating to students later. After 18 months the SSEC moved them to Walahuta which was a more central location for them to engage in youth ministry. After working hard to establish a youth ministry program and training leaders, in 1975 they were asked to teach for 6 months at CLTC. Sometime later in 1979 they received a letter from Peter Salisbury, the General Secretary of the SSEM in Sydney, asking them if Bruce would accept the appointment of General Director of SSEM based in Sydney. How quickly could they come? The transition into this role was not well handled as the position description was not clear about the expectations of the Board. After two years, Bruce realised from feedback he was receiving that the Board wanted a fundraiser and public relations/marketing person, and this was not his gifting. Following a meeting with the Board, Bruce and Retta sensed they should resign their position, even although SSEM asked them to return to PNG. Then followed a period of 'leave of absence' which was for them a 'wilderness experience' as they struggled to understand what the Lord wanted them to do. During this time Bruce had a conversation with Gil about the mismatch of his SSEM role in Sydney and found Gil's fatherly compassion and care a great encouragement as he affirmed their call to follow the Lord wherever He led them.

In late 1981, they received a call from David Price, the Principal of CLTC, asking if they would join the faculty. Bruce's immediate response, though the desire of his heart was otherwise, was 'No.' There were still relational issues to be resolved as a result of their experience with SSEM, and he knew that without resolution any future ministry would be hindered. But in a wonderful way these issues were soon resolved so that when David rang a second time to ask they said 'Yes.' They packed up or sold everything in two weeks and returned to the USA for partnership development, arriving at CLTC in early 1983 where they received a very warm welcome.

Since 1983, Bruce and Retta, with Nathan, Joshua, and Michelle, have served CLTC until today. When he arrived in 1983 Bruce was a faculty member, then Dean of Studies, then Principal of CLTC from 1992-1995. After this extended time in ministry in PNG the family returned to Chicago. With Retta's support, Bruce gained his MA in Intercultural Studies at Wheaton College. Then while Missions Pastor at their home church, the Village Church of Barrington (ILL, USA), Bruce completed his Doctorate in Education studies in 2007 with Northern Illinois University where he researched and wrote on, 'The Transmission of Knowledge: Perspectives on the Change from Traditional to Modern Settings in Papua New Guinea.'

They returned to the Faculty of CLTC in September 2011 where Bruce was soon appointed to the position of Dean of Graduate Studies providing leadership in the newly established MTh program. In 2012 he was appointed Vice Principal – Education with responsibility for the oversight of the whole of the Education Division on the Banz and urban campuses. Retta has used her remarkable secretarial and administrative skills, along with her gift in teaching and a pastoral heart to bring her own outstanding contribution to the life of the College. In recent years Retta has faced some serious health challenges which have required regular travel for specialist treatment in the USA. As I write, while they continue serving on the Banz campus (where Bruce is currently Dean of Associate Schools Development), they have been advised by the doctors in PNG that they can no longer provide the care Retta needs for her chronic kidney condition. They are currently making plans to reside in the USA from February 2019. Bruce plans to continue his involvement in regular visits to CLTC.

Gil's legacy is seen in the years of service that Bruce and Retta have given first to the SSEM and SSEC in the Sepik province of PNG and then to CLTC. They look back on all that they have experienced and say that they can see the hand of God all along the way shaping them for the next tasks ahead – sometimes new experiences to move them on in ministry, but other times just to equip them to help and counsel others. What Gil saw in them in that first encounter north of Chicago they do not know, but they do know that he was a visionary man of God who could not only exercise discernment, but also had a heart for building young people into vessels fit for God's use. That is their experience of Gil, and that is the passion they saw poured into CLTC and why they have always loved the work. The possibilities for lives trained at CLTC are unlimited, now reaching out through PNG national missionaries to take the Gospel from what was considered the end of the earth on again to those in other 'ends of the earth' who are still without Christ.[11]

William and Iru Longgar

Christian Leaders' Training College Papua New Guinea, Malmaluan Training College, Melanesian Institute, Rarongo Theological College, Constitutional and Law Reform Commission of Papua New Guinea

William and Iru Longgar

William Longgar, current Principal of CLTC, was not

---

11. Bruce and Retta Renich, 'Gil McArthur and Bruce and Retta Renich', 2 August 2018, 1-3.

only touched by Gil's influence in his early Christian life but entered directly into Gil's legacy as the current Principal of CLTC. William was a student at the University of PNG in the early 1970s, and while there became involved in the Everyman's Centre in Port Moresby. He was led to faith in Christ in his final year of law by Mari Kapi the first national judge in PNG, and later Chief Justice. Sir Mari Kapi was a close friend and partner with Gil in the PLF gatherings in Port Moresby. Gil sometimes visited and spoke at the Everyman's Centre when passing through Port Moresby during his time at CLTC. William was challenged by Gil's messages. He said (as did others) that you needed a dictionary with you when you listened to Gil because of his profound use of theological truth and his well-known phrases like 'the cosmic Christ'. But Gil's passion for God and his commitment to the Gospel, and the mission of God in the world left its mark in William's life: 'the heart of the man came through'. William became involved in ministry to students and on the streets in Port Moresby. He later attended two of the PLF gatherings in Port Moresby in 1980 and 1983.[12]

William was sponsored by CLTC through the final years of his university and CLTC studies when he completed a Bachelor of Arts in Religious Studies at the University of PNG. He then completed a Bachelor of Theology at CLTC where he also had a faculty teaching role from 1977 until 1986. In 1987-1988 he was Coordinator of the United Church Urban Ministry Program in Port Moresby. In 1989-1990 he was on the faculty of Rarongo Theological College in Rabaul, and then moved to teach from 1991 to 1994 at the United Church Training in Mission and Leadership Centre. He joined the faculty of the Melanesian Institute in Goroka before being awarded a scholarship to complete his PhD studies in 2002-2006 at Asbury Seminary in Wilmore, Kentucky USA. He returned to take up appointment as the Director of the Melanesian Institute 2007-2009. Following this he became Principal of the United Church School of Theology and Mission at Rarongo in Rabaul 2010-2012. In recent years William has been appointed a member of the Constitutional and Law Reform Commission of PNG. Few Papua New Guineans have had this breadth of training and experience.

William and Iru's study and ministry journey prepared them in a remarkable way to return to CLTC as a faculty member in 2013. William returned after 27 years involved in other ministries, 'because as I served

---

12. Longgar, 'Memories of Gilbert McArthur'.

at CLTC for the first ten years, so I wanted to give back to CLTC in the last ten years of my service for the Lord'. He was appointed the fifth national Principal of CLTC at the August Council Meetings in 2013.[13] He has been a leader of great integrity, providing a godly example and a servant heart together with his wife Iru.

* * * * * * * *

Reviewing just these few examples of Gil's legacy in those who became involved in biblical training and equipping leaders for church and community, highlights that developing leaders is essentially about growing people into their full God-given potential.

> Older leadership theory assumed that the work of leaders was to accomplish a task through people. The task was to make sales, build buildings, win elections, mobilise armies or mow the grass. People were seen as human resources rather than resourceful humans. But what if that formula is turned around? What if the real task is not primarily to accomplish work, but to develop people?
> *Effective leaders use the task to develop people.*[14]

Some felt that at times Gil erred on the side of seeing people primarily as human resources. But the stories of these examples emphasise that he not only saw people with potential to enable the fulfilment of a vision, but he was also committed to developing those people to their full God-given potential. In the outworking of this commitment who can measure the impact upon literally thousands of students in PNG, the Pacific, Australia and New Zealand who were enabled to grow towards their full potential through the training institutions of these and the many others whose stories could also have been included.

---

13. Longgar, 'Memories of Gilbert McArthur'.
14. James E. Plueddemann, *Leading Across Cultures* (Intervarsity Press, 2009), 179.

Garth Morgan, Mark Baiai, Ross Weymouth and Chris Alu surveying the progress of growing wet and dry rice

CLTC Beef Cattle

Poultry Program including both eggs, meat and day-old chicken production

CLTC Hatchery now has the capacity to produce 100,000 meat chickens each week

18
LEGACY IN MISSIONAL BUSINESS ENTREPRENEURS

Where there are no oxen, the manger is empty,
but from the strength of an ox come abundant harvests.[1]

One of the more common trends in mission today is the development of strategies integrating business and mission. The world of business should be more than simply sitting on the sidelines of God's mission and sending funds. Rather, the business world can be the arena for people to participate directly in the mission of God through their vocations and professional careers. Kingdom businesses can be set up in places where there is no 'missionary visa' available, providing opportunity for Christian professionals and entrepreneurs to be on the cutting edge of mission. Paul's activity in tentmaking is a good biblical example of this principle, and over the history of the Christian mission there are many examples of missionary entrepreneurs and churches engaging in the business world in their missionary activities.

During the 1970s there was a growing call for Christians to engage in Business as Mission (BAM), attempting to overcome the sacred/secular divide that has so infected the Western Church. BAM is not simply a fundraising tactic or a visa platform (although it can function as both), but a primary and relevant strategy for the 21st Century – especially in the 10/40 Window area of unreached peoples.

> [BAM] includes God's concerns for such business-related issues as economic development, employment and unemployment, economic justice and the use and distribution of natural and creative resources among the human family. These are aspects of God's redemptive work through Jesus Christ and the Church. Ted Yamamori, former International Director of the Lausanne movement has said that 'the use of business in global outreach is a strategy of choice for the context of the 21st Century mission'.[2]

---

1. Proverbs 14:4.

The PNG mission story is replete with many examples of 'Kingdom business' activities.

> Charles William Abel (1862-1930), was an Englishman…
> who arrived in British Papua in 1890 to work with the London Missionary Society. The following year, with his fellow missionary E W Walker, he established the base of an LMS missionary district on Kwato Island, near Samarai to the south of Milne Bay. Abel's vision for Kwato was of a 'total' community in which Papuans, separated from the 'darkness' of their past traditions, would develop Protestant Christian values and learn industrial skills to ensure their survival in a changing world. An ordained Congregational minister, Abel nevertheless had an essentially lay view of ministry. The Kwato Extension Association, which he was to establish, would run plantations in the Milne Bay area and a boatbuilding enterprise and dairy farm on Kwato Island; it would train teachers and evangelists and promote the sports of cricket and football.[3]

Other later examples in the mid to late 20th Century include the establishment of the trading company Namasu by the Lutheran Church, Pasuwe by APCM, Menduli by the United Church Mendi, and Baptist trade stores in the Telefolmin area among others. With the transfer from mission to church and the departure of the missionaries, most of these business activities declined in the late 20th Century.

As we have seen, Gil held strongly to an integrated biblical worldview that understood 'God established the institution and practice of business as a means of fulfilling His creation mandate to steward and care for all of creation. He is releasing the power of business to aid in the task of fulfilling the great commission making disciples of all nations. God longs to be glorified through our business activities.'[4] It was this basic 'holistic' theology that meant Gil had no hesitation engaging in the business world in his strategy in the establishment and development of CLTC. He believed that the College community embedded in a Melanesian

---

2. Lausanne Committee for World Evangelization, *Business as Mission – Lausanne Occasional Paper No. 59*, Orlando, Florida, USA: Lausanne Committee for World Evangelization, 2004, 5. This paper provides an excellent introduction to this important topic.
3. Mary McDonald, 'Charles Abel and the Kwato Mission of Papua New Guinea 1891-1975' (Project Muse, 2001), 1, in Charles Abel and the Kwato Mission of PNG 1891-1975, https://muse.jhu.edu/article/8318/summary.
4. Lausanne Committee for World Evangelization, *Business as Mission – Lausanne Occasional Paper No. 59*, 6.

context should demonstrate an integrated holistic worldview as a model for the students that had been lost by many of the churches and professional leaders. The CLTC and ATA business and support programs provided financial resources, but also examples of Christians engaging in the commercial world taking opportunity for training witnesses for kingdom impact upon the social fabric of the nation.

To achieve this objective, Gil recruited team members for CLTC and ATA who were missional business entrepreneurs committed to business as mission in their service at CLTC. This is another significant aspect of his leadership legacy.

Garth and Ruth Morgan
Christian Leaders' Training College Papua New Guinea, Alliance Training Association, New Zealand CLTC Advisory Council

Garth and Ruth were among the 'spontaneous seven' responses to Gil's passionate plea in 1964 in New Zealand. That plea was a Spirit-given life-changing moment for them.

Garth and Ruth Morgan

But it was to be two and a half years of testing, waiting and persevering in faith, before Garth and Ruth arrived on the Banz campus in August 1966. Like others before and since, they brought with them their unique gifts, special skills and experience that were vital to the healthy development of the financial and operational management of the College. Garth was a university graduate in accountancy with a focus on cost and management accounting, and sound work experience. Ruth was an experienced accounting machine operator and instructor in one of the city banks. Both were graduates of the then New Zealand Bible Training Institute (now Laidlaw College). While Gil had plenty of experience in the biblical theological training aspect of the College, he was not a qualified accountant. As a result, Gil's mentoring relationship with Garth was different to that of John. At times, it caused tensions for Garth in his financial management role. After they arrived at CLTC, Garth recalls:

> In one of my first formal meetings with Gil he told me, 'You are responsible for the College finances, administration and anything else which is not John's responsibility, (the training and teaching of the students) or not Graham's (the highway trucks, the logging and sawmilling), and you will ensure that every department that can earn money will maximise every opportunity to do so, otherwise the development of the College will suffer'.[5]

Beyond the above, Garth does not recall being given a detailed written Position Description for his role as Registrar, nor seeing one for any of his Executive colleagues in what was then a comparatively small staff team. In this rather flexible and general approach in Gil's leadership:

> Somehow, he conveyed, and we learned to understand, who was responsible for what, and we worked hard to ensure that nothing fell through the cracks between our respective responsibilities.
>
> Gil assigned responsibilities to those who were accountable to him, and trusted them to complete the tasks within the time frames he set, but with minimal input from Gil, unless we got it wrong or failed to complete the task by the set date.
>
> I do not recall any time when Gil actually spent time helping me to understand all the details of the tasks he would assign to me as the Registrar. Gil preferred to task me with a project, giving the very broad but limited guidelines, and left me to work it out, while he was away from College on some other networking or ministry assignment.'[6]

Gil held each of his lieutenants accountable for everything that other staff members responsible to them did or failed to do. Garth recalls:

> The only way I knew how to 'maximise every opportunity' was to set up an accounting system which recorded as much relevant data by quantities and values in numerically-coded accounts, which identified the various College departments, (gardens, cattle, poultry, logging, sawmill, building, engineering, transport, property, theological education, and administration) plus numerous cost centres linked to those departments for each vehicle, highway truck, tractor, generator, college store, haus sik (clinic) etc. That research during that first fortnight and praying through Jeremiah

---

5. Morgan, 'Gilbert McArthur Information', 5.
6. Morgan, 'Gilbert McArthur Information', 4–6.

33:3 resulted in a set of handwritten cash books, using 1200 coded accounts, with monthly totals 'posted' by hand on to pages with twelve columns, (recording for example, the fuel usage for each vehicle and a total for the fleet of vehicles), and these 100 plus pages formed a loose-leaf general ledger. Various financial statements and reports were then extracted by hand for the College executive and Council meetings.

Later, when Gil saw the extent and benefits of the information being extracted from those records, especially for the Council meetings, with no mechanical means to help with calculations of percentages or long columns of additions, to his credit, in 1969 he supported the request and the Council agreed to purchase from Port Moresby, a Remington book-keeping ledger-card machine. The cost of $1,600 was a major investment, being 40% of the cost of building a three-bedroomed staff house in 1968!

That first fortnight in August 1966 set the foundations of the accounting system that has recorded the financial history of the College for fifty years. The system was eventually computerised using a Canon desk-top computer, brought from NZ in 1977 at a cost of $7,000, the same amount as the fifteen-seater Toyota mini bus cost the College in the same year![7]

The fruit of the accounting and reporting system that Garth and Ruth implemented became clearer to Gil as time progressed. In 1967, when preparing budgets for each College department, Garth included amounts for depreciation as normal accounting practice required. However, when Garth presented the budgets to the College Executive, Gil exclaimed, 'What is this depreciation amount I see in these budgets? There are far more urgent and necessary priorities than depreciation.' Garth responded; 'Excuse me, Gil, but we are going to have to replace and/or buy more highway trucks, and this is a professional and acceptable way to achieve such a goal.' He noticed the astonishment on the faces of John Hitchen and Graham Walker, as they watched a young accountant challenge his Principal! 'You will remove this depreciation from these budgets. We are not going to spend our limited cash on depreciation.'[8]

Despite the protests, Gil was emphatic that the depreciation be removed from the budgets. However, that was not the end of the story.

---

7. Morgan, 'Gilbert McArthur Information', 5.
8. Morgan, 'Gilbert McArthur Information', 4.

Garth was convinced that the College would need funds to replace and purchase more trucks. So, without informing the other Executive members, he decided for each round trip a truck made to Lae, secretly to deposit $50 into a special PNG Bank account reserved for furlough fares, allowances, medical needs and designated funds etc. Sometime later, Graham Walker the Business Manager, came to Garth asking how the College could finance another highway truck. The College needs, plus those of other missions and requests from Shell and BP to transport fuel, meant more capacity was needed. Garth recalls: 'The secret depreciation provision provided the answer to Graham's question.'[9] Garth has no recollection of Gil discussing depreciation with him ever again! This regular ongoing provision provided for six more trucks by 1970, before all the highway trucks were gifted to ATA in 1971.

In the establishment phase of the College, financial resources were under constant pressure. Gil went to great lengths to control costs and maximise income, using his Registrar as an internal financial auditor to minimise expenditure where he could so that he would have the resources for major projects.

> Four months into his new experience at CLTC in 1966, Gil asked Garth to take 13 large sacks of surplus cabbages from the College gardens to Madang on the return freezer flight, to sell them to a person with whom Gil had made arrangements. On arrival in Madang, no one was expecting them, and Garth and Ruth ended up selling the cabbages on the street for the total sum of $13.30! Did Gil send them as part of some sort of orientation? Garth believed it was a test of his creativity, rather than sales of $13.30 that was behind this assignment![10]

> Monthly household accounts of all staff were closely scrutinised to ensure staff were not overspending their monthly food allowance of $20 per adult, plus the allowances for children and visitors. One of Garth's very difficult tasks was to speak with those who had overdrawn their allowances. This responsibility at times, and knowing the details of all staff accounts, impacted Garth and Ruth's relationships with other staff members. Gil regularly caused Garth embarrassment when he would introduce him to visitors as the College Registrar, 'who knows the number of toilet rolls each

---

9. Morgan, 'Gilbert McArthur Information', 4.
10. Morgan, 'Gilbert McArthur Information', 5.

household uses.' However, despite this difficulty over the years, they developed very close relationships with many staff who appreciated Garth and Ruth's important role.[11]

When the first airstrip was constructed at the College in 1966, Gil from his aviation background chose an appropriate location for gradient and prevailing winds. But in supervising the construction, he left sufficient topsoil, and planted a selection of grasses that meant the grass airstrip could also provide pasture for the developing dairy cattle herd, and so make some direct productive contribution. When completed, Gil asked MAF Chief Pilot Max Meyers to open the airstrip. Garth recalls that the meeting between Gil and Max went something like this: the three pilots were leaning over the fuselage of one of the aircraft, initially engaged in some small talk.

Gil asked Max, 'When are you going to do what you have come to do?'

In typical Max Meyers fashion, Max responded, 'The decision is yours Gil, not mine.' Gil said, 'Max, you're the chief pilot, not me.'

Max clarified the issue when he said, 'Gil, this is your campus, and your decision. What do you want? An airstrip or a cow paddock?'

Gil could not have both! It was one of those rare occasions when Gil did not achieve his goal![12]

Gil kept vehicle travel off campus to an absolute minimum. He insisted people walk to meetings, and not use work vehicles for personal use, irrespective of where you lived on the 413 acres. He required the Registrar to maximise passengers on medical travel to the hospital and ensure all travel to Mount Hagen was planned for maximum efficiency in movement of people and produce.[13]

Gil would not allow any tinned fruit to be trucked up the highway for the staff store, when fresh pineapples, paw paws, and bananas were available around College, and other 'luxuries' were to be kept to a minimum.[14]

---

11. Morgan, 'Gilbert McArthur Information', 7.
12. Morgan, 'Gilbert McArthur Information', 3.
13. Morgan, 'Gilbert McArthur Information', 8.
14. Morgan, 'Gilbert McArthur Information', 9.

Garth recalls Gil's leadership legacy of total sacrifice and commitment to the fulfilment of the vision and the tasks at hand – perhaps sometimes to the extreme:

> Gil drove himself hard seven days a week and long into the nights. He also conveyed by example and expectations, if not in actual words, to his College Executive members, that they were on the campus to do likewise, when the work required that commitment. The problem was that there was always much more work to do than it was possible to accomplish in a 6.00am to 10.00pm day, six days a week.[15]

Sometimes when the pressure was on, Gil would call a College Executive meeting for several hours on a Sunday afternoon, despite this being the only really free time in the whole week. One senior staff member, after the stress of the excessive workload over a period of months, wrote his resignation when one of these meetings was called. His neighbour, also an Executive member, called in on his way to the meeting and was told by the staff member that he was not attending because he was resigning. The neighbour graciously took the letter but did not deliver it. He told Gil the person was not well enough to attend. Later that night the neighbour counselled, encouraged and prayed with the couple, and arranged some rest days without responsibilities. They resumed work a week or so later. The situation was never raised by the Principal, other than to send a couple of tablets in an envelope the next morning suggesting that these would help. They remained in the envelope!

Most staff not only had demanding responsibilities, but because accommodation was short, some were required to live with other staff for extended periods because housing was not ready for them.

Working alongside Gil, Garth also saw another aspect of Gil's legacy that follows the theme that *Excellence honours God and inspires people*.[16]

> Gil had a compulsion to always present the 'Front Door' of the College in the best possible way, whether that be a letter, or no clothes visible on clothes lines as visitors drove in the main entrance road to the College campus, or the first lecture room building, or the administration building, or the guest house, or the auditorium. He requested that all of these buildings incorporate some special

---

15. Morgan, 'Gilbert McArthur Information', 8.
16. Hybels, *Courageous Leadership*, 174. One of Willow Creek Community Church's core values states, 'We believe excellence honours God and inspires people.'

architectural features using special designs, or river stones and/or selected, unique, natural-grained timbers. Every main building and the staff houses have quality tongue-and-groove hardwood flooring machined in the College's joinery shop. The quality of the main College buildings, some fifty years later, is a tribute to the design and workmanship Gil requested and the creativity and skills of those who led the building teams during Gil's Principalship, including Ron Youngman, John Woodbridge, Bob Elphick, and Ron Finger. Yes, it cost more, but it was an 'investment' for the future of the College. Gil 'saved' for these 'investments' by sacrificing or controlling the daily routine costs.[17]

Gil also had a networking gift that gave him confidence to go to the highest rank of an organisation and ask for the help he believed he needed to develop different aspects of the College. On one occasion, he asked Garth and Ruth to prepare an application to *Bread for the World*, the development and relief agency of the Protestant churches in Germany. The application was for funding to develop 100 acres of pasture for beef cattle grazing, including fences, races and cattle yards, plus a herd of twenty breeding Brahmin cattle. He made his approach through his contact with the Lutheran Bishop in Lae. Although the Lutheran churches in PNG had their own theological colleges, and only a few Lutheran students came to CLTC, the application was successful, and a substantial grant was received. The staff of that time have vivid memories of the stirring arrival of the rather feisty Brahmin cattle on the campus![18]

Gil's leadership left a legacy that continues in the lives of Garth and Ruth, and the national staff who became part of the business programs. Garth and Ruth's honest recollections illustrate that like all leaders Gil had his own idiosyncrasies and weaknesses:

> All of us who were members of the College Executive during Gil's Principalship, would agree that despite all that we experienced, learned and 'suffered' as we lived and worked within the extremely tight and often unexpected expectations that were placed before us, we knew of no one else, who could have led and achieved the development of the College, within the seven-year time frame, that he did it in. Gil was an instigator, who was driven by a challenge – a visionary, a networker, an eloquent speaker, who drew people

---

17. Morgan, 'Gilbert McArthur Information', 8.
18. Morgan, 'Gilbert McArthur Information', 6.

around him, whom he then relied upon and expected to 'produce the goods' and manage the day-to-day details.[19]

Garth also observed the humility of Gil's leadership, and his continuing growth in understanding servant leadership: 'It is to Gil's credit, that during a visit to the College in the early 1970s (subsequent to his retirement as Principal in 1970), that he apologised for putting programs before people during his Principalship.'[20]

Graham and Joyce Walker
Christian Leaders' Training College Papua New Guinea, Alliance Training Association, Beechwood Pty Ltd and other associated companies

Graham and Joyce met Gil when he came to Syndal Baptist Church in 1964, and were yet another family who responded to the call of God mediated through Gil's passion and commitment.

Graham and Joyce Walker

Graham was one in heart with Gil and Chairman Len Buck in their missional entrepreneurial mindset to develop the College transport operations and other businesses, creating ATA and moving the Head Office off the CLTC campus in 1970. Gil's legacy through Graham's life is evident in the record of his continuing service after Gil left CLTC to reside in Australia, and in the influence of the various ATA businesses on the economy of PNG.

In later years ATA focused strongly on developing the use of national sub-contractors in the transport business, and under mounting financial pressures, sold their subsidiary companies to national business men or other similar established businesses. Graham and Joyce Walker finally returned to Australia in July 1992, 27 years after they first set foot in PNG.

At the 10th Annual Meeting of the Directors of ATA on 25-26 March 1980, the Board recorded its appreciation for Graham's 10 years of

---

19. Morgan, 'Gilbert McArthur Information', 10.
20. Morgan, 'Gilbert McArthur Information', 8.

management leadership of ATA through some very difficult periods. It is an accurate commendation of all 27 years of his life invested into business as mission with the people of PNG:

> The contribution of Graham's vision, drive, grinding hard work, doggedness and sacrifice have characterised this saga. But above all, submission to the will of God, and obedience to the call of God, and loyalty in the work of God, have exemplified Graham's splendid committal to Christ. A man less determined to 'see it through' would have surrendered at many periods along the pioneer track that ATA has pursued... Graham has resisted the temptation to quit when the going was rough and can now justifiably rejoice with us in the success and blessing which God is vouchsafing in this God-given work of training the young manhood of PNG. The financial stewardship made possible by the success of ATA is due to the gifts and grace of its Managing Director.[21]

Jacob Luke

Alliance Training Association, Mapai Transport Pty Ltd, Papua New Guinea and New Zealand

Jacob's story is a significant example of the legacy of ATA in the life of one Papua New Guinean.[22] He lived as a young boy in Monokam village near Wabag in the Enga Province in the Highlands of PNG, where his father was a Lutheran pastor. When he was expelled from high school for challenging the competence of his national teachers, the Lutheran missionary recognised his potential and took him into Mount Hagen where he was given the opportunity to start work in the ATA depot as a 'kagoboi' (loading trucks). ATA Mount Hagen Manager Harry Wakerley saw the leadership and entrepreneurial qualities in Jacob and gave him the opportunity to develop his abilities as a young man. He

Jacob Luke

---

21. Alliance Training Association, 'Minutes of the Tenth Annual Meeting of Directors', 25-26 March 1980. CLTC Archives.
22. Jacob Luke, 'Jacob Luke's Story', November 14 2017. The information for this story originated from a conversation with Paul McArthur. Jacob edited the document and returned it via email 12 November 2017.

was eventually promoted to be Harry's assistant when Harry managed ATA Hagen during 1980-1985. His main responsibility was distributing the cargo to customers when it arrived in Mount Hagen and arranging backloading for trucks returning to Lae. He stood out among the ATA employees for his leadership qualities, and as a person of character and integrity, with an unusual ability to 'get things done'. He was offered the opportunity to work with Highway Motors (another ATA business), that held the Mazda dealership in Mount Hagen, and was very successful in selling vehicles to national clients.

In 1985 he told Graham and the ATA management that the time had come for him to 'do his own thing'. He started Mapai Transport with one Izuzu twin-steer truck, moving cargo from Lae to Porgera for the newly developing Pogera Gold Mine – a business relationship that still remains today. In a very difficult and competitive industry, his company has seen amazing success and growth. Mapai Transport now operates a fleet of 70 Kenworth T650 and T659s (with 10 more now on order), around 200 flat-top, drop-deck and tanker-trailers, five depots including Auckland, New Zealand and Brisbane, Australia, and employs 300+ people.[23] There are also a dozen Japanese cab-overs in his fleet, which are generally restricted to town work because of the appalling conditions on the highways, which is why Jacob has three custom built 6x6 recovery vehicles to support his fleet. Jacob's workshop does all the maintenance and repair, from minor parts replacements to complete engine and transmission rebuilds, and has always had a very strong emphasis on training staff. Jacob currently holds a significant share of the transport market on the Highlands Highway and uses very sophisticated IT technology to control his fleet for maximum efficiency, including the latest GPS tracking and cloud based operational software. From his office, he can see where trucks are, what they are doing, speak to the drivers, and disable a truck if he wants to do so.[24]

In 2008 Jacob established Mapai Customs & Forwarding Agency services, primarily as an added value service to ensure the smooth movement of Mapai's clients' freight into PNG, which has now developed into a stand-alone Logistics Service business with its own Freight Consolidation Depot. Jacob has become a wealthy and successful businessman who is looking south for the next venture, and the scope is broader than transport and logistics. A New Zealand company, Mapai (NZ) Ltd., was established in

---

23. David Meredith, 'The Perils of Working in PNG', *Big Rigs*, 10 November 2012, https://www.bigrigs.com.au/news/perils-of-working-in-png/1575665/.
24. Paul McArthur, 'Jacob Luke and Mapai Transport', Telephone interview, 7 January 2017.

2015. Grant Wakerley,[25] was appointed International Logistics Manager in 2012. 'Jacob has clearly given the board the mandate to move the company from just a purely transport and logistics business to a training business that does transport and logistics to pay the bills', Wakerley told *Business Advantage* PNG from his office in Auckland. 'This is a fundamental mind shift within the business and establishing a branch in NZ is part of that shift. The main driver for establishing an office in NZ is to boost export and import activities between PNG and NZ, particularly those companies that are working on exporting products from PNG to NZ.'[26]

On the 'Think Big Start Small' Group Facebook page, Des Yaninen posted a blog entitled 'What's Your Excuse?' which indicates the challenge of Jacob's achievement in developing Mapai Transport:

> Owner of Mapai New Zealand Ltd, Mr Jacob Luke (from Enga) went from being a mechanic [actually a truck cleaner] in Mt Hagen to establishing a small trucking company that turned into the largest in PNG, and now with business interests in shipping and logistics abroad. No school fees. No degree. No government funding. No rich family. No bank loans. No political connections. No internet. No Facebook marketing. No media advertising. Mr Luke started Mapai with none of the prerequisites we use as excuses today. All he had was hard work, discipline, vision and a stubborn determination never to give up. If he can do it, you can do it too. What's your excuse? Don't let it steal your dreams.[27]

Jacob has been generous with his wealth in donating a generator to CLTC, supporting Martin Luther Seminary in Lae, and other church and community projects, although it is not clear to the writer how deeply embedded the 'business as mission ethos' has actually gripped the leadership of Mapai.[28]

---

25. Grant is Harry Wakerley's son, whose friendship with Jacob started back at ATA in Mt Hagen. He has been Jacob's Business Development Manager since late 2012.
26. Kevin McQuillan, 'Mapai Transport Branches out to "Rebalance" Trade Links between PNG and NZ', *Business Advantage PNG*, 16 12AD, http://www.businessadvantagepng.com/mapai-transport-branches-out-to-rebalance-trade-links-between-papua-new-guinea-and-nz/. Blog Post, 5 December 2016.
27. Kay Liddle, 'Mapai New Zealand Ltd and Jacob Luke', 2 May 2018, The email of this Blog (Menti Ogarz notification+kjdmhu-juuh@facebookmail.com) from Kay Liddle to Garth Morgan was forwarded to the writer 6 February 2018.
28. Garth Morgan, 'Re: Legacy Chapter - Jacob Luke', 22 November 2017. This email provided some information for this section from Eric Crabbe, who worked with ATA during the time that Jacob was employed.

Suren Martin

Christian Brethren Church Leader and Pastor, CLTC Council Member

Suren and Yipoki Martin

Suren was among the second group of students to enroll at CLTC in 1966. Following his graduation, he was involved for many years in faithful pastoral ministry in the Brethren churches in the Sepik province. From his observations of support businesses while at CLTC, he also developed a number of agricultural projects over the years including a vanilla plantation and helped others in the community to develop similar projects. He was appointed to the new national Council of CLTC when the governance passed from Melbourne to PNG and continued in that role for many years.

* * * * * * * *

The stories of this chapter are a few examples of Gil's legacy in business as mission providing insight into how the Spirit of God worked through him inspiring people to network and teamwork in combining business and mission. As Kouzes and Posner comment:

> Leadership is a team effort… Exemplary leaders enlist the support and assistance of all those who must make the project work. This sense of teamwork goes far beyond a few direct reports or close confidants… Leaders involve, in some way, all those who must live with the results, and they make it possible for others to do good work. *They enable others to act.* Leaders know that no one does his or her best when feeling weak, incompetent, or alienated; they know that those who are expected to produce the results must feel a sense of ownership.[29, 30]

---

29. Kouzes and Posner, *The Leadership Challenge*, 11,12.
30. Please also refer to Appendix Six on page 446 for one late additional but remarkable story about Graham Salisbury and the CLTC Poultry Program.

19

LEGACY IN THE WIDER PACIFIC AND BEYOND

Vision imparts venturesomeness,
the willingness to take fresh steps of faith
when there is a seeming void beneath.[1]

After ten years in the role of Field Director for the World Vision South Pacific Office, Gil's sense of urgency to impact the top level Pacific national leaders had become even more pressing. In 1983 he wrote an inspirational paper entitled 'A Civilization in Crisis', which revealed the biblical Kingdom perspectives for his intentional focus on developing the top level Pacific leaders in the context of what he believed was a 20th Century civilisation crisis. Gil saw this global crisis arising from two sources: the problem of overpopulation, with its attendant issues of hunger, social injustice and human deprivation on a massive scale, and the problem of ecological pollution, depletion of energy and the imminent threat of a nuclear holocaust. He believed the one hope for resolving the crisis lay with the Gospel message in transforming leaders, thus empowering them to follow the servant leadership of Jesus Christ.

> The dreadful brutality, the senseless killing of innocent women and children, the chambers of human atrocity as perpetrated by the diabolical dictatorships of Central America, Southeast Asia and Africa, linked with the brutal genocide of the Middle East Arab factions, all testify to the fact that it is the inhuman action of people to each other that makes countless thousands mourn and a fitting description of today's world is that of a 'hobnailed boot stamped upon a human face.'
>
> On the leadership level at which these contemporary 'horrors' are being enacted it would appear that there are no appropriate forums

---

1. Sanders, *Spiritual Leadership*, 51.

by which the Gospel of sacrificial love, human equality, and the message of peace and reconciliation, can reach the specific target audiences that so desperately need a confrontation with the Man of History: the Galilean Christ – the Cosmic Christ. The great secular forums such as the United Nations, together with other worthy regional bodies like NATO, ASEAN, etc., have, in terms of dealing with the problems of humanity, clearly demonstrated a common 'Achilles Heel'. True it is that, for the most part, these forums are comprised of men and women of good intent. True it is that they provide an amalgam of the world's greatest minds, and yet tragically true it is that in the vital areas that really count for the well-being of the nations, they are **impotent bodies** – and in the words of the Indian adage, 'the great elephant has given birth to a mouse'! Multitudes of words are spoken and recorded, copious resolutions are framed and agreed upon but little of any consequence towards the healing of the nations takes place.

Why is this so? The answer is, **because there is no basis of trust.** Such secular forums are controlled by a humanistic value system. There is no place for any vertical dimension that will lift the horizons of the mind and spirit to an encounter with Transcendent Reality, and therefore no link with a moral and ethical servant-leadership code that will alone transform values, attitudes and relationships.[2]

Gil's commitment to the PLF was to open opportunities with Pacific leaders to apply biblical redemptive values to the urgent issues he saw in this civilization crisis. John Key was one who came alongside Gil in World Vision enabling him to give more time to the development of the PLF.

John Key
World Vision South Pacific Office, Pacific Leaders' Fellowship

John Key first met Gil in PNG in 1969 when John was involved in Anglican ministry, and Secretary of the MCC. They developed a firm friendship. In 1981, after John had returned home to the UK, Gil invited him to join him as Associate Director of World Vision South Pacific Office, based in Sydney. John, who had been impacted by Gil's passion and vision for the

---

2. Gilbert J McArthur, 'A Civilization Crisis', November 1983, 1, 2., McArthur Family Archives. Adjusted for gender inclusive language.

needs and opportunities of the Pacific, agreed to come. But by the time John arrived, Gil had persuaded World Vision to appoint John to take over his role so that Gil could concentrate on the development of the PLF and give his energy to this emerging ministry.

Gil's influence on John was immediately evident during his five years of ministry (1982-1987) with World Vision in the South Pacific, when part of his role was working closely with Gil on PLF matters. John recalls particularly those aspects of Gil's life that had a deep impact upon him:

John Key

> Gilbert McArthur was an unusually gifted and anointed man, driven by his love for the Lord Jesus Christ and his passion for the Kingdom of God. I believe he was a significant prophet and pioneer in his generation. He was persistent, often to the point of doggedness (one example, he persuaded me to buy a block of land in Laurieton, opposite the site of the PTI he was planning!). He was also a courageous and capable connector and networker. He spent the last five or six years of his earthly pilgrimage in retirement in Lake Cathie, lovingly cared for during a period of failing health by his amazing wife Pat and as active as he could be in the local Baptist Church. My last visit with him was in 1993, when we renewed many memories of shared ministry.
>
> I give thanks to the Lord for the huge privilege, honour and blessing of knowing Gil and working with him for five precious years.[3]

Heather Ford

South Sea Evangelical Mission Australian Office, Alliance Training Association Mount Hagen Papua New Guinea, World Vision South Pacific Office

When Gil was appointed the Executive Director of SSEM in 1972, he appointed Heather Ford to work part-time as his girl Friday (Personal

---

3. Key, 'Dr Gilbert McArthur - Some Recollections by John Key'.

Assistant) through 1973. Gil was impressed with her initiative, capacity and ability to multi-task without requiring close supervision, as he was often away from the office. Heather was deeply impacted by Gil's life during this period, and provides interesting insights into how Gil's vision, deep biblical faith and commitment became his legacy to her in shaping her life journey.

Heather Ford

At the SSEM office, the only time we had ever discussed the content of his work was when he mentioned that the information I was typing up was not to be repeated anywhere. I never mentioned it, but I was fascinated by the concepts I was privy to! Gil was issuing all kinds of directives to the heads of the SSEM missionary stations right across the Pacific, on how to adjust to the emergence of independence. He based and adapted many of his principles from historical precedence which had occurred in mainly African countries as they moved toward or simply demanded independence from their colonial masters. Gil's *insight and understanding* in those Confidential Papers was a real eye opener. These directives would now be considered normal practice, but I think back then, Gil's *grasp of the implications of cultural evolution* was pragmatically realistic, way ahead of his time, and made him such a worthy leader. A couple of examples I can remember: (a) whatever language the 'new' leadership of a country decided to adopt, instigate it *immediately* and change all signs, letterheads and communications to reflect this including verbal speech *even in-house*; if they change their minds a week later, change again as above; (b) issues of security arrangements and signs to watch for were quite detailed and specific. There were myriad and exhaustive directives around every aspect of life in regard to possible changes and ways of dealing with potential threats. It was quite obvious that he intended to create minimal chance of possible blood baths happening due to naivety or ignorance or slow adaptation in these waves of shifting national power.[4]

---

4. Heather Ford, 'Gil McArthur', Email, 16 September 2016, 2.

At the end of 1973 Gil asked Heather to move up to PNG to train ATA Mount Hagen staff in book-keeping.

> And so, in 1974, I came to Papua New Guinea. Landing in Lae, the ATA staff (the wives I expect) were horrified that Gil intended to send a single female to work at Hagen! Single women were not meant to be IN Hagen at that time: it was not considered safe. So my trip up into the Highlands was delayed until Gilbert arrived about a week later. They called him to a meeting and asked him to justify his choice. He simply invited me in to the meeting, to listen to the staff concerns and then to respond. When I explained what the youth work I had been training in for the past two years had involved, the staff backed off and the next day I was on a truck bound for Mt Hagen. Gil didn't let details get in the way of the task! On the other hand, had I not felt safe he made it quite clear that he would not send me. And the next three years offered me a plethora of treasured experience for which I am truly thankful, with no security threats![5]

In 1979 Gil offered Heather the opportunity to join him as his Executive Administrator/Accountant in the World Vision South Pacific Office in Sydney. She had never thought of Gil as a theologian, but rather as a visionary. But on reflection she remembers he was both, and her recollections capture, in a unique way, aspects of Gil's later life and ministry:

> It was his practical grasp of large principles, his willingness to grapple with untenable issues, his creative lateral thinking which dreamed of meaningful integration of the human and divine where I saw Christianity live in Gil. Christ dwelt amongst human beings and theology made sense on the ground – that is how I experienced Gil's primary expression of faith. However, I only saw Gil from a work perspective. I expect I saw Gil in his softer years – where he had mellowed, having faced something of life's pain, allowed it to humble him, and had the courage to integrate that and use it to further enrich his ministry, not limit it.

> I idealised Gil because he believed in me. He saw potential in me and trusted me with lots of responsibility which stimulated and satisfied me. I just 'got' his vision and was able to support it because he was able to communicate it so succinctly – and it made sense! It resonated deeply with something in my own spirit.

---

5. Ford, 'Gil McArthur', 2.

I guess what I'm saying is that the memory of Gil is very positive and my relationship with him helped shape my adult life in really healthy ways.⁶

Ted and Peggy Fletcher
Wall Street Journal, Mission to Unreached Peoples, World Evangelical Outreach, Pioneers International

It was while the Lord was stirring Ted Fletcher to consider moving out of the world of sales management with the *Wall Street Journal* that Gil's friendship was influential in confirming his conviction. While it may be said that Gil's time with Ted was minimal – mainly during his visits to the USA – nevertheless God's influence through Gil came at 'just the right time', resulting in a powerful legacy as Ted moved in obedience to start a new mission agency which today is known around the world as Pioneers International. While we have previously quoted Ted's record of these days in his autobiography *When God comes Calling*, Ted's son John has recently written of his memories of Gil's visits and the impact on his father:

Ted & Peggy Fletcher

> He [Gil] is someone dear to our family history, and to the history of Pioneers [USA and International]. He stayed in my parents' home in May 1968 – my Dad was district Sales Manager for the *Wall Street Journal*. I was 10 years old. Gil spoke to my Dad about the Scripture, 'We spend our years as a tale that is told'... from the Psalms. 'Ted, what story is God telling in and through your life?' It was that very month (May 1968) that my Dad heard a word from the Lord in Psalm 2:8 and wrote in the margin of his Bible, 'God's Promise to Me'. Eleven years later, in May 1979, something of that promise was realised as my Dad (and Mom) started Pioneers in the USA.
>
> I remember that same year in 1979, that Gil was in our home again, this time in northern VA as he attended the National Prayer

---
6. Ford, 'Gil McArthur', 2.

Breakfast. He was leading a contingent from the Solomon Islands that included Sir Peter Kenilorea, who just the year previously, at the age of 35, had become the first Prime Minister of the newly-independent Solomon Islands. One evening, a group of interested friends of my parents, and a number of my fellow students from the nearby Washington Bible College, gathered in our living room to hear Gil challenge us about the needs in the Pacific, and in the world, and once again he spoke about 'We spend our years as a tale that is told'.

For those of us who know and remember the history of Pioneers USA, we would regard Gil as a spiritual giant, one of our spiritual forefathers who paved the way for the work of God in Ted and Peggy's hearts by his personal interest in them and encouragement that they pursue the will of God – nothing more, nothing less, nothing else, anywhere, everywhere, and at all costs. Gil served on the founding Advisory Council of Pioneers USA, and together with Bill Clack and Len Buck, helped to forge the relationship between this small start-up mission and APCM and SSEC.[7]

On 12 May 1979, Ted and Peggy Fletcher officially founded 'World Evangelical Outreach'. The name was later changed to Pioneers in 1984.[8]

The legacy created by Gil's vision, faith and radical obedience in mission can be discerned in Ted and Peggy Fletcher, their obedience to step out in the risk and obedience of faith, and in the exploding growth of Pioneers.

The Bigger Picture

Gil's personal impact on the lives of those mentioned are only snapshots. In addition we cannot forget:

- The countless national peoples of the Baliem Valley in DNG and those of the Telefolmin area who through God's work in Gil came under the influence of the Gospel for the first time, came to faith in Christ, and were formed into active churches.

- The congregation of the Clemton Park Baptist Church in NSW Australia, who were impacted by Gil's passionate biblical teaching and vision to see the church grow and establish new facilities

---

7. John Fletcher, 'Re: Price Kneemail Sept 16', 14 September 2016.
8. Fletcher, *When God Comes Calling*, 151. Appendix 'Milestones in Pioneers History'.

and ministries to evangelise their community and reach out in mission to the wider world.

- The builders, agriculturalists, accountants, mechanics, farmers, managers, clerks, scholars and teachers who over the years committed to the vision of CLTC, ATA and Beechwood, and came from Australia, New Zealand, the USA and around the world, and experienced the total change of life and perspective that is the direct result of cross cultural service in the name of Christ.

- The early graduates of CLTC who were directly influenced by Gil's leadership, followed by generations of Council members, Faculty and students, whose varied ministries have extended across the churches and communities of the nations of PNG, Australia, New Zealand, the Pacific and even to the ends of the earth.

- The soldiers and police of the nation of PNG who were impacted by Gil's biblically-based teaching, training and ministry, and the values of integrity and truth that shaped their service.

- The numerous political leaders of the island nations of the Pacific who were drawn together and impacted by Gil's passion for the message of the Kingdom of God, and the vital importance of leadership integrity and unity at a crucial time, as they emerged as independent nations at the close of the colonial era.

20
LEGACY IN ORGANISATIONS AND MINISTRIES

*A legacy is different from a trophy or souvenir
in that it doesn't just mark something that happened in the past:
it lives on and continues to make an impact in the present.
It's a gift given to the next generation.*[1]

The primary influence of any leader is on people, but inevitably, as those people catch the vision, ministries themselves will reflect the conviction that drives its members. It is fascinating to see how many ministries were influenced by Gil's passion for mission, relentless work ethic, and faith in the God of the impossible, and how many exist today partly due to his dogged, prayerful perseverance.

The Dani Baptist Churches of Dutch New Guinea

Gil was only in DNG (today Indonesian Papua) in 1955/1956. Yet it was at that crucial time when, as we have seen, the first pioneer Baptist missionaries trekked into the Baliem Valley. Gil was involved in those first tough treks to where around 40,000 tribes peoples lived, isolated from the outside world, and unreached by the Gospel. Norm Draper, Gil's team leader, describes the people as 'excitable, turbulent and bold.'

> They were daring thieves and constantly at war with one another. Tension always ran high as traditional enemies were brought together by curiosity and any sudden movement or unexpected noise caused everyone to run, yelling! Masses of 12-foot-long, black palm spears surrounded us daily. With neither police nor government support, those initial months and years were uneasy ones, made more difficult because of lack of communication, and little knowledge of the culture or language.[2]

---

1. John Maxwell, *The 21 Most Powerful Minutes in a Leader's Day* (Nashville, Tennessee: Thomas Nelson Publishers, 2000), 354.
2. Draper, *Daring to Believe*, 202.

Dani Baptist Churches DNG Baptismal Service 1962

Following aerial surveys, early contacts were sometimes very difficult and dangerous exploits. The early contacts in which Gil was involved paved the way for the construction of four airstrips and the location of missionaries at Tiom, Maki, Pit River and Yukwa, and the subsequent emergence and growth of the young churches. In 1990 Norm Draper described the impact of those early mission years:

> Today the North Baliem Valley is a vastly different place from that which we found in 1956. Scattered along its length are between 100-200 village churches, their aluminium roofs glittering in the sun. However, much of village life and buildings have remained the same. Villagers still live in their traditional, round grass-thatched houses. War and conflict are almost non-existent; almost everyone rejoices in the new era of freedom from fear of spirits, and the climate of peace that the Christian faith has brought. Most menfolk carry their Dani New Testaments in their shoulder bags, and Bible teaching schools, (whether the teaching is in Dani or in Indonesian), find it difficult to accommodate the pressure of would-be students.[3]

---

3. Draper, *Daring to Believe*, 205.

Sixty years after Gil and others first trekked into the Baliem Valley, Baptist churches now number over 300 across Indonesian Papua, and can rightly be spoken of as part of Gil's legacy today.[4]

The Min Baptist Union Churches of Papua New Guinea

Early in 1957, after two years in DNG, Gil and the family were transferred across the border to the relatively new initiative of the Baptist Mission at Telefolmin in Papua New Guinea. Gil's family joined the Vaughan and Doull families. Don Doull was the leader and with Gil and Doug they worked well as a unified team. Gil threw himself into the task of learning the Telefol language so that Bible translation would provide the basis for conducting Bible Studies as they focused on their two-fold strategy:

- Get young men into Bible School to equip them to become evangelists and pastors in remote areas; and
- Work towards building airstrips in the many remote areas, to enable the travel and placement of evangelists to evangelise, disciple believers and nurture young churches.

Min Baptist Churches PNG, Early Baptisms

---

4. Rod Bensley, 'Empowering Leaders in Papua', *Vision Magazine*, n.d., 8.

In early 1958 Don recalled:

> With our first out-station airstrip open and in regular use we felt that we were beginning to realise our plan. The mission station base now had a functioning Bible School with about twenty young men being taught the truths of the Bible, and many of them were now at the stage where we could say they were literate. We were beginning to reach out to the surrounding valleys where large pockets of unreached people were living.
>
> We believed that the people who had been nearest to us over the years who had been in our immediate Telefolmin area, were now close to a real understanding of what it meant to be a follower of Jesus Christ. These things gave us confidence to expect that God would soon give us the satisfaction of seeing some of these people make that heart response which would place them in the Kingdom of God.[5]

Their confidence was rewarded in August 1958, when: 'God heard and answered the prayers not only of the immediate past, but also the prayers of years, on Sunday 24 August 1958. A few days later I [Don] wrote an article headed "Harvest Has Come".'[6]

From the initial 130 who came to a meeting desiring to respond to the Gospel, many more joined them in the following weeks as the movement gained momentum. The first baptisms took place before a crowd of some 400-500 witnesses on 9 August 1959.[7] More followed the next year as new airstrips were constructed to open up new areas. Gil, through his language study and translation work before he left Telefolmin, made a vital contribution to the follow-up and discipling of these first believers:

> Their initial reading was of the Bible stories and their application to life. These were available in the Pidgin language through the book of Bible stories produced by the Lutheran Mission and also the booklets produced by SSEM referred to earlier. We also had a loose equivalent of 40 of those stories which Gil McArthur produced in booklets in the vernacular.[8]

In God's purpose, another aspect of Gil's legacy in the Min Baptist Union came years later. In 1977, as a direct outcome of Gil's strategy to

---

5. Doull, *One Passion: Church Planting in Papua New Guinea*, 116.
6. Doull, *One Passion: Church Planting in Papua New Guinea*, 117.
7. Doull, *One Passion: Church Planting in Papua New Guinea*, 121.
8. Doull, *One Passion: Church Planting in Papua New Guinea*, 126.

bring Senior SSEC Solomon Island pastors to the special Senior Pastor's courses at CLTC, they had opportunity to share with PNG church leaders the spiritual awakening that their churches were experiencing. Norm Draper records the impact on the Min Baptist churches:

> The Revival, as a significant spiritual awakening is commonly called, has had a marked effect on the growth of the Christian church in the Telefolmin area, just as it has done in the Baiyer/Lumusa districts to the east. It broke out in Telefolmin through Diyos Wapnok, who had attended a pastors' seminar at Banz. At this seminar held at the Christian Leaders' Training College, the main speakers were pastors from the Solomon Islands who told of the spiritual awakening that had taken place in their own home areas. Diyos became greatly concerned for the Holy Spirit's outpouring in the life of the churches in his area. In 1977, his prayers were answered when God began His work in the Sepik Baptist Bible College at Duranmin, where Diyos was Principal. Duranmin is only fifteen minutes' flying time from both Telefolmin and Tekin, and soon the whole area became alive with a new enthusiasm for Christian faith and practice. People became eager to study God's Word. Prayer became the fabric of everyday life. God's power was seen in healings of various kinds. Many young people who had stood on the sidelines were stirred and motivated and became deeply involved in the worship of the church.[9]

As the Solomon Island pastors shared their experiences of revival, the Spirit of God also birthed similar revival movements in other churches. As in the Sepik area revival there were 'some who were charlatans, working for selfish ends and display. Some disrupted worship... by excessive shaking, noise and dancing. But with time, the people themselves learned to sift the false from the true, encouraging, restraining, guiding – but never suppressing'.[10]

Today the churches that began in the Telefolmin area have spread across the mountains and valleys of the Min people, and now together they comprise the Min Baptist Union of PNG. Pastor Jeffrey Modua, the President of the Baptist Union of PNG, advises that since the arrival of the Gospel in 1952, the Min Baptist Union has grown to a total membership of 168 churches![11] While many were called by the Lord of

---

9. Draper, *Daring to Believe*, 136, 137.
10. Draper, *Daring to Believe*, 137.
11. Jeffrey Moduwa, 'Min Baptist Union Churches', 2 July 2017.

the harvest to serve among the Min people over the years, these churches also can rightly be spoken of as part of the legacy of Gil McArthur, and his pioneering passion to reach out to the Min people with the Gospel, and see the first of what became a great harvest for God's glory.

The Clemton Park Baptist Church

After four years of pastoral leadership at the Clemton Park Baptist Church honing his preaching and pastoral skills, Gil left a legacy of Sunday attendances that had increased from 40 to over 400 people, a congregation with mature leadership and a vision for evangelism and mission, with a new Worship and Education Centre and pastor's house. The church 'saw' the vision of CLTC and commended him to go in obedience to God's direction.

Gil's last message at Clemton Park Baptist Church Golden Jubilee

The Christian Leaders' Training College of Papua New Guinea

It is often difficult to discern whether one legacy of a leader is more significant than others. However, almost unanimously, when people were asked 'what do you believe is Gil's most significant legacy today?' the immediate response was 'CLTC'. For over fifty years, CLTC has been the interdenominational, English language, higher level church and community leadership theological education program serving the Evangelical Alliance group of churches in the Pacific.[12]

---

12. The core founding churches (and the missions from which they grew), included: Baptist Union of PNG (Australian Baptist Missionary Society); Evangelical Church of Papua New Guinea (Unevangelized Fields Mission/Asia Pacific Christian Mission/Pioneers); South Sea Evangelical Church (SSEC); Christian Brethren Churches (Christian Missions in Many Lands); Churches of Christ PNG (Australian Churches of Christ); Assemblies of God; Apostolic Christian Churches (Apostolic Christian Mission); and Evangelical Church of Manus (Manus Evangelical Mission). Students were drawn from these and a wide circle of other churches including the Church of the Nazarene; Wesleyan Church; various Synods of the United Church, and a number of independent churches and mission groups. Growing numbers of students from other mainline churches in PNG have enrolled as students in more recent years.

The first training program began in 1965 at Certificate level. In response to consultations with the evangelical churches, other programs were added: Certificate of Christian Education in 1968; Diploma in 1969; Single Women's Course in 1970; Bachelor of Theology in 1978; and Master of Theology in 2008. In addition, other agricultural and vocationally based programs have been in place according to demand over the years.

CLTC was a founding member of the Melanesian Association of Theological Schools (MATS) from 1968, and its programs were accredited through MATS until, with the PNG Government delegating educational quality assurance and accreditation to its Department of Higher Education, Research, Science and Technology, in 2014 CLTC was formally recognised as a Tertiary Education Institution with accreditation now authorised by DHERST.[13]

In recognition of 50 years of CLTC equipping Christian leaders for church and community, present National Principal William Longgar wrote of the continuing legacy of the founders of CLTC in the College News 50th Anniversary Edition under the text 'My face will go with you' (see Exodus 33):

> Fifty years ago under the leadership of Dr. Gil McArthur, the Christian Leaders' Training College of Papua New Guinea began its journey as a theological institution to train young men and women as leaders for the churches and the nations of the Pacific. From a small and a humble beginning the 'tiny acorn' planted in a vast swamp land in the Wahgi valley in 1964 has become a very beautiful sprawling campus, with the possibility of greater expansion, infrastructurally, logistically and academically. In the words of J O Sanders, it 'has grown into a spreading oak

Celebrating 50 years of Equipping Christian Leaders in Melanesia
1965 – 2015

---

13. The curriculum philosophy and development stages of CLTC's theological teaching program are explained in, John M. Hitchen, 'Evangelicals Equipping Melanesian men and women', 110-136.
14. William Longgar, 'My Face will Go with You – Exodus 33:1-23', *College News*, June 2015, 3, citing Sanders, *Planting Men in Melanesia*, 9.

LIVE IN TENTS – BUILD ONLY ALTARS

Traditionally dressed students lead the Jubilee procession on Sunday

Guests and Pioneers at the Jubilee Sunday Celebration

Thomas Elling (local leader), Silas Pokikau (Pioneer Student), Wilma Paka (Dept of Higher Education) and William Longgar (Principal) cut the Jubilee cake

under whose branches cluster a number of related enterprises, each of which remains true to the original vision – to plant throughout Melanesia [and the Pacific] men [and women] of God who will be effective messengers to their own generation.'[14]

The men to whom the vision of such a College was given, 'had their eyes on tomorrow's horizon, and planned for a harvest where the horizons lift. Theirs was a vision, not for one year or even ten years, but for eternity'.[15] Today two thousand-plus graduates are spread across the full breadth of the Pacific impacting their churches and nations with the gospel of Jesus Christ.

In many ways, 'the face of God' has journeyed with the College for the last fifty years. Through pains and toils, death and sicknesses, the 'face of God' sustained, protected and enabled the men and women who had led CLTC through those fifty years. Today we celebrate a success story that came in the midst of a lot of sacrifices. The unmarked graves at the main campus in Banz are testimonies to the great price paid for success.[16]

The 50th Jubilee Celebrations of CLTC also took place in Port Moresby and Lae, and in Australia and New Zealand.

The 50th Jubilee Celebrations of CLTC – MiCamp Lake Taupo, New Zealand

---

15. William Longgar, 'My Face will Go with You', citing Sanders *Planting Men in Melanesia*, 9.
16. William Longgar, 'My Face will Go with You', - Exodus 33:1-23, *College News*, June 2015,3. CLTC Archives.

LIVE IN TENTS – BUILD ONLY ALTARS

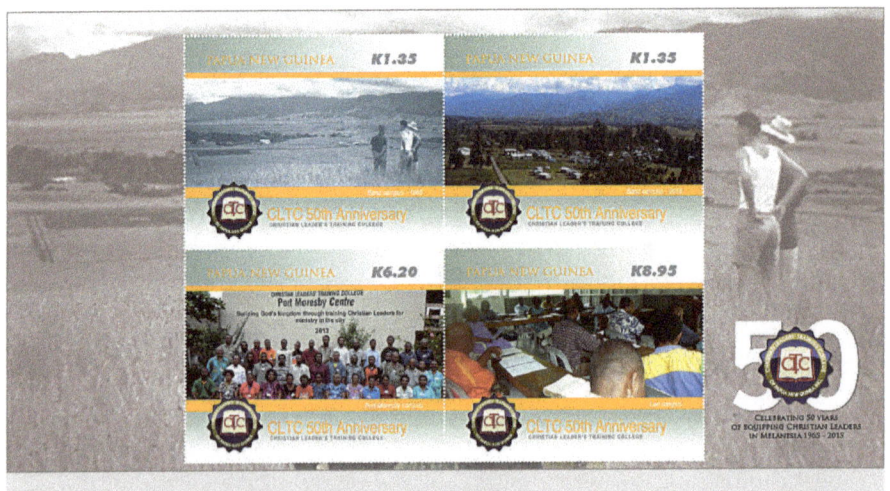

The Australian Jubilee celebration cake was cut by
William and Iru Longgar (centre), Alan Baker (left) and Marg and
Ade Rickard (longest serving staff members)

CLTC Jubilee Stamp Issue

What is the legacy that CLTC has provided to this point? Many churches would echo the commendation in the history of the Australian Baptists in mission:

> The inter-denominational Christian Leaders' Training College (CLTC) had begun at Banz in the Western highlands in 1964. It did not cater for the training of pastors at the village level (so was not adequate for all the training needs among the Engas) but was designed to foster and equip leaders for evangelical missions throughout New Guinea. Its medium of instruction was English. Four leading young Engas were part of the initial intake. Three of these, Kongoe Sipwanje, Traimya Kambipi and Mapusiya Kolo became outstanding leaders in Baptist and community affairs in PNG. Many younger future leaders, both Enga and Min, graduated from CLTC. It provided an invaluable service to the Baptist cause by providing solid Bible training on a beautiful campus with good facilities and a very capable faculty.[17]

A major component of the legacy of CLTC today is the ministries of over 2000 graduates across the Pacific and beyond.

But John Hitchen, in a chapter to which we have already referred, expands our view under his final section – *'Aspects of CLTC's Contribution to South West Pacific evangelical identity'*.[18] He discusses the CLTC legacies of:

- *Contributing to an inclusive rather than exclusive evangelicalism*
  CLTC has been committed from the outset to serve the full range of evangelical churches in PNG and the Pacific. This commitment has been tested along the way, particularly in regard to the charismatic and Pentecostal churches. However, through a careful biblical and inclusive approach these churches continue to utilise the training ministries of CLTC.

- *Developing standards and credibility within the tertiary theological sector*
  In assisting the establishment of MATS, and the *Melanesian Journal of Theology*, CLTC has contributed to the credibility of theological education in the educational sector of public services.

---

17. Eds, Tony Cupit, Ros Gooden and Ken Manley, *From Five Barley Loaves*, 219.
18. Hitchen, 'Evangelicals Equipping Melanesian Men and Women', 110-136.

- *Fostering the development of the Evangelical Alliance and a healthy evangelical ecumenism contributing to holistic National development*
  CLTC took a major lead in the establishment of the Evangelical Alliance of the South Pacific Islands, in which Gil had direct personal involvement. CLTC has provided a community for students from all churches to discover their unity in Christ as they study and live together. Evangelical leaders have found opportunity to meet on the campus to discuss mutual concerns, and an open relationship to the MCC has been encouraged, and cooperative ventures activated in a Christian Education in Schools syllabus, input into the National Youth Movement, a National Seminar on Evangelism, and media standards.

- *Stimulating awareness of global mission contributions*
  Through the CLTC community, a cross cultural mission awareness of the needs of the unreached peoples of the world developed in the late 1970s and through the 1980s which has seen churches being awakened, graduates moving into missionary ministries and the birth of PNG missionary organisations.

- *Demonstrating the holistic interdependence of the body of Christ in developing a ministry for God, and in influencing the ethical tone of society*
  CLTC from the beginning has brought together people of diverse backgrounds, gifts, ministry and support skills by its integration of the theological training and support divisions on the one campus and in the one organisation. This interdependence of the spiritual and the material has demonstrated powerfully the reality of the Kingdom of God in action. As a result, CLTC/ATA has fostered holistic awareness in its graduates, and made a profound impact upon the poultry, cattle, building and transport sectors of the economy.

It can also be claimed that CLTC has been a formative influence on shaping leadership in Australasian and global evangelicalism. Many expatriate and national staff and faculty have gone on into significant evangelical and theological leadership ministries beyond PNG.[19]

---

19. Hitchen, 'Evangelicals Equipping Melanesian Men and Women', 128-136.

In a more recent paper, John Hitchen discusses more fully how CLTC's legacy through involvement in commercial support programs has also contributed to the economic well-being of the peoples of PNG. In this, the College has challenged previous patterns where Christian agencies separated 'Christian' work from involvement in 'secular' business activity. CLTC has been a community where, 'Successive generations of leadership students... have shared their educational campus and social, leisure and worship activities with a diverse range of vocationally skilled expatriate and national personnel, all committed to business ventures to underwrite the operation of this Christian educational service.'[20]

John suggests that this CLTC business experience offers a strong database for evaluating what CLTC has learned about equipping national people for involvement in these various industries:

> CLTC's participation in Melanesian societal and economic development over the past fifty years has highlighted one fundamental issue: for long-term, sustainable development merely teaching pragmatic, technical, professional or practical competency, even with appropriate theoretical understanding and adaptation to local needs, is not sufficient. Development needs to address the worldview or social imaginary level change, or transformation, necessary for the desired development to become culturally embedded. Without deep-level worldview transformation the [business] developments remain superficial and dependent on external input to continue long-term. Moreover, changes necessary to embed healthy development within Melanesian cultures do not take place through appropriating merely physical, material, technological or professional (or we might say 'secular'), concepts and processes. Development involves spiritual and theological aspects if cultural embedding is to be permanent. In reaching this conviction, CLTC has been drawing on some of the wealth of Christian mission experience, both positive and negative, particularly since the beginning of the modern Protestant missionary movement in the late eighteenth century. The lessons gleaned from missiologists can enrich the wealth of insight into worldview transformation available from social anthropologists and the increasing understanding of changing social imaginaries being offered from historical philosophers.[21]

---

20. Hitchen, 'The Christian Leaders' Training College of Papua New Guinea – A Case Study of a Christian Contribution to Economic Development...', 2.
21. Hitchen, 'The Christian Leaders' Training College of Papua New Guinea – A Case Study of a Christian Contribution to Economic Development...', 10.

In his analysis John draws on the work of the late Harold Turner, a New Zealand 'primal religions' scholar. He employs Turner's framework in discussing the five cultural themes of cosmology, epistemology and technical effectiveness, understanding of time, understanding humanity, human nature and social values, and ethics and moral causality, to establish his proposition. He believes that each point is necessary to a deep worldview level transition to firmly root healthy development within Melanesian societies. John concludes:

> In analysing the components of an adequate worldview for the new challenges facing Melanesian nations today, there is a danger that in focusing on the parts we ignore the whole. Each of these themes has confirmed that Melanesian and Pacific societies are deeply imbued with religious consciousness. This is not a peripheral interest of a few, but a basic focus of their holistic worldviews. This openness to input from the Other, or the Transcendent beyond the human, serves as an integrative factor holding together the various strands we have discussed. It has been summed up helpfully as the search for salvation at the heart of Melanesian worldviews. Any adequate approach to development in the Pacific needs to ask whether this search is itself being developed adequately to embrace and consolidate the desired developments in the various other worldview aspects? Or, reframing the question, how is this traditional religious consciousness and quest best served at this point in the historical development of the Pacific nations?...
>
> ... we suggest the Christian Gospel... has with depth of contextual awareness, the seed sowing potential more adequately to provide the needed integrative basis. The Gospel offers a way for retaining and enriching the 'noble traditions' of Melanesian heritage, and also guiding the ongoing transitions of worldview necessary for meaningful, dignified Pacific participation in social, political, economic, environmental and spiritual development which is firmly embedded within our Pacific cultures. Theological Education's most significant contribution to such holistic development is the way it builds and renews the worldview basics, thereby equipping gardeners to tend the roots and ongoing health of the trees of cultural flourishing, not just focusing on the means of harvesting currently accessible fruit.[22]

---

22. Hitchen, 'The Christian Leaders' Training College of Papua New Guinea – A Case Study of a Christian Contribution to Economic Development...', 14, 15.

CLTC however, does not simply rest on these legacies. Looking forward, following an intensive review and discussion process led by Rod and Denise Edwards, which included Council, Advisory Councils, supporters, staff, faculty, and students, the CLTC Council formally adopted a Strategic Plan in 2013 in line with the original vision of those who established CLTC. The Vision Statement affirms:

> The CLTC's vision is to excel in providing training programs which:
> - Integrate spiritual growth, scholarship, ministry and interpersonal skills in an environment of discipleship through the teaching of the Scriptures;
> - Equip students in mind and heart for ministry and vocation;
> - Are based on a Christian world view to live and work as mature servants of Christ in their community, church and mission.[23]

How CLTC is seeking to achieve this vision today is developed in the extensive College Mission Statement.[24] Many involved with Gil in the establishment of CLTC would agree with Garth Morgan:

> Rev Dr Gilbert McArthur left a lifelong legacy in our personal lives that has enabled, encouraged and even compelled us, to care for the God-given vision that Gil transplanted into our own lives as we journeyed with him for seven years. And only God knows what impact the legacy of the Christian Leaders' Training College of PNG Inc. will have in the nations of the South Pacific through the ministries of the College's 2,000 plus graduates as they live and serve in their respective churches, communities and countries.[25]

The Evangelical Alliance of the South Pacific Islands

We have noted that Gil gave very strong support to the formation and development of the Evangelical Alliance, which was launched in 1964, just as he arrived to live at CLTC. In the years following, along with others, he saw the important role of the EASPI for the evangelical churches and provided leadership and support to the developing EASPI influence.

As Kay Liddle has observed, the EASPI achieved much more in co-operation than originally envisaged. Their activities and projects over the years have included:

---

23. CLTC Council, 'Christian Leaders Training College – Strategic Plan', 2013.
24. The CLTC Mission Statement is included in Appendix Five.
25. Morgan, 'Gilbert McArthur Information', 10.

Participants at National Conference on Evangelism in Lae 1976

- Forming and maintaining cordial relationships with the MCC;
- Working together in education with regional High Schools catering for EA Primary School students;
- Establishing an evangelical Christian Teachers College;
- Forming committees to study educational, sociological and development issues;
- Mission Education Officers of EASPI and MCC producing a 'Philosophy of Education' to provide programs designed to best meet the needs and problems of the country;
- Involving Mission theological educators in 1968 to prepare a Christian Education in Schools Syllabus for use in Administration schools;
- Establishing a Christian Broadcasting Service, which was eventually set up on the CLTC Campus;
- Preparing Christian radio programs for government stations;

- Establishing with MCC a Churches Council for Media Coordination;

- Cooperating with MCC on an Inter-Mission Committee to liaise with the University regarding Religious Studies and Chaplaincy;

- Developing cooperation between mission hospitals – sharing lecture notes for nurses and orderlies, exchanging of staff and nurses, and orderlies training at each other's training centres;

- Similar sharing of staff in the education field;

- Forming a Churches Medical Council with the MCC and PNG government;

- Organising the first Keswick Convention and Christian Endeavour Convention at CLTC;

- Interfacing year by year with Christian Leaders' Training College, informing the College of members specific needs related to equipping and training men and women for ministry in both rural and urban environments. Also ensuring that the CLTC relationship with other Bible Schools was healthy in the overall task of preparing leaders;

- Organising a National Seminar on Evangelism for all EASPI and MCC members following the Lausanne I International Congress on World Evangelisation held in 1974;

- Establishing community development and environmental projects among rural communities; and

- Contributing to research and leadership in developing policies and programs for urban youth in collaboration with the PNG government.[26]

It is significant that as the Alliance (now known as the Evangelical Alliance of Papua New Guinea EAPNG) developed over the years, national Christian leaders have been mentored and drawn into its leadership. Joshua Daimoi, the first Melanesian Principal of CLTC, expressed well this acceptance of responsibility to provide evangelical

---

26. Liddle, *Into the Heart of Papua New Guinea*, 366ff.

leadership in 1983: 'Having observed and been convinced by what you our missionary brothers stood for to advance the cause of the Evangelical Faith, we became enthusiastic and committed to carry on the torch of evangelical faith taken over from the pioneers that brought that faith to our nation.'[27]

While it is recognised that Gil's leadership in the development of the EASPI was one among many, all that flowed from the life of EASPI can be said to be another dimension of his legacy.

Alliance Training Association Inc., Beechwood Pty Ltd, Highway Motors Pty Ltd, Timberline Pty Ltd

We have seen how ATA was born out of the need for CLTC to transport supplies economically into the highlands of PNG.[28] Gil and Graham Walker, with the support of the CLTC Council, saw the opportunity to solve the CLTC supply problem, generate financial support for the CLTC programs, service other mission agencies and churches, and create new pathways for national people to receive training and opportunities for apprenticeships, employment and starting their own business ventures.

But at the core of the vision that brought CLTC to birth was the determination to see leadership development in the emerging nation

ATA's initial Lae Workshop and Hostel built in 1971 by Ron Youngman

---

27. Liddle, *Into the Heart of Papua New Guinea*, 367.
28. Initially supplies were flown in from Madang, but this proved to be too expensive.

of PNG, at a time when some analysts believe that the Australian administration had not invested adequately in the education and preparation of leaders for independence.[29] In the cultural context of PNG, where there is no secular/sacred divide, the birth of ATA was the opportunity to demonstrate and model holistic Christian leadership in the world of business and industry embedded in a community centred upon God and his revealed Word through his Son Jesus Christ. It was this primary driver in those who brought ATA to birth that produced its most significant legacy – national people with character and integrity, equipped with skills to contribute to a developing nation.

In 2012, Kay Liddle, retired PNG Brethren missionary and close friend of Gil's through the years of his leadership in PNG, recorded his observation of the legacy of ATA:[30]

> During the next twenty years, ATA continued to provide practical training and a Christian work ethic through its various business activities: It acquired the Kenworth truck agency for PNG and through its saw-milling subsidiary Beechwood Pty Ltd, it supplied timber to meet the rapidly growing needs of the highlands region and was a major employer in the Southern Highlands Province. ATA was instrumental in setting up and supporting many national sub-contractor groups to run successful businesses within the transport and timber industries. ATA's business operations were finally sold to the Papua New Guineans they had trained and employed.[31]

The Pacific Leaders' Fellowship

In his visionary, networking and administrative capacity, Gil left a legacy of influence through the PLF in the lives of many political and church leaders around the Pacific. Driving him forward in establishing this interface of leaders was the conviction that only through their encounter with the living God through Christ incarnate, crucified and risen would they be liberated from self-seeking, aware of their accountability to God, and encourage each other to develop policies and make decisions in the best interests of the people they were called to serve:

---

29. Dorney, *The Embarassed Colonialist - A Lowy Institute Paper*, 22.
30. Kay Liddle, a veteran PNG missionary, was appointed Acting Principal in 1971 following Gil's resignation from CLTC. In this position Kay was a Board member of ATA and Beechwood, and so had opportunity to closely familiarise himself with the impact of both companies.
31. Liddle, *Into the Heart of Papua New Guinea*, 346.

Max Meyers, Fiji Governor-General Ratu Sir George Cakobau, Gil and Sir Peter Kenilorea

The nations and their leaders, the rich and the powerful will be called before the bar of divine Justice and asked to give an account. The great question will be: 'What have you done for the least of these my brethren?' (Matthew 25:40). The awesome verdict is that the people of many affluent nations will follow their leaders to damnation because, even by default, they gave their assent to the exploitation of the weak and the needy in the plundering of the deprived multitudes by the powerful and did not share the benefits of the earth's resources with those bereft of daily sustenance.[32]

The ministry of the PLF impacted many Pacific Island leaders. On one occasion Max Meyers recalls that they experienced great difficulty in getting permission to land on the small island of Kosrae in the North Pacific. They pondered what they should do. Gil's passion and perseverance were such that he urged the team 'Let's just do it!' Probably not an acceptable approach in aviation today! When they landed, the President of the island arrived. Sir Peter Kenilorea, Prime Minister of the Solomon Islands, who was the PLF leader, was first off the aircraft. Max recalls his opening introduction went something like this:

---

32. McArthur, 'A Civilization Crisis', 4.

My name is Peter. Many years ago sailing ships came over the oceans to the islands of the Pacific, and drew lines that divided us forever. We are just an informal group from the South Pacific who want to do something about this. So, we have come here just to be with you, meet with you, and talk about leadership.[33]

The President sent them on to their accommodation, and later returned with all the leaders of the tribal groups of the island. They spent a wonderful time together, sharing about God's call to lead as servants. When the meetings were over, and it was time to take off to their next destination, (as we have already noted) the Lieutenant Governor said to Sir Peter, 'this visit… will perhaps turn out to be the most honourable visit that Kosrae State has ever had!'[34]

John Key, who served with Gil in this remarkable ministry in the Pacific, offers his own evaluation of Gil's legacy through the PLF:

It is hard to evaluate the longer-term impact and legacy of the PLF, because its seeds were sown and its fruit harvested in the personal, intimate lives and journeys of each man who was blessed to participate. I believe we should thank the Lord for what he did through Gil's ministry in –

- Providing prayerful and personal support for newly elected leaders in times of uncertainty and vulnerability;
- Connecting national leaders, particularly the younger ones, across national and island boundaries as brothers in Christ;
- Imparting Kingdom vision, values and principles into the leadership and governance of island nations, rediscovering their identity and purpose in the turmoil of national and regional changes and challenges.[35]

An Ongoing New Zealand Legacy

Maxim Institute, Venn Foundation, Masters Institute, New Zealand Education Development Foundation

One day in mid-1990, Ron Youngman came into the office of another Gil McArthur protégé, the then Principal of the Bible College of New

---
33. Max Meyers, 'Gil McArthur and the Pacific Leaders' Fellowship', Telephone Interview, 21 February 2017.
34. Meyers, 'Gil McArthur and the Pacific Leaders' Fellowship'.
35. Key, 'Dr Gilbert McArthur – Some Recollections by John Key', 1.

Zealand (now Laidlaw College), and said, 'John, what are we going to do about the moral deterioration in our nation and the loss of any Christian values or godly influences in our schools?'

A discussion ensued in which Ron expressed his frustration that he had written and spoken to his Church pastors and denominational leaders asking what they were doing about our godless education system, but they had just ignored his questions. He had likewise written to his local MP and even the Prime Minister and had received only bland responses thanking him for his concern and rehearsing the policies to which they were committed, but which did nothing to address his concerns.

John Hitchen and Ron agreed that to make any changes the teachers' colleges equipping the next generation of teachers were strategically important, the school curriculum had to be enhanced, and somehow public opinion needed to be stirred up to want a change for the better. When John asked if Ron had any ideas where to start, Ron said he had been impressed by a recent *NZ Herald* article written by the Head of English at Rangitoto College, a leading Auckland Secondary School. It lamented the way the Judaeo-Christian heritage and values promoted by the traditional classic English texts had been replaced in recent High School curriculum revisions by superficial ideologically slanted texts which undermined those foundational values. Ron had been wondering whether, if he put up some money, they could get that English teacher, Bruce Logan, to take a year out and do more writing to stir up public opinion to try to move the education system in a more positive direction. Ron and John didn't pause to think how foolish that might seem to others, because they had both seen what McArthur-like vision could do from small beginnings in PNG, and they took it for granted that Gil's kind of vision could bring comparable change, even in God's own country, New Zealand. So when, to their delight, Bruce Logan eagerly grasped the opportunity to influence public opinion for a year, they gathered a small group comprising two other respected State school teachers, a principal of a Christian School who was also developing a small Christian teachers' college (which would become Masters Institute), a lecturer in the state-run Auckland College of Education, John's fellow lecturer in Christian Education at BCNZ, and one other Christian businessman, to form the NZ Education Development Foundation (NZEDF), which was formally incorporated on 23 December 1991, with Bruce Logan as its one staff member and

Director.[36] After his first year, Bruce Logan agreed to continue long-term as NZEDF Director, producing a regular Journal, *Cutting Edge* with articles covering a range of educational and family value concerns, and regular editorials and opinion pieces in several national newspapers. Conferences, seminars and pamphlets followed.

Ron provided the central funding for the Foundation for its initial decade. But his role in shaping educational opinion went further. One of his last 'retirement' building projects had been extending the influential Christian School, Kingsway College, and he added membership on their Board to his NZEDF commitment. By the late-1990s, Masters Institute had grown and needed better premises. So, with the support of his Roskill Christian Trust funding group, on which Garth Morgan served as the major financial guide, Ron re-furbished one of his original warehouses and set it up as an effective teachers' college for Masters Institute to relocate and continue to extend both in numbers and influence. More recently, Masters Institute amalgamated with BCNZ to become what is now Laidlaw College's School of Education, equipping teachers with primary degrees in both Worldview Studies and Teaching Practice.

In 2001, with John and Ron still actively serving its Board, NZEDF was joined by a new group of entrepreneurial visionary Board members who appointed a new CEO skilled in fundraising to broaden NZEDF's scope to become Maxim Institute, a Gospel-based think-tank addressing not only educational, but wider social, economic and policy concerns shaping the heart of national development. With a greatly increased research team, new internship program and an annual Conference to prepare High School leavers for the worldview and faith challenges of university study, since 2001 Maxim has significantly influenced discussions and policy formation on constitutional reform, taxation matters, foreign policy in the South Pacific, poverty issues and planning for NZ rural communities facing decline in coming years. The Institute's research has also made key contributions to nation-wide discussions on the nature of marriage and family life, euthanasia and, of course, educational matters. More recently two key aspects of Maxim's work, the 'Internship' formation and educational program and the already

---

36. The foundational trust signatories were Rod Edwards, Dean of Students at BCNZ, Ron Youngman, retired builder, Roger Moses, Bruce Logan and Graham Smith, all teachers, Bev Norsworthy Principal of Hebron Christian School, George Stonehouse, Lecturer at Auckland College of Education, Wyn Fountain, retired businessman and John Hitchen, Principal of BCNZ.

independent 'Compass' High School-leavers' conference, have been formed into a second organisation, the Venn Foundation, to continue to develop people to live as opinion-formers and social change agents in needy Aotearoa New Zealand.[37]

It is not hard to see the roots of these developments in the Gil McArthur vision for Christian influence in the South Pacific region of the world. Gil's lieutenants, Ron, John and Garth, have ensured key educational aspects of Gil's rich heritage are being well adapted to address national policy formation, for the Kiwi context.[38]

The South Sea Evangelical Mission and Churches

Prior to Gil's involvement, Ken Griffiths had faithfully and effectively led the SSEM from 1943. Ken's leadership style was strongly consultative. He was not one to push his own views.

Gil, on the other hand, was a strong visionary leader. He looked to the future. He was a missionary theologian, deeply committed to articulating the biblical foundations of the strategies he proposed to strengthen indigenous churches. With the capacity to inspire and motivate others, he took decisive action to put the vision and strategies into place. In the SSEM work in the Sepik, he was a catalyst in introducing a formal structure for the church that opened the way for consolidation and new initiatives in evangelism and church planting in the PNG islands.

His vision involved (as always) the development of competent spiritual leaders. It was far-reaching, not just for the strengthening of the SSEC churches themselves, but for the impact of the spiritual power of the Kingdom of God upon the new nations of the Pacific. In Gil's words:

> These great movements of the Spirit must be viewed within the context of emerging nationhood. The heady wine of nationalism provides another kind of intoxication that must be recognised for what it is, and a way found to ensure that the young church fulfils its God-given purpose in bringing spiritual integrity and moral judgement to the life of the young nation at this crucial period.

---

37. John Hitchen, 'Ron Youngman – Later Developments', 10 October 2017. John who worked so closely with Ron provided detailed information for this section.
38. Ron Youngman continued on the NZEDF and Maxim Boards until retiring only a few years before his death. John Hitchen chaired the NZEDF Board till 1999 (when he was Principal of BCNZ) and has continued as the only original Board member still active on the Maxim Board today, 28 years after NZEDF's commencement.

This leads us to address ourselves in prayer commitment to the task of preparing the New Wineskins.[39]

Gil's decisive and assertive leadership brought new energy into the life of SSEM, both to the missionaries, and to the national leaders of the SSEC churches. He wanted to give them a strong basis of independence in the important positions they held and equip them to be effective.

Gil's legacy in SSEM meant that the work in the Solomon Island and Sepik churches consolidated to the point where they themselves began to emerge as missionary sending communities, reaching out across PNG and beyond. For SSEM the issue had very much become *where to next?* which directly led to the story of the birth of Pioneers International.

Pioneers International

Ted and Peggy Fletcher were influenced by Gil, and others, to commence a new mission agency in 1979 focussing specifically on unreached peoples. What began as World Evangelical Outreach changed to Pioneers in 1984 because:

> God sent us more and more young people who wanted to blaze new paths to the unreached. In fact, we decided to change our name to describe more accurately the call that the Lord had given us. We also needed a name that would be more 'security' sensitive – one that didn't sound like a Christian mission, so that we could protect our missionaries in restricted access countries. I remembered hearing that only one out of every ten missionaries is pioneering new frontiers. We wanted a mission in which ten out of ten were pioneering, so we chose the new name 'Pioneers' to reflect our desire not to follow the worn paths, but to blaze new ones.[40]

The Pioneers Board formalised this focus in their Mission Statement: 'Pioneers mobilises teams to glorify God amongst unreached peoples by initiating church planting movements in partnership with local churches.' The Pioneers ethos and culture is further defined in the Doctrinal Statement and eight Core Values to which all members are asked to commit: Passion for God, Unreached People Groups, Church Planting Movements, Teams, Ethos of Grace, Local Church Partnership, Servant Leadership, and Creativity and Innovation.[41]

---

39. McArthur, 'New Wineskins for New Wine', 5.
40. Fletcher, *When God Comes Calling*, 77.
41. See Appendix 3 for the complete Core Values statement.

The introduction to the original bylaws of WEO read:

> All that follows in these bylaws comes only after prayer. Prayer is always to be the first priority, the highest purpose, the moving force, the vital energizer of this Mission. The overriding prerequisite in every provision of these bylaws is earnest, travailing prayer to the Father that the world might hear of His Son through our heart and lips made ready by prayer.
>
> All who serve the Lord in this sacred organisation are charged with this sacred trust – to pray for the blessed will of the Father to be accomplished through us.[42]

Although the priority of prayer was not explicitly expressed as one of the Core Values, prayer is reinforced as a central emphasis in the life of Pioneers today through the Soli Deo Group.[43]

Initially, Pioneers experienced some real opposition from other traditional mission agencies in inter-mission forums and conferences – particularly around their identification of six unreached people groups, their commitment to innovative and flexible approaches, and policy of sending missionaries into people groups where other missions were already working but not covering all the people in those areas.[44]

It was some years later, in 1997, that APCM and then SSEM in Australia and New Zealand, both long-standing traditional mission agencies, came to a decision to merge with Pioneers and form Pioneers International. Both APCM and SSEM had been in decline for some time, with aging missionaries and missionary numbers decreasing in their traditional areas of operation, and where now vigorous young churches were carrying on the mission of evangelism and church planting. Len Buck (a former General Director of UFM/APCM and close friend of Gil and Ted and Peggy Fletcher) in his last years lamented that APCM was no longer really reaching unreached peoples: 'We need to start a new mission agency! We need to inspire a new generation of people with

---

42. Fletcher, *When God Comes Calling*, 54.
43. Soli Deo – God Alone, is a group of advocates within Pioneers International. They stimulate passion for the glory of God alone throughout all teams and other conferences and retreats. They develop resources for biblical devotionals, worship, prayer and fasting, and for the Pioneers Monthly Day of Prayer and Fasting.
44. Fletcher, *When God Comes Calling*, 77–82. See Ted Fletcher's first description of the Core Values and his discussion of the opposition experienced from established mission agencies.

Pioneers International Conference Chiang Mai Thailand 2017

a heart for the lost!'[45] The respective boards of APCM and SSEM both took great steps of faith in 1997 to recognise it was time for a new day. The merger with Pioneers created an international mission movement committed to opening new doors to reach the unreached peoples around the world. Over the past 38 years, Pioneers International has experienced remarkable growth under God's blessing and currently has 3248 International Members.

Pioneers Australia today has over 220 adult cross-cultural workers (85 in 2005), and over fifty more Australians preparing to leave, so the flow of workers continues in a remarkable way and fulfils the yearning and prayers of Len Buck to see a new mission thrust to unreached peoples out of Australia.[46]

Ray Laird was Chairman of SSEM at the time Gil was initiating the PTI at the new SSEM base in Laurieton. As he looks back to that time when Gil's health was declining, and he faced the difficulty of trying to find a suitable person to appoint as the PTI Director in Gil's place, Ray makes this astute observation:

> In retrospect, seeing what has occurred in the last 25 years to SSEM, now absorbed into Pioneers, I think that our Lord was pointing to His answer to something that several SSEM members had been asking as we struggled to discern our future: Is our Mission in PNG and the Solomons coming to an end? The SSEC in PNG and in the Solomons had both received their independence with good indigenous leaders on hand, and it seems that we had become a mission looking for a new field to evangelise. Well, that is what happened, and today as part of Pioneers we are involved with a

---

45. Len Buck said this in personal conversation with David Price in the Principal's office at the Bible College of Victoria circa. 1991.
46. Details of the Pioneers International Director's Office statistics for 2017 are available in Appendix 3.

ministry of 250 teams in 101 countries of unreached peoples. I think that Gil would be happy![47]

At the point where Gil wanted to reinstate an older, out-dated approach to SSEM's future by establishing the PTI at Laurieton, God brought SSEM under the fresh vision and direction of Ted Fletcher, whom Gil himself had influenced so significantly at an earlier stage in each of their journeys. God's ways of transition and continuance in our stories are not always those even his most faithful servants expect. Gil's legacy and his passion to see the Gospel arrive among unreached peoples continues through Pioneers International today!

CLTC Faculty 2018
Standing: Isaac Pulupe; Patrick Hall, Steven Duncan, Joseph Mango, Dan Anderson, Rebekah Yandit, Samuel Waripi, Johanna Smith, Retta Renich, Bruce Renich, Abel Haon, and Phil Tait
Seated back: Sharon Lepper, Jenny Tobul, Dorothy Sanga, Alison Weymouth, Rachelle Haon, Celestial Yejerla, John Prasad, and Roland Lubett
Seated: Moses Bakura, Marguerite Tom, Iru Longgar, William Longgar, Duli Asi, and Lucy Korema
Seated floor: Allan Sanga, Jubal Boto, Gordon Tobul, Kirine Yandit, Henoma Ttopoqogo, Aaron Abia, and Lionel Tom

---

47. Laird, 'Gil McArthur', 2.

21

A LOVING LOYAL PARTNER AND FAMILY

Who can find a virtuous and capable wife?
She is more precious than rubies.
Her husband can trust her,
and she will greatly enrich his life.
She brings him good, not harm,
all the days of her life.[1]

Marjory Foyle, one of the pioneers of the member-care/development movement in mission agencies writes:

> Both husband and wife should be called. Sometimes the husband may be pushed into missionary service because of his wife's call, and vice versa. Married couples are a unit, and although the timing may be different, if God calls one he also calls the other. Some wives have told me they had no sense of calling at all and were resentful of being 'taken along like a piece of baggage'. One wife, able to laugh at it later on told me 'At least I wasn't checked into the hold with the rest of the luggage, I had a seat!'[2]

From their early response to the challenge to take the Gospel to unreached people Pat and Gil were totally united in their sense of call. Their letter of application to the Baptist Mission declared: 'My wife and I are deeply conscious of our Lord's leading in respect to Him requiring us to devote our lives to the proclamation of His riches, to souls in need where'er those souls may be found.'[3] Pat was not a reluctant piece of baggage!

This account of the life and ministry of Gil would be inexcusably incomplete without recognition of Pat McArthur who was alongside Gil co-authoring each page of his story. His children Robyn, Jenny, Paul,

---

1. Proverbs 31:10-12 NLT.
2. Marjory Foyle, *Honourably Wounded: Stress Among Christian Workers*, First Edition (Bromiley, Kent: MARC, 1987), 42, 43.
3. McArthur, 'Application for Service in New Guinea', 1.

Wendy, and Sandra were also a vital aspect of his personal support and encouragement who shared in the joy and pain of the journey.

When Pat died on 20 May 2002, Ann and John Hitchen wrote a tribute to her which opens a great window into the life of this grace-filled lady. Ann and John had served as colleagues under Gil and Pat in the establishment phase of CLTC, from 1964 until the McArthurs left PNG in 1971. Few are better qualified to speak of Pat's ministry and legacy alongside Gil.

> By her personal commitment, faithfulness and self-sacrifice, Pat made a colossal contribution to the setting up of what has become the major evangelical theological and biblical education centre for church and community leaders in Papua New Guinea and the Solomon Islands. In 1963 Gilbert was appointed... the founding Principal of CLTC. When Gilbert took up the job, no one thought to write a job-description for the Principal's wife! But everyone, especially Gilbert, took it for granted that Pat would do whatever was necessary to assist him in his pioneering task of transforming 413 acres of swamp land in the Highlands into an effective educational centre.
>
> Pat had already proven her ability to cope with the virtually impossible when she and Gilbert had pioneered the Baptist Mission work both in Irian Jaya and at Telefolmin in the Sepik, or Sandaun, Province of PNG.
>
> In 1964 Pat took her five children to join Gilbert at the CLTC site in the Western Highlands of PNG. Theirs was the only European style building completed on the property and, under Pat's cool, hard-working hands it was internally decorated and furnished to become their family home; the College office; an auxiliary boarding house for new staff or building helpers; the College meeting place for church services, staff meetings, medical clinics; and the point of contact for purchasing fruit and vegetables from the local people – a veritable market place on a daily basis in the early days. Each of these extra functions would be moved step by step to custom-built facilities, but at the beginning the McArthur home was the starting point for everything, supervised and coordinated capably and uncomplainingly by Pat.
>
> I lived in the McArthur home for my first 8 weeks at the College, as did numerous others who followed. Pat played a major role in those

Gil and Pat, Robyn, Jenny, Paul, Sandra and Wendy

early days driving the College's four-wheel drive Land Rover over only partially formed clay tracks into all the surrounding hills. At each group of local houses, she would buy kaukau (sweet potato) and vegetables and fruit – bananas, pineapples and pawpaw – by the Land Rover load, to provide the basic food requirements of all the building team, administrative, agricultural and teaching staff, plus the students of the College. This meant she had to be an excellent linguist, bartering in the trade language of Pidgin. She had to be a shrewd psychologist, distinguishing between the sob stories pleading for a higher price and the genuine needs of local people. She had to be ever alert to those who tried to recycle what she had already bought to sneak it back to her for a second payment. She had to calmly but strongly stand up to the local men who, with no traditional respect for women in any business role, would seek to manipulate the occasion forcefully for their own advantage.

I learned heaps about cross-cultural communication, true respect for Papua New Guineans, and firm, impartial dealing in tricky situations when I accompanied her on a number of occasions on those food-buying trips. Nothing ever seemed to faze Pat. She could handle the most-irate or the most insistent local people with a laid-back poise that few of us ever achieve.

Pat also served as hostess for numerous visitors and dignitaries to the College, including the Governor General, Chief of PNG Defence Force, Chief of Police from Queensland, the District Commissioner and various other Government Officers, Members of the PNG Parliament; visiting Australian MHAs as well as many church and mission leaders. Again, Pat was never flustered and always rose to the occasion humbly and with dignity.

Such visits often meant Pat drove the seven miles into the local airstrip, or the 37 miles to the District airport at Mt Hagen to pick up and return the visitors to their public transport. And that was over the then unsealed, heavily pot-holed roads of the time.

Facilities at the College were primitive by Western standards. Washing with tubs and copper, using a kerosene or shellite powered iron, caring for a kerosene fridge and tilley lamps, or maintaining the two-stroke battery charger for her battery-powered lights, Pat was an expert do-it-yourself handywoman. Gilbert was often away on College business – or overseas studying for an extended period before Pat was able to join him on one occasion. Gilbert's work habits and sleep patterns were very difficult for any spouse to appreciate. But Pat accepted and supported Gilbert whatever the personal cost to her and did so uncomplainingly.

Pat was very self-contained. She was a rather private person throughout those years establishing CLTC. She took her place leading the other staff wives, welcoming each one as they arrived, helping them settle in and encouraging them in times of personal difficulty or sorrow. She was always available if one of the wives needed a listening ear, but seldom asked for, or expected help for herself. Gilbert was seen by some as a hard taskmaster – expecting others to be able to measure up to his own very high standards of sacrificial commitment. And Pat was always totally loyal to him, setting her own example of gladly going the second mile whether on College business or to help others in the College community or for the sake of her family. Only eternity will reveal the importance of the foundations she helped lay for training and equipping so many Papua New Guinean, Solomon Island, Vanuatuan, and Tongan church and national leaders through the ongoing ministry of CLTC.

Pat carried the major responsibility in bringing up the five children. Robyn was in her late teens and Jenny entering hers when they came to CLTC. The College Campus was an ideal place for bringing up younger children – with agricultural, mechanical, and building projects aplenty to occupy growing children, as well as an excellent primary school at the local township of Banz, with Pat doing most of the twice-daily fourteen-mile return-trip school runs. But with Jenny at secondary level that meant home-schooling as well… Pat ensured each of the children developed full-orbed and well-rounded lives. We honoured Pat as a home-maker, mother and friend to her children as they grew up at the College.

Ann and I, and I am sure the large number of other Kiwis who served at CLTC during the McArthur period, cherish only the utmost respect for Pat McArthur. She was a woman of strong faith and self-sacrificing commitment. She loved and enjoyed life at CLTC – participating fully in the worship, social and fun times as well as in her awesome contribution to practical administrative tasks… She was easy-going and quietly assured in all she did. Those of us who are privileged to have known her as a friend as well as a colleague, found she respected and accepted us as we actually were. She encouraged and supported us. Ann and I have particularly thankful memories for her support when we lost our baby son. Pat had known personal grief herself and her quiet trust and steady service for her Lord and Master, Jesus Christ, strengthened and upheld us in our time of need.

Pat never put on airs. She knew who she was in Christ. On the few times that we have met her since the McArthurs left CLTC, the years quickly rolled away and we would pick up again just as if we had never been apart – for Pat was constant and dependable in every way. We thank God for the privilege of having been enriched by her partnership and friendship.[4]

John's tribute ended by expressing the whole CLTC family's sympathy to each of the children, and grandchildren, and reminding them Pat was, 'a great Mother and Grandmother,' thanking them, 'for sharing her with us.' He concluded with the prayer…

> that Pat's faith, her friendship and her example may continue to rub off on each of you as we also pray we may live worthy of all she meant to us. It is not difficult to picture Pat now in the presence of Our Lord Himself. Her honest humility, straightforward trust and

---

4. John Hitchen, 'Tribute to Pat McArthur', 2002, McArthur Family Archives.

easy relationships with all her work-mates suggest heaven will mean only greater fulfilment and greater enrichment for her. May the Good Shepherd Pat served so gladly and well uphold and support each of you at this time.

Number two daughter Jenny provides a family 'insiders' last word of appreciation for 'my Mum':

> I have always had the most incredible admiration for my mother, knowing that she came from such a quiet sheltered life, to the life of ministry first in Sydney, then New Guinea… was so not what Mum had expected her life to be when she married Dad. She rose to all the challenges that came her way, speaking at meetings, home schooling, entertaining and so many more. Never once did I see her give up, complain, have a cry (there were plenty of reasons for her to do so). Mum was always there for us, patiently holding the family together, never cross, always loving, a great sense of humour that could lead to so much laughter. Never could there have been a more perfect partner for Dad than Mum – her loyalty, calmness, common sense, smartness, entertaining skills and her enduring love for Dad her life's partner, were the reasons Dad was able to do what he did. Mum was always there in the background, supporting him no matter where it led. Mum was so capable, there was hardly a thing she couldn't put her hand to – super clever at fixing most things, the lawnmower or light fittings to name a few. A wonderful cook, gardener and homemaker, Dad often said how Mum always could make any place we had be a 'Home', and he was really proud of that gift she had.
>
> What she accomplished in her own right is truly amazing, and we acknowledge those talents. Her loving care of Dad in his illness was beautiful to watch, and his adoration and thankfulness were conveyed to her in just a look. The saying 'Behind Every Good Man, is a Great Woman' says it all in our Mum.[5]

The story of Pat McArthur's journey alongside Gil illustrates what those today who provide member care for missionary families affirm:

> It cannot be stressed enough that the husband and the wife must each have a calling to ministry abroad… Missionary life itself is a huge challenge involving much loss and change. With the added

---

5. Jenny Fitzsimons, 'Mum', Email, 22 January 2018.

strain of separation from family and friends, loneliness, adjusting to a new culture and possibly a difficult climate, learning a new language, coping with previously unknown illnesses, arranging for or doing schooling, etc., it would be unwise to venture out without a personal call on the part of each person. If the wife has not chosen this step out of her own conviction and calling, and unless she is extremely adaptable and easy-going, she will struggle with resentment toward the people and culture, as well as toward her husband. She may subconsciously blame him for her ill-feelings. Women struggling in this area tend either to internalize their conflict and suffer from various psychosomatic disorders or depression, or they get very angry and confrontational. It is to everyone's advantage for sending agencies to be sure that each partner has a calling.[6]

There is no doubt that Pat with Gil shared and demonstrated that 'equal calling'.

Pat McArthur – morning run to Banz International Primary School

---

6. Annemie Grosshauser, 'Chapter Forty One: Supporting Expatriate Women in Difficult Settings', in Kelly O' Donnell, (Ed), *Doing Member Care Well: Perspectives and Practices From Around the World* (Pasadena, California: William Carey Library, 2002), 424.

Pat McArthur with local Wahgi people

— WITH CHRIST —

The **REV GILBERT J. McARTHUR**, MA, LLD, AM, OBE, was called Home on 3 February 1994 after a long illness. He was the founding principal of the Christian Leaders' Training College, Banz, PNG, from 1963-70.

He had lived a full and adventurous life, coming to Christ as a young man at a Christian Brethren service.

After service in World War II, he married Miss Patricia May Miller, of Tamworth (NSW), who shared fully in her husband's vision. An encounter with Dr J. Oswald Sanders in 1950 led to his call to missionary service, and after studies at the NSW Baptist Theological College, he went to Irian Jaya with ABMS, preparing airstrips in isolated areas.

The McArthurs later moved across the border to Telefomin in the West Sepik area of Papua New Guinea. Once more they found themselves involved in a pioneering enterprise. In addition to their normal evangelistic work, a vernacular Bible school was commenced, the language reduced to writing, and portions of Scripture translated into the local dialect. Twenty young men entered the Bible school and all became Christians. A real breakthrough took place, and the church began to prosper.

Late in 1960 the education of their children made it necessary for Mr and Mrs McArthur to return to Australia, where he accepted a call to the Clemton Park Baptist Church in Sydney, a ministry that continued until he accepted the invitation to become principal of a college in Papua New Guinea that as yet existed only in vision.

Dr McArthur also served as president of the NSW Missionary Aviation Fellowship council and as Pacific area representative of World Vision, as well as with South Sea Evangelical Mission.

'New Life' associate editor, Clifford Wilson, says of him:

'I had the privilege of knowing Gilbert McArthur for over 50 years. In his late teens Gil was an outstanding Gospel preacher, especially in the open air. He was knowledgeable, convincing, interesting, fervent.

'He joined the Royal Australian Navy as a seaman and he bore an excellent testimony.

'His vision and drive in the early years of establishing the Christian Leaders' Training College in PNG were wonderful to behold. His colleagues in leadership rightly regarded him as a visionary who had the capacity to deliver. In various ways he was a leader of leaders.'

Gil McArthur's 'New Life' Obituary, 10 Feb 1994

22

A LEADER'S CHARACTER

*May you always be filled with the fruit of your salvation
—the righteous character produced in your life by Jesus Christ—
for this will bring much glory and praise to God.[1]*

In reading the chapters of the Gilbert McArthur Story-Book, we have seen throughout the core principle of his life, 'Learn to live in tents – build only altars'. There has been much to reflect on, to give thanks for, and to challenge our lives and ministries.

Gil McArthur, like each one of us, was not perfect, but he was willing to be God's instrument for his time – always hungry to keep growing in his knowledge of God, and to be obedient to God's will for his life.

Gil McArthur

In reviewing the lasting impressions of Gil's life and leadership, let us give thanks to the Lord Jesus Christ for his servant who has gone ahead of us, and the legacy he has left. In doing so we respond to the biblical call to 'Remember your leaders, who spoke the word of God to you. Consider the outcome of their way of life and imitate their faith. Jesus Christ is the same yesterday and today and forever.'[2]

Man of God

A W Tozer wrote many years ago: 'What comes into our minds when we think about God is the most important thing about us… A right

---

1. Philippians 1:11 NLT.
2. Hebrews 13:7.

conception of God is basic not only to systematic theology but to practical Christian living as well.'[3]

Leaving the world of aviation, Gil was profoundly impacted by his time in Theological College. He developed a great confidence in the authority and power of the Bible as the living Word of God. He matured in his growing knowledge of God, his deep relationship with him, and what response that relationship required of him. His Principal, George Morling, understood and lived what some have called 'the deeper Christian life': the life which recognises sin and its consequences; the saving work of Christ in his death and resurrection; conversion through repentance; faith and surrender to Christ as Lord; living a holy life; and the gift of the Spirit to transform lives and empower followers of Jesus to serve in his mission to the world. Gil embraced this biblical framework, and led others into its truths throughout his ministry. It was behind the inauguration of the 'Keswick' conventions held in the early years at CLTC.

The prevailing theme in all his preaching and teaching (even if perhaps for some the words were difficult to grasp), was his sense of the majesty, holiness, greatness, power and grace of the Triune God – Father, Son and Holy Spirit, and his absolute confidence in the Gospel as the power of God for salvation.[4]

In his application to the Baptist Mission in 1951, Gil expressed how he understood what relationship with God required: 'It is my humble endeavour through daily fellowship to place Him at the very centre of my life, praying that by his Spirit He will control my thinking, determine my attitudes, and bring me to the place of willing obedience to His will.'[5] It was one of those 'altar moments'.

Gil's story provides many examples of this working out in his life. When Gil, Pat and the family faced packing up and leaving the pioneering work into the Baliem, and the language learning and translation work which was just becoming effective, it must have been a very difficult period. Their move was precipitated by the tensions between Gil and Norm Draper the Field Leader, both men wanting to be where the action was. Gil must have felt some deep anguish about the decision

---

3. Tozer, Aiden Wilson, *The Knowledge of the Holy - The Attributes of God - Their Meaning in the Christian Life* (London: James Clarke and Co. Ltd, 1961), 9.
4. Romans 1:16,17.
5. McArthur, 'Application for Service in New Guinea', See Schedule C, Section 11.

of the Mission Board, but demonstrating his commitment to the call of God upon his life, and respect for the decision of the mission leadership, he agreed to the move. We have referred several times to the memorable line to his church and supporting partners at that testing time: *'Keep on keeping on – Ephesians 6 – there's much to do whilst it is day. We must measure our work in the light of eternity, therefore, learn to live in tents, build only altars.'*[6]

Gil moved his tent from Sentani to Telefolmin because of the altar of sacrifice he had built in his life to the Lord Jesus.[7] Before departing for his study leave at Columbia Bible College, Gil gave a powerful message to staff and students at CLTC. It was based on the words of King David when he purchased land from Araunah the Jebusite to build an altar to the Lord to stop the deadly plague on his people. Araunah offered the land free to David, but his response was: 'No, I insist on paying you for it. I will not sacrifice to the Lord my God burnt offerings that cost me nothing.'[8] Gil said to the staff and students:

> A look around the College campus enables us to properly say that in the goodness of God we have in these three years builded together an Altar upon which to worship and serve the Lord. And I think, that in a proper way, without any wrong pride in our hearts we can say that what we have offered to the Lord has cost us all something, and we would not have it otherwise.[9]

Like Elijah the Old Testament prophet, Gil was not a perfect man, but 'human just like us'.[10] But he was a man of God surrendered as a living sacrifice to the Lord who saved him.

Man of Biblical/Theological Maturity

Gil was gifted in his way with concepts and words. He often used unusual or unfamiliar words and phrases to express the profound biblical truths that had gripped his mind and spirit about God, the Word of God, the Gospel and the mission of God to the nations of the world. We have noted that it was not unusual for some to feel his mind-stretching thoughts and language were beyond them, or to be critical of language that was above

---

6. McArthur, 'The McArthur Diary Extracts', Number 12, January 1957.
7. Romans 12:1,2.
8. 2 Samuel 24:24.
9. Gilbert J McArthur, 'Address to Students and Staff at CLTC from 2 Samuel 2:24', 1967, McArthur Family Archives.
10. James 5:17.

his audience. Heather Ford, Gil's Executive Administrator/Accountant in the World Vision office tells an interesting story about this:

> Pat McArthur would often come and do some secretarial work there [SSEM office], due to staff shortage. She was delightful. Very occasionally she would give me glimpses of some personal aspect of their life. One time I was commenting on Gil's vocabulary – probably as I was looking up the dictionary for yet another meaning and spelling! She told me that when they were in USA while Gil was doing his Doctorate, they would sit up in bed and she would test him on a page of the dictionary every night before they went to sleep!!! In my opinion Gil was a wordsmith, and it seems he worked hard at developing this skill to do justice to the breadth and depth of the vision he bore in his heart. He was an orator of dreams, yet had a head for strategy, and a street wise canniness for trouble shooting.[11]

Gil not only engaged deeply with his Bible, but also with his dictionary to build his word capacity. His language at times may have stretched his readers and listeners – especially Grade 6 level students at CLTC! But he spoke with such conviction, passion and authority that people sensed God was speaking powerfully to them, inspiring and calling them through his writing and preaching to think great thoughts of a great God and Saviour who had revealed himself through the living and written Word.

His language and communication emerged out of his deep biblical and theological spirituality. Ray Laird (Chairman of SSEM 1981-1990) said 'He possessed one of the finest minds I have ever encountered, and with that was joined a remarkable combination of energy, wisdom and grace.'[12]

Gil's sharp mind engaged at a deep level with his Bible. He held a very high view of Scripture, and how God's Spirit worked through his Word to reveal himself and his love for people. To that end he was committed to translating, teaching, preaching and contextualising the message of the Bible into the cultural context of his listeners. He believed that there was an urgent need for a robust, scriptural Christianity embodied by Christians and churches who were holy, and who were deeply engaging in ways which demonstrate not how much we are really like our culture, but rather the stunning alternative to which the Word of God calls us.

---

11. Ford, 'Gil McArthur', 2.
12. Laird, 'Gil McArthur'.

In speaking to the assembled Faculty and Students at Columbia Bible College in 1976, he aligned himself with how J B Phillips felt when he was translating the book of Acts:

> He said he felt something like an electrician trying to rewire an old house, and he could not shut off the power! As he took this Holy Writ and began to work on it and articulate it in the language of his day and generation, he discovered a movement, a dimension of power, a current flowing that did something to his own life. He realised that it was not just the routine usage of words, but there was a vibrant something here which began to dominate his own life and thinking and control the very translation he was working on. And how true that is! Every missionary discovers that the Word of God is alive. I think it is Williams' translation that says: 'God's Word is alive and in action full of power'.
>
> And it's good to know after you have done all your theological studies, and you have fulfilled the discipline of learning the apostles' doctrine, studying the Word of God line upon line, that as you go forward to another people to share that truth from life to life, and heart to heart, that you do not need to give this Word its power. You do not need to resort to gimmicks. It's not the formula, the pattern or even the biblical outline which you may have received in the lecture room. This Word has its own inherent dynamic, and it pulsates with the divine nature and character of the living Christ. He is evident within it, and it is pregnant with all the fullness of the godhead bodily in Jesus Christ. It has its own power, it speaks with its own authority, and it is our blessed privilege simply to take it and put it into action.
>
> This is the mystery of God in choosing people like you and me, earthen vessels into which he can place this treasure, that across our lives the revelation of God in Christ may be communicated in the language and thought forms of your day and generation to a people that have never known and never heard.'[13]

Gil's theological worldview was framed by the Kingdom of God. It was not narrow and individualistic. He understood the work of the 'Cosmic Christ' to have profound implications not only for personal salvation, but indeed for the Christian community and the whole of creation in transforming the very heart and fabric of every society and the moral ethics of every people group.

---

13. McArthur, *The Dynamic of the Word of God in Action*.

Man of Vision

Right through his life, from EWA days through to his final years with the Pacific Training Institute, Gil was a Spirit-gifted visionary. He was always looking to the future, able to see further than others.

In 1968, Will Renshaw was appointed a member and Treasurer of both the MBI Council and the MBI CLTC Committee. He had opportunity to observe Gil in the emerging and consolidating years of CLTC, and believes that there was a certain uniqueness to the way vision operated in Gil's ministry:

> Gil was a visionary with the ability to overcome seemingly insurmountable challenges, build airstrips, gifted in languages, timber logging, and take calculated risks that would daunt others. While Len [Buck] shared the same vision as Gil to get things done, he did not have Gil's practical gifts, yet Gil could not have accomplished what he did in the development of the College without Len being alongside with his missions experience and accountability to the MBI Council. The two men complemented each other.[14]

Over the years, a strong consistency in Gil's vision was expressed in one particular strategy that developed in a variety of ways. He often spoke of the Strategy of the Gospel as it works out in the calling, training, equipping and life-long learning of Christian leaders. Whether it was in the early Gospel response of the Dani or Telefol people to the Gospel, or growing the congregation at Clemton Park, or meeting the leadership needs of the Pacific churches, or political leaders of the newly independent nations – he could see the vital need to build faith and integrity in leadership as one of the most critical strategies in the mission of God to the nations of the world.

> Gil was a Change Agent, always seeking to move with the moment – that is the needs of developing peoples, to move them from paths that belonged to the past, and which had lost their viability in their changing worlds. He was aware of the moment and gave himself to the task of finding ways to bring them into grip with the challenges that they faced in their transition to a fast-changing world.
>
> As a wise Strategist, Gil saw the need to introduce the indigenous peoples to new skills, and provided the wherewithal for them

---

14. Renshaw, 'Gilbert McArthur Lecture – The Mission', 3.

A LEADER'S CHARACTER

CLTC Faculty Banz Campus 1983
Standing at Back from left: Charles Stilwell, Ian Malins, Jim Ikinum, Greg Crawford, David Price, Ewan Stilwell, William Longgar, Usa Hesa, Stephen Horne, Joshua Daimoi
Seated in front: Makapiya Selese, Marilyn Rowsome, Lorraine Mitchell, Bob Fergie, Joe Taruna, Bruce Renich, Nataya Peu, (Ade Rickard absent)

to receive appropriate training in those skills. This included projects on the fields, and for some in Colleges in Australia and New Zealand. Among those skills were woodwork, building and furniture, agriculture, forestry, modern transport (on land and sea), and health ministries and principles. Education was high on his list to make the younger generations adequate and able to take their place in the new world emerging before their eyes. In particular, Gil was aware of the need of training in biblical and theological knowledge. Apart from his great contribution to CLTC, he saw the value of the local, indigenous Bible colleges, and of providing wider experience for some in Bible Colleges in Australia and New Zealand. Part of his strategy was making friends in high places, seeking out the decision-makers and leaders in Government, those who were responsible for adaptation to the new world, ensuring that the Churches marched together with the Government into the future, and not at cross purposes.[15]

The fact that today it is estimated that large numbers of the world's pastors (90+ percent) are untrained (and therefore serve their churches

---

15. Laird, 'Gil McArthur', 1.

with limited fruitfulness), and that effective and mature pastors and Christian leaders need a process of life-long learning to bring the Word of Christ to engage the lives of their people, surely means that *equipping leaders remains a vital strategy in the mission of God to the nations of the world.*[16]

Man of Action

Garth Morgan, who worked closely with Gil over the years believes: 'Gil's words are not what passed the "vision" on to me. It was Gil in action!... Gil's story is also about his words, but without Gil in action, there would not have been the depth of inspiration that inspired others to both follow and pursue the goals that Gil implanted in us.'[17] In his farewell to Gil from the leadership of CLTC, John Hitchen also affirmed:

> Gil was not only a visionary and a strategist, but also a man of action: Under the hand of God, Mr McArthur has been responsible for seeing the need for various things, for bringing them into being, for getting them off the ground, for getting them started, and under God's good hand, laying a firm foundation to ensure that they can continue.[18]

Gil's leadership demonstrated a unique determination and magnetic power to persuade and draw missions, missionaries, national pastors, young people and the emerging national leaders to the College campus, exposing them to the College development, facilities and potential to serve the emerging churches and the nation. Garth Morgan recalls:

> In the first week of January 1967, the first South Pacific Keswick Convention was held at College with about 70 missionaries and 50 Papua New Guineans present. Many came via MAF aircraft. Visitors were accommodated in student houses or classrooms as there was little accommodation available in staff homes. The messages were simultaneously translated into Pidgin and Police Motu. CLTC staff prepared all the meals on their wood stoves in their homes. Some MAF aircraft, which flew the Keswick participants home, returned with about 50 young PNG women and men for the first Christian Endeavour Conference, held over the next 10 days. In May 1968, The Evangelical Alliance of the South Pacific Islands Conference was hosted at CLTC with around 70 attending. This was followed by

---

16. Richard, 'Training of Pastors', 1.
17. Garth Morgan, 'Re: Conclusion', 2 December 2018, 1.
18. Hitchen, 'Appreciation of Rev G. J. McArthur', 1.

The British and Foreign Bible Society Bible Translators Institute for three weeks in August/September, with some 100 delegates attending. Other Keswick Conventions followed in 1968 and 1969 when more facilities made catering much easier, and in the following years the College often became the preferred venue for many conferences, conventions, and visits from prominent leaders. We have already noted that in July 1969 the Governor General of Australia, Sir Paul Hasluck and Lady Hasluck, together with the Administrator of PNG Mr David and Mrs Hay, plus several administration officials visited the College during Sir Paul's four-day tour of the country.[19]

But not everybody liked Gil, and his pursuit of turning vision into reality. That did not surprise him, for he had learned what being a leader meant:

> The truth... is if you lead anything, someone will disagree with your decisions and you will divide people into different opinions. There will be supporters and detractors. (Keep in mind, there has never been a president of the United States – or any country – with 100% approval ratings.) Leading is hard, because it takes people into the unknown. Leadership challenges the status quo. It stretches people and organizations. It brings change and change is always attached to an emotion. Leaders must be prepared to lead towards the vision of the organization, even when it means losing approval ratings.[20]

Gil was a catalyst, a man of action totally committed and disciplined to achieving the vision and getting the task done – whatever it was. He was disciplined and tough on himself, and this impacted Pat and the family at times. He expected those with him to match that same level of discipline and action. He was in a real sense a product of his missionary generation in terms of the discipline and sacrifice he modelled and expected of others. But for Gil this was what discipleship and fruitfulness in ministry required.

He expressed this clearly in a message he gave to a farming community at Georgetown Baptist Church in South Australia, shortly before moving once again into PNG in his responsibilities with ATA and SSEM. He shared that he had expected to stay home in Australia and send others,

---

19. Morgan, 'Gilbert McArthur Information', 9.
20. Ron Edmondson, 'One Hard Truth of Leadership', 8 February 2017, https://www.sermoncentral.com/pastors-preaching-articles/ron-edmondson-one-hard-truth-of-leadership 2988?ref=?utm_source=newsletter&utm_medium=email&utm_content=button&utm_campaign=scbpuSeptember%205th,%202017&maropost_id=742756920&mpweb=256-4425125-742756920.

and that leaving would be hard on them both – particularly Pat with the grandchildren no longer close by. He preached from John 12:20-26.

> Now there were some Greeks among those who went up to worship at the festival. They came to Philip, who was from Bethsaida in Galilee, with a request. 'Sir,' they said, 'we would like to see Jesus.' Philip went to tell Andrew; Andrew and Philip in turn told Jesus.
>
> Jesus replied, 'The hour has come for the Son of Man to be glorified. Very truly I tell you, unless a kernel of wheat falls to the ground and dies, it remains only a single seed. But if it dies, it produces many seeds. Anyone who loves their life will lose it, while anyone who hates their life in this world will keep it for eternal life. Whoever serves me must follow me; and where I am, my servant also will be. My Father will honour the one who serves me.'[21]

Gil emphasised that this was a twofold message about spiritual multiplication. It was about the ministry of the Lord Jesus Christ, and that in God's purpose he had a spiritual harvest in view. But for this to happen Christ must die to bear the judgement of our sin, that we might come to the Saviour as the 'many seeds' of his work. But it was also a message about being a disciple and witness to Christ today as co-workers with God in a world harvest. To achieve a harvest, like God we must have clear objectives – work hard, not take many holidays, get our priorities right – and there will be some areas of life we need to say no to, not because they are wrong themselves, but because we are committed to a spiritual harvest, and that means dying to ourselves, our ambitions and comfort. Gil lamented that in his day so many seeds remain single seeds – alone, because they are not willing to die to themselves and sow their lives into another culture through their prayers, financial partnership or in being open to personally go in response to the call of God. In concluding he said:

> 'The most profound philosophical statement that has ever fallen on human ears is this,
>
> Then he called the crowd to him along with his disciples and said: "Whoever wants to be my disciple must deny themselves and take up their cross and follow me. For whoever wants to save their life will lose it, but whoever loses their life for me and for the gospel will save it. What good is it for someone to gain the whole world, yet forfeit their soul?" '[22]

---

21. John 12:20-26.
22. Luke 9:23-25.

Gil urged the congregation to join the mainstream of God's purpose and come alive to a new dimension of productivity in the eternal implications of planting and sowing for a spiritual harvest for God's glory.

In his commitment to action and to see the vision realised, Gil was a networker of people. He initiated and fostered relationships with those he thought could offer a contribution in one way or another to see the vision into reality: people of influence; people with resources; people with skills and experience; people with potential for leadership development. But he also connected people to create relationships and synergy that would be an encouragement to them personally and build resilience in their ministries.

Man of Compassion

Some who served with Gil may find it strange to say that Gil was not only a man of action, but also a man of compassion with a pastoral heart. Some thought he put programs before the care of people in his leadership.

But in his passionate commitment to reaching lost people, it is very clear that like the Lord Jesus Christ, 'When he saw the crowds he had compassion on them, because they were harassed and helpless, like sheep without a shepherd.'[23] Gil's deep compassion for unreached people was one of the primary drivers in his missionary engagement.

Those who worked closely with Gil also testify to his compassion and concern for the people he led, although clearly for some this was not as apparent as for others. Some thought Gil had a greater compassion for the national people or his students, than for his staff and team members. Ray Laird, former Chairman of SSEM has sensitively expressed his assessment of this tension:

> Gil was a true friend of the nationals, making sure of giving the indigenous leaders of the Churches confidence, assuring them of support, but instilling in them a sense of independence in their critical roles in their communities. He was a great encourager, standing with them in giving guidance when appropriate.
> I remember on one trip up to the Sepik, he took me to one of the villages where a good work had been going on for some years. As we strolled through the village we met many beautiful young people, early and mid-teens. Gil remarked that these young

---

23. Matthew 9:36.

people were facing a dilemma, because the old village life was disappearing, and these young folk did not have enough education to go to the next levels of schooling; they could not get jobs with the Government, or with businesses. They would probably drift to the big towns, get into trouble and come back and terrorise the village people. He was very concerned, his heart ached for them.

I never doubted that Gil was a genius with a great capacity for multiple tasking, although I admit that I thought at times he may have been attempting too much, too soon. Gil asked a lot from people, a possible failing of many who have been born with the blessing of a great capacity for thought, industry, and production. Thankfully, most who had dealings with Gil were able to rise to the challenges he set before them. There were, however, some who could not. Our missionaries, if still alive, could affirm this or otherwise, but I believe Gil had much more patience with the indigenous peoples and leaders than he did with some of our missionaries and other workers attached in various posts in SSEM. I cannot give you a portfolio of names, but there were some who found Gil casting them off abruptly as not being up to the tasks allotted to them. At times, I shared his chagrin, but could not give my approval to the mode of his action. I think I had learned that leaders must never expect any or all their team members to be able to do as much the leader him/herself. Each has a certain God-given capacity, and it is the duty of a leader to discern what it is in each member, and how to allot appropriate tasks to them.[24]

John Hitchen made detailed reference to Gil's compassion when he spoke at his farewell from CLTC. After describing Gil's wide ministry in CLTC, PNG, and beyond – a man of vision, an administrator who gets things done despite the problems, a catalyst, a man who sees the need and takes steps to get things moving – he added:

> But that's not the only Mr McArthur. There's another Mr McArthur who is the Counsellor, the very sensitive shepherd-hearted leader. This is the Mr McArthur who through these past six years has often been in tears for the students, counselling those who have been in trouble. He's the man who has never been happy to accept defeat in the life of a student. But through the concern of his own heart, and the counsel of God's Word, he has fought and struggled to overcome each of the problems which for a time have knocked down the various students.

---

24. Laird, 'Gil McArthur', 1, 2.

> But not only in the lives of students, but in his relationships with the staff. To establish CLTC and to build it to what it is today, it has been necessary to have real drive and to give dominant leadership. But not many even of the staff know of what it has cost Mr McArthur to do this. Perhaps of the staff I'm the only one who's had the privilege of being with Mr McArthur when he's been in tears as he's shared and discussed with me what it is going to cost to work out the decisions he knows God wants him to make…
>
> Not what it is going to cost in money. But what it is going to cost to the staff members in the way it's going to cut across their family life; in the way they are going to have to sacrifice the rights of their children; in the way in which the husband won't have time to be the kind of husband that his wife needs. And few of the staff know the tears that Mr McArthur has shed in demanding of them what God has asked him to demand. Few have any idea of the lonely nights where the pressure of the work of CLTC has stopped Mr McArthur from sleeping and when his body has been in physical torment because of the things he's been carrying in each different part of the programme. The next day he's always back at work. Nobody knows, except his wife and perhaps one or two others that he hasn't been able to sleep for pain through the night. Yes, not many of us know Mr McArthur, the sensitive shepherd-hearted leader of this College.[25]

A little later, Heather Ford worked closely with Gil in the SSEM office in 1973, and then later in 1979 in the World Vision South Pacific Office.[26] In her work with Gil she experienced his compassion firsthand:

> It wasn't really until 1979, when I joined World Vision International South Pacific, that I worked with Gil quite closely. As his executive administrator/accountant I organised his Diary, his trips, organised his staff and office, dealt with the international and local issues and dignitaries as they arose… Gil and I seemed to work pretty seamlessly and without conflict, as I was excited about the principles and practice that Gil was formulating. It was busy but not stressful, and Gil was an appreciative and considerate boss. And the few times I did disagree with him, he always listened, and never over-rode my personal values. I really appreciated his respect. And I have never met another human being to equal his maturity of character. I guess our

---

25. Hitchen, 'Appreciation of Rev G. J. McArthur', 2, 3.
26. Following the intervening period during which Gil had asked her to work in PNG with ATA.

work ethics were compatible. What stands out in the memory are the unusual little stories that would occasionally fall out of the regular day's work... To me, Gil was a man of great humility. I understand not everyone remembers him that way. I experienced Gil as kind and compassionate with a profound understanding of human need. Gil adored Pat and loved his children. From where I sat, he appeared to grieve but accept when people close to him – kin or missionary family – chose differently to what he thought was right. I believe Gil was a realist and accepted what he could not change. Nor did he allow other people's perceptions to determine his own agenda.[27]

* * * * * * *

This concludes the Story Book of Gilbert McArthur – man of God, man of biblical and theological maturity, man of vision, man of action and man of compassion.

Finally, brothers,
whatever is true, whatever is noble, whatever is right,
whatever is pure, whatever is lovely, whatever is admirable
– if anything is excellent or praiseworthy –
think about such things.
Whatever you have learned or received or heard from me, or seen in me
– put it into practice.
And the God of peace will be with you.[28]

---

27. Ford, 'Gil McArthur', 3, 4.
28. Philippians 4:8-9.

TIME FOR MEDITATION?

If you are planning for one year, plant rice (or wheat!),
If you are planning for ten years plant trees, but
If you are planning for one hundred years plant men and women.[1]

Eugene Peterson says that anyone who has seen a dog with a bone can understand meditation. He tells the story of his little dog who loved large bones. Those who have owned a dog know the routine – dog is given a bone – great excitement, tail wagging and growling if you try to take it back – dog chews the bone with great satisfaction – dog drags the bone to a secret place and buries it – later dog digs up the bone and the routine repeats – dog enjoys getting more off the bone than we can ever imagine! One day, when Peterson was reading the prophet Isaiah, he came to the words 'as a lion growls over his prey' (Isaiah 31:4). The word 'growl' caught his attention. What the lion does over his prey, his dog does over his bone! But Peterson was also excited to notice, that the Hebrew word translated 'growl' was the same word as in Psalm 1 translated 'meditate'.[2]

The invitation here is to pause and meditate on the Story-Book of Gil McArthur – which will obviously take longer than simply reading the words and putting the book on your shelf! The encouragement to such meditation is not because Gil was perfect or the greatest leader of all – but to understand more of what God does when his grace takes hold of flawed people who yield to his Spirit. The invitation now is to take time to mentally and spiritually 'chew over' the story – and respond to the Spirit of God as his work in and through Gil takes hold of you and shapes your daily life in new steps of obedience.

I believe in his characteristic forthright way, Gil would challenge us to meditate on at least two aspects of his journey that are reflected in the images of a tent and an altar, and the vision that drove his life-purpose.

---

1. An old Chinese proverb, which J Oswald Sanders quotes in his introduction to *Planting Men in Melanesia*, the Story-Book of the first ten formative years of CLTC, which Gil quoted with the bracketed contextualised addition when preaching to wheat farmers in South Australia in the early 1970s.
2. Eugene Peterson, *Eat This Book - A Conversation in the Art of Spiritual Reading* (London, Sydney, Auckland: Hodder and Stoughton, 2006), 1–4.

First, that we live our lives with passionate surrender to the Lord Jesus Christ, learning to live in tents, and build only altars for the glory of God and his mission to the nations.

In a world where 'God' still makes sense to four out of five people today,[3] we need a devotion to someone beyond ourselves to give life ultimate purpose. Gil led from a spiritual centre. He found meaning, direction and total fulfilment not based in personal achievement, possessions or circumstances, but in relationship with God through Jesus Christ. In Christ Gil found the fulness of the revelation of the transcendent God to a humanity in denial of his existence, choosing to follow their selfish ambitions and expectations in a myriad of ways. He experienced the forgiveness of God's grace and the transforming work of the Spirit in his personal journey of dying and rising in Christ. Gil was counter-cultural in his call 'to live in tents' and not seek ultimate security, contentment or fulfilment in self-serving and material things.

In the contemporary world people are building for their own names and gains. But the 'altar' moments in Gil's story indicate the priority he gave to growing and maintaining his relationship with God. This was not simply in a 'one-off' surrender – he was building altars in all the decisions along the way 'not to be disobedient to the heavenly vision'. He was willing to sacrifice – and it cost him, his family and those he led.

Second, that in the mission of God to the nations, the development of Christ-like servant leaders is a critical strategy at all levels that calls for urgent priority.

The Chinese character for 'crisis' combines two characters — one for 'danger' and the other for 'opportunity'. Today we frequently hear that there is a crisis of leadership that is evident across the whole spectrum of life – in families, local communities, work and professional life, politics and national government, and in the Church and its mission today. It is a moment of danger and opportunity.

In his call to mission, Gil became increasingly aware of the vital role of leaders, and he saw the critical need to intentionally develop

---

3. Timothy Keller, *Making Sense of God - An Invitation to the Sceptical* (London: Hodder and Stoughton, 2016), 11. See Timothy Keller's book for a clear presentation on the relevance of Christianity in an age of scepticism, because as human beings 'we cannot live without meaning, satisfaction, freedom, identity, justice and hope – and Christianity provides us with unsurpassed resources to meet these needs'.

leaders with character and integrity who modelled Kingdom values and the servant leadership of Christ. Such leaders are the key to healthy churches and nations where there will be peace, freedom, righteousness and justice for all. Remember the passion of Gil's focus that:

> One of the most vital resources of any nation is its leaders. The social fabric of any society is a reflection of its moral and spiritual values. The political, economic and spiritual life of a nation revolves around the behaviour and actions of the leaders at every level of society (elected as well as the non-elected).[4]

In the context in which we currently live and serve, what personal leadership influence and opportunities do we have? As we look around us, what are the wider leadership needs, and how can we intentionally address the development of leaders in our sphere of influence?

What chapter are you writing today in your story-book of life? Gil's life calls us to make sure it is written bearing fruit in a lasting legacy built on the solid rock of Christ.

Rightly, Gil himself has the last word! Not that with Gil words were ever enough. Those of us who lived and worked with him, and caught his vision for strategic leadership training, did so not because of his words alone, but because we saw those words worked out in his daily priorities, his sacrificial living, and his disciplined, unswerving commitment to fulfilling the vision. His life-style gave authority and influence to his words. So, we invite you to meditate on his legacy with our personal testimony to the way Gil's life confirmed and validated his words. The conclusion of his paper *A Civilization Crisis*, brings a challenge which has a strangely contemporary ring for today. He wrote in the maturity of his vision and experience to see the Australasian continent rise to acknowledge that 'our national and spiritual destiny is intimately joined with the Afro – Asia – Oceania – Pacific nations whose same oceans wash our shores':

> 'The kingdoms of this world are soon to become the kingdom of our God and His Christ.' (Revelation 11:15)

> Therefore, as Christ became a human among humans to provide for the shared needs of a common humanity, so must we close ranks

---

4. While this quotation from Gil is used in a PowerPoint on the CLTC story, I have been unable to source the original context in which it was made.

and by wise and godly legislation ensure that we become a nation among nations that shares in mutual responsibility for the well-being of one another. Only by our contemporary identification at both personal and national levels with the great Redemptive Act of History, will we overcome the 'fear of the nations' which holds our leaders in terrible bondage to an ever-escalating arms-race, and the resultant false security of trusting in the might and power of nuclear weaponry rather than in the Fatherhood of God.

To this end must we dare to believe that God will open up the forums of leaders to listen to the voice of the seemingly foolish, as they hearken to the Creator and Sustainer of the Universe when he declares in Colossians 1:15-20 that the world will not end by the act of an individual pressing a nuclear button. It will end by the same divine fiat that brought it into being, when the Cosmic Christ as the 'Coordinating Principle' of the Universe, upholding all things by the word of his power, folds up this world like a worn-out garment and ushers in the new heavens and the new earth (Hebrews 1:10-12).

Therefore, what manner of people ought we to be, and how urgently and fearlessly should we exploit the opportunities of the moment to impact the decision-making forums of the world with these God-given values so necessary to the reconciliation and well-being of the nations?[5]

---

5. McArthur, 'A Civilization Crisis', 4-5. Edited for expression in gender inclusive language, emphasis added.

APPENDIX ONE

THE McARTHUR DIARY EXTRACTS
*EXTRACT No. 1**

M.V. Sibigo,
At Sea.
25th November, 1955.

Hullo Folks,

Greetings to you all from way out on the briny; there's a 35 knot wind blowing and the old girl (i.e. the ship, not my wife) is finding the going rather heavy as she ploughs her nose into the deep troughs. Incidentally, I have discovered why a ship is referred to as a 'she'. Because 'it takes a good man to handle her right, and because it's not the initial expense that breaks you, it's the upkeep.' All of which is very true when you see the pounding she gets from the tons of water dumped consistently upon her decks.

We have all settled down well on board ship; Robyn and Paul have been sharing their meals with the fishes occasionally but we have no real casualties amongst us, and are really enjoying the hitherto unknown experience of just eating and sleeping with intermittent bursts of reading. Wendy is basking in the sunshine of all the added attention we are now able to give her, and it's going to be hard not to spoil her over these next two weeks. Jenny is obviously going to get the language before any of us, and in her own way will be a real little missionary for whenever we notice her missing she may be found entertaining the Chinese crew, and apparently making herself quite well understood.

It is somewhat hard to realise that we have now left our homeland far behind and severed our physical connections with you dear folk with whom we have been so closely united these past years. The parting has not been really hard for us, it has seemed to be but a natural transition into that sphere of service for which we have so long prepared, and in which you are all so completely one with us. The sense of our great partnership as together we work out the purposes of God on earth outweighs such things as human separation and distance and links us all together at the Mercy Seat in strong eternal ties.

---

* The Diary Extracts have been included in the original wording, grammar and terminology, except for a few minor adjustments.

As there is very little news of interest at this stage of our journey we shall record some basic information which will be helpful for future reference.

1. These news items will come to you regularly through the kindness of Miss Dorothy Clack of the Parramatta Secretarial Services; should you want other copies or know of others who would like to join the prayer partnership, please contact Miss Clack through – Box 72, P.O., Parramatta, N.S.W. (Phone: YL 8482)

2. Our postal address is as follows: Rev. G.J. McArthur,
   Baptist Mission,
   Sentani Airstrip
   HOLLANDIA. D.N.G.

3. There is no parcel post to Dutch New Guinea as yet, and by way of overcoming this very real problem a group of young men from the Stanmore Y.M.M.L. have undertaken to receive all parcels and packets and pack and crate them and take out export licenses re their export to D.N.G. If at any time you desire to forward certain goods to us would you kindly pack them well, indicating who they are from and the nature of the contents, together with an estimated value, and post to: Mr. E. Pink, 14 Bruce Street, Ashfield, N.S.W. The cost of the shipment to D.N.G. will be borne by the Stanmore Y.M.M.L. and if you would like to have fellowship with them in this regard please contact Mr. Pink.

One other matter – would you please endeavour to post your parcels etc. so that they will arrive at the Ashfield address about the first week of any given month. This will allow the despatchers to complete the formalities in sufficient time to catch the ship.

Well folks, that's all for now – our next letter will tell you of our arrival in Dutch New Guinea and the first impressions gained; in the mean-time join with us in prayer, that each day shall find us keeping faithful in mind, in heart, in spirit to Him Who has so graciously called us to be co-workers with Himself in the great harvest field of the world. Pray too that the hearts of the hitherto untouched people of the North Baliem Valley shall be prepared for the coming of the Evangel.

With warmest regards,

   Yours in fellowship,

      Pat & Gilbert.

McARTHUR DIARY
EXTRACT No. 2

> Rev. G. J. McArthur,
> Baptist Mission
> Sentani Airstrip,
> Hollandia. D.N.G.
> *M.S. Sibigo*
> At Sea – 3.12.1955

Hullo Folks,

Greetings once more from the briny, but as I write the sea has lost something of its salty tang, for we are now abreast of where the mighty Sepik River spills out its mountain waters into the sea. The time and place of writing are of peculiar moment, for if we were to fly directly inland from here we would arrive at Telefolmin, there to meet the Doulls and the Vaughans – our missionaries in one of the loneliest outposts of the world – how much they need help and fellowship in that most difficult work, and yet we move on past them. On across the border, to meet a new challenge. God is indeed causing us to 'lengthen the cords' of our missionary enterprise, but let us not forget to 'strengthen the stakes'. Will you pray for our Telefolmin work – right now. We sent them a cable this morning it cost 4/- a word: we wanted them to know that they are a vital part of this new venture. Then we knelt together and looking off unto the hills invoked the blessing of our Father which maketh rich and addeth no sorrow to be their portion. In a new way and with deep meaning the sense of our oneness in the Lord and in His work became real. Ah! yes, the throne of grace is the place where we all can, and must, often meet.

Well, our sea trip is nearly over now – tomorrow we shall be in Hollandia, and into the work. It's been a good trip, plenty of food, plenty of sleep, all of which has made us ready for the task ahead. The children have been very good, and seem to have won the hearts of all ship's officers and crew, including the Captain whose cabin they invade daily. Wendy as usual brings joy into every day, and seems to be quite content to lie and 'coo' as mummy gives the children their lessons.

Tuesday 6th:

This is an historic moment, for I now write to you from what we call 'Missionary Hill' in Dutch New Guinea. We landed on Sunday and 'boy' was it a thrill to meet that much loved missionary veteran, Rev. Victor White and together with him and Rev. Norman Draper talk over the results of their last survey into the Baliem Valley. Do you know that they flew for an hour and a half in a straight line up the valley and for the whole time they were over the top of dense population, and in an area where the white man, as yet, has never been. The opportunities are tremendous, it's a wonderful privilege to have a share in such a work; may the Lord find us worthy servants.

We are in the process now of settling in, and establishing the coastal base so as to be ready to move into the interior as soon as other personnel are available and the time is ripe for the Baptist advance to take place. Spent most of Monday clearing the goods through Customs and meeting other Government Officials. Today have been working on the Aluminium house getting same ready for habitation; it will take a little while before we are unpacked and into the house but in the meantime we have been able to move into a home normally occupied by American missionaries, but as they are away at Conference they have kindly invited us to make use of their place, which of course is a real blessing to us and allows one to get on with preparing our own home without being concerned about the family.

Our own house site is a particularly good one, and Rev. Victor White has done a sterling job in all the preparatory work, making it so much easier for us to get settled in and get on with the job. Mr. White leaves tomorrow for Sydney and will be taking this letter with him; make sure you rally to hear him at the various meetings he may take – He's one of God's gentlemen and has a story to tell that will thrill your soul.

That's all for today. The children send their love and we shall write again when the Diary reveals some more news of interest.

Cheerio for now, and praying that this letter finds you and yours all well and happy in the Lord.

    Yours in the Advance,

    Pat & Gilbert.

APPENDIX ONE

THE McARTHUR DIARY
EXTRACT No. 3

Sentani,
29th December, 1955.

Hullo Folks,

Or perhaps I should say 'Hi Folks', for here on Missionary Hill we are surrounded by American personnel and the children have completely spurned our attempts to keep them Australianised. For instance, this is how young Paul usually greets me now: 'Wa:al da:ad how'd ya be?'
I expect they will lose it all when we move into the interior.

Now what does the Diary reveal that is of interest since last we wrote? Hmm, I'm afraid that the first part of the story is rather a sorry one so won't burden you with too much of it. From the day of our arrival here we have just worked to the limit each day collapsing into bed at night completely exhausted. The shell of the house was up when we arrived but the cement floors had to be put in, basic furniture erected (we still haven't got our chairs together), sanitary arrangements effected, and water facilities arranged, plus additions to the house and making same waterproof, etc. All our goods and chattels were outside in crates covered up with roofing iron. As we wanted something so we rummaged around, identified the right crate, opened same up, located the article, repacked the crate, covered it up again and so it went on.

I picked up tinea of the feet whilst up this way during the war years, and although it did not worry me much in Australia, it broke out here again and during the cementing programme I was foolish enough to work in bare feet for a while. The cement burned into where the tinea had opened up the flesh and the result was a horrible infection on both feet. Boy! it was just plain agony to have all my weight on those feet whilst trowelling out the floors.

When putting in the drainage system the Diary states that I would stand in the blistering sun with the heavy crowbar held in hands that were so sore that every jab at the tough concrete felt like hot needles, and I wonder why I spent five years studying theology and Greek etc., as a preparation for missionary service.

Well, let's turn over the page… We are now living quite comfortably in the house, having moved from our temporary quarters. A 10 foot veranda has been added to the front of the building which gives us a little more breathing room. The water is connected, the plumbing and drainage is just about finished. All our gear is out of the weather, either in the house or sheltered in a 10 x 12 shed that I threw up, and 'lo and behold' is still standing. My feet are just about right, and my hands are just about tough enough to tackle any labouring job about the place. Also, my back ceases to protest as much as it did at being bent for the best part of the day. Pat has really worked hard and got the children settled in well and the place looking quite nice. Wendy, who has been feeling rather bad with prickly heat looks like becoming acclimatised. So, in the words of 2 Cor. 4:17 'Our light affliction was but for a moment'.

Christmas Day:

We have had a lovely time today. A large bundle of mail and Christmas cards arrived from you good folk. Thanks so much, it was a real thrill to hear all the news and know you were all thinking of us. And what do you think? We had roast duck for dinner! Rev. Norman Draper bought one off some of the locals and with a few other things thrown in we did really well. Tonight, all the folk on Missionary Hill are getting together for a time of fellowship, singing carols etc. and praising God for the gift of His Son. But what about the people way over those great mountains that I can see from here locked away in those virtually inaccessible valleys and gorges? They have no Christmas, they sing no carol, only the mournful funeral chant comes echoing across the hills. This week in the Baliem Valley seven people died, all over some petty incident. They know of no way of settling their disputes other than by killing. Out of the abyss of their spiritual darkness they unconsciously call us to share with them the true meaning of Christmas – 'Emmanuel, God with us!' Oh! beloved, let us continue to pray, continue to live, in the glory of that great fact – 'God with us!' Firstly, for our own salvation and then with us, that in Christ's stead we may beseech men everywhere to be reconciled to God

This extract is perhaps, a little too long. But in many of your letters you have asked that we share with you, 'our hopes, our joys, our fears'. The Diary faithfully records these changes in the tempo of missionary living. It could not be more personal, and we trust that it is both acceptable in its form and helpful in its purpose of stimulating intelligent prayer fellowship.

Warmly yours,

Pat & Gilbert.

APPENDIX ONE

THE McARTHUR DIARY
EXTRACT No. 4

Rev. G.J. McArthur,
Baptist Mission
Sentani Airstrip,
Hollandia. D.N.G.
February, 1956.

Hullo Folks,

Greetings once again from Missionary Hill. The time of writing finds us just having returned from our Sunday morning worship gathering. There are five Missionary Societies represented here, and our times of collective fellowship are of very real spiritual value. And not only so, for they also inspire one to engage in happy retrospect – reliving the times of blessed fellowship spent with you all in other days.

This time the pages of the Diary contain matters full of real missionary significance. Perhaps it would be wise at this stage to acquaint you with the overall programme of the Evangelical Missions based here on the hill. There are movements afoot, the ramifications of which are very great, and decisions to be reached that will have real bearing upon the indigenous church yet to be born in the highlands of D.N.G.

In order that your thinking will be clear and your praying specific a sketch map is enclosed, which, together with the following information will bring you right into the picture as it really exists on the field.

A. Missionary Groups and Areas of Operation

1. The Christian and Missionary Alliance – C.M.A.

An American mission, well organised, well equipped with their own aircraft etc., and enjoying considerable financial backing from a strong group of home churches in the United States. This mission pioneered the advance into the rugged highlands and have constructed an airstrip on a site near the Baliem River in the Southern end of the valley. They now have two married couples and a male linguist stationed there (see map point No. 1 – *Map overpage*).

2. The Regions Beyond Missionary Union – R.B.M.U.

An American group comprising two married couples and one single nursing sister. The personnel of this group obtain their support on an individual basis, and have little or no organised backing from the home front. Lack of funds and availability of additional personnel have kept this group at the coast here for over two years. Their ultimate objective is the Swartz Valley (see map point No. 2).

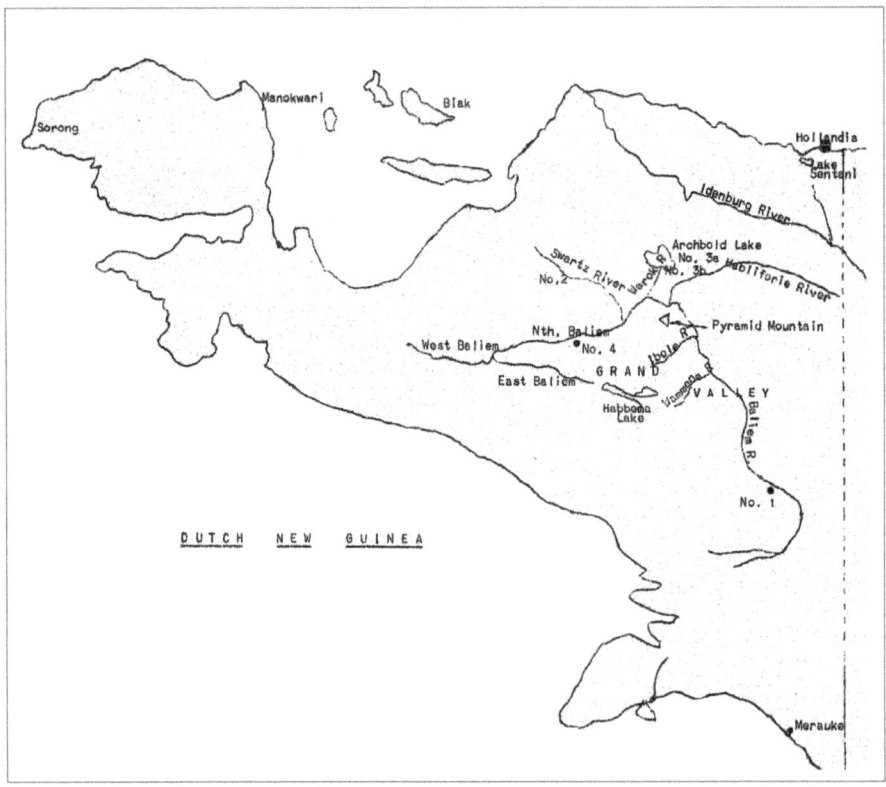

3. The Unevangelised Fields Mission – U.F.M.

A world-wide missionary society but represented here by Australian personnel and supported by Australian Christian giving. The present areas of operation are at Sengee and the Archbold Lake with intended advances into the Hablifoerie and north to the junction of the Warok and Baliem Rivers (see map points No. 3a and 3b).

The personnel of this group comprise at the moment – two married couples, two single women, two single men with possible additions in the near future.

4. The Missionary Aviation Fellowship – M.A.F.

An American body represented here by Mr. David Steiger and family. They are supported by funds from America with the aircraft operations being maintained by the charges levied against the missions using same. The services of Mr. Steiger and the aeroplane are at the disposal of all the evangelical missionary societies.

5. The Australian Baptist Foreign Mission – A.B.F.M

Represented at the moment by the Rev. & Mrs Draper and the McArthur family. The area of operation that we believe the Lord wants us to reach in His Name is the North Baliem and the tributaries to the SW and NE (see map point No. 4).

B. The Vision Glorious

A glance at the map and a perusal of the Missions involved brings home to one the fact that here, under God, is an opportunity perhaps unique in the history of missionary enterprise, viz: Five evangelical mission groups with independent and world-wide support, enjoying a oneness of faith and having no major doctrinal differences, now entrusted with separate areas of heavily populated country having possible dialectical changes yet all dove-tailing into one another. The contemplation of this united advance into these places of spiritual darkness, and the ultimate outcome for the Kingdom of God moves one with deep emotion. Granted that, due to the warring nature of the people, there will be years of real spiritual warfare on our part. All of which will doubtless take its toll on missionary health and even life, but at last, from every valley there will surely be heard the glorious note of redemption, thereby mystically uniting these warring tribes-people who for centuries have lived in mutual hate and fear.

C. The Difficulties Involved

As is usual in any advance into areas where Satan sits enthroned there are problems to be faced up to and overcome. Problems of personnel, supplies, finance, organisation etc. All very real in themselves and requiring much consecrated time and effort to deal with same. But finally, the real problem is a spiritual one and can only be met and dealt with on the spiritual level. The Word of God truly says that the weapons of our warfare are not carnal but spiritual, and only when used as such will they be mighty to the pulling down of strongholds.

We are convinced then, that only the all-prevailing prayer of God's people who are themselves fully cognizant of the facts will thwart Satan in his current attempt to block this united advance of the gospel into his territory.

D. The Problem Itself

The Foreign Department of the C.M.A. with headquarters in New York has vetoed a request made by the members of its field conference that the North Baliem area be conceded to some other evangelical missionary body. New York feel that C.M.A. have some moral claim to the whole of the Grand Valley including also the North Baliem system (see map Extract No. 5). Whilst in some measure we may agree with this moral claim, yet, it is important to note that the C.M.A. field staff clearly recognise the fact that it is an impossible task for them to evangelise the North Baliem for many years to come. It has been mooted that numerous additions to the staff will shortly be forthcoming, but again it is recognised that such additions will in no way fully exploit the missionary potential of the Grand Valley itself. Now the problem is:

1. If we go forward with our plans for an advance into the North Baliem we shall be doing so in opposition to the official C.M.A. ruling even though its field members are, in the main, in complete sympathy with our programme. This would create an embarrassing situation and tend to future disunity.

2. If, as the problem goes to the higher conference level, there are stall moves put forward with a resultant lengthy delay, then we may find that the evil one has kept us all out of this area just long enough to allow the R.C.s to move in and occupy the area in strength, thereby forever thwarting the possibility of a united and co-ordinated evangelical witness throughout the highlands.

E. What Now?

Discussions on the field have resulted in further recommendations being forwarded to the respective home committees. The one great desire now being that a policy statement be forthcoming which will provide for the early occupation of this area, and that it be done in such a spirit of Christian love and fellowship as to invoke the manifest blessing of God.

Well, dear friends, you now have the facts. Will you all lay hold on God re these vital matters. Pray for the C.M.A. Board in New York that the Holy Spirit will enable them to see this matter in true perspective. Pray for the Secretary and members of our own New Guinea Regional Committee, that they may be endued with power from on high as they deliberate this vital matter. Pray for us here on the field that we may be granted the necessary wisdom, patience, and added Christian grace in all our inter-mission relationships, and also that there be no lessening of the missionary fervour during the time of waiting and uncertainty. Pray that in everything God will so govern the decisions of men as to get glory to Himself in this 20th Century advance into the land of primitive darkness.

This has been a lengthy, but, we judge, necessary epistle. And so, until next time the Diary tells its story – Pray on!

Yours in Warm Fellowship

Pat & Gilbert

APPENDIX ONE

THE McARTHUR DIARY
EXTRACT No. 5

Rev. G.J. McArthur,
Baptist Mission,
Sentani Airstrip,
Hollandia. D.N.G.
March, 1956,

Hello Everybody,

Christian love and greetings from all here at Sentani. We trust that this letter finds you all well and happy in the Lord.

Things are moving along smoothly at Missionary Hill. Many things have been recorded in the Diary, since last we wrote, that are of real interest, much of which gives occasion for thanksgiving and prayer.

1. The visit of Rev. V. White to D.N.G. and the subsequent spiritual tonic to the folk here, plus his wise council and advice in the important inter-mission conferences.

2. The formation of a united evangelical mission committee, and the decision for an early co-operative advance into the highlands.

3. Discussions with the Governor of the territory have been most favourable, and there is no official barrier to in anyway hinder our proposed trek inland.

4. The M.A.F. Pilot, Mr. D. Steiger, has been advised that a Cessna 180 aircraft will shortly be allocated to D.N.G. This will be of great value in the difficult highland operations, particularly when floats are required for landing on the lakes and rivers, etc.

Matters for prayer:

1. As an exploratory probe and orientation programme we plan, early in April to move into the Archbold Lake area, where the U.F.M. are working, and together with them and the R.B.M.U., trek through to a site about four days journey away where it is hoped we shall be able to quickly construct a temporary airstrip. The reaction of the natives in this area will be assessed as we live among them, and if conditions are favourable further probes will be made in the direction of the North Baliem, and possibly the Swartz Valley.

2. The allocation of personnel for the various jobs, and the flying of such personnel and equipment into the Archbold Lake, also a

large proportion of goods will need to be dropped from the air as the team near the intended airstrip site – altogether a difficult operation.

3. The acceptance of the team by the various native groups as we pass through, and the availability of carriers and finally, labourers for the construction of the airstrip.

4. The folks left out on the coast as they follow the progress of the team by radio and the keeping open of the vital supply line to the inland.

Well, that's about all the news of interest for now, and I trust that your many questions are being in some way answered by these Diary extracts.

Thank you all for your genuine prayer interest, rest assured that we shall endeavour to keep you right up to date with the news, as together we share in the working out of the purposes of God for these people.

All the family are well and send their love.

Cheerio for now,

Warmly Yours,

Pat & Gilbert

THE McARTHUR DIARY.
EXTRACT No. 6

Rev. G. J. McArthur,
Baptist Mission
Sentani Airstrip,
Hollandia, D.N.G.
20th April, 1956

Hullo Everybody,

Once again, the Diary tells its story. But firstly, allow us to borrow the language of the first great missionary and say: 'Spiritual blessing and peace from God our Father and the Lord Jesus Christ.' Also, we could again say with Paul the Apostle that we 'thank God upon every remembrance of you', for our link with you is made doubly precious as separation invokes constant reminiscence.

As missionary enthusiasts you will be vitally interested in the happenings of the past two weeks or so, as we have been finalising all our preparations in readiness for the advance inland. As the Diary tells its story we trust you will catch something of the missionary thrill and get caught up in the general air of expectancy that has been abroad these days.

After having spent ten days in hospital with a tropical ulcer, I was discharged on the basis that I keep off my leg. Well, such has been impossible in the rush of affairs, and now I'm pumping heavy doses of penicillin into myself in an endeavour to halt a further outbreak. Perhaps it's a good thing in one way, as I'm able to give some of the other members of the team a practical demonstration on the correct procedure for intramuscular injections. However, being the guinea pig, as well as the instructor is a little unorthodox and also tends to make one a little 'sore'.

In addition to being a patient at the hospital, I have also had the opportunity to complete a course of basic medical instruction, and am now certified by the Dutch authorities to administer their medicines, covering a large number of treatments, give injections, perform minor operations, such as opening up abscesses, cleaning and sewing up wounds, etc. – altogether a useful fund of knowledge. Be wary, though, for should I ever return to Australia, then you may well find yourself invited into the outpatients' department rather than the pastor's vestry.

The setting up of the radio network, necessary for the coast to inland communications, has been an interesting part of the work, and we are fortunate in having Rev. N. Draper as part of the team, for he is also a radio technician whose knowledge has been of great value in this regard.

We were very fortunate in securing, at no cost to the mission, two fifty-six foot radio masts. But they were five miles away at the top of a 2,000 foot climb, and have you ever tried carting an object 56 feet long on a jeep and trailer? Well, we did it, and I provided the motor cycle escort, clearing the traffic on the little Bantam B.S.A. The native policeman insisted that we have a large red flag on the rear of the mast before letting us begin the haul to base. But as we had nothing on but our shorts, at long last he reluctantly acquiesced to the Rev. Draper's bright red socks being used as a substitute. We have heard it said that it was not the colour of the socks alone that kept all and sundry away from the end of the mast!

Some of our well-meaning friends have advised that the Diary notes should not be just a sort of synopsis of events, but rather a story of human interest. So! Put on your trekking boots and let's ramble around together. What do we see?

Here's the Revs. N. Draper and G. J. McArthur clothed in perspiration and a pair of shorts, out in the tropical sun sinking a 6 foot hole for the base of the radio mast. John Betteridge and Ian Gruber are hacksawing through some 2 inch pipe which will be hammered 3 feet into the ground and used as stakes for the stay-wires.

Where's Hendick Noordyke? Ah yes, there he is sawing up eighty pieces of wood from which handles will be made for the long pieces of hoop-iron which when sharpened will be the weapons given to the natives in the interior for the clearing of the airstrip site.

Well that accounts for the menfolk, what about the women? Over there on the concrete slab alongside a small mountain of soiled clothes stands a somewhat perplexed Mrs. Draper. She happened to suggest to our latest arrival, Mr. H. Noordyke, that she would do his washing for him. (These jolly bachelors, why don't some of you girls take them off our hands?)

Heh! What's that commotion over there to the east? Oh, it's only Mrs. McArthur dragging Jenny back to school lessons. It's the second time she's ducked off this morning – no wonder her mother's getting so thin (or was she ever fat?).

Sunrise 14th April. Another day dawns as Baby Wendy supplants the cock-crow with an early morning 'Da:da'. Today we finish weighing up and packing all the goods for the aerial drops. You can imagine what packing is involved when they have to be thrown out of an aircraft travelling at 80 m.p.h.

April 16th. D-Day. The Piper Pacer aircraft fitted with a new engine and floats is to make the first trip into the Archbold Lake today. It will carry one man and his gear or a total payload of 280 lbs. This will go on for about ten days or so, until all the personnel are gathered at the lake, and then the first advance into the hinterland will begin.

April 17th. We received a cable from the New South Wales Regional Committee today assuring all members of the team of the Committee's prayerful support at this time. Thank you, brethren. We welcome and appreciate the backing of such men of God.

April 18th. First trips successful. Radio communications with the inland working well. Medical kits for the team to be sorted out and packed. Tonight we shall gather for a final communion service with loved ones before the separation of many weeks takes place.

April 19th. Must finalise the packing of my own kit, and also say goodbye to you all for perhaps two months, as I will be moving inland shortly after this mail closes.

Pat, who is a vital partner in the story the Diary tells will be keeping you acquainted with the news, as my only communication with the coast for some time will be by radio.

We would love to hear from many of you. Please drop a line when you can. Let us meet daily at the Mercy Seat,

    Your Friends and Co-Workers,

    Pat & Gilbert

THE McARTHUR DIARY.
EXTRACT No. 7

Rev. G. J. McArthur,
c/- Baptist Mission
Sentani Airstrip,
Hollandia. D.N.G.
21–30 April, 1956

Hullo Everybody!

Christian love and greetings from all in D.N.G. As Gilbert has gone into the interior it's my privilege to write the Diary this week, and to keep you in touch with everything.

Things have been moving here during the past week. Gilbert went into Lake Archbold ten days ago and he seems to have had a lively time in there as this extract from a letter reveals:

'Yesterday Garnet Ericson from the U.F.M., John Betteridge and myself, together with two native boys went up to see what would be involved in crossing the river which has been in flood for some time. All the bridges were washed away and as there was no tall timber close to the bank we were unable to in any way bridge the deep channel.

Garnet, who is a strong swimmer, thought he would try to cross. Boy!! You should have been there – the current caught him and within seconds he was a hundred yards or more downstream but managed to make his way to the other bank. The next to try was a Christian native boy, but he could not get across the current and managed to scramble out on the same side as he went in only much further down the river.

As the water has always been my strong suit, I thought I would have a try because even if I didn't make it, I reasoned that I would hit the same bank somewhere down the river and I particularly wanted to test the strength of such a current as it would be valuable experience and help to determine future decisions.

Fortunately, I took my heavy trekking boots off, and tied them strong over my back because had I left them on I certainly would not have been able to swim as I needed to. I reasoned that if I could get some place to dive from, that such would give me a good start across the current. So finding a high bank I threw myself in, hoping that there were no snags.

Boy!! Did I have to swim and when I reached the other bank I found that my new trekking boots had gone – the strong leather laces apparently pulled right out. Also my waterproof watch which I had quite forgotten about, and which had a strong strap, had also been pulled off and was somewhere in the Hablifoerie River.

The recrossing of the river was just as much fun, only this time we had John Betteridge and the native boys to grab us as we got near the bank.

All together it was quite an expensive venture but was valuable experience as now I know just what can and cannot be accomplished in strong flowing river crossings. The trekking party would never make it and equipment would be lost.

As a result of yesterday's episode, we are all going up to the river today in an attempt to find a suitable site that we can bridge. Then we shall spend many valuable, but necessary, hours in felling trees and carting same in order to bridge the gulf.

Last night was also a moving experience as the members of the trekking party gathered together for prayer. The setting certainly added meaning to the moment – that little lake, hidden away up in the mountains, shut off from the rest of the world. The bush timber house set up on great foundation poles eight feet high. Inside, on heavy bush chairs which look all askew as they stand on a floor made out of strips of bark, are to be seen seven weary men. A closer look made in the light of the tilley lamp reveals that they are all well covered from head to toe, and one wonders why, for it is not so very cold. Then is heard the high drone of hundreds of big black mosquitoes and all is understood. A further glance reveals that in every hand is to be seen an open bible, for these men are servants of the most-High God and as such need daily direction from His Word. To the almost deafening sound of the tropical rain one after the other of these men rises to pray. In a moment of time, the bounds of time and space are lifted, and heart is joined to heart at the divine meeting place. The content of the prayer is all-embracive, confession, personal need, loved ones, mission leaders, other mission groups, prayer partners, and finally a strong confident note is reached as God the Holy Spirit works in the midst and gives to these lonely men the assurance of the faithfulness of God in meeting all the many and varied needs relative to the trek into the unknown. The perils of the river and all that lies ahead, the concern for all loved ones left behind are all resolved in the presence of the Lord. Thank God for the place of prayer and daily strength, the 'Open door' has deeper meaning these days.'

That is the end of the first extract but there is another short piece here just to let you know how they got over the river:

'We are all tired out here today as we went up to the river to try another crossing. Bert and Garnet and I got across O.K. but there's no chance of the others making it. We tried to bridge it with big trees, but the current tossed them about like matchwood. Tomorrow morning we are going to try the dinghy. Two of the boys will swim over and I will sit in the dinghy as they pull me over. If it works O.K. then we will get the gear across, and then I am thinking the trekking party will move off on Saturday morning.'

The trekking party are in touch with us by radio now – they got away safely from the Archbold [Lake] on Saturday afternoon. Today's sked on the radio said they were going very well and by tomorrow afternoon they should be very close to the airstrip site where they intend making an airstrip.

Well, I have filled this letter with news from Gilbert and I was going to tell you of my impressions of D.N.G. so perhaps the next extract from our Diary will contain such things.

The children and I have been well except for these tropical sores which the children seem to get from some kind of insect bite. They have to be kept covered because if they are left exposed they quickly become infected and can develop into a tropical ulcer.

Gilbert was unfortunate to have one of these horrible ulcers and was ordered to hospital by the doctor and had penicillin injections each day for ten days. On returning home however, he went off to work again and the ulcer soon started to deteriorate, and he was again ordered penicillin. I am very thankful to say though, that since going into the Archbold it was healing very quickly – the change of climate would help considerably.

I would like to thank you all for your prayers, for your gifts and your letters. These are all very much appreciated, and we think of you all and of the wonderful times spent in fellowship together and we can say 'I thank my God for every remembrance of you'.

Cheerio for now and love to you all,
    Yours in His Service,

        Pat & Gilbert

APPENDIX ONE

THE McARTHUR DIARY.
EXTRACT No. 8

Rev. G. J. McArthur,
Baptist Mission
Sentani Airstrip,
Hollandia. D.N.G.
24th June, 1956

Hullo Everybody!

Greetings once again from Missionary Hill in D.N.G. Many things of interest have taken place since last we wrote, so let's open the pages of the Diary and read its story.

The Sequel to the Hablifoerie Trek from Lake Archbold

A total of twelve flights were made into this small highland lake, carrying all the personnel and equipment necessary for the trek through to the proposed airstrip site at a place we now know as 'Bokindini'.* After safely negotiating the flooded Hablifoerie River the party moved along through the various population groups, at all times meeting with complete acceptance by the people. On the fourth day the airstrip site was reached and the little Piper Pacer aircraft, commenced to drop more supplies and equipment to the party. After burning off the tall kunai grass the strip surface was found to be covered with thousands of stones, both large and small, deeply embedded into the ground. At first sight it looked like a long project to clear the area and make it suitable for landing aircraft. But here again your prayer support was honoured, for upwards of a thousand natives arrived at the camp, 99% of whom had never before seen a white man, and yet all willing and eager to work – and that, for the large sum of one cowrie shell per day. At the end of four weeks an area of 600 metres by 30 was cleared and hardened, and the first landings accomplished successfully. A mission station will now be established at this Bokondini site by the U.F.M. but we shall make good use of same as a forward base from which to move off, in our next venture into the hitherto untouched North Baliem.

Future Plans

It is expected that the major composite trek to the Pyramid Mountain site at the entrance to the North Baliem will take place towards the end of July. This next move will bring us right to the gateway of the proposed area

---
* Gil uses spelling 'Bokindini' later 'Bokondini'.

of our missionary enterprise. After the establishment of a co-operative airstrip at this point, ground surveys will then be made up the North Baliem Valley floor with a view to determining population density within tribal and language groupings, and the choosing of the best sites for the establishment of future mission stations. Meanwhile the routine work of preparation goes on. The last move took us to within sight of the promised land, now we regroup and organise prior to going in to possess the land. The Baptist team is now gathering in strength at the Bokondini site, whilst the C.M.A. party at their station in the south are putting together a flat-bottomed boat, which, powered by a 25 h.p. outboard engine will be used for pushing up against the strong current of the Baliem River. It is hoped that by using the boat the troublesome tribespeople of the centre Grand Valley will be bypassed. Tentative plans indicate that a two-pronged advance will be made, i.e. (a) the C.M.A. moving up the river and (b) the Baptists climbing the range out of the Hablifoerie Basin and coming in from the North. It is imperative that in moving into an uncontrolled area such as this that a retreat route back to a safe area be established in case of any major tribal hostility being encountered. At the moment the local inhabitants of this area are constantly engaged in local wars and their attitude to the settlement of a white party is unpredictable.

In Retrospect

It is now just over six months since we arrived in D.N.G. and one ponders with some amazement and thankfulness to God, on what has been accomplished. The coastal base, consisting of four well-appointed buildings, together with all plumbing, painting and sewerage, is just about completed. We have also helped our brethren of the M.A.F. in the erection of the framework of a large aircraft hangar, and that, all out of scrap material. The great heavy trusses of 50 foot span, we salvaged from the iron work of an ex-American army gasoline dump. The 12 foot uprights consist of 6 inch caste-iron sewerage pipes which we dug out of the ground below our house. The roofing framework was originally the floor members of our Quonset huts. In addition to this we have been inland and the airstrip at Bokondini is now completed, whilst at the Archbold Lake another airstrip, blasted out of virgin forest, with the aid of gelignite and tree-pullers is also nearing completion. The language problem has not been really tackled as yet, for when your body is tired, mental concentration is not easy. We will need to have someone specially set aside for this important work when we finally settle down in the interior.

The Home Circle

It's good to be with the family again, before separating once more for the next trek. However, I expect to be away for only a few weeks on that occasion as the coastal administration and the maintaining of the supply route is to be my responsibility for the time being. You will be pleased to know that little Wendy is coming along fine now and certainly brings joy to our hearts with her delightful baby ways. She had her first birthday about two weeks ago and has already taken her first steps. Robyn, Jenny and Paul are well and happy, although they don' t take too kindly to school work in the tropical heat and require a little 'encouragement' from father every now and again, and even Mother is beginning to understand why school teachers need so many vacations. Really, though, we are all well and happy in the work, being well provided for in every way, and rejoicing at the opportunity of making some contribution to the establishment of this new mission field. It was a real joy to have so many of you write letters of such interest whilst I was away inland. It was a great help to Pat, and as they floated down to me out of the sky on being dropped from the aircraft, I lifted my heart in thankfulness for such a fellowship of kindred hearts and minds. It is impossible for us to answer them all personally as I believe that the Diary is now reaching, either directly or indirectly, some 500-odd people. However, every expression of interest is noted, every question listed, and each one thought of, as the story is put together. We do trust that the personal touch is being maintained in this way.

Let us now say in closing, that this D.N.G. venture, the development of which is to be reconsidered at our Foreign Mission Board Meeting in August, is, in many ways, going to be a costly undertaking. The mission leaders of our home committees will be faced with real problems of both economic and spiritual content. The budget for this current fiscal year will be a heavy one. Only as God's people get the missionary passion and rise to heights of self-sacrifice and personal dedication to the principle of world evangelism will the overall need be met, and those who now sit in darkness and the shadow of death see at long last the 'light upon the mountains' heralding the dawning of a new day to be found through personal experience of a Saviour God.

The Lord bless you and keep you; The Lord make His face shine upon you and be gracious unto you; The Lord lift up His countenance upon you, and give you peace. Numbers 6:24-26

Your co-workers in the fellowship of the Gospel.

The McArthur Family

THE McARTHUR DIARY.
EXTRACT No. 9

Rev. G. J. McArthur,
Baptist Mission
Sentani Airstrip,
Hollandia – Binnen. D.N.G.
August 1956

Hullo Everybody,

Greetings from D.NG. Once again, the Diary has much to tell, so let's turn the pages and read its story:

1. The day scheduled for the beginning of the great composite advance towards Pyramid Mountain dawned on Friday 27th July, when Rev. N. Draper and myself flew from Sentani into Bokondini to join the rest of the Baptist team already assembled there. Previously, some 2,000 lbs. of supplies and equipment specially packed for aerial drops had been flown into this recently constructed highland airstrip, which was now to become the springboard for the current advance. On arrival at Bokindini, Friday and Saturday were spent in working out and assembling the actual loads each man would carry over the rugged terrain into the Baliem Valley system. Sunday gave for that spiritual preparation and fellowship so necessary for any onslaught upon Satan's territory.

2. Monday turned out to be a wet, awful day with lots of low cloud covering the ranges we had to climb. Nevertheless, we must needs move off as by Wednesday noon we were scheduled to have crossed the Baliem River and joined up with the C.M.A. party who were coming up river by powerful motor boat from their station way down the South-East. However, just before leaving Bokondini we heard the sound of an aircraft overhead on top of the cloud. It was the C.M.A. aircraft that had been turned back by bad weather and was now trying to find a way into Bokondini. Knowing just how the pilot was feeling, I searched the sky for a hole in the cloud, through which he could let down without hitting the mountains. At last I saw one – the only one – and prayed that he would find it too. As we watched the plane found it and quickly spiralled down to safety. On board was the wife and two young children of an American missionary. As they stepped out of the aircraft a mighty shout went up, followed

by a spontaneous movement towards the plane by hundreds of natives who were gazing upon a white woman and children for the first time. The excitement was great, and it really was a moving spectacle to behold, also an indication that to take one's wife and children amongst these people is to be immediately accepted by them, for in their thinking, when a man brings his wife and family, it is with obvious peaceful intent.

And now back to trekking party:
3. We moved off in pouring rain, which for the most part stayed with us all day. Heavy climbing confronted us for some time and I was secretly glad that the local carriers, usually so agile, were slowed down by such loads as 50 pounds, battery and radio. It was all I could do to keep pace with them, and my load consisted of a camera and the hat on top of my head.

I soon got my second wind though and rather enjoyed slithering down the mountain on the other side. Nightfall on the first day found us moving up the slopes of another mountain and near to a native village. The folk were quite friendly and invited us to stay in one of their huts. We had had enough of the wet by this time, so suppressing any thoughts of pigs, bugs, and fleas we crawled into one of the little round houses. The various oddments adorning the walls as revealed in the light of a torch, defy description, but as I endeavoured to clean an area in which to lay my sleeping bag, I had the feeling, that on this night, I would be closely associated with the venerable ancestors of the highlanders.

Sleep did not come easily, for reasons best left to your imagination. Also, the men gathered in one of the adjoining huts entertained us until 3 a.m. with vigorous, if not musical chants. At last our voices were raised in protest to this prolonged serenade, and to our amazement it ceased immediately. Oh that we had spoken a few hours earlier. Well at last the morning dawned, at least finding us dry, if not refreshed.

Tuesday 31st July.

We pulled on our socks, still wet from the previous day's soaking, ate some boiled rice and tinned fruit, packed up our gear, stood for reading and prayer, whilst bewildered highlanders looked on, then off once more towards our objective. The natives on these first two days were quite friendly and co-operative, although as we walked down the narrow gorge towards the Baliem River, large numbers of them armed with spears and bows and arrows pressed hard upon the party. For those of us in the rear of the line it was rather eerie to be able both to smell and to hear them whispering together, and then to be startled as they would break into a mighty shout.

By 2 p.m. we had reached a 'No man's Land', and our local carriers would go no further. So, shouldering the packs ourselves we moved off to accompaniment of 'Barbi' 'Barbi', which meant that we were going into the territory of the enemy. Below us we could now see the mighty Baliem River, and beyond in the distance, our objective – Pyramid Mountain could be discerned. We walked for about two hours, feeling the silence now as each one was occupied with carrying his load, and perhaps, contemplating just what reception would be forthcoming from the next group of people as we come upon them from the country of their enemies.

We had passed through two or three deserted villages and were abreast of another, when we were spotted for the first time by the locals. All these villages are quite strongly fortified by a high wall completely encircling the houses. As the young men saw us, so they immediately rushed for their weapons to the accompaniment of the shrieks of the women and children. However, as we stood and called greetings to them, so they stopped and took stock of us. Finally realising that we were not their traditional enemies but 'white men', they became quite friendly and carried our gear down to the river.

The recent rains had caused the river to rise and it was running quite swiftly. Whilst considering how we would get across with all our equipment etc., two men appeared on a raft made of three long tree trunks lashed together and propelled by one of the men pushing a long pole into the bed of the river – just like a punt. Rev. N. Draper hopped on and asked them to take him across, but they refused to do so. This stalemate was broken as l, taking hold of the pole, jumped on and commenced to push off. This provided the necessary impetus for one of the chiefs to hop on and take over, which I was quite happy for him to do, as it required skilful and experienced handling to get that thing across the current without capsizing same. Hendrik Noordyke and myself eventually swam the river both ways, just to show them that it could be done without their aid if necessary. However, they were very helpful and numerous trips were made without incident, until at last all our gear was safely across.

Darkness was now falling, so we cut some poles and erected the tent fly, filling in each end with leafy branches for the dual purpose of shutting out the breeze and the prying eyes of the natives. A number of times before midnight we heard the sound of stealthy feet, but the warning of 'Spot' – our watchdog, plus the flashing of a torch was enough to deal with the visitors. However, on the morrow, our Dutch friend – Mr. H. Noordyke, was heard mumbling profusely in his mother tongue, which, being interpreted, meant that he was highly offended because some of the natives had stolen his socks. Perhaps, he may have judged the natives wrongly though, for the nature of the trek thus far may well have caused the said socks to be capable of walking off by themselves.

Wednesday 1st August.

Moving quickly along the river now, our original intention was to contact the C.M.A. party by radio, thus determining each others position and eventually joining forces before converging on Pyramid Mountain, which was known to be a troublesome area. However, we were not able to contact the C.M.A. party (subsequently we learned that their radio battery had shorted out) and so decided to move towards our objective.

As we neared the area large groups of young warriors appeared from all directions, and we had real difficulty in keeping our party with all its equipment from being completely enveloped. Those of us at the rear became quite hoarse from shouting at them to keep back. On reaching the site we made them all sit down so that we could watch them carefully whilst we had another try at making radio contact. We had no sooner turned round than 'lo and behold' the aerial wire had disappeared.

These young warriors were certainly a playful bunch of fellows. Ian Gruber and I went to look for some water, and on returning I had a long stick, pointed like a spear, thrown at me. Fortunately, it ricocheted off the top of my head, a little lower and it might have hurt more than my feelings. Thereafter, whenever any of us went to the creek, we would be pelted with sticks and stones by these young bucks hiding in the trees. Then when we erected the tents, long lengths of bamboo were thrown, but no serious damage was done, and we can be thankful that no barbed arrows and proper fighting spears were used. I discovered later, that one contributing factor to all this horse-play was, that we white men were considered to be spirits, and they wanted to see if we could really be hurt just like anybody else.

Fortunately, the attention of these young warriors was soon distracted from us by the arrival of the MA.F. plane which swooped over and drove them all back into the trees. But after our first load of supplies had been dropped and the plane headed back for Bokondini, they soon came out of hiding and crowded around again.

The C.M.A. party arrived that night and we put them up in our tents around which we had erected an electric fence as a deterrent against night marauders.

Thursday and Friday 2nd and 3rd August
The situation was rather tense, goods were stolen sometimes forcibly, and it was not easy to decide just what our attitude to these thefts should be. Also, we learnt by radio that the C.M.A. relief party coming up the river by boat had been driven back by hostile warrior groups. However, we quietly left it to the Lord believing that He, having led us here would give us acceptance with the people.

Saturday 4th August
Large crowds of natives were around when suddenly a cry went up from one whom later we determined to be the witch doctor. He kept shouting out one word only, which resulted in all the women and children running away and the menfolk separating into two groups one on either side of the camp. We were all wondering what would happen next, when into the picture stepped the big chief and beckoned us towards him. As we came near so he motioned us to sit down and the other tribal elders came and did likewise. Fortunately, Mr Myron Bromley, the C.M.A. linguist was with us, and though the dialect is somewhat different from that of the other end of the valley where he had been working, he was still able to converse with the chief and interpret the proceedings to us.

It transpired that the elders had ruled that we should stay, but that to do so, a ceremony of removing the heat from the ground had to be enacted. We had passed through enemy territory in coming amongst them and the bad influences of such associations had to be removed if we were to remain. Naturally we had to concede to this request even though we knew not what it might entail. But as it turned out it was quite a harmless, yet very interesting procedure. Long lengths of bamboo were placed on the ground, together with pieces of sweet potato. Each one of us in turn was selected to stand alongside one of these lengths of bamboo, whilst a warrior partner was selected to stand opposite and join hands with us. To the accompaniment of much 'mumbo jumbo' on the part of the witch doctor and the chief, the lengths of bamboo were jumped on and crushed. Two separate pieces, representing the alien influences were taken away and dealt with as enemies apparently should be.

All this had the effect of getting the heat out of the ground, and we were then solemnly informed that the ground was now cold and that we could be seated again. But if you have been there sitting out under the blazing sun, you would doubtless have thought otherwise. We now settled down to the serious business of making friends. First there was an exchange of gifts – axes, mirrors, beads, and shells on our part and pigs on theirs. Then came the smoking of the traditional 'pipe of peace' which in this case was a dirty cigarette made of a certain type of leaf. The chief would take one puff and then place it in each of our mouths for us to inhale likewise. The whole thing was really very humorous. I managed to evade this part of the ceremony by telling the chief, in the few Dani words that I knew, that I was only a little fellow of no significance, whilst the fellow next to me was a big chief and better to give him two puffs. Next there followed the 'feast'. The old chief was certainly a persistent fellow and tried to make us consume large quantities of sweet potato, baked banana, sugar cane and a type of spinach which tasted like castor oil. I was fortunate to have the dog alongside of me, and between the two of us, plus what I managed to give away to the young bucks behind me, I think I acquitted myself rather well and made the old chief proud to have me around.

Sunday 5th August

The feast proceedings continued, but during the course of same Myron Bromley was able to tell them something of the purpose for which we had come and they all quietened down whilst he led in prayer. Also, some of the worst cases of natives suffering from tropical yaws were treated on this occasion. One woman had the whole of her face eaten away, eyes, nose, lips completely indistinguishable. It will surely be in this field that our best contacts with the people will be maintained during the early days of the work.

We were deeply thankful to our Heavenly Father on this day for the marked change in the attitude of the people. The articles stolen were returned, and the boisterousness of the young men diminished. The evening hours of this day were poignant with meaning. To native eyes watching from the darkness of the trees would be seen gathered under a tent fly and illuminated by two tilley lamps a group of white men sitting down and strangely quiet. One after another would stand and with eyes closed and face pointed skywards would utter many fervent words. Then one man takes something in his hands – the Bible, and looking at it begins to speak whilst all the rest listen intently. Ah! Little do these dark watchers realise that the coming of this Book marks a new era for them. For the message of this Book is not bound and has penetrated every realm of darkness, coming as it does with power and speaking with its own authority to the souls of men.

It was my very real privilege to be the first to minister the Word of God in this area, and as the words rolled out into the night I could not help but be thrilled and yet strangely awed by the thought of what the content of this Book could, and ultimately would do even for such a heathen community as now surrounded us.

Conclusion

The time arrived for Mr. J. Betteridge. who had made such a valuable contribution to our pioneering programme to leave for home, and as there was much work banking up out of the coast for me to do in the way of keeping the supply line moving, we two then, once more shouldered our packs and moved out to trek back to Bokondini. On arrival at this station now occupied by the U.F.M. we picked up the M.A.F. plane and flew back over our track in order to make another drop of supplies to the party at Pyramid Mountain. We were pleased to see that large numbers of natives were working on the strip site, and it should not be long before the missionary aircraft can land on yet another highland airfield.

Such then is the story of our latest advance into the hitherto untouched highland valleys of D.N.G. We feel that for those of you who have prayed this thing though with us, the very real evidence of God's continued guidance and protection in every aspect of the programme will have been sufficient reward. But to this we add our grateful thanks for your fellowship.

Our pioneering programme in this land is by no means over. We have yet to reach the people of the upper North Baliem – another valley system entirely apart from that so far reached. Continue to support up here by the way you live down there, and the job will be done to God's glory.

Yours in Him,

The McArthur Family.

APPENDIX ONE

THE McARTHUR DIARY.
EXTRACT No. 10

Rev. G. J. McArthur, L. Th.,
Baptist Mission
Sentani Airstrip,
Hollandia – Binnen.
Dutch New Guinea
October, 1956.

Hullo Everybody!

We send you greetings from Mount Sion with the prayer that this extract will find you all thoroughly enjoying the presence of the Lord and occupied in the business of the Kingdom.

In this part of the harvest field things have settled down somewhat, much of the spectacular is over and in this extract we want to answer some of your questions regarding the facets of the more normal missionary life.

Inland – Pyramid Mountain Camp Site…

The Baptist party now consists of Rev. & Mrs. Draper, Mr. Ian Gruber, Mr. H. Noordyke, and the five Christian native boys we took in from the coast. Grass houses now take the place of tents, the airstrip is in operation, the third we have built in six months. The local inhabitants still remain friendly, although continue to steal at every opportunity. A few days ago, an argument broke out between members of different clans whilst working on the airstrip. Within no time a local war had developed with the Mission camp plumb in the centre of the battleground. One side would surge forward past the camp, shouting as they charged 'Bardi Lek'. Within no time they would come running back with the other side in hot pursuit, who in turn, would again assure the startled missionary that they were 'Bardi Lek' – not enemies. During the night villages and fences were burned down and altogether everybody had a wonderful time. I'm quite sure the menfolk, as least, enjoy themselves on these occasions, and really, the casualty rate is very low. They bounce around on the balls of their feet, dodging arrows etc. – it looks more like a football game than anything else. Spear wounds seem to do the most damage and on this occasion one man was killed and another seriously wounded. The whole thing ended with the presentation of peace offerings by both sides, the party that killed the man and inflicted the most damage having to make the most compensation.

I trust that I don't appear too casual in relating such matters as these, but having been associated with three separate battlefronts of the last 'white-man's' war, and having in mind the awful potential of the next, I'm afraid I can't strike any such sentimental note as to a 'plea for the primitive'. On this level they have nothing advantageous to learn from the Western cultural pattern. The problem of these stone-age people, like that of the modern world, still remains the same. The veneer of advancing civilisation has not effected a change – it is still basically a spiritual problem. Man will never be adjusted to man or nation reconciled to nation until there is firstly, a great reconciliation with God, through personal faith in a great Saviour who is to be owned as both Christ and Lord – for such He is. Let those of us who own Him thus, glory in the fact that this message of reconciliation has been committed to us – a divine trust, given on the basis that we share it with others. The motivating power of Paul's missionary endeavours was the consciousness of his debtorship to man, which must needs be discharged to Jew, Greek and Barbarian alike – for all have a like need. In this spirit of Pauline debtorship we too must find our place.

Sentani...

Each of the five evangelical missions operating in the interior has its supply line administered from Sentani. Therefore, we who are members of the Base personnel, find ourselves with a common objective – that of keeping the missionaries inland supplied with everything essential to living. In the case of the A.B.F.M. this 'life-line' has its beginning in the office of the New Guinea Regional Secretary – Rev. A. G. Dube, where together with his capable assistant – Mrs. Jensen, all D.N.G. requirements are received and expedited. The supplies relative to a pioneering programme range from whole houses to boot tacks, and in this regard it is gratifying to note that the speed and efficiency in which the A.B.F.M. has both established itself on the coast and in the interior, together with the maintenance of continuity of supply, has been a source of amazement and evoked the admiration of all local officialdom, and in addition, raised a testimony to the faithfulness of our God, from who each member of the team, daily receives wisdom and guidance and strength.

HOW WE LIVE… The cost of living here is very high – in the first place we lose 25% of the value of our money due to being on the sterling rate of exchange, then just about everything that one requires to live, other than paw-paw and bananas, has to be imported which, of course, makes the final cost rather prohibitive. But thanks to our own efficient supply line and the many extras supplied by you good people, we find ourselves wanting for little. We are, however, endeavouring now to establish a few projects; our own paw-paw trees will soon be bearing and in about another six months or so, the banana trees should also produce. Although the soil is poor and the tropical sun a real scorcher we have finally won through with our first crop of tomatoes. Other vegetables are in the process of being nursed along, but like my beans, which were eaten right out of the ground, I'm afraid the insects are going to win the first round. Never fear, however, for eventually something will be found to keep them at bay. A chook-yard up here needs to be both dog-proof and snake-proof, and my recently constructed masterpiece has proved to be so – thus far anyway, for the other night I chased a dog that had apparently failed to get in, and a python took my missionary neighbour's fowls in preference to mine. We are really very happy to have these chooks in operation, for a recent medical examination indicated that Robyn in particular, needed plenty of this type of food vitamin.

Around the Home...

The children are just about all acclimatised now. Where once a little scratch would rapidly develop into a nasty sore, nowadays it soon dries up and disappears. Schooling of course, is a real problem, and becomes very trying for both teacher and scholar. Our little home is the only world they know; they eat, sleep, go to school, and for the most part, play within its precincts. We are so thankful that in answer to prayer, they are beginning to understand something of what is involved and endeavouring to help their Mummie with her very full programme. Sometimes when I go into Hollandia – a distance of about 25-30 miles – we load up the old Jeep, and deposit the family on the beach, whilst I attend to Mission business. They really enjoy that, and it does them all a lot of good.

Language Work...

Pat and I are working hard at the Indonesian language now, and it's a real thrill to see how Pat is mastering both the grammar and the vocabulary. The language around the coast here is a type of Low Malay – something after the style of Pidgin English, in that a sentence is made up of a series of simple statements. The High Malay or Indonesian language is rather beautiful, having a complicated system of affixes, which greatly vary the meanings of the root words. We feel that with some 52,000,0000 Indonesians living close to our Australian borders and having in mind the rapidly changing pattern of the Asiatic world, the acquirement of some proficiency in this language will be of great value in the realm of World

Evangelism. Pray with us, that we may be found continuing faithful to the routine tasks at hand, and yet ever sensitive to His voice as new doors of opportunity are opened.

We do thank you for your fellowship in these things and lovingly commend you to God… Acts 20:32

With kindest Regards,

    Your Missionary Family,

    The McArthurs

APPENDIX ONE

THE McARTHUR DIARY.
EXTRACT No. 11

Rev. G. J. McARTHUR,
Baptist Mission
Sentani Airstrip,
Hollandia. Binnen. D.N.G.
December, 1956

Hullo Everybody,

Warmest greetings from Sentani, and as this letter will reach you during the Christmas season, we would therefore send our most sincere expressions of Christian love, praying that the 'joy of the Lord' will be your portion throughout all the coming united meetings and family gatherings.

Here in D.N.G. we are having sorrow in some things, joy in many things, and overall, a real consciousness of the Lord's interest in our affairs. Share with us in the following:

1. We have been deeply shocked and grieved here by the recent loss of two mission aircraft. One overturning whilst landing for the first time on a new highland airstrip, and the other, completely demolished during an uprising of hostile natives in the Wissel Lakes area. During this uprising a number of Christian workers lost their lives, and the whole mission work in this area is being threatened by the powers of darkness. We were in touch, by wireless, with this mission station only today, and even as I now write, the natives are massing for another attack. We are confident that the police will hold them off, but oh! the loss of life involved and the resultant damage to the work. Let us pray that even here the Lord will 'cause the wrath of man to praise Him', and get glory to Himself out of the midst of this seeming chaos.

2. We are rejoicing in the successful opening of our new airstrip in the North Baliem and the establishment of the first Baptist mission station in this needy field, which, throughout the centuries, has never heard the name of Christ. It is now just twelve months since our pioneering work began in D.N.G., and after the building of four airstrips and undertaking many treks the great objective of reaching and settling among the people of the North Baliem has been achieved. There are some 30-40,000 people locked away in this rugged mountainous system – pray that God will give us men to match these mountains, and in turn,

raise up prayer supporters at home to overcome the mountainous problems of supply and support.

3. Last week I preached my first message in Malay without the aid of an interpreter to a mixed congregation of about sixty. My wife commented that it was the first time she had seen me stuck for words! But, oh! how hard it is to think in the local idiom and express oneself clearly in another language. We are so thankful, however that there are those locals who have trusted the Lord as Saviour, and further rejoice that one man has now commenced holding a Bible study group in his own home. These babes in Christ need you – think of them often.

4. It seems to be clearly indicated that it is the will of God for us to leave Sentani and move over to Australian New Guinea in order to strengthen the work at Telefolmin. Our mission work at Telefolmin has, in the past, been hindered somewhat by the unavailability of a suitable linguist to tackle the difficult tonal language. It is the feeling of our Regional Committee that we should be the ones to undertake this work. We surely respect the confidence of our brethren in this and rejoice at such an opportunity for a life of service amongst these people. However, let it be said, that our own personal equipment is, at the present, not all that it could be in order to break open this difficult language, and we earnestly covet your fellowship in prayer, that the Divine enablement shall be ours.

5. We have been further blessed by the discovery of a small Dutch trawler which is going to Australian New Guinea in January and has undertaken to deposit all our goods at Wewak, and in addition, to call again on the way back and pick up the goods of the Craig family who have been posted to D.N.G., thus saving the mission the heavy cost of air freight. To capitalise on this arrangement, it will be necessary for Pat and the children to go on ahead, and myself to remain here until a relief can be arranged. Our co-workers at Telefolmin will be the Rev. Doug Vaughan – an old college chum and his wife Rosemary who is well known and loved by Pat and the children, so there will be no problem as to the family being looked after and settled in until I arrive. Also, soon to join us at Telefolmin is the Doull family who know the area so well and have such a deep love for the people. We are looking forward to a time of rich fellowship and fruitful service with these

dear folk. It is good that this move comes at a time when a holiday for Pat and the children is so needful. This year's consistent heavy routine in the coastal heat has taken its toll, and those of you who have expressed concern will be heartened to know that Telefolmin will mean a complete and invigorating change of climate and will also cause the children's schooling programme to be eased considerably, in that, the humidity which is so wearing to teacher and scholars will no longer obtain.

6. We shall shortly be having our second Christmas in Sentani and we have noticed that the children in their prayers are thinking a good deal about a ship due to arrive within the next week or so, with a crate of 'good things' on board for the four little Macs. Thank you so much kind friends, we believe that the resultant joy to the children will be ample reward for your kindness.

Much packing, crating and planning is now before us again, so the pages of the Diary, for the next few weeks, will record little else but the sound of the hammer. We shall write again before leaving, so please continue to address your mail to Sentani until we advise you otherwise.

May God grant you a very happy Christmas.

    All our love,

        Your Missionary Family,

            The McArthurs.

THE McARTHUR DIARY
EXTRACT No. 12

Rev. G. J. McArthur.
Baptist Mission,
Telefolmin.
Via Wewak, T.N.G.
18th January, 1957.

Hullo Everybody,

This letter is being written from Sentani, although you will note the above change of address. Pat and the Kiddies left this week for Telefolmin, and I now have the honourable role of 'bachelor'! It's really quite amazing what these past 10½ years of married life have taught me. My ability in the use of the tin opener and other sundry weapons of the kitchen makes one glow with inward pride – the indigestible type. I invited one dear brother to share my festive board, but as he nearly lost a hand searching among the opened tins for the salt, I have refrained from extending any further hospitality to other than those possessing at least ten years of married service, and thereby of comparable ability as myself, in the use of the recognised weapons of warfare.

Saying 'goodbye' to the children was quite an event. Dawn was just breaking as we boarded the jeep and drove down to the airstrip. There was quite a send-off committee awaiting comprised of all the missionary folk on the hill, and I noted that the children were taut like a violin string as they said 'goodbye' to their playmates of the last twelve months and climbed on board the little single engine, four-seater aeroplane. It's literally amazing what went into that aeroplane, viz: the pilot, my wife, the four children, two suitcases, a clothes wringer, an ironing board, two folding chairs, two pillows, one large carton of saucepans, crockery etc., and one biscuit tin, plus another tin – designed to catch any unwanted breakfast that might in due course be offering. The children had never travelled on a light aircraft before, and as they were all keyed up, the idea was to take their minds off the rather frightening roar of the engine and the initial take off surge. This required a little clowning on the part of father – not a very difficult transition for him of course – so setting the jeep alongside the aircraft where all the children could see, father went through the same take off motions as the pilot, and both the aeroplane and jeep roared down the strip together. Believe me, I gave that old jeep full flap, full throttle, and pulled right back on the stick, but she just would not leave the old terra firma, and laughingly the youngsters flew away into the rising sun and the dawn of a new sphere of service. 'God bless them!'

How we thank Him for them, may we ever be worthy of their charge.

And so, the McArthur family left Sentani. You might pray for them as they settle in at Telefolmin. I asked Dave Steiger – the American missionary pilot who flew them into Wewak – how they got on during the trip. Herewith his answer: 'Waa-l, they did alright I guess, when the kids got all through fighting to look out the window, they just went to sleep.' Then he added: 'Good thing though, they don't weigh much (the five of them weighed only 260 pounds) for when we got to Wewak the Government were flying extra police into Telefolmin to deal with another outbreak of cannibalism in the area, in which thirty odd people were reputedly killed and eaten.' He further added, 'But don't get to worrying though, your bunch don't rustle up a good feed between the lot of them.' Well, we laughed with him for there really is no immediate danger. There is a strong patrol post at Telefolmin, and all this fighting and killing is common practice amongst the untouched peoples of the interior. What a challenge though, to the Christian Gospel. Let us covenant together to reach and win these people for Christ, and to finally present them with God's Word in their mother tongue. One's heart tends to quail at times at the immensity of the task, but when we get into God's programme we get God's provision, and so, in His strength, and in fellowship with you, the job will be done to His glory.

I leave shortly for Tiom – our new station in the North Baliem, there to see the work and say farewell to our D.N.G. missionary team, and thence to Bokondini for some language analysis and phonetic revision, prior to coming back out to Sentani, handing over the work to Mr I. Gruber, and then moving on to join the family at Telefolmin about the second week in February.

The next pages of the Diary will tell you all about the 'beginnings for God' at Tiom, but from now on, please address all mail to the above Telefolmin address, and many, many thanks for all the very kind expressions of Christian love and fellowship over the Christmas period. It was a real thrill to us here to know that we were being remembered by you.

Keep on keeping on – Ephesians 6 – there's much to do whilst it is day. *We must measure our work in the light of eternity, therefore, learn to live in tents, build only altars.*

    Yours affectionately,

        The McArthur Family.

THE McARTHUR DIARY
EXTRACT No. 13

Rev. G.J. McArthur,
Baptist Mission,
Telefolmin.
Via Wewak. T.N.G.
6th February, 1957.

Hullo Everybody,

Well, here I am back at Sentani after a trip inland to Tiom in the North Baliem and Bokondini in the Hablifoerie Basin, where I spent a week viewing the progress of the work, and in addition, was able to allocate many valuable hours to linguistic revision. I had hoped to be in Telefolmin by now, as the Grubers were due here to relieve me last week, but have heard that the M.A.F. aeroplane which took my family to Telefolmin has had some trouble and is now out of action on the Telefolmin strip with a damaged undercarriage, and, as this is the aircraft scheduled to bring the Grubers to Sentani, and accommodate me on the return flight, it is doubtful therefore, just when the Grubers' extended honeymoon and my batching days will really terminate. The position is rather more serious than you think, for Pat has the recipe book, my tin opener claims it has far exceeded its annual quota, and should the current crop of paw-paw and bananas fail – then I'm sunk! But let's change the subject and moving inland look at something very worthwhile, viz:

The Beginnings for God at Tiom

I took Mrs. Craig and her two young daughters with me on the flight into Tiom, there to meet her husband Charles, who has recently joined the D.N.G. staff. It was very moving to watch the reaction of the natives to the sight of the white woman and her two little girls. It must have real meaning to these people when a family comes and settles amongst them, for they get so excited and are obviously thrilled with the whole arrangement.

Our station at Tiom, situated at 6,300 feet on the northern slopes, occupies a commanding position of the whole North Baliem system, and it was a great experience for me to set foot on the actual spot which four months or so ago I had spotted during an aerial survey and recommended as a suitable site for an airstrip and the establishment of our first Baptist Mission station. Two grass houses, (one with an aluminium roof) plus other sundry buildings now adorn the site, good contacts with the local chiefs have been established and serious work on the language has begun.

Also, this week Messrs. Draper and Craig are out on trek to a site about two days walk away and situated on the southern slopes, where it is hoped shortly to open another station. The local inhabitants have already had their first lesson in way of moral obligations, for it was discovered that the pile of timber – to which each daily purchase is added, was to all appearances, changing overnight. So Messrs. Draper and Craig decided to mark each piece, and lo! and behold! the next day's purchases revealed that they were buying back their own timber. Well, the usual big palaver with the chiefs took place, and all buying operations were suspended until the culprits indicated their remorse by the gift of a pig, which being duly forthcoming restored relationships to normal. And so, this first essential lesson of honesty has been demonstrated. But you can understand something of the long difficult task that confronts your missionaries in this new area, and how much they need your prayerful understanding as they daily seek to exercise a ministry requiring a double portion of wisdom, tact, and patience. Remember also Mrs. Draper, who is now suffering from Hepatitis, which, coupled with a low blood count, requires careful attention, and has necessitated her being brought to the coast for hospitalisation.

The End of a Chapter

Herewith closes the D.N.G. chapter, at least for me, family gone, luggage gone there remains but myself and the cat. Very soon I hope, there will be only the cat. It is now fourteen months since we landed, and the story of such is recorded in pages of the Diary. But really the work is only just beginning, and we farewell our fellow workers in that affinity of spirit which is cognizant of the problems still to be met and overcome, and yet in the awareness also of the rich potential for God this field surely offers, and the harvest joy that will ultimately be theirs.

Opening of Another

Two years ago, whilst attending the School of Linguistics in Melbourne, I received my phonemics examination paper back from the instructor with the following words written on the top – 'Good work Gil, Telefolmin here I come.' He knew my concern for the people of Telefolmin – that they should hear the Gospel in their mother-tongue and was also aware of the difficulties of such language situation and had promised his aid in the unravelling of some of the technical complexities known to exist. And so, two years from that date, and six years from the time when on returning to my home in Tamworth, from a meeting of the Airline Executive, and being struck by the amount of time and energy being expended in the business world, I was moved in prayer to promise the Lord that He who is the First shall have the first of my life. Hence college, the ministry of the churches, D.N.G. and now – Telefolmin here I come! God grant that the intervening years have wrought something of the character of God into one's life that will be continuously and increasingly revealed in the ministry to which we now humbly and gratefully move.

Thank you all so much again, for your vital partnership. This is Sentani 'over and out' – will call you again from Telefolmin – stay tuned.

Yours in the new Advance,

The McArthur Family

Gil's final visit to the Tiom airstrip for language handover prior to his departure from DNG for Telefolmin PNG

APPENDIX ONE

THE McARTHUR DIARY
EXTRACT No. 14

Rev. G.J. McArthur,
Baptist Mission,
Telefolmin.
Via Wewak, T.N.G
March,1957.

Hullo Everybody,

Greetings from the 'Min' country. I'm sitting in my study – recently butted on to the front of our bamboo house and have just cleared away the pile of language material in order to spend a little time orientating you all with the Telefolmin picture. From my study window, facing a little to the East of South, I look out across swampy marsh land, of which, for the most part, the Telefolmin Basin is comprised. Five hundred yards away is the approach end of the airstrip which runs on at right angles up to the Government Station. Half a day's walk further South are the villages of the Feramin group, and then immediately behind and rising up to 12,000 feet are the great mountain peaks marking the Papuan border. From my other window looking West I can see the three nearby villages of the Telefolmin group, and beyond, the Sepik River winds around the foot of the mountains, which, coupled with their more Westward neighbours, separate us from Dutch New Guinea. Behind me to the North, and over an 8,000 feet range is the Eliptamin area where the killing of the Patrol Officers and native police took place. The next range further North houses the Mianmin group of cannibals who recently accounted for the demise of 19 of a neighbouring tribe. Half an hour's flying in this northerly direction would find us breaking out of the mountains and then, on turning a little to the West and flying for another hour we pass over the Sepik Basin, and skirting the Torricelli Range, finally arrive at Wewak – the coastal supply base and seat of Government for the Sepik district.

Coming back to Telefolmin, we must take you for another excursion. It is important that you come to know these areas and have their peoples upon your heart, for together we must work and pray for the many that will surely be His on that 'Day'. Walking Eastward through precipitous country for about ten days would bring us to the watershed of the Strickland River system, and amongst the Oksapmin group of people who are reputed to number about 12,000. This is still uncontrolled territory and it will be some time before we are able to work amongst such, but later on this year there is a strong Government patrol scheduled to move out into this area, and we hope to be able to join one of our missionaries to the party.

Now, having got your bearings, the following will serve to familiarise you with the more detailed aspects of the work:

The Mission Station

This comprises two houses, trade store, church, school, sawmill, cargo-boy houses, and school-boy houses. All of which, at this juncture, are built of bush materials, and therefore tend to deteriorate rather quickly. However, with the sawmill in production, future planning provides for buildings of a much more permanent construction.

The Work Itself

The Rev. and Mrs. Vaughan have been doing a marathon job of work here. The hard work of the timber mill, the maintenance of the machinery, the school programme, the trade store, plus general station management, and the current building programme, all form part of their responsibility. We hope shortly to be able to relieve them of some of the burden, but as no previous work has been undertaken in the vernacular, I must needs spend the better part of my time endeavouring to break open and master this essential adjunct to the reaching of the people with the message of life. Pidgin English is the present medium of instruction, but its scope is limited and gives us no contact with the people of the villages. Our work, therefore, will be considerably restricted until we have acquired some real facility in the everyday language of the people. Already we have been able to determine the basic construction of the Intransitive Verb and noted its changes according to vowel harmony with the various pronouns. But it's a long slow work, and we are eagerly awaiting the return of Mr. & Mrs. Doull from furlough to help us with the overall programme.

New Areas

Due to the constant tribal warring and uprising of the people, plus the fact of the rugged nature of the terrain this area has been rather difficult to bring under control, and for the past five years or so our mission work has been restricted to a very small radius. Recently however, we were given permits to undertake treks into the Eliptamin and Feramin areas. The permits stipulate that we must have at least two experienced Europeans in the party. We thank God for the opening up of these areas, and you will rejoice to know that Rev. D. Vaughan and myself together with a number of our school and cargo boys, have now returned from a week's trekking over the mountains, holding services in the villages and giving gifts to the headmen to mark the occasion of our coming amongst them. It was a moving experience to stand on the sites of the previous killings and to hear from the people themselves the vivid descriptions of what actually took place, and then to have them all sit down and haltingly explain that into this place of violence and death, there had at last come the message of life, love and reconciliation. We do thank you all for your prayer support as we went out and made these initial and vital contacts, and really believe that God answered prayer and gave us complete acceptance with the people. Never at any time during the day, or the long night hours as we slept amongst them, did we have any cause for alarm and we feel that there is a rich harvest awaiting us amongst these people. It is essential that we maintain our contact with these groups, but in order to do so, and making one short visit to the main villages, we find ourselves away from home and the work at base, for a part of two weeks out of every four, and we would value your prayers as we seek to formulate and present to the New Guinea Regional Committee, a suggested programme for this coming budget year.

I expect that you are now quite tired from all this trekking, so let's draw up a chair and spend a little time:

At Home

Our home was built by Mr. Don Doull some five years ago and it's a credit to his good workmanship that the only replacements needed during that time have been – outside walls, roofing and some windows, which, for a bush house, is by no means extensive. Even with our family of six the house is quite roomy and comfortable, and the children have settled down very happily. Little Wendy was over awed at first by the strangeness of the place and people and could not be left for a moment, but now she runs all over the station saying 'hullo' to everyone in general. The health of the children has improved no end and they are full of life. Their school programme is much more static now, although I'm afraid that with the past interruptions they are somewhat behind. Paul has passed his sixth birthday and should be well into his schooling, but as yet, his lessons have not arrived so he's still making the most of his freedom building aeroplanes and taking off up the track with a team of naked young aviators from the local village following in his slipstream. Another interesting sidelight on child education centres around our eldest girl Robyn – age 9 years. The other day whilst passing the laundry I heard a youthful, yet nevertheless authoritative voice of a true 'school-ma'am' giving instruction in multiplication, subtraction and writing. Taking a peep, I saw two dark young locals sitting on upturned boxes and equipped with pencil and paper paying rapt attention to their instructor. I was quite surprised, on examining their pads, to find that Robyn had been working from one of her earlier lessons and had apparently got her subject across as the youngsters had effected quite a true reproduction of the lesson. It may not be too long then, before we have another school teacher on the staff.

It's always cold and wet up here of an evening and we plan shortly to install some kind of heating arrangement as there is an abundance of firewood. Another recent acquisition is a Badminton court which we have covered with sawdust from the mill, and on which most afternoons at 5.15 p.m. the Vaughans and the McArthurs join battle. It not only provides good recreational exercise but is also a means of contact with the Government personnel comprised of five men and one woman. One dear fellow, who apparently has never been favourably disposed towards missions was invited over, and after having soundly thrashed us in most of the games, went away feeling much happier and decidedly more friendly. You might remember us in our contacts with those fellows. We want to be wise and honourable and witness a good confession before them, at the same time gaining their respect and confidence, minister Christ to their hearts.

This has been a weighty screed, and those of you who have been interested and gracious enough to see it through to the bitter end might go the 'extra mile' and drop a line in reply. We have not heard from some of you for quite a while now, and it would be a real thrill to have you say 'Hullo'.

All the family send their love. We shall spend some more time with you after the next trek. Until then – Hebrews 13: 18-21.

Yours in Rich Fellowship,

The McArthur Family

APPENDIX ONE

THE McARTHUR DIARY
EXTRACT No. 15

Rev. G.J. McArthur,
Baptist Mission,
Telefolmin. Via Wewak, T.N.G
26th April, 1957

Hullo Everybody,

Since last writing I have spent a week in the Baiyer Valley attending the Field Council meetings. Two village baptismal services took place whilst I was there, and for me to witness same provided real spiritual stimulus and gave deeper meaning to my life and future missionary service. The solemnity and quiet dignity of the whole proceedings coupled with the obvious sincerity of the candidates was impressive to behold. Sitting there and watching, my thoughts turned to the untouched heathen and cannibals of the Telefolmin area – only now opening up to missionary contact. What, I asked, had wrought the change in these Baiyer people? Here before me was an old man and his two wives, going down into the waters of baptism, there symbolically to die to the old life – its passions, superstitions, violence and bondage. What mighty weapon had been so effectively wielded so as to break through the fixed feelings and inhibitions of such a man and his many like-fellows? For on very few mission fields of the world has there been such marked success with the older generation. The answer, I feel sure, is Educational Evangelism, for whilst there are undoubtedly many contributing factors to be considered, yet central to all, is the emphasis on Adult Education in the local vernacular. This has brought many choice men and women to the stage where they can both read and write in their own language. Then into their hands has come the 'Living Word' – through the eye-gate and penetrating deep into the heart, there producing its own eternal result. The Gospel of Mark is now being translated, each chapter being duplicated and given to the Teacher Boys and other literates to digest and converse upon. And so they do – at work in the gardens, in the home, and around the fires at night. With right wonder and amazement we 20th Century Westerners may look on and watch this spiritual metamorphosis, as, through the working of the Holy Spirit the 'dynamic' of the Gospel breaks down the 'old' and establishes the 'new', by relating a primitive world to the Saviour God.

We greatly rejoice and thank God for the spiritual awakening now taking place amongst the Engas of the Baiyer Valley and return to the pioneering work of the Telefolmin District, confident that, though there are still difficult years ahead to be encountered and overcome, yet the spiritual harvest will one day assuredly be reaped.

Arriving back in the 'Min' country, my colleague – Rev. Doug. Vaughan met me with my trekking boots and we took off for another three days amongst the people of the Eliptamin Valley. Our reception was again very good. The folk were pleased to see us, and it was gratifying to have all the patients that we had previously treated for such things as tropical ulcers, axe wounds, pneumonia, conjunctivitis etc. come up and proudly display the healing results of penicillin and other sundry treatments. We are not able to stay long with the people whilst on these treks, and they are always disappointed when we pack up and leave them. However, we have marked out an airstrip site and the people are cutting the timber and clearing the area themselves, so it will not be too difficult to finish off the site and eventually visit the area more frequently, plus being able to spend more time with the people, by taking advantage of light aircraft transportation.

Back here at Base, I have just taken over the school work from Rev. Doug Vaughan, and spend each morning working with the boys in Pidgin English. The afternoons I endeavour to allocate to language work in the vernacular – but real progress has been hampered somewhat by other many and varied demands upon one's time, plus the fact that the informant I was using is now being employed fulltime at the Government Patrol Post. It is hoped that I will shortly be able to obtain another suitable informant and settle down to some consistent language research.

All is well on the home front, the children are fast becoming proficient in the art of the bow and arrow, and I'm afraid that young Paul's knowledge of the bush far exceeds his understanding of the three 'R's'. Baby Wendy continues to keep us all amused and is loved and spoilt by all the native cargo boys and school boys. The other day one of our long-delayed Christmas boxes arrived, and although some of the goods were spoiled, yet the youngsters had a great time. There they were – each with a mouthful of lollies (a rare treat up here) and all decked out in their new pyjamas, and running around displaying their finery to all and sundry. They are really appreciative of these kind gifts and it's a real joy to Pat and myself to see them so happy. It's also been a great thrill to get letters from so many of you. The mail plane is our only link with the outside world, and how we look forward to it!

Cheerio for now, and every blessing.

Yours in his Service,

The McArthur Family

APPENDIX ONE

THE McARTHUR DIARY
EXTRACT No 16

Rev. G.J. McArthur,
Baptist Mission,
Telefolmin.
Via Wewak, T.N.G.
June, 1957

Linguistic Edition

Hullo Everybody,

Or perhaps, in this edition, one should only greet those whose interest in language work is such that they are prepared to wade through the somewhat dry and technical contents of this particular extract. So many folk however, have asked questions relative to the breaking of a primitive language that we thought it would not go amiss if we brought you all up to date on the subject of our linguistic research thus far.

In the first place we had better acquaint you with our objectives. Just what are we aiming at?

1. Speech Like the Natives

This can only be achieved by analysing the basic sounds of a language in terms of the speech organs. Most languages contain sounds so like each other, and yet so unlike that which we ourselves are used to, that they can only be detected and then reproduced by one having a knowledge of how sounds are made and what points of articulation in the human speech mechanism are used in producing them. Hence, we are now recording phonetically, with a separate symbol, every separate sound heard in the language.

2. An Alphabet that is Easy to Read

Every school boy knows the horrors of our English spelling, that puts a 'k' in 'knife' and leaves the 'h' out of 'sure'. Therefore we take all our phonetic data, and by a process of elimination arrive at what is termed a 'Scientific Phonetic Alphabet'. Providing that one's analysis is accurate, this alphabet becomes the practical orthography and the very foundation stone for making the people literate. It eliminates all spelling troubles because you give the people a separate symbol for every sound in their language which has significant meaning. They then learn to spell a word as it is said. What a boon to a people learning to read in later life.

3. A Concise Grammar Statement

Contrary to generally accepted opinion, primitive languages do have most complex and yet fixed, grammatical constructions. Therefore, we must discover what holds the units of speech together, so that sentences are not meaningless, gibberish-like nonsense rhymes, but the expression of a people's soul. The idiomatic word order must also be accurately determined before the 'wonderful words of life' can be translated and presented in a manner acceptable to the people.

4. A Literacy Programme
The native himself must be able to read if he is ever to enter into the riches of the Word and feed upon it.

Thus, our objectives. But how far have we come? Well, we are very thankful to say that we have accomplished a little more than first expected. Let's open the language files and have a browse through:

(a) A phonetic dictionary of approximately 300 nouns, adjectives and prepositions.

(b) Plurality of nouns, possessive nouns and pronouns, and nouns with adjectives have all been worked through, checked and recorded .

(c) Forty odd verbs have been identified and each one conjugated with the six personal pronouns through the ten different tenses, covering various aspects of the Past, Present, Future and Perfect, and in this language there are different verbal endings for all the tenses with structural changes for the interrogative and negative.

(d) Nouns and pronouns have been used with the verbs in different constructions to determine change when subject becomes object etc.

e.g. The basic stem of the verb 'to kill' is 'ungko', which although never seen to appear in its own basic form has been proved by analysis to be such.

Kabo tanum ungkorala
(You man kill) = You kill the man – The verbal ending being 2nd person singular, Present Imperative and determined by the pronoun subject.

But now notice the change when the pronoun subject 'Kabo' becomes the object of the same verb:

Tanum kungkorago
(man you kill) = The man kills you – The first letter of the pronoun 'K' is prefixed to the verb, which is conjugated 3rd person singular, viz, He – the man, kills you.

Jolly interesting isn't it? – or is it? !!

Work has progressed so well that I was encouraged by our Baiyer linguist Rev. E. Kelly – to take out as soon as possible a tentative orthography, for they have found that in working with the literate school-boys many of the more doubtful aspects are clarified by the boys themselves in the usage of the language material. Well, as all our school boys have been away for the three weeks or so working in the family gardens, I was therefore able to make a concentrated attack on things and spend about eight hours or more each day on straight language research. The result: An orthography and syllable chart. Then came the first test of trying it out with the older school-boys who have reached a certain standard of literacy in Pidgin English.

The result: the brighter boys can slowly reproduce on paper short sentences in their own language. Hallelujah! What a thrill!

But more yet:

One particularly bright fellow, after only a week's instruction can now read off any vernacular word I put on the blackboard and tell me its equivalent meaning in Pidgin English. Which means of course that the tentative orthography, though doubtless subject to minor changes, is basically correct and of significant meaning to a literate who can associate the symbols with the sounds of his own language.

What next? I have since been spending all my mornings with this boy, working by aid of the tape recorder on straight narrative, with the result that we now have about twenty questions and answers on the subject of 'God the Father'. From there we shall move to the subject of 'God the Son' and 'God the Holy Spirit'. In this way a proper conception of the Godhead will be established right from the very beginning.

The next test: On Sunday 24th June, at the morning service, I am going to speak in the vernacular using these questions and answers on 'God the Father'. If my speech is understood by the people it will mean that a most significant step forward linguistically has been made. If the content of my talk is apprehended, then it will mean a most significant step forward evangelistically. Will you pray for us all on the above date? Herewith is a short extract from the subject matter that will be used:

Atum God beyo nuyo itamsa beleki?
(Father God he you & me looks at with knowledge?)
= Is Our Father God personally interested in you and me?

Beta nuyo itamsa, Beyoki nuyo itamsaKwa
(He you & me beholds He you & me has true knowledge)
= Father God is the only one who truly knows and understands us.

Beta numi wengtinang-kusa
(He belong you & me talk-hears)
= He hears and understands what we say.

Atum God beycki arugum utamsako
(Father God He alone all things has knowledge of)
= Father God is the only one who knows and understands all things.

Atum God beyoki numi agetem uyo utamsako
(Father God he alone you & me inward thinking has knowledge of)
= Father God is the only one who knows the thoughts of the heart.

 You have just read then, the first concept of 'God the Father in Heaven' ever recorded in the Telefolmin dialect. Let us pray that it will be the forerunner of much that will get glory to Himself from among these needy people. Allow me now to close with the following quotation, which, although rather lengthy, will amply repay the reader:

'The missionary aims at influencing, not the shallows of a people's life, but the deepest depths – to touch the springs of conduct, to reach down to the innermost recesses of their being. There is no path to the heart save through the mother-tongue. The mother-tongue! That in which the mother croons lullabies over the cradle – that in which the infant learns to lisp, that in which he first learns to pray at his mother's knee, that in which he jokes and plays with his fellows, that in which the youth whispers words of love into his sweetheart's ear, that which enters into all the sacred memories of a man's life. The mother-tongue – the music of the heart and home! Men may learn many languages but they pray in their own, as they make love in their own. Whenever they wish to express what is deepest in them they use the speech they drew in their mother's milk. And when the Gospel comes to them in those hallowed tones, it comes with a power it can never have in an alien tongue…' Edwin Smith, The Shrine of a People's Soul.

And so, on this occasion,
 I am,
 Yours Linguistically,

 Gilbert J McArthur.

'I have given them thy word.' John 17:14

THE McARTHUR DIARY
EXTRACT No. 17

Rev. G.J. McArthur,
Baptist Mission,
Telefolmin. Via Wewak,
T.N.G
July, 1957.

Hullo Everybody,

Greetings once again from the 'Min' country. This normally remote and lonely valley has been in the news of late, due to the stream of distinguished visitors who have dropped in for a 'looksee'. The Minister for Territories, Mr. Paul Hasluk, together with the Administrator, Brigadier Cleland, and other Government officials carried out an inspection of the area and whilst here, officially unveiled the monumental stone raised in honour of the two Patrol Officers and native policemen who lost their lives in the Eliptamin Valley in November 1953. It was an impressive ceremony, and we were fortunate enough to make a good tape recording of the whole proceedings, which, together with kodachrome slides, we shall send to the relatives concerned.

Another interesting visit was that of Baroness Von Trapp and Monséignor Wiseman. Madame Trapp is the mother of ten children which together comprise the world famous 'Trapp Family' of singers and instrumentalists. A devout Roman Catholic the Baroness is the author of a number of books and the originator of the slogan – 'The family that prays together stays together'. We found Madame Trapp to be a most interesting personality, and obviously sincere in her desire to serve God. I had been doing some word studies in the Greek Text of Ephesians, and the books were still on my study desk when the visitors entered. The Baroness took hold of one and animatedly discussed same with the family priest – Monsignor Wiseman. However, the honourable gentlemen had interests elsewhere and the Baroness thereupon entered into conversation with myself on the subject of the Word of God. We do pray that like many of the Augustinian Fathers of old, Madame Trapp may come to know and to hold the truth of Justification by Faith.

Veteran missionary, Rev. Victor White, recently returned from Australia, was another welcome visitor and we greatly appreciated his fellowship and wise counsel in the many important matters concerning our developmental programme.

Perhaps the most significant thing to take place of recent days is the return to Telefolmin of Mr. and Mrs. Doull and family. Mr. Doull pioneered the work here some five years ago and we have been eagerly awaiting his return before finally formulating our programme for the future relative to making the most impact with the Gospel upon the strongholds of Satan still standing in this needy field. Our times of group discussion and prayer were characterised by a real sense of the presence of Christ as the urgency of the need all around us, and the inadequacy of our own efforts caused us to definitely seek the working of the Holy Spirit in His gracious ministry of illumination, inspiration and guidance. Complete unity in decision and harmony in the proportioning of the work was paramount at all times, and it is felt that we now stand ready to make positive advances for our God and Saviour amongst these people.

The tentative orthography, upon which hinged so much in regard to the work in the vernacular, has thus far, stood the test and required no alteration. We now have nine young men who can read and understand anything in their own language that the hours of language work in the study can produce for them. At the Church service this morning I gave the story of the Sower in the vernacular, after which, Mr. Doull with the aid of an interpreter, endeavoured by questions and answers, to ascertain just how much of the spiritual import of the story we had got across. It was a thrilling experience for us to hear the most influential tribal chief in the area – a man by the name of 'Femsep', and one who it is believed played a major part in the previous uprising and killings, now coming forward with the answers, all of which showed clear evidence of his intelligent comprehension. O praying friends! Do lay hold on God for this man and another chief named 'Nifinim', for to win them for Christ would represent a major breach in the wall of opposition.

Another forward step is in the realm of adult literacy. We hope shortly to build our Teacher Pastor Training School, to which we shall relate select native personnel with a view to making them literate in their own language so as to be able to feed them the Living Word, that they in turn may be able to share its truths with the people of their own villages. The first basic primer is now ready and aims at teaching five vowels and three consonants, which, together with the resultant syllables should have the student reading numerous nouns and adjectives plus short sentences very early in the course, a factor which creates incentive and has them eagerly looking forward for the next book. It is hoped that the full orthography including all syllable drills and word construction as related to sentences will be completed by the conclusion of the fourth primer. Then serious reading exercises in the vernacular commences.

Well, these are truly exciting days. Be sure and share with us in the spiritual engagement. We have our weapons, the battle is the Lord's, victory is assured, the results eternal. What wondrous origin! What glorious destiny!

Yours because His,

The McArthur Family

'What have I to do anymore with idols?' Hosea 14:8.
Hast thou heard Him, seen Him, known Him?

Is not thine a captured heart?
'Chief among ten thousand' own Him,
Joyful choose the better part.
Idols once they won thee, charmed thee,
Lovely things of time and sense
Gilded, thus does sin disarm thee,
Honey'd, lest they turn thee thence.
What has stripped the seeming beauty
From the idols of the earth?
Not the sense of right or duty,
But the sight of peerless worth:

Not the crushing of those idols,
With its bitter void and smart,
But the beaming of His beauty,
The unveiling of His heart.

Tis the look that melted Peter,
Tis the face that Stephen saw,
Tis the heart that wept with Mary,
Can alone from idols draw —
 Draw and win, and FILL COMPLETELY,
Till the cup o'erflow the brim.
What have we to do with idols,
Who have companied with Him?

Evangelical Christian, May 1957.

THE McARTHUR DIARY
EXTRACT No. 18

Baptist Mission,
Telefolmin,
Via Wewak, T.N.G.
August, 1957

Hullo Everybody,

We know that you would like to share in the joy that has been ours of late as we have taken the first steps in implementing our Bible School programme. It was not an easy task to standardise our whole Evangelistic work here at the base, as we have some young men who have reached a certain standard of literacy in Pidgin English and who have developed quickly under concentrated teaching in the vernacular. Then there are the older cargo boys who work in the saw-mill, plus the house boys, all such being completely illiterate, but nevertheless containing good material which could, with training and the regenerating of the Holy Spirit become worthy Teacher Pastors.

All these men have reached the stage where they could obtain substantial wages by working for the government or by going out to the coast and working for the Traders etc. It should be known that one of the major problems confronting all missionary bodies in the realm of native secular education is the fact that having spent 10-15 years or more educating the youngsters and bringing them to a stage where they can be most useful to the mission, it is then found that the 'attractive' wages offered for various secular positions lures them away and so often the work of years is lost. In view of this it is our purpose to major in the realm of adult literacy in the vernacular, with the whole emphasis placed upon Bible teaching and the relating of great transforming truths to the life of the community. We challenged our lads with the proposal of them all being placed on the one common standard, and irrespective of previous position, to now be classified as Bible School Trainees and accept the small remuneration attached to same. We expected many to leave and obtain other work, but to our surprise, even when faced up with the set of standards expected from our Bible School Trainees, only one refrained from accepting.

We now have 23 trainees on the station and not one of them related to purely secular work. The working roster is such that every man spends half of each day in learning to read and write his own language and being instructed in the word of God.

Don Doull and Doug Vaughan work their respective teams in milling and building during the morning and school in the afternoon. I take the more advanced boys for schooling in the morning, and in the afternoon I work on straight Bible narrative in the vernacular, using same as a basis for language research and also for preaching material in our village itineration programme. From 4 o'clock to 5 o'clock each day the three missionary families all gather for language study.

And so, under God, we are really beginning to marshal our forces for the attack on Satan's strongholds, and one uses these terms related to spiritual wickedness advisedly, for the power of evil is manifestly felt in this lonely valley. I have just left a young man lying prostrate with fear, unable to speak, preparing to die because he is convinced that evil has been worked upon him.

Not so long ago a man was found with over 25 pieces of thin wire pushed in under his skin and hardly visible to the eye. Quick medical treatment at the coast saved his life. Within the past month 4 women have hanged themselves – two of them could not be revived and subsequently died. In the adjoining valleys and mountains cannibalism and violence still holds sway. Be assured then, that our request for prayer is no formal matter, but a plea from the heart to join with us in claiming the out pouring of the Holy Spirit's transforming power upon these people.

You can imagine what a joy it was to us all here on Sunday last to present our 23 Bible School boys, resplendent in royal blue lap laps and white belts, to the local congregation, and inform them that through these boys they would shortly be hearing the Words of Life in their own tongue. We do not expect the battle to be an easy one for Satan will not readily relinquish his seat of authority and demonic control, but we have thrown down the gauntlet and before these people, named him and his emissaries for what they are.

Only this week I finished the story of 'The Fall' in the vernacular and 'Wesani,' my informant, can hardly wait for me to use it in the Villages, for he wants his people to hear about the 'war in Heaven' – the pride and fall of Lucifer, the angel of light and his subsequent marring of God's handiwork in the defection of our first parents, and the resultant blight of sin upon mankind. Ah! Yes, to know sin's origin, to admit its power, to recognise its stain, to admit one's own bondage, is the first step towards looking off unto Jesus and finding in Him – the second Adam, the 'Quickening Spirit' who alone can 'break the power of cancelled sin and set the captive free' – may God in His mercy hasten the day when many of these lost tribes shall from the heart sing.

'My chains fell off, my bands snapped free,
I rose, went forth, and followed Thee.'
    Yours in the Fight

        The McArthur Family

THE McARTHUR DIARY
EXTRACT No. 19

Rev. G.J. McArthur,
Baptist Mission,
Telefolmin.
via Wewak, T.N.G.
October, 1957

Hullo Everybody,

What's news in the 'Min' country? Well, the most important thing that's happened here of late, is that we have discovered a jolly good word in the vernacular, the connotation of which is a very close equivalent to 'propitiation'. I was struggling away with the story of Cain and Abel and looking for something that would convey the thought of 'acceptable sacrifice'. It had to be accurate for in all these Old Testament stories I am endeavouring to make a New Testament application, and in this case, wanted to relate Abel's offering to the 'Lamb of God' that taketh away the sin of the world. Discussion with my informant 'Wesani' had roamed far and wide when it was discovered that, quite often, when an influential man is sick and near to death, a pig will be killed, its blood shed and offered up to the spirit world as an appeasement in the sense of atoning for the sick man's incurrence of the spirit's displeasure. And so, related to Christ and given deeper meaning, this word 'ungkotiwe' – to propitiate by sacrifice, will become a gateway to the spiritual enlightenment of these people.

'Not all the blood of beasts
On Telefolmin altars slain,
Could give the guilty conscience peace,
Or wash away the stain:
But Christ, the heavenly Lamb,
Takes all our guilt away;
An 'ungkotiwe' of nobler name
And richer blood than they.'

You know dear friends, that when it takes from two to three weeks hard work to produce one Bible story, it surely makes one sensitive to the fact of how appreciative we ought to be of our English Bible. Let us never forget that it took the ceaseless toil of scholars and the blood of the martyrs to put it into our hands in its present form. And as its precious thought forms, in rich cadence fall upon our ears, striking right at the very centre of our feelings, let us lift our hearts in thankfulness to God, that we have His Word, to us, in our own tongue. Such worship will then surely turn to prayerful intercession for the countless numbers who have yet to hear this Living Word in their own mother tongue.

Perhaps one is asking too much of you in the way of language assimilation, so let's see what the Diary has to say about some other interesting facets of our missionary work:

1. All Mod Cons!!

History was made the other day when the installation of the first bath in Telefolmin was completed in the Doull home. Many thanks to Bob Johnston of Metters for all the odds and ends of fittings and piping, etc. which allowed plumbing to be satisfactorily completed.

The installation of the bath coincided with a particularly wet week when seven inches of rain fell to commemorate the occasion and made it possible for us to use the bath without fear of wasting water!!

2. Ladies' Meeting

Roll call; three missionaries' wives and their children plus about twenty locals. The result: bedlam; opening hymn: a trio, background of 'giggle' accompaniment. However, the meeting soon settled down and reached a common level, as needles and thread were produced and the serious business of sewing lap-laps commenced. As you can well imagine, the approach to the primitive female is most difficult, requiring much tact and patience. You might remember this important aspect of the work in prayer, for unless the 'Mothers' are reached with the Gospel, then our impact upon the community as a whole is small indeed, being related only to the male population. There is a real need in this area for an itinerate Baby Clinic work, for it is felt that only by this means will we break down the fixed inhibitions of the family life and get through for Christ on the female level.

3. The Fisheries Department

Some time ago we introduced four Tilapia fish into our specially constructed pond. The progeny of the original four are now clearly visible in large numbers, and most times of the day an interested group of natives is to be seen hungrily eyeing the aquatic display. We plan to introduce these fish into the village pools eventually, as being a good protein food for all concerned.

4. The Sawmill

Silence reigns, the saw has lost its 'temper' and refuses to cut straight, so we must now await a replacement from South. When this arrives, our chief miller – Rev. Doug Vaughan – hopes to go right ahead with the cutting of the timber for the permanent Bible School buildings.

5. The Younger Fry

It's young Valerie Doull's 3rd birthday, and all the youngsters are busily engaged ferreting out and wrapping up suitable presents. There being no 'Woolworths' or 'Coles' up here, the usual practice on these occasions is to give something away in the hope that you'll get it back, or perhaps even something better, when your own turn comes. You know, one gets a real lump in the throat when he sees the little it takes to make these youngsters happy. Let a plane arrive carrying a letter or a card with their name on it, and they run from house to house to share their joy with all and sundry. We expect to send the two oldest girls, Robyn and Jenny, home for schooling at the end of the year, and although we shall miss them greatly, yet the companionship and competition of other children will mean much to them. In addition, it will give them twelve months of proper schooling before we arrive home on furlough, and thereby provide a basis for assessing the educational policy for the future.

6. Sporting Features

We have allocated one afternoon per week as being sports period for the Bible School Boys. I'm trying to teach them how to play soccer according to the rules – mostly 'Rafferty's' I'm afraid. You should see them! The whistle blows, someone gets the ball and off he goes with the whole field after him, and in any direction but the right one. Soon, ball and most of the players are off the field altogether and all you can see is numerous fuzzy heads bobbing up and down amongst the kunai grass. But never despair, they'll learn in good time, even if they do wear out a few missionary referees in the process.

    All for now

    With Christian Love,

        The McArthur Family

P.S. N.B. For those of you who have run out of ink – pencil will do!!

THE McARTHUR DIARY
EXTRACT No. 20

Rev. G.J. McArthur,
Baptist Mission,
Telefolmin.
Via Wewak. T.N.G.
December, 1957

Hullo Everybody,

The time of writing finds us out at the coast at Wewak enjoying the heat, the sandflies, the mosquitoes and the surf. Oh! the beautiful surf, how glorious it is to plunge into the cool waves and be tossed around on the crests, especially for one who spent a good deal of his life-time at Coogee and Bondi. The new Baptist Mission Guest House is situated only thirty yards or so from the beach, and it is here that we were able to spend a few days with Robyn and Jenny before putting them on the plane for Australia. They were happy days and little Wendy soon overcame her first fears and enjoyed the surf immensely.

Our 'farewells' with the girls were by no means tearful. That we shall miss each other is obvious, but the unity and fellowship of family prayer has become very meaningful to us all during the past two years, and we all seem to understand well that though the next twelve months will find us 'sundered far' yet by faith we shall meet, around one common mercy seat. Then again, we are all so busy, every day happily filled to the brim with constructive enterprise, that the twelve months will fly away and next Christmas (D.V.) will find us together as a family again.

All our Bible School boys are on leave at the moment having gone back to their villages in the adjoining valleys of Telefolmin. We would value your prayer fellowship for these boys at this time. We are confident that the Holy Ghost has already begun His gracious ministry in their hearts, and now is the time of testing as they go back to their own people, to relate all that they have heard concerning the Saviour of the World. The boys who are now literate in their own language have all taken home with them the ten Old Testament messages and story of the Incarnation which I was just able to complete and work through with them before leaving. As you good folk have opportunity during this Christmas season to ponder again the tremendous fact of God the Son choosing to enter into the stream of human history, to be born into our nature that He might thereby touch life at every point and triumph where we fail, and by the offering up of the quality of such a life, restore the Divine image within the soul of man. As you think of such, will you spare some thought for the numerous groups in the untouched valleys of the Telefolmin Ranges, who for the first time, will hear the story of the Babe Jesus in their own tongue read by one of their own people. Will they ridicule? Will they scoff at the message of these young men? Will they try to enforce the beliefs and superstitions of the tribe – the things of evil that have held sway for centuries? Or will the Gospel light begin to dawn in their hearts? O pray that it might. We have given them His Word, will you importune for the 'Quickening Spirit'? Thank you.

One very interesting point that has eventuated as a result of our holiday in Wewak concerns the Telefolmin prisoners who are out here serving a ten-year sentence for their part in the uprisings and killing of the Patrol Officers. Also, the Miyanmin cannibals are in the same jail. Sunday services in Pidgin English have been conducted regularly amongst them and recently both Doug Vaughan and Don Doull had opportunity to visit them and speak a message to them in their own language. Since arriving at Wewak 'Wesani', my informant, and I have been able to visit them a number of times, and as they have listened to the Bible Stories and seen evidence of Wesani's facility in reading and writing, a few of them have expressed the desire to be taught, so that they can then read for themselves the numerous stories we now have in the Telefolmin language. The answer to this great need has already been met by the willingness of a gracious Christian lady – Mrs. Bergin, who will be residing at Wewak for the next two years and who feels definitely called of God to undertake this teaching ministry. We will be giving Mrs. Bergin instruction in the teaching procedures of the Telefolmin Primers and Readers and then subject to approval by the Jail Authorities, Mrs. Bergin will visit the Jail twice weekly and hold classes amongst the prisoners. Now, this is a matter of great importance, it is hardly possible for us to assess the future results. These men are leaders of the Telefolmin and Eliptamin communities and should some of them become literate and fed continuously with the Bible material that we will be able to send out, then under God, it may well be that, in future years, instead of returning to their communities as embittered martyrs, they will come back as messengers of the Gospel. Will you pray for us as we contact the Jail Authorities that our proposal might meet with their acceptance, also remember Mrs. Bergin as she undertakes this important ministry. May their 'bonds turn out rather to the furtherance of the Gospel'. Phil. 1:12.

We shall be returning shortly to Telefolmin, there to enjoy fellowship over Christmas with our fellow Missionaries, and then eagerly launch out into the work of the new year. This will be our third Christmas away from Australia, and we do want to thank all you dear people for your love and fellowship, expressed in so many endearing ways over the past two years. It has been our joy and privilege to represent you here on the field and it is our sincere prayer that before too long we shall be able to rejoice together as the seed sown in dark hearts blossoms forth into new life.

May this Christmastide mean 'new beginnings' in each of our lives, and may the spiritual blessings vouchsafed to us in Christ be our happy portion,

    With kindest regards,
    Your Friends in Christ,

    The McArthur Family

THE McARTHUR DIARY
EXTRACT No. 21

Rev. G.J. McArthur,
Baptist Mission,
Telefomin.
Via Wewak. T.N.G.
January, 1958

Hello Everybody,

This edition brings to you all our New Year greetings. We do thank our Heavenly Father for your fellowship in the Gospel these past two years, and now, together with you, eagerly face up to the challenge of 1958. May we live it positively for Him.

Here in Telefomin we commenced the year with a week's trek into the Eliptamin Valley, contacting and preaching amongst the people of the villages. You will be interested to rewalk the track with us:

Leaving the station shortly after breakfast on Monday 28th December 1957, Don Doull and I, together with twelve of the Bible School Boys, commenced to climb the 8,000 foot mountain range that separates us from the people of the Eliptamin. Lunch time found us at the summit and walking in cloud and rain through the dense forest. We found shelter in a small 'lean-to' made of sticks and leaves and there enjoyed our lunch of potato puffs and a thermos of hot tea. The afternoon found us working our way down the steep gorge on the other side and feeling our path carefully across the mass of fallen rock and trees occasioned by the numerous landslides that take place as the water eats its way deeper and deeper into the heart of the mountain. Arriving at the village of Terapdawip we met with a happy reception on the part of the locals, and setting up camp settled down for a good night's rest. The next day we were up early and off to inspect a possible airstrip site previously sighted from the air. Most of the morning was spent hacking out a walking track on a compass bearing over a distance of 500 yards, through the thick bamboo and surrounding bush. Having satisfied ourselves to such things as: approach angle, ground surface, lateral and longitudinal gradients, plus the area necessary to be cleared, we then had lunch and moved off to inspect and compare another possible site previously examined by Doug Vaughan and myself. Late afternoon found us back at the camp and getting ready for the evening service. We had sent out runners to the other villages asking the people to come and meet with us and by nightfall there was a goodly company of folk assembled and waiting to hear what we had to say. The whole service was indeed a thrilling experience. Lit up by the light of the Tilly lantern were the somewhat amazed faces of the people, who for the first time were listening to a white man speaking in their own tongue and telling strange and wondrous things concerning the Great Father God and His purposes for men. Of similar significance to them, would be the fact of hearing some of their own young men – our Bible School Boys, reading the truths of God from our prepared scripts. We really felt that God moved in and by His Spirit brought conviction that night, for quite spontaneously the people began asking questions, and just as spontaneously the Bible School Boys provided the answers. Few of the people went home that night, most of them sleeping in the improvised shelters nearby, and long into the night, discussion regarding the content of the message was carried on amongst them. My informant – Wesani, came and told us the next morning, how that a man had come to him during the night asking all sorts of questions, one of which was: 'Can I pray to God just like you and the white man did tonight?' Ah! yes, surely breaches are being made in Satan's strongholds, and the Christ of the Cross will yet find a place within many dark hearts.

Before leaving Terapdawip, we heard that a young married man had just been killed by a wild pig, so learning the name of the village, we set out to visit same. On arrival we found the whole village in deep mourning. Gathering them around we commenced to tell them of the Saviour who had come to rob death of its power, take away its sting and sorrow, and had brought light and immortality to pass. The young wife and her father – the headman of the village, were very thankful for our coming, and after having prayer with them we departed, promising to come back again and give them more of the good talk of God. And so we continued our itinerate ministry, up and down the ridges of the Eliptamin system, visiting the villages and calling the people together to hear the 'wonderful words of life'. As Don Doull and I commenced the long trek back to base we both felt that each service held amongst the people had been full of real meaning. Of particular encouragement to us was the evident willingness of all the headmen to have their people help us with the construction of a proposed airstrip, so that we can then visit them more regularly and set up Teacher Boy Stations in their midst.

Now back in Telefolmin, we are prayerfully progressing the subject of who among us will be able to go and take up residence with the people of the Eliptamin for the purpose of directing the airstrip construction work. When this project is well in hand we hope to do the same thing in both the Feramin and Tifalmin areas, so that by such means, we will have ready and quick access to the four major areas of need. At the same time we must keep our Bible School and Literacy work at Base functioning well, so that by the end of the year we may rightly expect to reap a number of boys having both the academic and spiritual qualifications to warrant their being posted as Teacher Boys to the areas of need. We are hoping that we shall be able to send them out equipped with a series of some forty odd printed Bible messages, covering the essential truths of both the Old and New Testaments, and giving the teaching points to be highlighted in each lesson. At the conclusion of this syllabus the individual will have a clear outline of God's dealing with man from the Creation to the Second Coming of Christ. We ask you to join with us in praying; that as the great plan of Salvation is unfolded to them, they will be led of the Holy Spirit to see their place within it, through the provision freely given in Christ the Lord and Saviour.

We approach the year's work confident of the adequate resources vouchsafed to us in Christ. May we be found worthy of this sacred trust.

'Faith cometh by hearing, and hearing by the word of God.' Romans 10:17. 'How then shall they call on Him in whom they have not believed? and how shall they believe in Him of whom they have not heard? and how shall they hear with out a preacher? and how shall they preach except they be sent?' Romans 10: 14-15.

You will be glad to know that Robyn and Jenny have arrived safely in Australia and are being well cared for by Pat's family who reside at 10 East Street, Tamworth, N.S.W. Paul has stepped manfully into the breach and taken over responsibility for young Wendy and does a good job shepherding both her and Valerie Doull during their times of play. We are enjoying good health and have so much to be thankful for, and indeed, so we are.

    With kind regards,
    Yours in His Service,

        The McArthur Family

THE McARTHUR DIARY
EXTRACT No. 22

WOMEN'S EDITION
Pat McArthur
Telefolmin.
Via Wewak, T.N.G.
January, 1958

Dear Ladies,

Here at last is a short epistle from 'little me' and not before time I expect, but as so many lovely cards and parcels have arrived during the Christmas season I feel I must write to you all, per medium of our Diary letter, and say a big thank you for your kindness.

If you could have seen Paul and Wendy as they found a parcel, or present, as Wendy prefers to call them, addressed to them, and heard the shouts and squeals of delight as they displayed the contents of each surprise packet, well I'm sure you would have been amply rewarded for the part you played in making our Christmas such an enjoyable one. Even Gilbert is apparently not too old to enjoy a toy-train and can even fly a kite, too.

We both had a wonderful time undoing our parcels and enjoying the good food so kindly sent by all you dear folk.

No doubt you would be interested to hear something of our work amongst the native women and how we seek to minister to their needs. The womenfolk here, as in most primitive societies, are the beasts of burden and it's the usual thing to see a woman with a 'billum' (string bag) full of Kau-Kau and Taro on her back plus a great load of firewood, then perhaps, to top it all off would be the young 'pikinini', and all this whilst her husband walks along with his bows and arrows. When in a facetious mood my husband tells me that he thinks the menfolk here have got the right idea and that there should be more of it – all men are the same, aren't they? Although occasionally we do see a man deigning to share the load and we are forced to recognise that nature's gentleman can still be found in most places of the world.

We have a sewing class each Friday afternoon for all the women, but usually it's only the younger ones who come, the older folk say they are too old to learn to sew. It appears to be the usual thing I think for them to step into the background as they get older.

There is much fun and games in our classes with babies, pigs, etc. but some of the girls can really sew neatly and it has been encouraging and a real thrill to have this contact with the women of our valley. These sewing classes have been the only means of contacting the women who by nature are very reserved and unemotional. We hope to be teaching them later on to use the rush (grass) which grows quite close to our station and as these people have no arts and crafts we thought if we could introduce them to 'rush work' and as they learn the 'knack' of it and are producing mats, baskets, boxes etc. they would have some new interest and a means of making a little money also should we eventually be able to market these items. At the close of our class we read a Bible story which we missionaries take in turns to read in the vernacular, then perhaps one of us will close the meeting by reading a responsive prayer.

It is most encouraging to see the change which has come about in these people since we have been able to bring 'The Word of Life' to them in their own language. It really has got 'Life' for them now, whereas before they were disinterested now they are anxious to come and hear this message which can change their lives and bring them from darkness into His marvellous Light.

We have one aged woman, the mother of one of the Bible School Boys, who comes to Church regularly. She has had a tattered old lap-lap and a blouse which couldn't keep anybody warm, and she has to wear them constantly as she has nothing else in the way of clothes, so of course they are very dirty too. As I sat behind her one morning during the Church service I noticed how cold she was as she hasn't any flesh on her poor old bones to keep her warm, so next day I took an old cardigan of mine down to her and just put it around her shoulders. She was so grateful that she came and put her arms around me and gave me such a big hug and that was all the thanks I needed, because such an embrace from a Telefolmin woman really means something.

The native dress of the womenfolk here is not worth writing about really as there is nothing to it and the men's clothing is just the same but it's amazing how 'normal' such things become after a while.

There is no medical work being done here by our Mission as there is a government medical assistant close by. We do feel however that the only way we shall ever really get to know and gain fully the confidence of our womenfolk is by clinic work with the mothers and babies. There are such a crowd of young children and babies around just now and when you see them so dirty and in need of attention you just long to be able to go and help them, but the only way would be to go out to each village and spend a day or so amongst the people.

Although Robyn and Jeanette have gone back to Australia for their schooling, teaching Paul occupies the whole of each morning throughout the week and Wendy demands to do some school work too so I suppose it won't be too long before she will be keeping Paul company in the 'class room'.

We do ask you to pray for these dear women who surely are loved of God, for their need is great and we have so much that we can share with them by way of bringing them to know and experience the love of God in Christ which will give meaning and direction to their everyday living – and how much more so when we remember that 'The hand that rocks the cradle rules the world' and that to win these mothers for Christ, will also have such worthwhile results among the younger generation.

Once again thanking you for your prayers and for all the practical expressions of your love and asking that you continue to share with us in our work amongst the womenfolk here.

Kindest regards to you all,
Your Sister in Christ,

Pat McArthur

THE McARTHUR DIARY
EXTRACT No. 23

> Rev. G.J. McArthur, Baptist Mission,
> Telefolmin.
> Via Wewak, T.N.G.
> February, 1958

Hullo Everybody,

The Eliptamin Valley is occupied for Christ! For centuries past the evil one has reigned supreme over this remote Valley system. Then, when in 1952/53 it was seen that the Australian Baptists were knocking at the very doors, by subtlety, by unleashed violence and murder, the evil one again slammed the door in our faces, and the area was officially closed to the missionary. But who is he that would defy the armies of the living God? For in 1957 permission was granted for two missionaries to enter the Valley. On that occasion God graciously gave us acceptance with the people, and from then on, contact with the area by trekking parties has been maintained. The last of these forays resulted in a final decision being reached as to the airstrip site and future Teacher Boy Station. And now?...

Friday 14: The call sent out to the headmen of the Eliptamin villages, 'We want to come and sit down among you and build an airstrip. Will you send carriers for all the cargo?'

Saturday 15: The day spent in finalising all the details, gathering together of all the equipment, etc.

Sunday 16: A day of prayer, waiting upon God to equip us, make us ready, and more sensitive to His leading.

Monday 17: An answer to prayer – down the track come marching some fifty odd men of the Eliptamin… 'We have come to carry your cargo'.

Tuesday 18: Now fully loaded, the party line up, prayer is made, missionaries' wives say goodbye, and led by missionaries Doull and Vaughan the party moves off and slowly disappears into the bush at the base of the mountain range separating the Eliptamin from Telefolmin.

Someone made the remark, 'They look like the Children of Israel'. I'm inclined to think however, that the party was more reminiscent of another band that once crossed from Troas, and landing at Neapolis, marched across the Aegean highway to plant the 'Standard of the Cross' in Philippi – a frontier outpost of Imperial Rome. Truly the vanguard of Christ's army on its first westward march.

The Task Ahead

The task of recruiting and organising native labour forces, building the Teacher Boy Station, together with the planning and detailed supervision of the airstrip construction, now becomes largely the responsibility of our colleague Rev. Doug Vaughan. It is hoped that he will be able to stay permanently in the area and if possible, see the job through to its completion before going home on furlough. The Government has stipulated that the area is not considered safe enough for one missionary to remain on his own, so it means that Don Doull and I will be constantly on the move, alternating in fortnightly periods between the two areas, endeavouring thereby to keep all departments of the work functioning during the time of the airstrip construction.

We are all greatly rejoicing in the opportunities afforded by this latest move, and ask that you join with us in believing prayer, for the continued good health and safety of the personnel involved, for the abundant blessing of God upon all departments of the work, for the successful completion of the airstrip and our permanent occupancy of the Valley for Christ.

Warmly yours in Him,

The McArthur Family

THE McARTHUR DIARY
EXTRACT No. 24

Rev. G.J. McArthur,
Baptist Mission,
Telefolmin.
Via Wewak, T.N.G.
April, 1958

Hullo Everybody,

The time of writing finds Doug Vaughan and myself resident in a little log cabin – 12 feet x 6 feet, out in the Eliptamin Valley where we are progressing the construction of an airstrip. You will be interested to hear of what takes place out here, now that we are in more permanent contact with the people.

The Weekly Programme

We have split the valley population working potential into two halves, the top section working on the airstrip for two weeks whilst the lower group of villages look after their gardens, and then the following two weeks, the situation is reversed, and so it goes on. By this means the measure of demand upon the people, who in this area have to work very hard to ensure a proper food supply, is the more evenly proportioned.

Any time around 7.30 a.m. finds the folk breaking out of the bush from various points of the compass and converging on the little log cabin; spades, picks, crow-bars and sacks, are handed out and off they go to the airstrip site to commence the day's work. Usually, there is a sick parade of about twenty odd folk, with ills ranging from; sores, colds, malaria, burns, to severe pneumonia cases. The contact on this level is most worthwhile and gives us a ready acceptance with the people.

The forenoon hours find Doug Vaughan out on the airstrip constantly taking levels – marking high spots for removal and low spots for filling, and generally supervising the labour force.

When Don Doull is out here with Doug he usually sets up his Bible School class under the trees and spends the morning teaching, as it is imperative that we keep our literacy and Bible teaching work going well, in order that when the airstrip is finished, there will be those graduates competent to man the Teacher Boy Station. The afternoon periods are spent helping out in the general airstrip work.

During my fortnightly periods out here, I school my class of fellows and spend what time I can on language work, helping out on the strip as required. Don Doull is then found back at base, running the saw-mill in the mornings and schooling in the afternoons.

I have purposely taken a little time and space to explain these working details so that it will answer some of your questions as to what happens to the rest of the work when missionaries have to stop and build airstrips. You will now readily see, I think, that between the three families based at Telefolmin, every vital department of the work is being earnestly progressed, and also, that none of the many pressing and necessary practical duties are being allowed to deter us in our main aim of evangelism through the medium of literate, biblically educated indigenous converts.

And now back to the daily round: 12 noon has Doug blowing the whistle and all down tools and adjourn to their little grass 'lean-to's' for a feed of taro and a brief 'shut-eye'. The whistle blows again at 1.00 p.m. and the folk assemble for the daily Church service. Up until recently this consisted of one of us missionaries reading one of the Bible story translations, but you will be thrilled to hear, that now, quite a number of our young men have such facility in reading their own language, that they can stand up, and taking a portion of the message each, speedily tell it forth. When this is completed, one of the young men will hold forth and further develop the message and make its application to the hearers.

Ah yes! This is the kind of missionary work one dreamed about when swotting it out in the learned halls of his beloved Alma Mater – 'a tropical sun overhead, a jungle setting, and some hundreds of natives listening intently to one expounding the great redemptive truths so divinely prepared and suited to meet the need of every human heart where 'ere it may be found'. Well, it's all beginning to materialise now. The quiet but solid foundation work of the missionaries the past six years, plus the more recent months of consistent language work and Bible teaching, has now brought us to the very threshold of an effective evangelistic ministry. True, it is only the threshold, much still lies before us, but the story is being told, clearly and decisively in the language and thought forms of the people, and what is more important perhaps, their own young men — our Bible School boys — are standing forth and fearlessly naming the old evil practices for what they are, and telling of the deliverance to be found in Christ the Saviour.

Sunday Service

On Sunday, instead of the people coming to see us, we go to see them. Would you like to come? Good! The village we have selected is Tagatemtigin and leaving the airstrip we climb down into the gorge, and up the other side and into the bush. After about half an hours slopping along the muddy track we come to the top of another gorge system. From here we can see the village, all we have to do is to drop down 1000 feet into the river, wander along awhile, and then climb up 1500 feet to the Tagatemtigin village which is way up on the other side of the mountain range.

Well, here we are. I'm afraid our 'Sunday go to meeting clothes' have noticeably changed colour during our sliding around the mountains, but a glance at the attire of our present congregation indicates that the matter of dress is of little significance. Sitting down under the shade of one of the huts, we gather the folk around and commence to tell them of the Saviour's love. They listen very well, the only interruption being the pigs squealing and chasing each other, and the youngsters yelling out and throwing stones at them — (Oh! for a nice quiet church back home). The Service being finished we have an 'after Church fellowship' which consists of the weary missionaries disposing of a thermos of tea, whilst holding a conversation with the village headmen.

Of such then, is the nature of our 'Church in the Wild Wood'. All that remains to be done is to walk home. But tired muscles count for little when the heart is rejoicing at having once again shared the life-giving message. Glad you came? I 'm sure you are.

A Matter for Prayer

Can you recall the first time you ever heard the story of the Crucifixion? Do you remember the day when you first realised that there on the cross of Rejection and Shame, the Lord of Life and Glory died for you – paid the price to set you free from sin and death and hell? All of this coming week will be spent in translating this great fact into the language of the people and making its eternal application to their hearts. Will you join us in prayer? For we are asking that as we come to this point in the teaching syllabus, many of the young men of the Bible School will find it impossible to get past the Cross without a full surrender to its love demand. Thank you.

  Yours in warm fellowship,

    The McArthur Family

APPENDIX ONE

MISSIONARY SUPPLEMENT

Telefolmin
April, 1958

Dear Friends,

I have been specifically asked by a group of readers of the Diary to, in my capacity as a missionary, write an article as an attempt to reconcile the Sovereignty of God and the Freewill of Man, as set within the background of the Missionary Mandate. I have given much time and thought to the subject and hereunder is my contribution. I make no claim to have in any way solved the problem, but the study has served to strengthen my own approach to the subject. As the thoughts pour forth warm and real from my own heart may they invoke something of a like response and stimulus to other ready hearts and earnest minds.

1. The Sovereignty of God

I well remember the great agony of soul and mind that was occasioned me as I first faced up to the problem of God's elective purposes for men. In my study of Church History I found myself stirred with admiration for the great Puritan Reformers of the Calvinistic school of theology. Men who stood forth boldly, and in an age of spiritual decadence and moral corruption, fearlessly proclaimed the great truths of the Sovereignty of God, His Righteousness, His Holiness, His Wrath, His Judgment. Truly it is good for us to have great thoughts of God, to 'stand in awe and sin not,' to be mindful of His eternal Majesty and Power. And it is not a difficult transition to think of such a God arbitrarily legislating to that which He has created, and even to interpret Ephesians 1:5 and Romans 8:29-30 as being a royal mandate which, in accordance with infinite foreknowledge, ensures that all God's elective purposes will be completed, and that, quite apart from any participation on the part of His creature man. Coupled with all this development of thought however, is the remembrance of my own dealings with God, the witness of my own spirit as to the times that, in accordance with the motivating power of my own deep need, I have got beyond the Majesty of the Godhead, and found a loving Father's heart. Ah! yes, the mind, the intellect, can stand in awe and utter bewilderment at divine Sovereignty, but the troubled soul of a needy sinner needs a Father's heart upon which it can sob out its longings and make known its deepest needs. Turning the pages of my Bible I find that God the Father, as made known in God the Son, and brought within by God the Holy Spirit, is indeed a 'loving heart'. The mighty God of the Old Testament whose voice of authoritative majesty and power reverberated among the rocky crags of Sinai, demanding obedience or death, is yet indeed the same God who in Christ the Son stepped out of heaven into time, entered the stream of human history, was born into our nature, suffered a death of ignominy and shame – and why? Because, He Whose right it was to legislate to men and bend their wills to His own decrees, chose rather in His infinite wisdom and love, to draw men to Himself by another way. He Who once wrote with thunder His law upon the tablets of stone, now writes with redeeming love His new covenant upon the heart.

Here then, coupled with the known Sovereignty of God in the realm of all created things is to be found the Freewill of Man, for the New Covenant of redeeming love is one that breaks through to the deepest part of man's being – the heart, and any response that comes from there is individual and fully personal. Arbitrary legislation or election even though it be divine, cannot force true yieldedness at this point. But as from the Cross there comes that 'love demand' to give oneself away to Jesus, and the heart of man responds to the heart of the Saviour, so do we find the mystery of the Sovereignty of God and the Freewill of Man merging mystically together in a spiritual relationship, which, though eternal and foreknown, has now been experienced in time. True it is, that as Calvin and before him Augustine, asserted, it is all of Grace and not of man, but mysteriously woven into the fabric of it all is the irrevocable fact, that the only answer to the demonstration of the Cross that a Saviour God will accept, yea that He could accept, is; one involving the individual, personal response of the heart's affections, now brought into glad recognition of a Father's love as a result of the Holy Spirit's inworking and faith's appropriation of the atoning death of the Saviour to once and for ever deal with the problem of personal sin.

Perhaps one of the greatest lessons learned of recent years, is, that spiritual truth cannot be forced into artificial categories where everything is systematically tabulated and once and for all clearly defined. Man would love to have it that way, but the great verities of the Christian faith have the stamp of the Infinite upon them, and in that sense can never be fully contained or expressed by any one finite mind. The intrinsic value of scriptural truth is clearly evidenced in the fact, that all the great minds of all the ages have ever been able to dig deeper and deeper into the unfathomable treasure store of spiritual truth and come up with some new facet of glory or another rich gem for further meditation and enriching study. We shall do well to ever leave our minds and hearts open to greater revelation and deeper insight into truth.

Having reached this place of inward (not intellectual) reconciliation as to the seeming paradox of the Sovereignty of God and the Freewill of

Man, I find no great difficulty in moving beyond the glorious facade of Jehovah God's eternal majesty and power to rest in child-like trust upon the loving heart of a Father, so fully revealed in God the Son and made over to me by God the Holy Spirit.

Let me say now, that it is impossible for one to enter in and oft resort to this place of holy intimacy without being made conscious of the fact that the heart of God longs to make known its 'love call' to the heart of every man, and just as God the Son could not rest upon the Bosom of the Father without coming to reveal the Father's heart, and by the quality of His own life and sacrifice burst asunder every human and Divine barrier that prevented the heart of God reaching the heart of man and His life touching ours, so also, are we verily constrained, yea strangely impelled to do likewise – to go and to tell, that 'God would have all men to be saved and brought to a knowledge of the truth!' We find that such a 'heart' must be witnessed to, such 'love' must be shared, the story must be told. This leads us to a consideration of:

2. The Missionary Mandate

To the thoughtful reader who is interested in discovering God's overall purposes for the children of men, the Old Testament will provide evidence, that whilst not fully developed, the 'Missionary idea' is yet nevertheless wholly implicit within its pages. God first revealed His world-wide design when He told Adam and Eve to 'be fruitful and multiply and replenish the earth'. The commission was the same to Noah when mankind was given a fresh start. The words to the great missionary Abraham were, 'Get ye out' and as he obeyed in faith so there was channelled through him the great promise, 'In thee shall all nations of the earth be blessed'. And so, through the man and on through the family and the nation, do we see God desiring to make Himself known to the children of men.

As we commence to turn the pages of the New Testament, the missionary idea comes into clear perspective. Every single part thereof is written by a missionary with a missionary object in view. Would you like to have been with the disciples as the resurrected Lord met with them prior to His ascension? What days they must have been, how pregnant with meaning. Secondary issues would have no place there I'm sure, rather would it be the great primary objectives of the Kingdom that would be dealt with. And so it was, for it was here, that both the individual, and the Church of Jesus Christ as a whole was given a mandate that has never been revoked, or never will be, until the Heavenly Bridegroom returns to claim His cherished Bride. What is this mandate? In Matthew 28:18-20 it reads: 'All power is given unto me in heaven and in earth. Go ye therefore, and disciple all nations.... And, lo, I am with you always, even unto the end of the age' In Mark 16:15 'Go ye into all the world and preach the gospel to every creature.' In Luke 24:47 'That repentance and remission of sins should be preached in His name among all nations.' In John 20:21 'As my Father hath sent me, even so send I you.' Nor does it finish with the Gospels but is carried forth into the 'Acts of the Apostles' which title, might well translated 'the Doings of the Missionaries'. The context of the first eight verses of this book pictures the risen Lord breaking in upon a discussion of the disciples, and brushing aside their speculative questions, immediately relates them to their primary purpose and mission viz, 'ye shall be my witnesses... unto the uttermost part of the earth.' Dr. R. H. Glover referring to this verse says: 'How can we escape the obvious truth that Christ founded His Church upon the Great Commission as its charter of incorporation? And it follows logically that just as every incorporated institution on earth must strictly carry out the terms of its charter or at once forfeit its right to continue, so the Church of Christ only so long as it consistently observes and fulfils the terms of its divine charter, by giving itself faithfully to its appointed task and taking the Gospel to the whole world, has any right to retain Christ's name or to claim the promise of His continued presence and power, upon which its very life and work depend.'

My brethren and sisters in Christ are these words true? Who among us having an open Bible and an open mind can deny them? Yet how easily the Evil One can cause us to turn aside unto secondary issues that do not provoke unto love or good works and get us off the main track of witnessing. It is not so much a matter of holding to the truth as we understand it, but what is far more important, is how the truth holds us. What are we doing with what we have? And what is it that we have? 'All Power' and for what? – witnessing!... witnessing!... witnessing! Can our mission be anything less than that of our Lord's? viz; 'To seek and to save the lost.'

So then, by every God given faculty, by every nerve and energy of life, through every possible consecrated human agency must we witness. The local church through its various departments which allow for the exercise of its several members diverse gifts and abilities must take up the challenge of Samaria and be found witnessing to its own generation of men. But let it stop there, and it will perish there like the Babel builders of old whose one concern became: 'Let us make us a name.' Here is revealed that spirit of self-love and self-seeking which has ever since dominated men and nations and opposed and hindered the working out of His great missionary purpose. Be assured that the more missionary active we are in Samaria the less selfish we shall be in reaching out through the Home Mission to Judea. And can we stop even there? If we look at our cheque books we will. If we coldly analyse the church budget, we will. If we resent the demands of the 'extra mile' upon our energies and time, we will. And if we do, then be assured again that at that very point, the cruse of oil will dry up.

The Commission states: 'You must witness and go right through with your witnessing until the uttermost parts of the earth.' How can this be done? Beloved it is not our problem, for with the commission comes the provision – 'All Power' is given, obedience alone ensures the bestowal. The cruse of oil will only dry up if and when we stop drawing upon it. The promise: 'Lo I am with you always,' is not given to the little group that separates itself from the world's need to selfishly cultivate its own spiritual life. Read in its setting it is directly related to witnessing and that, ever on and outwards to the uttermost part of the world.

What then are our main conclusions? Surely, they are these; We are a race of men who have individually and personally been constrained by Calvary love, and whose hallmark as such is to 'witness'. We pray and we believe. We attempt because we expect. We are both commissioned and empowered to harvest in a world field. So then, Maranatha! Let us have done with lesser things, fulfil our commission, and be about our Father's business.

Sincerely Yours in Christ

Gilbert. J. McArthur

THE McARTHUR DIARY
EXTRACT No. 25

> Rev. G.J. McArthur,
> Baptist Mission,
> Telefolmin.
> Via Wewak, T.N.G.
> July, 1958

Hullo Everybody,

I am writing to you again from the little log cabin out in the Eliptamin Valley. We are most thankful to say that the airstrip construction programme in this area is completed and the first landings successfully accomplished. It was a particular thrill for us to have the airstrip opened just prior to the Rev. and Mrs. D. Vaughan leaving for Australia and furlough. Doug had borne a heavy share of the construction work and it certainly must have been very meaningful for Doug together with Rosemary his wife, to actually make the first landings on the airstrip and then leave for Australia, knowing that the first major step in opening up this difficult area for the Gospel has been realised.

Don Doull and I are now eagerly engaged in starting off an adult school and literacy programme in the area. We had planned to come out here today for the purpose of finishing off the Church School building, making desks etc., and initiating two of our Bible School boys into their first fortnight of teaching in the school and preaching around the villages. I came out on the first flight and brought young Paul with me to see the famous airstrip that had been the means of keeping his Daddy away from home so much. The aircraft was due to return within the hour, but the hours passed and darkness came and still no aircraft! How thankful we are then, for the little log cabin. Outside the rain is pouring down but young Paul with a cup of hot tea and two cobs of corn (picked tonight off the side of the airstrip) inside him is now happily snuggled down on the top bunk and already beginning to fabricate the story he is going to tell Mummy and Wendy of his day and night in the wilds of the Eliptamin.

Back at Telefolmin we have all been very much in prayer of late concerning the commencement of the Eliptamin itineration programme, and we want you all to stand right alongside of us in things and be able to intelligently evaluate the importance of the hour. In the first place it is an hour in which an effectual door of witness has been at last opened up for us to go in and present the claims of Christ to a needy people. Secondly it will ultimately provide the opportunity for the breaking through to the 'Mother's heart' by the ministry of regular baby clinics. Such clinics will also do much to halt the infant mortality rate, the incidence of which, is very high in this area. Thirdly it will become the proving ground for our Bible School boys. They will come out here in pairs and operate as a team, conducting school during the mornings, tending the airstrip in the afternoons, and on evenings and weekends, preaching in the villages in accordance with the printed vernacular Bible Syllabus which they are now, all able to read.

By the end of the first two weeks every village in the area will have heard the Creation Story in their own 'Mother-Tongue' and presented in their own idiomatic thought forms. The following two weeks finds another two boys coming out and in addition to carrying on the school programme, they will expound the message of 'The Fall' and make its application to the hearts of the people. Back at Base, we are careful to ensure that the fellows know their material well and are able to both read it and proclaim its truth. In this regard Don Doull is now spending each afternoon working back through the syllabus and prayerfully making the deeper application. I met Don as he came out of school the other day and he said to me: 'We dealt with the Judgment of God in the message of the Flood today, and the boys were all deeply moved as the Holy Spirit brought conviction. In fact, the atmosphere was such that we just had to stop and go into a session of prayer.' Thank God! for such indications of the Holy Spirit's working, and it is right here that we solicit your earnest prayer fellowship, for we need the life-giving fire to fall from heaven itself and clothe the work of our hands with spiritual meaning. Also, those young men of the Bible School are now being subjected to many strains and stresses – as the old life makes its claims, and yet is found contrary to the truth they are hearing. But at this point too, we have immediate cause for rejoicing. This week out in the Eliptamin there is being celebrated the most important stage in the initiation of the young men into the rites of manhood. The Government Station lost a number of its men from the permanent cargo-line, even though the warning was given that any man leaving would not be re-employed. At the Bible School, this call to tribal manhood was reacted to in different ways. Some openly told their head-men and even their fathers, that they were finished with such practices. Others however, under family pressure, wavered nearly to the point of capitulation. For such as these, prayer was made, and we rejoice to say that to date, not one of our young men has associated himself with these initiation ceremonies, surely another evidence of the enlightenment of the Holy Spirit.

And now for some family news: Pat leaves here this week for Baiyer River, there to await the arrival of number five in the McArthur-Miller clan. As Paul and Wendy will be staying with me, and as Robyn and Jenny are in Australia, you can well imagine that the weeks at Baiyer River will be somewhat lonely ones for Pat. So you dear folk who are just about to pen your next letter, please send it to Baptist Mission Baiyer River via Goroka, T.N.G. not Telefolmin, for what with Paul's school and young Wendy's loving demands, plus the normal daily round, why! I won't be able to read the mail let alone answer it.

Well, it's time for me to wrap the one remaining blanket around and try and keep warm for the next eight hours. The way the rain is coming down at the moment though we might still be here tomorrow night. We had about an inch and a half of rain yesterday and the two day total by morning will probably be over three inches, and it needs a really good surface for an airstrip to take that amount and still be safe for immediate operations. Tomorrow will tell the story. Good night to you all! – will call you again from Telefolmin.

Sincerely yours in Christ,

The McArthur Family

P.S. The airstrip took it all right and the landing hardly left a mark.

THE McARTHUR DIARY
EXTRACT No. 26

> Rev. G.J. McArthur,
> Baptist Mission,
> Telefolmin.
> Via Wewak, T.N.G.
> August, 1958

Hullo Everybody,

There is a new voice making itself felt in the Min country! At approximately 1:00 a.m. and 5.30 a.m. each morning, demanding cries are to be heard disturbing the peace of the hill country. Upon hearing such cries, there are those who awaken with great alarm, and in their feverish search for the flashlight, invariably meet with many an immovable object. All of which goes to show, that 'the joys of parenthood' are not quite so easily realised between the hours of 10.00 p.m. and 6.00 a.m.

Yes! you have guessed rightly – there's a new baby in the McArthur's bamboo mansion, viz: Sandra Joy – our little 6 lb. 5 oz. daughter. We are most thankful to say, that the complications usually anticipated with an RH-Factor baby did not eventuate, and Pat arrived back in Telefolmin two weeks after Sandra was born. This was much to Paul's and Wendy's delight, and of course, Dad was tickled pink, too (the tin-opener had become quite blunt). But four girls! Am I going to have trouble in a few years' time! However, Paul and I have agreed to stand together in the uneven contest of future years.

This is just a short family edition in order to let you know that all is well on the home front. Many thanks for your prayer fellowship, and for the many encouraging letters to Pat whilst at Baiyer River.

Here in Telefolmin there are sure evidences of the Holy Spirit's working in the lives of the Bible School men, and we are holding on in definite prayer that a break through may soon be realised. We will write again shortly and acquaint you with the various facets of this spiritual awakening. In the meantime, stay with us in prayer, and if possible, join with us in a specific way at 6.30 a.m. each Monday morning.

Cheerio for now. Kindest regards and every blessing.
    Yours in the thrilling work for the Saviour,

          The McArthur Family

THE McARTHUR DIARY
EXTRACT No. 27

Rev. G.J. McArthur,
Baptist Mission,
Telefolmin.
Via Wewak, T.N.G.
August, 1958

Hallelujah Edition

Hullo Everybody,

'It is of significance that every man earnestly engaged in the work sooner or later acquires a personal confidence in the growing triumph of the Kingdom, and in the secret miraculous energy of the Divine Spirit associated with his own feeble and seemingly futile endeavours.' William Carey.

And what has proved to be true in all places of the earth where Christ is preached, is now being evidenced in this remote valley of Telefolmin. Come and rejoice with us now, as the Diary record leads us into yet another 20th Century 'Journey into Pentecost'.

August 18th-23rd... Each morning at 6.30 a.m. of this week, Don Doull and I have been meeting together in a time of prayer fellowship. The matters upon our hearts have been: the forthcoming Baptisms at Baiyer River, the current Federal Board Meetings, and the evidence of a spiritual awakening amongst the men of the Bible School. Night after night here in Telefolmin we have retired to rest with the sound of hymn singing, followed by the hush of prayer, and then more singing, coming from the houses of the Bible School, telling us that God the Holy Spirit is surely at work in many hearts.

Sunday 24th 6.45 a.m... A voice at the window 'Masta Makata, mi laik mekim samfela tok-tok long yu,' (Mister McArthur, I would like to have a word, with you). On the way to open the door and let the speaker in, I thought to myself – 'oh dear! more trouble,' for invariably when the Bible School men have come to see us early in the morning, it has meant something amiss during the night. But, 'O ye of little faith,' for when I opened the door, there before me were two young men resplendent in their blue lap-laps and white belts, hair washed and combed, and faces aglow with the Joy of the Lord. 'Oh! Masta Makata, bel (heart) bilong mifela hapi tumas long Yesus, na mi tufela kam tokim yu.' (Oh, Master McArthur, two of us men want to speak with you because our hearts are so happy in Jesus.) I rejoiced with them briefly and then asked them to sit down in the study whilst I contacted Mr. Doull. On Don's arrival we had prayer with them and questioned them as to their experience. From their joyful answers it was obvious that for some time the Holy Spirit had been dealing with them and facing them up with the challenge of stepping right out for Christ, and there had now come this full surrender to His Lordship, and the desire to let the whole community know where they stood by following their Lord through the waters of baptism.

To fully appreciate the significance of the next event on this memorable day, it is necessary for you to know, that unlike the Enga people of the Baiyer River, there exists among the Min people an elaborate and rigid system of initiation, primarily having to do with bringing the youths through to the place of accepted and recognised manhood. In addition to this, there is the fact that the rituals associated with the House Tambaran (spirit house), form the basis for the major part of their social intercourse and inter-tribal relationships. In fact, the whole cultural pattern of the people centres around the various activities of the House Tambaran, many of which are evil in the extreme and cannot in any way be countenanced by the missionary.

It is for this reason that in our concentrated teaching programme, we have stressed positively the fact, that to enter into the new life in Christ, means death to the old life with all its former practices. So then, for the Min people to say 'Yes' to Christ, means saying 'No' to so much of that which hitherto has formed and fashioned their lives. With this in mind, we asked the young men viz: Wesani and Yemis, if they would stand up at the Church service, and tell their own people of the great decision. They readily agreed to do so, and we prayed with them asking the Lord to give courage and strength and the right words to say.

The Church Service… It was Don's turn to lead the village service, and the message for the day was the final one in the series on the Crucifixion. (You remember we asked you in Extract No, 24 to pray that many would not be able to get past the message of the Cross.) As the story was told and the application of how the Crucified Saviour met the need of the dying thief, and the two young men then followed with their testimony of how they too, had said 'Yes' to Christ, Don Doull felt constrained of the Holy Spirit to issue the challenge of the Cross to the people. This was no ordinary appeal (if one may, in this particular case, be permitted to use the term) – in content it went back to a day in December 1950, when Don Doull together with a party led by Rev. A. H. Orr and Rev. Prof. Burleigh, had flown across the mountains from Baiyer River and landed in the Telefolmin Valley. The intervening years had been filled with much toil, disappointment, and frustration, even to the complete closing down of the work following the uprising of 1953. But coupled with this was the knowledge that God's Word had been faithfully and consistently proclaimed, and that for the past eighteen months there had been the concentrated village preaching programme, where, through the medium of the Bible School men the message of Redemption had been systematically told forth in the language and thought forms of the people. It was fitting then, that Don should be used of the Holy Spirit to issue this challenge. But knowing all that was involved, Don asked the people to carefully count the cost and then if the answer was a personal one of, 'Christ for me and me for Christ', to come and see us that night and we would meet with them in the school room at the station.

Sunday Afternoon… The missionaries met for prayer. We felt deeply the need for our own spiritual preparation in being ready to stand by those whom we felt that night would throw off the works of darkness and move by faith into His most marvellous light.

Sunday 6.30 p.m… Now pouring with rain and very cold, a natural dampener to any light-hearted spirit intending to make the mile walk to the Mission station. Don and I quietly waited in the School to see what God would do among the Min people. By 7.00 p.m. the folk, began to gather, eagerly we watched the door, who would enter next? 'Hallelujahs' were more felt than expressed as we beheld husbands and wives, and in one case, a whole family, entering in. The gathering being complete, both Don and I in turn, spoke to the people for an hour, again stressing the need for complete sincerity and full awareness of all that was involved. It was then agreed that I should name each one individually in the presence of God, and if they had decided for Christ, they would answer in the affirmative. As each name was called, including those of the women folk, back came the strong affirmative 'Yes! Christ for me.'

In such a way then on this Sunday 24th August, 1958, was the Church of Jesus Christ born in the Telefolmin Valley as some fifty of the Min people including three village Headmen and nineteen of our Bible School men, were born again of the Holy Spirit in response to personal faith in a Crucified, Risen, and Coming Again Saviour. Hallelujah! His touch has still its ancient power.

You will all readily appreciate the need for prayer as we now seek to unfold to these dear folk the fullness of the new life in Christ. It is opportune that only this week Wesani and I completed the final translation in the teaching syllabus. This final book of the series has thirteen separate messages covering such things as; The Formation of the Church, The Fellowship of Believers, the Ministry of the Holy

Spirit, and a series of questions and answers on Baptism, and the Feast of Remembrance. Special classes will now be held for these confessed Christians, and Don and I will be majoring on the positive truths concerning the life and practice of the Believer. We all feel here, that in view of the necessity for there having been a definite break with the former accepted practices of the community, there must not therefore be any unnecessary prolonged delay in relating these Christians to a public confession of faith in Baptism and the resultant testimony of a Church fellowship in the community.

Well our hearts are full. We are so thankful to have had some small share in this spiritual harvest. Perhaps our only regret is that Doug and Rosemary Vaughan, who are now on furlough, were not here to share the joy with us. However, we know that they will be rejoicing with us, and it will give real meaning to their deputation ministry among the churches, as they will be able to acquaint you all with the interesting background of many of the personalities who have now taken their stand for the Saviour.

You dear friends who have so faithfully laboured in prayer will also rejoice in spirit with us. May we encourage one another to continue earnest in prayer, that the testimony of these 'firstfruits' might be so real and vital as to spread in its effectiveness to the surrounding valleys and be the means of ushering in a great spiritual harvest to the glory of our God and our Saviour. With every kind thought

Yours in the Telefolmin Awakening

The McArthur Family

THE McARTHUR DIARY
EXTRACT No. 28

c/- 10 East Street,
Tamworth. N.S.W.
November, 1958

Hullo Everybody,

Many of you are asking for details concerning the young Telefolmin Church, so herewith is a progress report which we trust will help you in maintaining that prayer-fellowship so essential to the spiritual content of our work.

In addition to the daily programme of teaching the men in the Bible School and sending them out to the villages to share the truth with their fellow-countrymen, we are also gathering the Christians together each Sunday afternoon between 4 and 5 o'clock. At this meeting we seek to introduce them to all the positive implications of the new life in Christ and to the joy of experiencing daily personal relationships with their Lord and Saviour through the indwelling Spirit. We also make a practice of having a time for discussion and then questions etc., and such times have enabled us to get right at the back of the native mind and understand the problems of these primitive people as they emerge from darkness into light. Here is a typical example of the type of problem now facing us: It will shortly be the responsibility for the three villages most affected by the spiritual awakening to play host to all the surrounding villages in regard to the great taro feast and sing-sing (celebration). Associated with such are certain ceremonies to appease the 'spirit' who looks after the taro crop, also the final night marks another stage in the initiation of the young men. Great fires are lit and the initiates are made to kneel down with their backs to the fire, then upon a given signal the old men upset the burning hot coals all over them. The Telefolmin Christians – which include some of the leading men of the area – had obviously been made sensitive by the Holy Spirit as to what their attitude to such a celebration should now be, and accordingly they asked us: 'Can we fulfil our commitments on this particular occasion, and then finish with it for the future?' We opened up to them the Scriptural truths concerning the dangers of compromise, and they finally decided for themselves that they would have no part with the celebration. And so we rejoiced as amongst some of these primitive Min folk there was re-echoed the words of Joshua 'As for me and my house we will serve the Lord'.

Our hearts have also been greatly cheered as other men and women of note in the area have come along of their own accord and identified themselves with Christ. Such men as Suni, the government interpreter;

APPENDIX ONE

Kusimnok, a policeman of real character; plus the two local doctor boys Bogosimnok and Muli and their wives, have come and clearly testified their allegiance to Christ, all of which indicate that the Holy Spirit is still calling out a people for His name in this Telefolmin Valley.

STOP PRESS... We have just returned from a strenuous trek into the uncontrolled area of the Tifalmin Valley. News of a tribal fight necessitated a government patrol going out, and Don and I were given the opportunity of travelling out with them and coming back on our own. The trip resulted in us being able to mark out an airstrip site and gain the support of the locals in constructing it. There is much less construction work involved in this site as compared with that of the Eliptamin, and we have left instructions with the local headmen as to what to do in clearing and preparing the main area. There is every possibility that on Doug Vaughan's return in January the major part of the work will have been completed and only a few weeks of European (on the spot) supervision will be required to have the airstrip ready for operations. Will you make it a definite matter of prayer that official permits will be forthcoming to enable us to enter the area, complete the airstrip and set up a teacher boy station.

FINALE... This Diary extract will in all probability be the last you will receive from us whilst at Telefolmin before our furlough. Three years ago this month we sailed through Sydney Heads en route for D.N.G. and now on Monday night, the 1st December, we expect to land at Mascot aerodrome.

A perusal of the 28 extracts of the Diary enables one to relive again the main features of the intervening years, and they will ever serve to be a reminder – both to you, our prayer partners, and to us as a family – that the promises of God vouchsafed to us in the unchanging Christ are ever 'Yea and Amen'. We feel that with some real measure of truth we are now able to say – as we have witnessed both the regenerating and moral dynamic of the Spirit of Christ at work in the lives of men – that our hitherto unconscious confidence in self has shifted, and now has for its object the Glorified Christ, ever at work in the world, in the Church and in the believer through the Holy Spirit.

We thank you all so much for your love and interest and we pray that as we meet with you again, we shall be able to share with you something of the 'Glory of the Gospel at Work' as we, your representatives, have been privileged to witness it.

Please continue to hold the work amongst the Min folk close to your hearts, and ever remember the labours of our Brethren, viz. the Doulls and the Vaughans as they continue to be God's messengers of the Evangel in this place of real need.

Sincerely yours in Christ,   The McArthur Family

APPENDIX TWO

PIONEERS INTERNATIONAL CORE VALUES

Passion for God

Our passion is to glorify God throughout the nations of the world, through obedience to the Bible and by living and proclaiming the message of salvation through Jesus Christ. It is an act of worship to actively participate in some way in the Great Commission.

Unreached People Groups

Some cultures in the world have no neighbours who can tell them about Jesus Christ. Our hope is to share God's love with those people in places where the gospel is yet to be effectively proclaimed.

Church Planting Movements

We are committed to helping people know and follow Jesus, and to the process of empowering and equipping those believers to become disciple makers of others – bodies of believers that, by the power of the Holy Spirit, are intentional about planting other churches.

Teams

We don't do lone rangers. We accomplish our mission through God's people mobilised from around the world. Our entire ethos and structure rests on the strength, growth, creativity, diversity and cohesiveness of our teams.

Ethos of Grace

International teams illustrate to the unreached that what we offer is Christ — not culture. We affirm that God's grace operates uniquely in the lives of all believers. In all our relationships we endeavour to cultivate an atmosphere of mutual acceptance and respect which encourages each of us to attain our full potential in Christ.

Local Church Partnership

The mandate for mission has everything to do with the church. So our work today has everything to do with the local church, from the beginning of the sending process to church-based movements around the world.

Servant Leadership

We empower our members through a decentralised structure that emphasises team-based servant leadership and an interactive approach to decision-making, based on mutual trust and accountability.

Creativity and Innovation

The message of God's love in Jesus Christ is timeless, and there are a thousand ways to make that message known. We encourage men and women to use their gifts, skills and personalities to communicate the gospel for the sake of precious people everywhere.[1]

---

1. Pioneers of Australia, *2018 Prayer Directory*. (Melbourne: Pioneers of Australia, 2018), 49.

APPENDIX THREE

PIONEERS INTERNATIONAL STATISTICS

Official Pioneers International Director's Office statistics for 2017 indicate that Pioneers currently has:

International Members

Team Members, Appointees and Associates	2824	86.9%
Mobilisation Staff and Board Members	462	14.2%
International Director's Office/Team	14	0.4%
Seconded Members (subtracted from the total)	-52	1.6%
Total International Members	**3248**	**100%**

Members are serving in 104 countries around the world with 202 different People Groups in 212 different languages.

Among the following religious groups:
- 60% Islam
- 11% Buddhism
- 6% Hinduism
- 6% Non-religious/Secular
- 6% Tribal Animistic
- 4% Catholicism
- 2% Chinese Traditional
- 3% Other
- 2% Protestant

APPENDIX FOUR

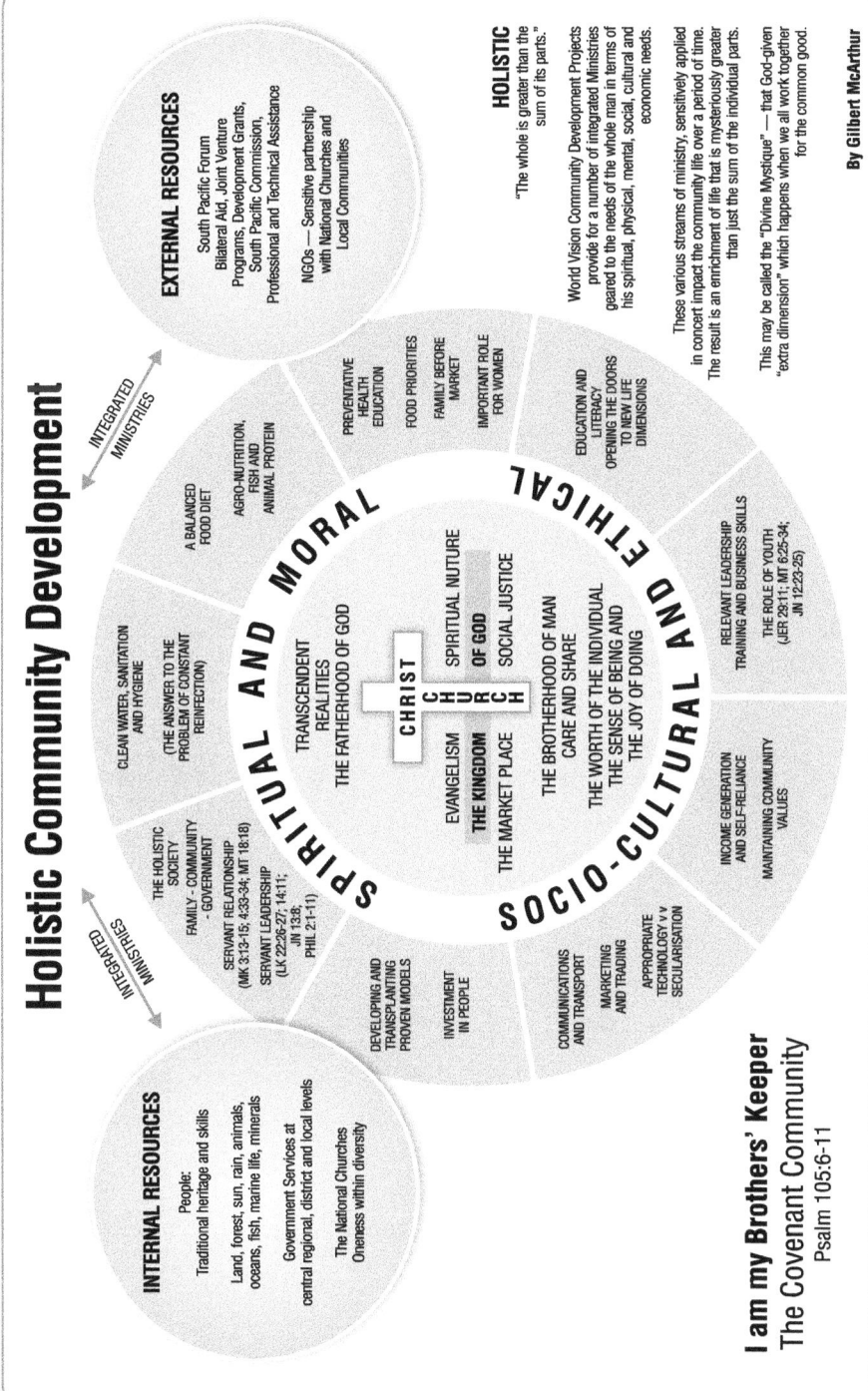

APPENDIX FIVE

CLTC Mission Statement

CLTC's mission is to glorify God by:

- Advancing the Evangelical Christian faith and promoting the gospel of Jesus Christ in Papua New Guinea, Melanesia and elsewhere, by providing biblical, theological and ministry training for recognised tertiary and graduate level certificate, diploma and degree qualifications. Such training will equip suitably qualified Papua New Guineans and other Melanesian and Pacific men and women for positions of leadership in church and society.

- Developing Christian leadership influence at all levels of national life in the nations of the South Pacific through formal certificate, diploma and degree qualifications and informal training programs and seminars.

- Providing for the financial support of the College through business programs which positively contribute to the physical and economic well-being of the people of Papua New Guinea. Such programs will provide in-service training for employees and aim to complement the financial partnership with the churches we serve.

- Providing agricultural, technical, commercial, industrial and other training courses as the governing body may decide; such courses to be seen as contributing to the social welfare and justice of the region and as proper practical applications of the gospel and the central theological education of the College.

- Pursuing the above objects as servants of and in co-operation with Christian churches and bodies of like faith, particularly those affiliated with the Evangelical Alliance of the South Pacific Islands.

- Engaging in continuous up-building of graduates and churches and promoting of their mission and service to the peoples of Melanesia, whether by theological encouragement; evangelistic, missional or practical service; and/or resource development and distribution, using such means and media as appropriate.

- Making the widest possible contribution to the welfare of the people of Papua New Guinea and Melanesia by participatory membership and sharing in programs, projects, or joint ventures with other church bodies, Christian service agencies, Government, business or voluntary associations as may be appropriate.

APPENDIX SIX

Graham Salisbury
The CLTC Poultry Program

Graham Salisbury

Graham Salisbury died on 17 January 2019. A third-generation poultry farmer in Wellington, New Zealand, he was one of many who first met Gil during his whirlwind recruiting visit to New Zealand in 1964, when so many were impacted by the vision and opportunity the establishment of CLTC presented. In his book *What Came First?* he wrote:

> The highlight of my trip [around the Pacific] was Papua New Guinea, where I went to initiate the development of a poultry unit at the Christian Leaders' Training College in the Highlands. I had met the Principal, Dr Gilbert McArthur [whom Graham describes as 'a rugged individualist'] when he visited New Zealand, and he invited me to come to the College…

> When I returned home, we sent the first consignment of chickens as a gift. Out of the 208 chicks (day old laying pullets), 200 were reared

by Erec Rosser... Over the next ten years, I watched Erec doing an extraordinary job with very little assistance.[1]

Garth Morgan records the amazing legacy of Gil's invitation for Graham to visit CLTC.

Graham planted three poultry seeds at CLTC.

The first seed was the 208-day old laying pullets, to commence the production of eggs for the communities in the Highlands. Today the CLTC layers unit has the capacity to produce 10 million eggs per year for human consumption!

The second seed was to encourage me, then Registrar of CLTC, to establish the PNG Poultry Industry Association (PIA) in 1971, along with Tablebirds poultry farm in Lae. The PIA has become the major voice in PNG to protect that country from importing poultry from other countries known to have poultry related diseases.

The third seed was Graham's guidance in helping establish a hatchery and breeding farm as the next step in long-term poultry production. The initial hatcher used one third of the space in the students' dining room. Graham was involved in identifying suitable parent stock, and the search and shipping of two second-hand incubators, an egg setting machine and a compatible hatching unit. Today the 900 square metre dedicated hatchery complex contains 5 setters and 5 hatchers with the weekly capacity to produce 100,000 meat chickens. These chickens are sold to village women who rear and sell them in their village markets. These women are then able to ensure their children are fed, clothed, medicated and educated.[2]

Today, CLTC earns more than 60% of its total annual income from the poultry business that has grown from these three seeds planted by Graham. There are now almost 100,000 poultry birds on the CLTC farm today.

Graham Salisbury is a wonderful example of a business entrepreneur having a profound impact in Christian mission, simply through seeing the vision, grasping an opportunity, developing a strategy, and providing seed funding and resources – all in the context of long-term prayerful partnership.

---

1. Graham Salisbury, *What Came First? – Including the Tegel Chicken Story*, (Auckland, New Zealand: Lighthouse Publishing, 2004) 128-129, 210.
2. Garth Morgan, 'Graham Salisbury', Email, 31 January 2019.

BIBLIOGRAPHY

Note: where no other location is given, the document is held by the Author and was received from the listed author for use in this biography. Multiple references by the same author are listed in chronological order.

Alliance Training Association. 'Minutes of the Annual Members' Meeting', 26 October 1971. Garth Morgan Archives.
———. 'Minutes of the ATA Directors Meeting', 19 August 1972. Garth Morgan Archives.
———. 'ATA Minutes of the Ninth Annual Meeting of Directors', 28 March 1979. CLTC Archives.
———. 'Minutes of the Tenth Annual Meeting of Directors', 25-26 March 1980. CLTC Archives.

Ambrose, Vic. 'Telefolmin Aircraft Program', 11 April 1957. Global Interaction Archives.

Australian Baptist Foreign Mission. 'Australian Baptist Foreign Mission Board Minutes of Annual Meeting', 26 August 1959. Global Interaction Archives.

Bensley, Rod. 'Empowering Leaders in Papua'. *Vision Magazine*, Summer 2015-2016.

Bignold, Gwen. 'Memories of Dr Gilbert McArthur', February 2016.

Box, Harry. *Don't Throw the Book at Them – Communicating the Christian Message to People Who Don't Read*. Pasadena, California: William Carey Library, 2014.

Carlyon, Ross. 'Evangelism and Church Building'. *Not in Vain*, November 1986. SSEM Archives.

Christian Leaders' Training College of PNG. 'Minutes of the Christian Leaders' Training College Consultative Committee Meeting', 15 November 1966.
———. 'Strategic Plan', 2013.

Clinton, Bobby. *The Making of a Leader – Recognising the Lessons and Stages of Leadership Development*. Colorado Springs USA: NavPress, 1988.

Coutu, Diane. 'How Resilience Works'. *Harvard Business Review*, May 2002.

Cowman, Lettie. *Charles E. Cowman: Missionary Warrior*. Los Angeles, California: The Oriental Missionary Society, 1928.

Cupit, Tony, Ros Gooden and Ken Manley, Eds. *From Five Barley Loaves – Australian Baptists in Global Mission 1864-2010*. Preston, Victoria, Australia: Mosaic Press, 2013.

Daimoi, Joshua. 'Recollections of Dr McArthur', Email, 5 April 2017.

Denton, Wal. 'South Pacific Leaders Fellowship', Letter, 18 July 1991. McArthur Family Archives.

Dorney, Sean. *The Embarassed Colonialist – A Lowy Institute Paper*. Sydney, NSW: Penguin Random House Australia, 2016.

Doull, Don. *One Passion: Church Planting in Papua New Guinea*. Springwood, NSW, Australia: Published by the Author, 2004.
———. 'Re: Gil McArthur', Letter, 29 January 2016.
———. 'Re: Gilbert McArthur', Telephone Interview, 29 August 2016.

Draper, Norm. *Daring to Believe: Personal Accounts of Life Changing Events in Papua New Guinea and Irian Jaya*. Lawson, NSW, Australia: Mission Publications of Australia, 1990.
———. 'Personal Re: Gil McArthur', Letter, 11 August 1956. Global Interaction Archives.

Dube, Albert. 'Albert Dube to Gil McArthur – Personal', Letter, 13 September 1956. Global Interaction Archives.
———. 'Letter to Gilbert McArthur', Letter, 13 December 1956. Global Interaction Archives.

Edmondson, Ron. 'One Hard Truth of Leadership', 2 August 2017. https://www.sermoncentral.com/pastors-preaching-articles/ron-edmondson-one-hard-truth-of-leadership-2988?ref=?utm_source=newsletter&utm_medium=email&utm_content=button&utm_campaign=scbpuSeptember%205th,%202017&maropost_id=742756920&mpweb=256-4425125-742756920.

Enlow Jr., Ralph. *The Leader's Palette: Seven Primary Colours*. Bloomington, Indiana, USA: WestBow Press, a Division of Thomas Nelson, 2013.

Fernando, Ajith. *Jesus Driven Ministry*. Leicester, UK: Inter Varsity Press, 2002.

Filoa, Jezreel. 'Islanders Called to New Guinea'. *Not in Vain*, June 1970. Rickard Family Archive.
———. 'Visit to Australia'. *Not in Vain*, September 1968.

Fitzsimons, Jenny. 'Birth Dates', Email, 17 May 2016.
———. Re: Gilbert McArthur's Last Days. Telephone Interview, 27 July 2016.
———. 'Mum', Email, 22 January 2018.

Fletcher, Ted. *When God Comes Calling – A Journey of Faith... Wall Street to the World*. Revised Edition. Orlando, Florida, USA: Bottomline – Pioneers USA, 2010.

Fletcher, John. 'Re: Price Kneemail Sept 16', Email, 14 September 2016.
———. 'Gil McArthur – as Told by Peggy Fletcher to Carin LeRoy', Email, 27 April 2018.

Ford, Heather. 'Gil McArthur', Email, 16 September 2016.

Foyle, Marjory. *Honourably Wounded: Stress Among Christian Workers*. Bromiley, Kent, UK: MARC, 1987.

Granberg-Michaelson, Wesley. *Leadership from Inside Out – Spirituality and Organizational Change*. New York: Crossroad Publishing, 2004.

Griffiths, Alison. *Fire in the Islands: The Acts of the Holy Spirit in the Solomons*. Wheaton Illinois, USA: Harold Shaw, 1977.

Griffiths, Gordon. 'Information and Observations about Gil McArthur', 25 January 2016.
———. 'More on Gil McArthur', Email, 21 August 2016.
———. 'More on Gil McArthur 2', Email, 19 September 2016.
———. 'Update on the SSEM Part of the Story', Email, 24 January 2017.
———. 'Ray Laird's Response to the SSEM Part of Gil's Story', Email, 28 January 2017.
———. 'SSEM HQ – Council of Advice, CEOs & Board Members', 11 February 2017. SSEM Archives.

Grosshauser, Annemie. 'Supporting Expatriate Women in Difficult Settings'. In *Doing Member Care Well: Perspectives and Practices from Around the World*, 419-434. Pasadena, California, USA: William Carey Library, 2002.

Hitchen, John. 'The Place of Vacation Ministries – and the Role of the Missionary in Such Ministries – in the Overall Training of CLTC Students', 15 November 1966.
———. 'Thinking Aloud – About English Bible School Programmes within the Framework of the Evangelical Alliance', 15 November 1966.
———. 'Appreciation of Rev. G. J. McArthur', 29 November 1970. McArthur Family Archives.
———. 'Tribute to Pat McArthur', 2002. McArthur Family Archives.
———. 'Evangelicals Equipping Melanesian Men and Women: An Interpretation of the Training Ministries of the Christian Leaders Training College of Papua New Guinea, 1965-2010'. In Tim Meadowcroft and Myk Habets (Eds.), *Gospel, Truth & Interpretation: Evangelical Identity in Aotearoa New Zealand*, 110–36. Auckland, New Zealand: Archer, 2011.
———. 'Early Timber Sources', Email, 15 August 2016.
———. 'The Christian Leaders' Training College of Papua New Guinea – A Case Study of a Christian Contribution to Economic Development and to Theological Change at World View and Social Imaginary Levels for Sustainable Development in Melanesia – A Paper Presented at the

"Woven Together" Conference on Christianity and Development in the Pacific', Victoria University Wellington, New Zealand, 9-10 June 2016', 6 September 2016.
———. 'Gilbert McArthur Lecture Series for CLTC', Email, 9 September 2016.
———. 'Gil McArthur as Mentor', 22 October 2016.
———. 'Joshua Daimoi – Comments from John Hitchen', 9 April 2017.
———. 'Part Two: "The Mission"', Email, 4 October 2017.
———. 'Ron Youngman – Later Developments', 10 October 2017.

Horne, Charles. 'Inter Mission Bible School', 19 October 1960. Melbourne School of Theology Archives.

Hunter, Brigadier Ian. 'Commendation of Rev. G. D. McArthur', Letter, 30 January 1967. McArthur Family Archives.

Hybels, Bill. *Courageous Leadership*. Grand Rapids Michigan, USA: Zondervan, 2002.

Keller, Timothy. *Making Sense of God – An Invitation to the Sceptical*. London, UK: Hodder and Stoughton, 2016.

Kenilorea, Peter. *Tell It as It Is: Autobiography of Rt. Hon. Sir Peter Kenilorea, KBE, PC Solomon Islands First Prime Minister*. Edited by Clive Moore. Taipei, Taiwan: Centre for Asia-Pacific Area Studies, 2008.

Kerr, Alan. 'In Appreciation of Leonard Buck'. *Light and Life* News-Line, September 1996. CLTC Archives.

Key, John. 'Dr Gilbert McArthur – Some Recollections by John Key', Email, February 2016.
———. 'Re: Gil McArthur Question', Email, 3 September 2018.

Kouzes, James M., and Barry Z Posner. *A Leader's Legacy*. San Francisco: Jossey-Bass, 2006.

Kouzes, James M, and Barry Z Posner. *The Leadership Challenge*. Second Edition. San Francisco: Jossey-Bass, 1995.
———. 'We Lead from the Inside Out'. *The Journal of Values Based Leadership*, No. 1 Winter/Spring (2008).

Kroll, Woodrow. 'When God Closes a Door He Always Opens a Window', n.d. https://www.christianquotes.info/images/woodrow-kroll-quote-closing-a-door/#axzz56HgD4Q90.

Laird, Ray. 'An Era of Transition'. *Not in Vain*, December 1990. SSEM Archives.
———. 'Gil McArthur', Email, 13 January 2017.
———. 'More About Gil McArthur', Email, 4 February 2017.

Lausanne Committee for World Evangelization. *Business as Mission – Lausanne Occasional Paper No. 59*. Orlando, Florida, USA: Lausanne Committee for World Evangelization, 2004.

Lawrence, James. *Growing Leaders – Reflections on Leadership, Life and Jesus*. Abingdon, UK: The Bible Reading Fellowship, 2004.

Liddle, Kay. *Into the Heart of Papua New Guinea: A Pioneering Mission Adventure, Book One*. Auckland, New Zealand: Kay Liddle Trust, 2012.
———.'Gil McArthur References in Kay Liddle's Books', Email, 27 August 2016.
———. 'Mapai New Zealand Ltd and Jacob Luke', Email, 2 May 2018.

Loane, Marcus. 'Pacific Islands Leadership'. *Not in Vain*, May 1984.

Longgar, William. 'My Face Will Go with You – Exodus 33:1-23'. *CLTC College News*, June 2015. CLTC Archives.
———. Memories of Gilbert McArthur. Telephone Interview, 24 January 2017.

Luke, Jacob. 'Jacob Luke's Story', Email, 14 November 2017.

McArthur, Gilbert and Pat. 'Application for Service in New Guinea', Letter, 17 July 1951. Global Interaction Archives.

BIBLIOGRAPHY

McArthur, Gilbert J. 'The Lockheed Hudson Saga', circa 1947. McArthur Family Archives.
———. 'Early EWA Reminiscences', circa 1949. McArthur Family Archives.
———. 'The McArthur Diary - Extracts', November 1955-November 1958, see Appendix One. McArthur Family Archives.
———. 'Making a Base'. *Vision Magazine*, March 1956. Global Interaction Archives.
———. 'Gil McArthur to Albert Dube', Letter, 20 August 1956. Global Interaction Archives.
———. 'From Here and There – A Description of Tiom'. *Vision Magazine*, April 1957. Global Interaction Archives.
———. 'The Sovereignty of God and the Free Will of Men', April 1958. McArthur Family Archives.
———. 'New Guinea Christian Leaders Training College'. *New Life*. 2 September 1965. Melbourne School of Theology Archives.
———. 'Christian Leaders' Training College Annual Report for the Year Ended 30 June 1967.' Melbourne, 25 July 1967. MBI Archives.
———. 'Address to Students and Staff at CLTC from 2 Samuel 2:24', circa. late 1967. McArthur Family Archives.
———. 'The Making of a Man', circa 1968. McArthur Family Archives.
———. 'Applied Christian Ethics for Melanesian Churches'. Master of Arts Thesis, Columbia Bible College, 1968. McArthur Family Archives.
———. 'Mission: Stratagem and Strategy'. *Not in Vain*, March 1972. SSEM Archives.
———. 'Our Sacred Deposit of Truth'. *Not in Vain*, June 1972. SSEM Archives.
———. 'New Guinea Churches – An Historic Moment'. *Not in Vain*, December 1972. SSEM Archives.
———. 'New Wineskins for New Wine'. *Not in Vain*, December 1972.
———. *The Strategy of the Gospel*. Cassette Tape. Baptist Church Georgetown South Australia, 1974. McArthur Family Archives.
———. 'Sepik Advance'. *Not in Vain*, March 1975. SSEM Archives.
———. *The Dynamic of the Word of God in Action*. Audio CD. Student Chapel Address at Columbia Bible College South Carolina, USA, 1976. McArthur Family Archives.
———. 'SSEM Centenary – 100 Years, 1882-1982'. *Not in Vain*, August 1982. SSEM Archives.
———. 'South Pacific Leaders' Fellowship: The Fruit of Mission in the Pacific'. *Not in Vain*, April 1983. SSEM Archives.
———. 'A Civilization Crisis', November 1983. McArthur Family Archives.
———. 'South Pacific Leaders' Fellowship Micronesian Good-Will Mission. *Not in Vain*, November 1983. SSEM Archives.
———. 'Why a P.T.I. in Australia?' *Not in Vain*, May 1987. SSEM Archives.
———. 'The Fellowship of the Committed Ones', 1988. McArthur Family Archives.
———. 'Address to the Gathered Community at the Pacific Training Institute at Laurieton', September 1989. McArthur Family Archives.
———. 'Holistic Community Development', n.d. McArthur Family Archives.
———. 'Jacob Luke and Mapai Transport', Telephone Interview, 7 January 2017.

McArthur, Gilbert J, and John Hitchen. 'Leadership in Rural Communities in Melanesia', Banz, PNG: March 1967. CLTC Archives.

McArthur, Paul. 'Gil McArthur Memories', Telephone Interview, 6 September 2016.
———. 'Re: Details about Gil McArthur', Telephone Interview, 16 October 2016.
———. 'Jacob Luke and Mapai Transport', 1 July 2017.

McDonald, Mary. 'Charles Abel and the Kwato Mission of Papua New Guinea 1891-1975'. Project Muse, 2001. Charles Abel and the Kwato Mission of PNG 1891-1975 https://muse.jhu.edu/article/8318/summary.

McQuillan, Kevin. 'Mapai Transport Branches out to "Rebalance" Trade Links between PNG and NZ'. *Business Advantage PNG*, Blog, 5 December 2016. http://www.businessadvantagepng.com/mapai-transport-branches-out-to-rebalance-trade-links-between-papua-new-guinea-and-nz/.

Maxwell, John. *The 21 Irrefutable Laws of Leadership*. Nashville, Tennessee, USA: Thomas Nelson, 1998.
———. *The 21 Most Powerful Minutes in a Leader's Day*. Nashville, Tennessee, USA: Thomas Nelson, 2000.

Melbourne Bible Institute CLTC Committee. 'Minutes of the New Guinea Christian Leaders' Training College Committee of MBI', 29 November 1962. Melbourne School of Theology Archives.
———. 'Minutes of the New Guinea Christian Leaders' Training College Committee of MBI', 20 January 1964.
———. 'Minutes of the New Guinea Christian Leaders' Training College Committee of MBI', 24 August 1965.

Melbourne Bible Institute Council. 'Minutes of the Council Meeting of the Melbourne Bible Institute', 25 July 1961.
———. 'Minutes of the Council Meeting of the Melbourne Bible Institute', 31 July 1962.
———. 'Minutes of the Council Meeting of the Melbourne Bible Institute', 30 July 1963.
———. 'Minutes of the Council Meeting of the Melbourne Bible Institute', 19 November 1963.
———. 'Minutes of the Council Meeting of the Melbourne Bible Institute', 26 July 1966.
———. 'Minutes of the Council Meeting of the Melbourne Bible Institute', 25 October 1966.

Melbourne Bible Institute Executive. 'Minutes of the Executive Meeting of the Melbourne Bible Institute', 28 February 1961.
———. 'Minutes of the Executive Meeting of the Melbourne Bible Institute', 28 March 1961.
———. 'Minutes of the Executive Meeting of the Melbourne Bible Institute', 27 June1961.
———. 'Minutes of the Executive Meeting of the Melbourne Bible Institute', 6 September1961.
———. 'Minutes of the Executive Meeting of the Melbourne Bible Institute', 26 December 1961.
———. 'Minutes of the Executive Meeting of the Melbourne Bible Institute', 27 February 1962.
———. 'Minutes of the Executive Meeting of the Melbourne Bible Institute', 25 September 1962.
———. 'Minutes of the Executive Meeting of the Melbourne Bible Institute', 18 June 1963.
———. 'Minutes of the Executive Meeting of the Melbourne Bible Institute', 25 February 1964.
———. 'Minutes of the Executive Meeting of the Melbourne Bible Institute', 19 March 1964.
———. 'Minutes of the Executive Meeting of the Melbourne Bible Institute', 21 August 1964. Melbourne School of Theology Archives.

Meredith, David. 'The Perils of Working in PNG'. *Big Rigs*, 11 October 2012. https://www.bigrigs.com.au/news/perils-of-working-in-png/1575665/

Meyers, Max. 'South Pacific Leaders' Fellowship Tour Report May 1982'. Box Hill, Melbourne: Missionary Aviation Fellowship, May 1982.
———. 'South Pacific Leaders Fellowship: Micronesian Tour Report'. Box Hill, Melbourne: Missionary Aviation Fellowship, July 1983. Will Renshaw Personal Archives.
———. Gil McArthur and the Pacific Leaders' Fellowship. Telephone Interview, 21 February 2017.
———. Pacific Leaders' Fellowship Ministry. Telephone Interview, 9 June 2017.

Milne, Bruce. *Acts: Witnesses to Him to the Ends of the Earth*. Ross-shire, UK: Christian Publications, 2010.

Moduwa, Jeffrey. 'Min Baptist Union Churches', 7 February 2017.

Moore, Clive. 'Pacific Islands Autobiography: Personal History and Diplomacy in the Solomon Islands'. *Journal of Historical Biography* 10 (2011).

Morgan, Garth. 'Christian Leaders Training College of Papua New Guinea Inc. 50th Jubilee Celebrations 2015 – A History of CLTC's Funding Over 50 Years'. Auckland New Zealand, 25 February 2015.
———. 'CLTC Financial History 1965-2014'. Auckland New Zealand: Christian Leaders Training College of Papua New Guinea, 2015.
———. 'Gilbert McArthur Information', Email, 6 November 2016.
———. 'Re: Peter Rowse', Email, 16 January 2017.
———. 'A Tribute to Ron and Peg Youngman', 22 February 2017.

———. 'Re: ATA 1970-1979 – McArthur', Email, 20 September 2017.
———. 'Re: Legacy Chapter – Jacob Luke', Email, 22 November 2017.
———. 'Re: Conclusion', Email, 12 February 2018.
———. 'Graham Salisbury', Email, 31 January 2019.

Morgan, Garth and Ruth. 'Timeline for CLTC for Garth and Ruth Morgan', 12 March 2016.

Morling, George. 'Letter to Max Knight from George Morling', n.d. Global Interaction Archives.

National Association of Evangelicals. 'What Is an Evangelical?', 30 November 2016. http://nae.net/what-is-an-evangelical/.

Orr, Harry. 'Aircraft in New Guinea'. Granville, NSW, 25 May 1951. Global Interaction Archives.

Orr, Harry, and Albert Dube. 'New Guinea Aircraft Scheme'. Sydney NSW, n.d. 1953. Global Interaction Archives.

Ortlund, Raymond. *Isaiah: God Saves Sinners*. Wheaton, Illinois, USA: Crossway Books, 2005.

Ott, Craig, and Stephen J. Strauss. *Encountering Theology of Mission – Biblical Foundations, Historical Developments, and Contemporary Issues*. Grand Rapids, Michigan, USA: Baker Academic, 2010.

Pacific Training Institute. 'The Official Opening'. *Pacific Training Institute Newsletter*, Volume 1, No 5 n.d. Will Renshaw Personal Archives.

Palmer, Ken. 'Clemton Park Baptist Church – Golden Jubilee 1940-1990'. Clemton Park, NSW, Australia: Clemton Park Baptist Church, 1990.

Papua New Guinea Leaders' Fellowship. 'Leadership News', *PNG Leaders Fellowship Newsletter*, September 1987. McArthur Family Archives.

Parkinson, Clyde. 'Christian Leaders Training College – October 1962 to October 1964', n.d.

Peterson, Eugene. *Eat This Book - A Conversation in the Art of Spiritual Reading*. London: Hodder and Stoughton, 2006.

Piggin, Stuart. *Spirit, Word and World*. Third Edition. Brunswick East, Victoria, Australia: Acorn Press, 2012.

Pioneers of Australia. *2016 Prayer Directory*. Melbourne: Pioneers of Australia, 2016.
———. 'Our Story'. Brochure, n.d.

Piper, John. *Let the Nations Be Glad – The Supremacy of God in Missions*. Leicester, UK: Inter Varsity Press, 1993.

Plueddemann, James E. *Leading Across Cultures*, Downers Grove, IL: Intervarsity Press, 2009.

Redman, Jess. *The Light Shines On*. Melbourne, Australia: Australian Baptist Missionary Society, 1982.

Renich, Bruce and Retta. 'Gil McArthur and Bruce and Retta Renich', 2 August 2018.

Renshaw, Will. 'PNG Leadership Retreat'. *New Life*, 24 September 1987, Vol 50, No 17. Will Renshaw Personal Archives.
———. 'Rev Dr Gilbert McArthur'. *Melbourne Notes and Comments*, Issue No. 7 (20 June 1994).
———. *Marvellous Melbourne and Spiritual Power – A Christian Revival and Its Lasting Legacy*. Melbourne, Australia: Acorn Press, 2014.
———. 'Gil McArthur', Email, 21 December 2015.
———. 'Re: Gil McArthur and Sir Peter Kenilorea', Email, 27 December 2016.
———. 'Gilbert McArthur Lecture – The Mission', Email, 13 January 2017.
———.Chief Justice Mari Kapi and his relationship with Gil McArthur, Email, 10 August 2017.

———. 'Progress with "The Mission"', Email, 11 October 2017.
———. 'The Mission – Last Section', Email, 20 October 2017.

Richard, Ramesh. 'Training of Pastors'. *Lausanne Global Analysis*. Orlando, Florida, USA: Lausanne Committee for World Evangelisation, September 2015.

Rogers, E. Ron. 'Morling, George Henry (1891-1974)'. *Australian Dictionary of Evangelical Biography*. Evangelical History Association of Australia, 2004.

Rowse, Peter. Re: Gilbert McArthur. Telephone Interview, 18 July 2016.

Salisbury, Graham. *What Came First? – Including the Tegel Chicken Story*. Auckland, New Zealand: Lighthouse Publishing, 2004.

Salisbury, Peter. 'Gil McArthur', Email, 27 October 2016.

Sanders, J. Oswald. *Spiritual Leadership*. London, UK: Lakeland – Marshall, Morgan and Scott, 1967.
———. *Planting Men in Melanesia*. Mount Hagen, Papua New Guinea: Christian Leaders Training College, 1978.
———. *Paul the Leader: A Vision for Christian Leadership Today*. Eastbourne, UK: Kingsway, 1983.

Siche, Fangalasuu Kaoni. 'Obituary – Jezreel Filoa – The Loss of a True Leader', October 1995. SSEM Archives.

Sinclair, Daniel. *A Vision of the Possible – Pioneer Church Planting in Teams*. Waynesboro, Georgia, USA: Authentic Media, 2005.

Smith, Archie. *East-West Eagles – The Story of East West Airlines*. Cairns, Queensland: Robert Brown and Associates, 1989.

Smith, Edwin. *The Shrine of a People's Soul*. London, UK: Edinburgh Press, 1929.

Somare, Michael. 'Speech by the Prime Minister, Mr Michael Somare, at the South Pacific Leaders Fellowship Dinner', 22 April 1983. McArthur Family Archives.

South Pacific Leaders' Fellowship. 'South Pacific Leaders Fellowship – Daily Program', 22 April 1983. McArthur Family Archives.

South Sea Evangelical Mission. 'SSEM Annual Conference Minutes', 1984. Melbourne School of Theology Archives.
———. 'South Sea Evangelical Mission Management Committee Meeting Minutes', 27 September 1985. Melbourne School of Theology Archives.
———. 'Only the Best for God'. *Not in Vain*, November 1986. SSEM Archives.
———. 'South Sea Evangelical Mission Director's Meeting Minutes', 15 July 1986. Melbourne School of Theology Archives.
———. 'South Sea Evangelical Mission Director's Meeting Minutes', 24 July 1987. Melbourne School of Theology Archives.

Stott, John R.W. *The Contemporary Christian*. Downers Grove, Illinois, USA: Inter Varsity Press, 1992.

Tanner, John. Re: Dr Gilbert McArthur. Telephone Interview, 17 January 2017.

Thomas, J.H. 'Leaving Certificate' School Report. Waterloo-with-Seaforth Secondary School, April 1937. McArthur Family Archives.

Thorp, Russell. 'Re: ATA Demise', 5 February 2018.

Tidball, Derek J. *Who Are the Evangelicals? Tracing the Roots of Today's Movements*. London, UK: Marshall Pickering, 1994.

Tozer, Aiden Wilson. *The Knowledge of the Holy - The Attributes of God - Their Meaning in the Christian Life*. London, UK: James Clarke and Co. 1961.

Tweedale, George. *Not Counting the Cost - Missionary Experiences in New Guinea, Ethiopia and Liberia*. Burpengary, Queensland, Australia: George Tweedale, 2016.

Unknown. 'Stranded in England'. *Argus Newspaper*. May 1937. McArthur Family Archives.
———. 'Trawler Arrives - Hardships of Voyage'. 21 July 1937. McArthur Family Archives.
———. 'Cabin Boy's Trip to Aid Family'. *Daily Telegraph*, 21 July 1937. McArthur Family Archives.
———. 'Pygmy Killers Used Women as Decoys'. *Herald Newspaper*. 10 November 1953. McArthur Family Archives.
———. 'Brief Mention'. *Vision Magazine*, March 1954. Global Interaction Archives.
———. 'Missionary Movements'. *Vision Magazine*, December 1955. Global Interaction Archives.
———. 'Walked into Danger'. *Herald Newspaper*. 11 March 1957. McArthur Family Archives.
———. 'Double Honour for Baptist Minister and Other Articles'. Publications Unknown, 1986. McArthur Family Archives.
———. 'We Live Our Years as a Tale That Is Told - Notes of Eulogy at the Funeral of Gilbert McArthur', February 1994. McArthur Family Archives.

Webber, Geoff. 'Some Hazy and Some Vivid Recollections of Rev Gil McArthur', Email, 20 January 2016.

Wiggins, John. 'Tribute to Unity Unasi (Blakey) at the Thanksgiving Service for Her Life.' *Not in Vain*, 1988.
———. 'Section One: Gilbert J McArthur', 25 January 2017.

Wikipedia, 'Chief Justice Sir Mari Kapi'. *Wikipedia*. Accessed 6 June 2017. https://en.wikipedia.org/wiki/Mari_Kapi.

Woolford, Don. *Papua New Guinea: Initiation and Independence*. St Lucia, Queensland, Australia: University of Queensland Press, 1976.

Wright, Walter. *Relational Leadership - A Biblical Model for Influence and Service*. Kindle Edition. Carlisle, UK: Paternoster Press, 2009.

Yandit, Kirine. '"Ownership" and Support of Theological Educational Institutions in Papua New Guinea: The Case of the Christian Leader's Training College of Papua New Guinea Inc.' DMin. Dissertation. Melbourne School of Theology, 2016.

Index

A

Abram/Abraham xvii, xviii, 427
Adams, James 3, 9
Airstrips/Aviation:
- value in mission 23-25, 66-67, 75, 97, 228, 230, 283, 300-302, 340, 359, 363, 364, 374, 385, 390, 415, 430
- construction 38, 42, 46, 47, 55, 58, 69, 74, 82, 366, 370, 371, 372, 398, 414, 420-423, 439

Akesim, Judah 147, 237
Alliance Training Association ATA vi, 140, 142, 145, 151, 156, 165-167, 168, 169, 170, 171, 199, 200, 249, 252, 253, 255, 256, 257, 279, 282, 286, 287, 288, 293, 295, 310, 316, 317, 343
Alliance Training Association Solomon Islands ATASI vi, 171, 199
Altar(s) xvii, xviii, xix, 25, 28, 60, 99, 217, 335, 336, 337, 349, 350, 389, 408
Ambrose, Vic 25
American, Samoa 179
Applied Christian Ethics for Melanesian Churches – McArthur MA Thesis 163-165, 196, 339
Archbold Lake 42, 43, 360, 363, 366, 368, 370, 371, 372
Asia Pacific Christian Mission APCM – see also UFM vi, 89, 205, 278, 297, 324, 325
Australian Baptist Foreign Mission ABFM/ABMS vi, 22, 38, 41, 55, 67, 82, 98, 156, 262

B

Baiyer River Valley 38, 67, 69, 77, 81, 110, 236, 261, 265, 303, 397, 401, 431, 432, 433, 434, 435
Baliem Valley vii, 25, 38, 41, 42, 48, 49, 55, 58, 60, 66, 82, 230, 297, 299, 300, 301, 336, 354, 356, 358, 359, 360, 361, 362, 363, 371, 372, 374, 376, 380, 385, 389, 390, 462
Banz PNG 103, 104, 105, 107, 108, 109, 110, 111, 119, 121, 137, 144, 147, 150, 151, 163, 166, 265, 272, 273, 279, 303, 307, 309, 331
Baptist College of New South Wales xii, 12, 130, 225, 267

Barnard, Victor 15, 21, 37, 105, 106, 107, 249
Baskett, Geoff 152, 154, 162
Bebbington, David 224
Beechwood xix, 145, 167, 252, 286, 316, 317
Belgrave Heights Convention 92, 94, 95, 96
Bible College of New Zealand BCNZ – see also Laidlaw College vi, 120, 259, 263, 320, 321, 322
Bible College of Victoria BCV – see also MBI vi, viii, 92, 266, 269, 325, 461
Bible:
- its Message xviii, 226, 237, 336, 407, 415, 418, 424, 425-429, 435
- in Training and Mission 16, 46, 54, 72-76, 81, 90-93, 105, 108, 118, 120, 127, 130, 131, 133, 140, 159, 165, 169, 187, 195-198, 211, 223-225, 230, 241, 247, 250, 260, 262, 268, 300, 302, 309, 315, 338, 341, 379, 386, 406-408, 411-412, 415-416, 422-424, 431, 434-436, 438, 440
- translation: 25, 62, 67-69, 73-74, 76, 230, 234, 301, 399-402, 408-409, 423-424

Binege, Yemis 79, 80, 435
Blakey, see Unasi, Unity
Bokondini 42, 46, 47, 48, 51, 55, 60, 371, 372, 374, 377, 380, 389, 390
Boroko Baptist Church 264, 265
Bromley, Myron 52, 54, 378, 379
Brugam 193, 197, 198
Buck, Leonard Edmund xiv, 91, 92, 93, 94, 96, 98, 100, 103, 104, 108, 109, 118, 127, 140, 147, 156, 165, 166, 211, 212, 238, 256, 269, 286, 297, 324, 325, 340
Burleigh, Professor 81, 435
Business as Mission BAM vi, 277, 278

C

Campaigners for Christ 92, 96
Cape Hoskins 197
Carey, William xvii, 77, 333, 434
Carlyon, Ross 201
Chaplaincy 156, 160, 161, 315

INDEX

Christian Brethren Churches CBC 132, 290, 304
Christian Broadcasting Service/Kristen Redio 154, 162, 314
Christian and Missionary Alliance C&MA vi, 41, 42, 48, 50, 51, 52, 359
Christian Leaders' Training College CLTC vi, xii, xiii, xv
- acquiring Banz property 103-114
- appointing founding Principal 97-101, 227
- contribution and influence 229, 230, 231, 235, 236, 237, 240, 243-245, 266, 304-311
- Consultative Committee, CLTCCC 124-126, 130-131
- early students/student life 101, 122, 123-126, 128, 131-133, 147, 152, 154, 165, 169, 191-192, 210, 234-237, 239-245, 261-262, 265, 274, 277-278, 285, 290, 298, 303, 304, 306, 309, 310, 311, 337-338, 345, 346-347
- finances 146-152, 256-257, 278-279, 280-283
- localisation of staff 130, 264, 265-266, 269
- MBI CLTC Committee 97, 98, 100-101, 107, 123, 126, 130, 135, 136, 137, 152, 153, 165, 232, 243, 340
- mission statement 443-444
- and other Christian Agencies 202, 210, 211
- orientation of staff 260-263, 268, 274, 280
- origins, in PNG and MBI 89-90, 91-96
- poultry program 150, 151, 254, 280, 310, 446-447
- prayer support 152-154
- recruiting early staff 115-123, 259-263, 264-265, 266-268
- relations with ATA 140-143, 151, 156, 165-167, 168, 199-200, 252, 255, 279, 282, 286-287, 310, 316-317
- relations with EASPI/EAPNG 156-160, 313-316, 342
- and Solomon Islanders/SSEC 191-192, 197, 303
- supply lines, infrastructure and support services 135-145, 165-167, 250-251, 252-256, 257, 286-287
- training curriculum 123-127, 263-264
- training issues and emphases 128-131, 304-311
- sundry other references 30, 42, 248, 263, 264, 265, 269, 270, 271, 272, 273, 274, 275, 278, 282, 285, 286, 287, 289, 290, 298, 303, 313, 314, 315, 316, 317, 328, 330, 331, 336, 337, 338, 340, 341, 342, 346, 347, 349, 351

Christian Mission in Many Lands CMML see also CBC vi, 157, 158, 227, 262
Churches of Christ Mission 157
Clack, William (Bill) 93, 94, 97, 98, 99, 100, 107, 136, 137, 143, 147, 152, 153, 165, 212, 252, 267, 269, 297
Clemton Park Baptist Church vi, xix, 82-85, 98, 112, 213, 230, 250, 297, 304, 340
Clinton, Bobby 32
Columbia Bible College xix, 154, 162, 163, 164, 234, 235, 337, 339
Conley, Bill and Joyce 156, 165
Contextualisation 128-129, 169, 202, 338
Coster, Aubrey 200, 257
Cowie, Robyn 118, 153, 253

D

Daimoi, Joshua and Mone 130, 147, 190, 227, 264, 265, 266, 267, 269, 315
Dani Baptist Churches 299, 300
Dani People 25, 36, 38, 52, 300, 340, 379
Davis, Ralph 94
Deasey, Dudley 158, 262
Deck, Norman 158
Department of Higher Education, Research, Science and Technology DHERST 305
Doull, Don and Elaine 59, 62, 66, 67, 70, 74, 75, 79, 80, 81, 156, 227, 228, 230, 235, 262, 301, 302, 355, 386, 394, 395, 403, 404, 406, 409, 410, 412, 414, 415, 416, 420, 421, 422, 430, 431, 434, 435, 439
Draper, Norman 39, 48, 50, 55, 56, 59, 299, 300, 303, 336, 355, 358, 360, 365, 366, 374, 376, 381, 391
Dube, Albert 24, 55, 56, 57, 58, 59, 382
Duranmin 65, 303
Dutch New Guinea vi, vii, xiv, xv, xix, 25, 26, 37, 84, 217, 222, 234, 261, 299, 354, 355, 381, 393

E

East West Airlines New South Wales EWA vi, 16, 18, 19, 20, 21, 230
Edwards, Rod and Denise 313, 321
Eliptamin 62, 65, 69, 74, 75, 76, 77, 393, 394, 398, 403, 412, 414, 415, 420, 422, 430, 431, 439
Erekali, Silas 210
Evangelical Alliance of Papua New Guinea EAPNG vi, 157, 262, 263, 264, 315
Evangelical Alliance of the South Pacific Islands EASPI vi, 156, 158, 310, 313, 342, 444
Evangelism 67, 84, 168, 172, 201, 224, 304, 310, 314, 315, 322, 324, 373, 384, 397, 423
Everyman's Centres 92, 238, 274

F

Fiji 174, 175, 177, 179, 183, 184, 186, 201, 247, 318
Filoa, Jezreel and Bethemek 242-245
Finger, Ken 243
Fletcher, John 174, 297
Fletcher, Ted and Peggy 147, 174, 208, 209, 210, 211, 212, 269, 296, 297, 323, 324, 326
Ford, Heather 293, 294, 295, 296, 338, 347, 348

G

Graham, Billy 96, 207, 208, 267
Griffiths, Gordon xiii, 175, 193, 197, 202, 251, 257
Griffiths, Ken 103, 192, 322
Gruber, Ian 51, 55, 60, 366, 377, 381, 389, 390

H

Hablifoerie River 42, 45, 360, 369, 371, 372, 390
Hasluck, Sir Paul 87, 154, 155, 343
Hawke, Bob 189
Highway Motors Pty Ltd 167, 288, 316
Hitchen, John and Ann xii, 30, 98, 120-121, 122, 123, 124, 125, 126, 127, 128, 130, 131, 142, 144, 147, 148, 155, 159, 161, 166, 168, 203, 259-264, 265, 266, 268, 269, 281, 305, 309, 310, 311, 312, 320, 321, 322, 328, 331, 342, 346, 347

Holistic Theology / Community Development 123, 124, 171, 172, 201, 216, 278, 279, 310, 312, 317
Hollandia 40, 354, 355, 359, 363, 365, 368, 371, 374, 381, 383, 385
Holy Spirit, role 37, 46, 67, 69, 70, 72, 77, 79, 81, 82, 100, 122, 164, 169, 187, 192, 194, 203, 217, 221, 224, 225, 229, 243, 336, 362, 369, 397, 401, 404, 406, 407, 416, 425, 426, 427, 431, 433, 434, 435, 436, 438, 439, 440
 – movements 95, 191-192, 303, 322
Horne, Charles 97, 98, 147, 262

I

Iwoksim, Wesani 69, 71, 73, 74, 79, 80, 81, 234-235, 407, 408, 412, 415, 435, 436

K

Kambipi, Traimya 165, 236, 309
Kapi, Sir Mari 177, 187, 238-239, 247, 274
Kenilorea, Sir Peter 174, 175, 177-189, 201, 245-248, 297, 318
Keswick Convention 226, 315, 336, 342, 343
Key, John xiii, 173, 174, 175, 177, 179, 187, 188, 292, 293, 319
Kingdom of God 77, 96, 107, 152, 171, 172, 175, 187, 203, 219, 221, 222, 230, 238, 239, 258, 277, 278, 291, 293, 298, 302, 310, 319, 322, 339, 351, 361, 381, 427, 434
Kiribati 174, 179, 185
Kolo, Mapusiya 309
Kristen Redio 154, 156, 162, 171
Kudjip 103, 144

L

Lae xix, 107, 119, 127, 136, 137, 138, 140, 150, 151, 159, 166, 169, 174, 199, 252, 254, 255, 282, 285, 288, 289, 295, 307, 316
Laidlaw College 120, 259, 263, 279, 320, 321
Laird, Ray 202, 204, 205, 213, 214, 228, 251, 257, 325, 326, 338, 341, 345, 346
Lamont, Sam and Anne 145, 153, 254

Language learning in mission xviii, 39, 48, 55, 58, 59, 61, 62, 67, 69, 70, 72, 73, 74, 75, 76, 81, 84, 100, 109, 124, 132, 133, 154, 159, 169, 260, 261, 292, 294, 299, 301, 302, 304, 329, 333, 336, 337, 338, 339, 340, 352, 353, 365, 372, 383, 386, 389, 390, 391, 393, 394, 397, 398, 399, 400, 401, 402, 404, 406, 407, 409, 411, 412, 418, 422, 423, 424, 436, 442

Laurieton 200, 202, 203, 204, 217, 257, 293, 325, 326

Lawrence, James 27, 28, 29, 30

Leadership:
– church and mission viii, xi, 89, 92, 96, 100, 132, 160-161, 182, 195, 198, 199, 230, 231, 234, 245, 259, 262, 266, 270, 304, 337, 340, 350, 351
  – code/manifesto 187-188
  – God's xix, 33
  – national/political 89, 133, 160, 171, 172, 180, 182, 187, 195, 238, 248, 253, 266, 298, 317, 319
  – nature and qualities of, viii, 16, 27, 28, 29, 30, 32, 115, 135, 173, 175, 179, 182, 188, 191, 195, 207, 219, 221-222, 226, 239, 247, 275, 290, 291, 292, 294, 322, 343
  – task of, particularly McArthur's xv, xvi, 1, 25, 27, 28, 30, 33, 55, 57, 62, 85, 89, 130, 131, 136, 145, 148, 153, 156, 159, 162, 165, 166, 167, 171, 182, 192, 193, 195, 199, 213, 216, 232, 233, 238, 247, 249, 261, 263, 264, 279, 280, 284, 285, 286, 287, 288, 290, 291, 298, 305, 313, 315, 316, 322, 323, 335, 342, 345, 347, 351
  – training and development, particularly at CLTC viii, 123, 124, 126, 128, 132, 140, 154, 160, 165, 196, 197, 213, 229, 231, 236, 237, 241, 244, 251, 257, 263, 272, 274, 304, 310, 311, 316, 444
  – see also, Pacific Leaders Fellowship PLF and Pacific Leaders' Training Institute PTI

Liddle, Kay and Gwen 131, 132-133, 158, 159, 227, 262, 271, 289, 313, 315, 316, 317

Longgar, William and Iru xi, xii, xiii, 31, 248, 273-275, 305, 306, 307, 326

Luke, Jacob 287-290

M

Madang 104, 136, 150, 282, 316

Mapai Transport Pty Ltd 287-290

Martin, Suren 147, 290

Maxim Institute 319-322

McArthur, Gilbert James:
– assessments/awards/ commendations of, xiii, 22, 30, 82-83, 84, 101, 122, 216, 219, 295,
– CLTC Principal/Principalship, xii, 89-100, 112, 136-140, 153-154, 168, see also McArthur legacy under organisations & ministries (CLTC),
– contribution to leadership development, viii, 87, 115, 126-131, 163-165, 168, 172-173, 191-192, 194, 199, 249, 266, see also McArthur legacy under theological educators, organisations and ministries,
– Diary extracts, In full, *Appendix One*, 39, 41, 45-46, 58-59, 61, 65-66, 69, 70, 76, 77, 79, 81, 82,
– final years/death, 207ff, 213-215, 325-326
– his story, ix, xi, xii, xiii, xv, xvi, xix, 214, 348-351
– influence on others, viii, xii, xiii, 30-31, 106-107, 118, 119, 120-121, 130-131, 139, 143-144, 155-162, 174, 210-212, 226-227, 230-231, see also next entry, McArthur Legacy
– marriage/family life, 15, 27, 33, 38, 59-60, 62, 68, 73, 74, 77, 82, 99, 214-215, 217, 301, 327-333
– military service, 13-15
– ministry/mission service/priorities, xv, 16,
– personal qualities, 10-11, 16-17, 21, 27-33, 66, 104, 121-122, 148, 202, 222ff, 242, 251, 275, 284, 285, 286, 335-348, 350
– upbringing & other formative influences, xv, Part One *passim*, 1, 3-12, 15, 16, 22, 24, 25, 27, 32, 38, 162, 173

Part Two *passim*, 38, 41, 62, 66, 68-69, 70, 75, 76, 87, 109, 121, 122, 131, 135ff, 145, 150, 159, 160, 161, 165, 168, 171-172, 174, 193-196, 197-198, 199, 201, 217, 219, 230-231, 234, 241, 270, 278, 294, 350-351,

- relations with colleagues, 55-58, 59, 66, 70, 75, 97 fn27, 101, 144, 165, 166 fn21, 231-232, 251, 260-261, 279ff, 347-348,
- relations with political leaders, 177-187, 291ff, 317-319, see also McArthur legacy under community leaders and wider Pacific, below.
- sayings/writings/archives, xi, xiv, 22-23, 23-24, 37-38, 39, 41, 45-48, 55-56, 58-59, 69, 70, 76, 79, 81, 82, 99, 100, 117, 131-132, 163-165, 172, 173, 188, 191-192, 193, 194, 195-196, 197-198, 201, 203-204, 216, 217, 302, 351-352, see also Appendix One, McArthur Diaries.
- spiritual commitment/call to mission, 11-12, 21-22, 28-29, 37, 38, 61, 79, 85, 87, 98, 99, 100, 106, 130, 152, 217, 222-228, 345-348
- transitions/tent-moving, xviii-xix, 3, 4-6, 11, 13, 16, 22, 25, 32, 37, 39, 58-59, 60-62, 82, 85, 99-100, 162-163, 168, 169, 188, 204
- vision/sense of purpose, xviii, 23, 28, 29, 66, 75, 84, 87, 92, 97-98, 103, 109, 111, 116, 175, 193, 196, 200, 202, 203, 217, 226-228, 231, 264, 340-342
- wider Pacific ministries/tours, 169-170, 171-212,

McArthur Legacy:
221-334, 221-232 (as leader),
- in church and community leaders, 233-248, 235 (Wesani Iwoksim), 236 (Traimya Kambipi), 237 (Judah Akesim), 238-239 (Sir Mari Kapi), 239-241(Unity Blakey), 242-245 (Jezreel Filoa), 245-248 (Sir Peter Kenilorea)
- in infrastructure builders, 249-258, 249-250 (George Tweedale), 251-253 (Peter & Margaret Rowse), 253-257 (Ron & Peg Youngman), 257 (Aubrey Coster)
- in theological educators, 259-275, 259-264 (John & Ann Hitchen), 264-266 (Joshua & Mone Daimoi), 266-270 (David & Margaret Price), 270-273 (Bruce & Retta Renich), 273-275 (William & Iru Longgar)
- in missional business entrepreneurs, 277-290, 279-286 (Garth & Ruth Morgan), 286-287 (Graham & Joyce Walker), 286-290 (Jacob Luke), 290 (Suren Martin)
- in the wider Pacific and beyond, 291-298, 292-293 (John Key), 293-296 (Heather Ford), 296-297 (Ted & Peggy Fletcher)
- in various categories of people influenced, 297-298
- in organisations and ministries, 299-326, 299-301 (Dani Churches), 301-304 (Baptist Churches PNG), 304 (Clemton Park Baptist Church), 304-313 (CLTC), 313-316 (EASPI), 316-317 (ATA/Beechwood/Highway Motors / Timberline), 317-319 (PLF), 319-322 (NZEDF/ Maxim Institute/ Venn Foundation/Masters Institute), 322-323 (SSEM/SSEC), 323-326 (Pioneers International)
- in his wife and family, 327-334

McArthur, Jenny xii, xiv, xix, 15, 22, 39, 74, 82, 214, 215, 327, 329, 330, 331, 332, 353, 366, 373, 410, 411, 416, 432

McArthur, Patricia xix, 12, 13, 15, 21, 22, 25, 26, 28, 38, 39, 42, 45, 55, 60, 62, 73, 74, 77, 82, 83, 84, 98, 99, 125, 155, 163, 169, 213, 214, 216, 217, 260, 293, 327, 328, 329, 330, 331, 332, 333, 334, 336, 338, 343, 344, 348, 354, 356, 358, 362, 364, 367, 370, 373, 383, 386, 387, 388, 390, 398, 416, 417, 419, 431, 432, 433

McArthur, Paul xii, xix, 15, 22, 39, 77, 106, 114, 213, 214, 222, 287, 288, 327, 329, 353, 357, 373, 395, 398, 416, 417, 418, 419, 430, 432, 433

McArthur, Robyn 15, 22, 39, 74, 82, 214, 327, 329, 330, 353, 373, 383, 395, 410, 411, 416, 418, 432

McArthur, Sandra 15, 77, 328, 329, 433

McArthur, Wendy 15, 39, 77, 214, 328, 329, 353, 355, 358, 366, 373, 395, 398, 411, 416, 417, 418, 430, 432, 433

Meditation 349, 426

Melanesian Association of Theological Schools MATS 305, 309

Melanesian Council of Churches MCC vi, 173, 264, 292, 310, 314, 315

Melanesian Institute 273, 274

Melanesian Journal of Theology 309

Melbourne Bible Institute MBI vi, viii, xii, xiii, xix, 91, 92, 93, 94, 95, 96, 97, 98, 100, 101, 103, 104, 107, 108, 112, 113, 116, 117, 118, 123, 124, 126, 127, 130, 131, 132, 135, 136, 137, 139, 143, 144, 146, 149, 152, 153, 154, 155, 162, 165, 166, 168, 192, 232, 243, 250, 267, 268, 340, 461

Melbourne School of Theology MST ii, iv, viii, ix, 92, 94, 97, 149, 188, 200, 205, 461

Mellis, Charles 38

Merritt, Roy V 93, 162, 268

Meyer, Frederick Brotherton 27

Meyers, Max xiii, 175, 177, 179, 180, 183, 184, 185, 186, 247, 248, 283, 318, 319

Meyers, Tim ix, 269

Mianmin 65, 393

Micronesia 179, 185, 186

Mienel, Werner 167

Miles, Helen and Bill 144, 153

Milne, Bruce 68, 69

Min Baptist Churches/Union 301, 302, 303

Mission:
- agencies/structures, xiii, 22, 23, 24, 25, 28, 38, 41, 42, 48, 56, 67, 69, 82, 89, 90, 91, 93, 107, 108, 124, 125, 129, 132, 137, 139, 140, 150, 154, 156, 157, 159, 169, 174, 192, 197, 198, 204, 205, 210, 211, 213, 214, 225, 227, 229, 246, 257, 261, 262, 265, 269, 270, 278, 282, 293, 296, 297, 300, 301, 304, 316, 322, 323, 324, 325, 327, 328, 336, 337, 359-361
- call to, 37, 97, 106, 120, 209, 221, 225, 244, 268, 271, 274, 350,
- history, viii, 41, 168, 277,
- leaders/leadership in, viii, xi, xviii, 89, 90, 92, 94, 96, 100, 103, 123, 131, 132, 158, 193, 195, 199, 207, 212, 217, 225, 229, 233, 262, 309, 322, 330, 342
- literature, xii,
- motives/motivation, 37, 194, 195, 216, 228, 229, 247, 345
- of God, xiii, xvi, xviii, xix, 129, 168, 211, 217, 224, 266, 270, 277, 336, 337, 340, 342, 350, 428
- of McArthur, xii, xv, 35ff., 37, 38, 84, 100, 221, 222, 263, 274, 290, 297, 299, 323
- prayer for, 46, 73, 75, 132, 195, 198, 224, 324, 355, 369,
- promotion of, 21, 96, 101, 106, 116-117, 310
- spirituality, 37, 222-225
- statements, xi, 146, 443, 313, 323, 427-429, 444-445
- task/fields/stations, viii, ix, 22, 23, 29, 38, 41, 42, 48, 55, 58,59, 62, 65, 66, 67, 70, 73, 74, 110, 120, 133, 135, 159, 164, 171, 173, 175, 193, 194, 198, 200, 212, 217, 224, 229, 242, 243, 249, 261, 262, 269, 271, 277, 278, 279, 287, 290, 298, 302, 311, 313, 314, 315, 324, 325, 327, 332, 340, 350, 358, 359, 361, 362, 372, 373, 385, 386, 394, 402, 409
- thinking/strategy, viii, 23, 68, 81, 93, 131, 158, 168, 193, 196, 197, 198, 203, 205, 217, 219, 259, 266, 268, 277, 322, 340, 342, 350,
- vision/purpose, 30, 116, 123, 135,196, 208, 304

Mission(ary) Aviation Fellowship MAF vi, viii, 24, 25, 38, 41, 42, 46, 55, 60, 66, 67, 94, 96, 97, 107, 108, 150, 171, 174, 175, 177, 178, 179, 185, 196, 197, 229, 247, 283, 342, 360

Missionary Diary Extracts/The McArthur xiv, xvii, 39, 41, 42, 45, 46, 48, 54, 55, 58, 59, 60, 61, 62, 65, 66, 68, 69, 70, 72, 73, 74, 75, 76, 77, 79, 81, 82, 337, 353, 364, 439, and Appendix One

Moore, Clive 245, 246, 247

Morgan, Garth and Ruth xii, 117, 118, 119, 120, 125, 131, 139, 142, 147, 148, 150, 151, 155, 167, 227, 231, 232, 253, 254, 255, 256, 257, 279-286, 289, 290, 313, 321, 342, 343, 447

Morling, Professor George/Morling College 22, 25, 30, 37, 225, 226, 264, 267, 336

Mount Hagen xv, 108, 109, 112, 127, 137, 138, 150, 166, 256, 283, 287, 288, 293, 295

N

Nauru 180, 205

Neuendorf, Alwyn and Fay 262

New Zealand Educational Development

Foundation NZEDF/Maxim Institute vi, 319-322
Niue 174, 179, 184
Nondugl Bush Lease 144
Noordyke, Hendrik 50, 55, 366, 376, 377, 381
Not in Vain Magazine of SSEM 186, 187, 191, 192, 193, 194, 197, 198, 199, 200, 201, 202, 241, 243, 244

O

Orr, Rev Harry 23, 24, 81, 435
Ortlund, Ray Jr 59, 60

P

Pacific Leaders' Fellowship PLF vi, 172, 173, 174, 175, 177, 179, 180, 182, 185, 186, 187, 188, 189, 200, 231, 238, 245, 247, 248, 249, 274, 292, 293, 317, 318, 319
Pacific Training Institute PTI vi, 200, 201, 202, 203, 204, 206, 207, 217, 249, 257, 293, 325, 326, 340
Parkinson, Clyde 104, 105, 107, 108, 109, 113, 115, 153, 250
Pidgin English (Neo-Melanesian) 62, 69, 72, 271, 302, 329, 342, 383, 394, 398, 401, 406, 412
Piggin, Stuart 94, 95, 462
Pioneers International/Pioneers Australia ii, vi, xiii, xvi, 89, 132, 204, 212, 213, 266, 269, 270, 296, 297, 304, 306, 323, 324, 325, 326, 440, 442, 461
Piper, John 73
Pokikau, Silas Blaisip 306
Port Moresby 107, 112, 127, 151, 158, 159, 160, 161, 174, 179, 182, 238, 248, 264, 265, 266, 274, 281, 307
Prayer xv, 11, 42, 46, 48, 49, 54, 59, 61, 65, 70, 72, 73, 76, 77, 79, 80, 97, 98, 100, 101, 103, 111, 115, 116, 130, 132, 136, 152, 165, 171, 173, 174, 175, 177, 179, 182, 186, 200, 201, 203, 212, 223, 224, 238, 247, 250, 252, 268, 269, 296, 303, 323, 324, 331, 354, 358, 361, 363, 364, 369, 371, 375, 379, 381, 383, 386, 392, 395, 404, 407, 409, 411, 413, 415, 418, 420, 421, 424, 430, 431, 433, 434, 435, 436, 437, 438, 439, 442, 462
Presidential Prayer Breakfast Washington 165, 171, 173, 212

Price, David and Margaret viii, ix, xi, xiii, xvi, 15, 97, 131, 147, 211, 237, 249, 266-270, 272, 325, 461, 462
Prison Fellowship 92, 238
Pyramid Mountain 48, 49, 51, 55, 371, 374, 376, 377, 380, 381

R

Rarongo Theological College 273, 274
Regions Beyond Missionary Union RBMU vi, 41, 42, 359
Renich, Bruce and Retta 270-273, 326
Renshaw, William xii, xiv, xv, 94, 96, 97, 98, 101, 127, 135, 147, 148, 165, 169, 186, 187, 202, 212, 247, 340
Revival 95, 192, 205, 303
Rickard, Adrian and Margaret xiii, 131, 147, 243, 308
Rosser, Erec 153, 447
Rowse, Ian 137
Rowse, Peter and Margaret xii, 101, 136, 137-138, 144, 153, 165, 251-253, 255, 267

S

Salisbury, Graham 446-447
Samoa 133, 174, 179
Sanders, James Oswald xv, 21, 28, 37, 87, 89, 91, 92, 96, 98, 99, 100, 111, 112, 113, 116, 118, 120, 121, 122, 123, 135, 136, 139, 140, 142, 144, 147, 154, 209, 211, 225, 226, 236, 263, 291, 305, 307, 349
Satan 70, 72, 164, 361, 374, 404, 407, 415
Sentani xix, 38, 39, 43, 48, 55, 57, 59, 60, 61, 337, 354, 355, 357, 359, 363, 365, 368, 371, 374, 381, 382, 385, 386, 387, 388, 389, 390, 392
Sepik River/Province/District/Basin 24, 62, 65, 237, 262, 290, 303, 328, 345, 355, 393
– work of SSEM/SSEC 191, 192, 197-199, 228, 243, 244, 271, 273, 322-323, 345
Sexton, George 89, 91, 92, 93, 97
Shields, Bruce and Kathy 262
Sipwanje, Kongoe 309
Solomon Islands 127, 158, 159, 169, 171, 174, 177, 179, 180, 182, 185, 186, 189, 191, 192, 196, 197, 199, 201, 204, 205, 228, 233, 239, 240, 241, 242, 243, 244, 245, 246, 247, 297, 303, 318, 323, 325, 328, 330

INDEX

Somare, Michael 89, 182, 185

South Sea Evangelical Mission SSEM vi, xiii, 132, 157, 158, 169, 171, 187, 188, 191, 192, 193, 194, 196, 197, 198, 199, 200, 201, 202, 204, 205, 210, 213, 217, 228, 231, 237, 239, 240, 242, 243, 249, 251, 257, 262, 270, 271, 272, 273, 293, 294, 302, 322, 323, 324, 325, 326, 338, 343, 345, 346, 347, 462

South Seas Evangelical Church SSEC vi, 158, 171, 174, 191, 192, 193, 197, 198, 199, 201, 204, 205, 217, 228, 237, 239, 242, 244, 245, 246, 271, 273, 297, 304, 322, 323, 325

Spirituality xi, xv, 37, 191, 201, 207, 222, 223, 224, 225, 338, 461

Steiger, David 42, 60, 360, 363, 389

Strahan, Thomas and Heather 118, 125, 144, 153, 253

T

Tagatemtigin 76, 423, 424

Tamworth xix, 13, 15, 17, 18, 19, 20, 21, 22, 29, 61, 74, 106, 391, 416, 438

Tanner, John 189, 202, 204

Telefolmin xiv, xix, 23, 24, 25, 38, 58, 59, 60, 61, 62, 63, 65, 66, 67, 68, 69, 74, 75, 77, 78, 79, 80, 81, 82, 84, 100, 112, 148, 156, 157, 227, 228, 230, 231, 234, 235, 249, 261, 278, 297, 301, 302, 303, 328, 337, 355, 386, 387, 388, 389, 390, 391, 392, 393, 397, 399, 402, 403, 406, 408, 409, 411, 412, 414, 415, 417, 418, 420, 422, 423, 425, 430, 432, 433, 434, 435, 436, 437, 438, 439, 462

Tents xvii, xviii, xix, 51, 60, 335, 337, 350, 377, 378, 381, 389

Tidball, Derek 223, 224

Tifalmin 65, 82, 415, 439

Timberline Pty Ltd 167, 256, 316

Tonga 133, 174, 177, 179, 184, 186

Transport, its use in mission 24, 128, 136, 139, 140, 141, 142, 150, 165, 167, 252, 280, 282, 286, 310, 316, 317, 341

Transwest Pty Ltd 167

Turner, Harold 312

Tuvalu 174, 179, 185

Tweedale, George 105-114, 115, 153, 249-250

U

Unasi, (Blakey) Unity 239, 241

Unevangelised Fields Mission UFM vi, 41, 42, 48, 55, 89, 91, 92, 94, 96, 98, 137, 157, 158, 213, 262, 324, 360

Urban Centres 128

V

Vanuatu 171, 174, 177, 179, 181, 182, 186, 205, 260

Vaughan, Doug and Rosemary 23, 59, 62, 65, 75, 76, 228, 230, 301, 355, 386, 394, 396, 398, 406, 410, 412, 414, 420, 421, 422, 430, 437, 439

Venn Foundations 319-322

Venz, Karl 145

Vision:

- characterising McArthur viii, xi, 21, 32, 46, 55, 66, 100, 104, 106, 111, 118, 148, 159, 162, 165, 170, 193, 196, 197, 199, 200, 202, 210, 217, 227, 228, 229, 231, 233, 238, 249, 251, 252, 253, 263, 264, 273, 275, 285, 294, 295, 297, 313, 317, 319, 320, 322, 338, 340, 342, 343, 345, 346, 348, 349, 350, 351

- for equipping leaders, particularly CLTC xviii, 66, 75, 87, 89-92, 96, 97, 100-101, 106, 109, 115, 117, 119, 120, 121, 122, 127, 130, 138, 147, 152, 153, 154, 155, 165-166, 168, 210, 217, 226, 228, 231, 250, 251, 252, 260, 264, 266, 267, 268, 271, 284, 298, 304, 307, 313, 316, 322, 340

- for wider Pacific/PLF/PTI 171ff, 172, 173, 175, 177, 188, 191ff, 200, 202, 203, 204, 207, 238, 247, 249, 257, 291, 299, 317

- nature of 29, 30, 98, 228, 229, 291, 299, 343

- for aviation in mission 23, 97, 196-197, 228

- for cooperation in mission 41, 160, 203, 247, 263, 361

- for evangelism and mission 84, 116, 196, 199, 205, 212, 227, 228, 229, 269, 278, 304, 326

- of God 223

- in business 287, 289

463

– 'vision hill' 103, 111-112, 113, 114, 119, 137, 227, 258
Vision Magazine of ABFM/ABMS 24, 39, 41, 301

W

Wakerley, Grant 289
Walker, Graham and Joyce 133, 138, 139, 140, 142, 144, 147, 153, 156, 165, 281, 282, 286-287, 316
Wapnok, Diyos 303
Warena, Glaimi 165, 243
Webber, Geoff and Margaret 125, 143, 144, 153
Western, Samoa 179, 185
Wewak 38, 60, 74, 157, 158, 185, 271, 386, 388, 389, 390, 393, 397, 399, 403, 406, 408, 411, 412, 414, 417, 420, 422, 430, 433, 434
White, Victor 38, 39, 56, 57, 355, 356, 363, 403
Wiggins, John 192, 239, 241
Woodbridge, John and Greta 153, 254, 285
World Council of Churches vi, 158
World Evangelical Outreach vi, 212, 296, 297, 323
World Vision South Pacific 169, 171, 172, 173, 174, 177, 188, 189, 200, 201, 231, 247, 249, 291, 292, 293, 295, 338, 347, 462
Wright, Walter 29, 30, 33, 135
Wycliffe Bible Translators WBT vi, 38, 94, 96

Y

Yandit, Kirine 7, 159, 453
Young, Florence 204
Youngman, Ron and Peg 117, 119-120, 137, 153, 165, 166, 169, 253-255, 256, 257, 285, 316, 319-322

www.ingramcontent.com/pod-product-compliance
Lightning Source LLC
Chambersburg PA
CBHW040320300426
44112CB00020B/2817